ENTERTAINMENT
ON THE NET

BARGAIN BOOK
$4.98

ISBN# 0681031077

9 780681 031074

JOE WILLIAMS

que®

Entertainment on the Net

Copyright © 1995 by Que® Corporation

Library of Congress Catalog No.: 95-78873

ISBN: 0-7897-0122-7

97 96 95   6 5 4 3 2 1

Interpretation of the printing code: the rightmost double-digit number is the year of the book's printing; the rightmost single-digit number, the number of the book's printing. For example, a printing code of 95-1 shows that the first printing of the book occurred in 1995.

All terms mentioned in this book that are known to be trademarks or service marks have been appropriately capitalized. Que cannot attest to the accuracy of this information. Use of a term in this book should not be regarded as affecting the validity of any trademark or service mark.

Screen reproductions in this book were created using Collage Plus from Inner Media, Inc., Hollis, NH.

Credits

PRESIDENT AND PUBLISHER
Roland Elgey

ASSOCIATE PUBLISHER
Stacy Hiquet

PUBLISHING DIRECTOR
Brad R. Koch

EDITORIAL SERVICES DIRECTOR
Elizabeth Keaffaber

MANAGING EDITOR
Sandy Doell

DIRECTOR OF MARKETING
Lynn E. Zingraf

ACQUISITIONS EDITOR
Cheryl D. Willoughby

PRODUCT DIRECTOR
Ned Snell

PRODUCTION EDITOR
Mitzi Foster Gianakos

ASSISTANT PRODUCT MARKETING MANAGER
Kim Margolius

TECHNICAL EDITORS
Alp Berker
Pete Durso
Doug Welch

ACQUISITIONS COORDINATOR
Ruth Slates

OPERATIONS COORDINATOR
Patty Brooks

EDITORIAL ASSISTANT
Andrea Duvall

BOOK DESIGNERS
Ruth Harvey
Kim Scott

COVER DESIGNER
Ruth Harvey

PRODUCTION TEAM
Angela D. Bannan
Jason Carr
John Hulse
Amy Gornik
Damon Jordan
Daryl Kessler
Bob LaRoche
Bobbi Satterfield
Kelly Warner
Jody York

INDEXER
Carol Sheehan

Composed in *Futura Book* and *Improv* by Que Corporation.

About the Author

Joe Williams has traveled the American landscape from the Jersey shore to the Hollywood hills, in search of twisted kicks and four-leaf clovers. He has worked as a rock critic, beat reporter, movie extra, computer-book editor, and ice-cream-truck driver. For the moment, he lives in a middle-American state that recently voted for riverboat gambling.

This book is dedicated to my mother, Marie Lucille Williams (née Formato), who forced me to watch television every night of my childhood when all I wanted to do was finish my homework and eat a healthy vegetable snack before bedtime. Thanks, Mom.

Acknowledgments

I'm speechless. Really.

Well, first let me say what an honor it is just being *nominated* in the same category as Robert deNiro, Kenneth Branagh, Dustin Hoffman, and Macauley Culkin. I think I speak for everyone here and for all the people watching this broadcast throughout the Global Village when I say that we are *all* winners tonight.

I'd like to thank the executives at Que Studios: Stacey Hiquet, Brad Koch, Tom Bennett, Jim Minatel, and especially Cheryl Willoughby. I owe a special thanks to my manager, Sandy Doell, who got me this gig, and to my booking agent, Cindy Morrow, who allowed me to take it.

I say a heartfelt *gracias* to my dialog coach, Ned Snell, who is a fine actor in his own right. And I offer a big cookie to my personal stylist, Mitzi Foster Gianakos, who helped me look the part and gave me inspiration in ways that I will never be able to tell her.

(Yes, I see the red light blinking. Just be patient.)

I have to thank my family and especially my parents, Wallace and Marie Williams, who paid for my tap-dance lessons and thus got me started in this business we call Show.

I'd like to thank the many people who helped me along the way: my loan shark, Michael Arko; my people on the Coast— Matt Flynn, Robb Moore, Stephanie and John Hughes, Millicent Morris, and Pam Caudle; Ann Marie Matheus, my eyes and ears on the street; the Goerisch Family Foundation, for providing me with research assistance; Fran Hatton and Dean Miller, for reminding me of what's important in life; Sean Medlock and all the kids at Sam's Hideaway, for the many hours of incoherent babble that helped me define a uniquely distorted worldview; Bob Temple and Bill Mann, for their contributions to the script; and especially Kathryn R. Welch, my personal healer.

I'd also like to thank Joel Hodgson and the producers of *Mystery Science Theater 3000,* which provided me with a substitute for sanity on those nights when I thought that I couldn't go on.

And finally, to Susan, I'd like to say—

Wait, I'm not finished!

We'd Like to Hear from You!

As part of our continuing effort to produce books of the highest possible quality, Que would like to hear your comments. To stay competitive, we *really* want you, as a computer book reader and user, to let us know what you like or dislike most about this book or other Que products.

You can mail comments, ideas, or suggestions for improving future editions to the address below, or send us a fax at (317) 581-4663. For the online inclined, Macmillan Computer Publishing has a forum on CompuServe (type **GO QUEBOOKS** at any prompt) through which our staff and authors are available for questions and comments. The address of our Internet site is **http://www.mcp.com** (World Wide Web).

Thanks in advance—your comments will help us to continue publishing the best books available on computer topics in today's market.

Que Corporation
201 W. 103rd Street
Indianapolis, Indiana 46290
USA

Contents at a Glance

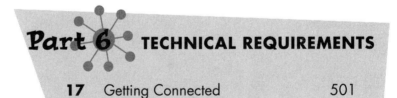

Contents

Part 1   General Entertainment Resources

Part 2 Movies

Part 3 · Television

5 GENERAL TV RESOURCES 101

6 NEWS AND TALK 125

Part 4 · Music

11   COUNTRY-WESTERN AND FOLK MUSIC   303

Part 5 Fun and Games

13 HUMOR   361

16 INTERNET ODDITIES   467

Part 6 Technical Requirements

Introduction

The Internet is *not* the CB radio of the '90s.

It is not a fad, it is not going to disappear, and it is not going to wait for the slowpokes to catch up to it before it starts to rearrange our culture.

The Internet has grown so much so quickly that a newcomer is likely to be intimidated by the abundance of information available there. Fortunately, much of that information pertains to a topic about which many people are naturally curious: entertainment.

Entertainment is the tail that is wagging the dog of the Internet. The Net may have arisen from an alliance of government, academia, and defense contractors, but today the developer base is increasingly dominated by two factions: college students, and businesses with something to sell. (Often the businesses are trying to sell something to college students.)

College students inevitably build Web sites about the things they are most interested in: late-night TV, alternative music, and scantily clad spokesmodels. Thus the Internet is dominated not just by entertainment-related sites but by the kind of entertainment that appeals to a twenty-something demographic.

Yet within the larger demographic of Internet developers, there is a remarkable diversity of interests, and this diversity is reflected in the variety of Web sites that you can access. Unlike movies, TV series, or books, a Web site is not affected by popularity ratings or sales. Thus any obsession, no matter how obscure, can have a viable home on the Internet. On the Net you can find sites devoted to everything from *Taxi* to tax law to taxidermy. And of course, if you can't find what you're interested in, you can always build a site of your *own*.

With all this diverse activity online, the average user could benefit from a guide that covers the broad sweep of Internet resources, everything from Aardvarks to Zygotes. Unfortunately, this ain't it. However, your author knows quite a bit about the considerable subset of Internet activity that is devoted to entertainment and pop culture, and that's where this particular book comes in handy. It's all about the fun stuff, and it won't waste your time telling you how to find online information about soybean production or how to send e-mail to the IRS.

What This Book Has To Offer—and What It Doesn't

This book is a selective introduction to the entertainment-related resources that are available on the Internet today. Given the staggering number of entertainment sites that already exist and the rate at which new ones are added, the author of this book has not attempted to be comprehensive. Many worthwhile sites were excluded from this book, and not all of the sites that were included will appeal to all readers. This is merely a rough map—from a rather opinionated driver.

Most of the sites in this book pertain to the central components of popular culture: movies, television, and music. There are also chapters on sports, games, humor, and unclassifiable Internet oddities.

There is little mention in this book of theatre or literature. For the purposes of this discussion, I consider theatre and literature to be examples of the "fine arts" (along with such things as painting, sculpture, and dance). I apologize to those who are seeking such information here. A comprehensive book about online arts and culture is surely in the works, and I'm certain that the author of *that* book will treat the subject matter with all of the heavy-handed respect that it deserves.

There is also very little information in this book about buying a computer, choosing an Internet provider, and configuring your software. Although the technical requirements for using the Internet are discussed in Chapter 17, "Getting Connected," this book is primarily a guided tour for users who are already up and running. (However, here's a bit of unsolicited advice to start things off: *Buy the fastest modem you can afford, or you will live to regret it.*)

Be aware, also, that there is very little in this book about the so-called online services, such as Prodigy, CompuServe, Genie, and America Online. These services have their purpose (in particular they enable you to *buy* things), and they have introduced a lot of people to the possibilities of online computing. Indeed, most of them are now starting to offer the Internet as one of their ancillary services. But for now, the most interesting online activity is taking place outside of the control of the online services, within the free-for-all environment called the World Wide Web.

At least 80 percent of the sites that are discussed in this book can be accessed via the World Wide Web. The remainder are FTP sites, Gopher sites, and UseNet newsgroups. (If you don't know what these terms mean, see Chapter 17, "Getting Connected.") Unlike the services of the commercial online companies, there is no built-in charge to use the Internet, because it isn't owned by anybody. It's free. (Of course, nothing outside of a mother's love is genuinely "free." To access the Net, you either have to be a freeloading college student or pay an Internet service provider a monthly fee; but unless your service provider happens to be one of the commercial online companies that offers the Internet as an "extra," this monthly fee is usually for unlimited usage. And the Internet beats the heck out of cable TV.)

Know Your Author

Obviously the information in this book is filtered through the perspective of some guy that you don't even know. Can you trust him? That depends.

Yours truly is a longtime entertainment reporter and Hollywood denizen of no particular importance. Although I have been writing about the entertainment industry for a decade and a half, I have only recently pointed my rickety Rambler toward the Expressway of Knowledge (or whatever they're calling it this week). Like many of you, I have learned about life—and the Internet—by continually forking down new paths. I've been a rock critic, a movie extra, a correspondent for *People* magazine, a voice-over announcer, and generally the kind of restless character that is not uncommon at the fringes of the show-business community. Along the way, I've hung backstage at the MTV Music Awards, been homeless in the back streets of Hollywood, and huddled in the back seat of a limousine with O.J. Simpson and Nicole Brown on a lonely highway outside of Birmingham, Alabama. Lucky for you, I took notes, and a lot of those observations about the show-business machinery have found their way into these pages.

Therefore, if you're looking for a catalog of Internet sites that is bleached of all personality and opinion, you're liable to be disappointed. This is Net-O-Rama *à la* Joe.

Except for the site names, their addresses, and their descriptions (which have been checked and double-checked), you should be prepared to take anything else that you read in this book with a small grain of salt. Just to keep things lively, there are a handful of misstatements and distortions of history (along with the author's debatable opinions) sprinkled through these pages like fairy dust. (I wasn't going to include a warning, because I thought these little jokes would be self-evident, until an early reader of the manuscript exclaimed, "Hey, wait a minute—there wasn't a guy in the Beatles named *Gus!*".)

On a more mundane note of warning, be advised that there is no guarantee that everything in this book will still be accurate as of the day of purchase. Internet connections are notoriously unreliable. A site that you access on Monday may not be available on Tuesday—and it might come back by Wednesday. If you get an error message when you're trying to connect, try again later. Maybe the site's just busy—a particular hazard during the daytime business hours—or maybe it has moved. Usually a site that moves to a new address will leave behind a pointer, but not always. If you still can't get to the site you want, consider exploring another. There's more than enough interesting stuff to go around.

How This Book Is Organized

There are six sections of this book, as follows:

* General Entertainment Resources
* Movies
* Television
* Music
* Fun and Games
* Technical Requirements

The first section will point you to some all-purpose online entertainment magazines and celebrity gossip sites. This is followed by the three major sections of this book: Movies, Television, and Music. The next section, Fun and Games, encompasses humor, games, sports, and oddball sites that don't fit into any other category. The final section, Technical Requirements, gives you the lowdown on actually getting connected to the Internet and using it effectively.

Each of the "major" sections—Movies, Television, and Music—begins with a chapter on general-interest resources for that medium, including home sites for some of the corporate entities that feed us our entertainment. These general chapters are followed by chapters on specific genres. For instance, the Movies section has a chapter called "Cult Cinema and Fantasy Film," the Television section has a chapter called "News and Talk," the Music section has a chapter called "Rock & Roll," and so on.

The organization of the individual chapters follows the model for the book as a whole. The first sites that are mentioned are general-interest databases, archives, or link sites. On the Web, a good general-interest resource will usually contain links to other sites containing more specific information. Thus, if you know the whereabouts of a few good archives or link resources, you can get just about anywhere else that pertains to a given subject. (That's why you don't have to be fanatical about memorizing and typing specific addresses. Between general indexes, link sites, and bookmarks, you can bounce around the Internet for weeks without ever typing an address.)

Another kind of general-interest site that is mentioned often in these pages is the online magazine. There are two types of online magazines. First, there are sites that are affiliated with existing print publications. Often this is a selected digest of articles from the print version (as in the online version of *People* magazine) or a teaser to lure new subscribers. If the entire magazine is duplicated online, it usually is not available until after the newsstand date. The second kind of online magazine site is the Internet-specific electronic magazine (or *e-zine*). These are original "publications" that mimic the look and content of a newsstand magazine but are only available online. A good example would be the terrific music publication called Strobe at *http:///www.iuma.com/strobe.*

Following the general sites are descriptions of more narrowly focused sites that you may find interesting. Usually the best or most comprehensive sites within a given subcategory are described first, and most of these descriptions are accompanied by a photograph (or "screen capture," as we say in the trade). A few particularly ambitious sites are mentioned in more than one chapter.

Finally, each chapter ends with The List, a catalog of all the sites and addresses that were mentioned in the chapter, along with a smattering of other worthwhile sites that you might want to explore on your own. The List is a good place to wander if you get tired of this author's opinions. (Remember, just because my name's on the cover of this book doesn't mean that I'm more qualified to pass judgment than you are.)

That's it, folks. Have at it. And don't forget to write.

Your friend,
Joe Williams

jwilliams@sams.mcp.com

or

414 Auber Dr.
Manchester, MO 63011

PART

I

GENERAL ENTERTAINMENT RESOURCES

1 Entertainment News and Celebrity Culture

CHAPTER 1

Entertainment News and Celebrity Culture

IN THIS CHAPTER:

> *Online entertainment publications*

> *Wire-service entertainment news*

> *Gossip sites*

> *Celebrity home pages*

IN OTHER CHAPTERS:

> *Getting connected to the Internet is discussed in Chapter 17.*

It is written in Groucho 3:16 that entertainment is the opiate of the masses; and as we approach the millennium, this ancient prescription is truer than ever. If you're anything like me, you think a day without O.J. is like a day without sunshine, and if you don't receive regular doses of Michael, Madonna, and Mister Ed, you're liable to go into convulsions.

For many young moderns who are surfing the Net, entertainment is a single entity, an oceanic trough of pop-cultural residue that contains equal portions of movies, music, TV, sports, games, and celebrity gossip. Unlike the world outside of your computing environment, the Net doesn't require that you choose a particular medium upon which to squander your money and your attention. You don't have to choose between movies and sports, or between television and music. Information about every facet of the entertainment experience is available from a single, friendly source on your desktop, and with a good all-purpose entertainment-info site, switching between the different media is as easy as a mouse click.

This chapter will examine the general-interest entertainment resources that are available on the Internet. It will also take a peek at some celebrity home pages and supermodel sites. Specific sites related to particular media will be found in each of the other sections of this book.

General Online Entertainment Sites

If you want to be part of a mushrooming trend, start an online entertainment site. Supersites that combine entertainment news, reviews of new releases, and downloadable multimedia files are everywhere on the Net these days—an indication of how important entertainment is to the consumers who are just now jumping aboard the Internet bandwagon. Many of these sites have high-profile sponsorship.

The following sites provide news, opinion, and online excerpts from the broad sweep of entertainment media.

Mr. Showbiz

http://web3.starwave.com/showbiz

The Mr. Showbiz site has just the right combination of skeptical attitude, straightforward news, playful graphics, and helpful info to qualify as the most nearly indispensable entertainment site on the Internet. (See figure 1.1.)

FIGURE 1.1

The opening page for Mr. Showbiz, the best and funniest entertainment-news site on the Internet.

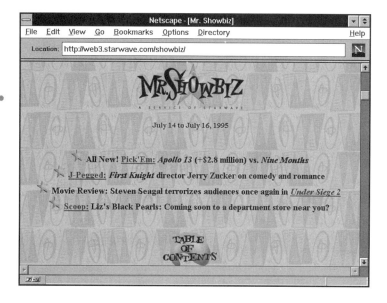

The site is divided between the Daily Dose (random news and notes), Mouth Off (letters and spirited cyber chat from visitors to the Mr. Showbiz site), Scoop (the latest entertainment news), Movie Reviews, Music Reviews, and Flash (the offbeat gossip and celebrity feature site, which is described later in this chapter). It also features up-to-date box-office, TV-rating, and music sales information, and it has a link to a fine account of the behind-the-scenes history of the Academy Awards.

The Gigaplex

http://www.gigaplex.com/wow

The Gigaplex is a glimpse into the possible future of entertainment news. It is a huge (600-page), timely, good-looking, all-purpose entertainment site that isn't padded with intrusive graphics or yesterday's press-releases.

The Gigaplex is divided into sites for Movies, Music, TV, Food, Books, Theatre, Golf (go figure), Top Ten Lists, and Yoga (yes, it's called The Yogaplex). Within these sites you will find interviews, features, excerpts, and upcoming-release information. One interesting recent feature, taken from *Interactive Week* magazine, was a report on the disturbing number of upcoming movies with an Internet/cyberspace theme. (We can look forward to at least a dozen "online stalker" movies, and I can almost guarantee that they all will be lousy.)

The Gigaplex is oriented toward mainstream popular entertainment (see figure 1.2), but that's understandable for a site of this type. And yes, they have a few things to sell you (including gourmet popcorn); but that aspect of the enterprise is handled very discreetly. As Jerry Lazar, the developer of this site, remarks in a great article called "The 10 Biggest Blunders Made by Web Builders," you have to offer the user something useful and free before you ask for a sale.

FIGURE 1.2

A list of the top-grossing films of all time, from the Gigaplex entertainment site. (Animal House is still hanging tough at #51.)

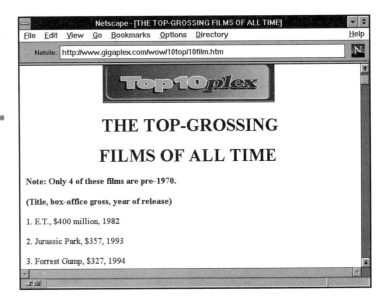

The Internet Entertainment Network
http://www.hollywoodnetwork.com

This is a bountiful but somewhat puzzling commercial site that invites you to "chat with celebrities, play games, go shopping, and network with industry professionals." There is a lot of stuff here for budding screenwriters and industry wanna-bes, as well as some of the weirdest online chatting I've ever seen. Example: *Price Is Right* hostess Janice Pennington turns to the cyber community for information about her missing spy husband.

The Electronic Newsstand
gopher://gopher.enews.com

Entertainment is a new category within the Electronic Newsstand gopher site, which is a potpourri of lifestyle information that you can access with either a gopher client or a Web browser. Within the Entertainment section, you can find a bit of info about movies, television, and music. In addition, you can access a number of online entertainment publications (albeit such little publications as *Irish Voice, Stage Direction, The Learning Channel Magazine,* and *Satellite Direct*).

Magazine, Newspaper, and Wire Service Resources

A growing number of newspapers and magazines have established an online presence. With some of these outlets, you will get headlines or scanty text-only information, while others are a sophisticated hybrid of the newsstand and an interactive Web page.

Be forewarned that many of the well-known media properties are charging money to access their online facilities. (Usually these sites require that you register from an online form and enter your credit card number. On general principles regarding the free flow of information and the inherent evil of credit cards, few of those sites are discussed in this book.)

Online Entertainment Magazines

If you like your entertainment news divided into handy little chunks (this is what *People* magazine calls the "bathroom factor"), you'll find several of the leading middle-brow, mass-market entertainment magazines online.

Pathfinder

http://www.pathfinder.com

The Pathfinder is a site sponsored by Time Warner Electronic Publishing. Here you'll find an access point to all of Time Inc.'s online magazines, including electronic excerpts from *Life*, *People*, *Vibe*, *Grooves*, and *Entertainment Weekly*. (See figure 1.3.) It also features a site devoted to political humor (which is gearing up for the next election) and an inevitable section called "O.J. Central," complete with e-mail feedback from the masses. If you fill out a survey and register a password, you can access the search engine for back issues of these magazines.

FIGURE 1.3

Pathfinder's welcome page will take you directly to the online version of the news or entertainment magazine of your choice—after you register, choose a password, and agree not to reveal any secrets you learn along the way.

People Magazine

http://www.pathfinder.com

The electronic digest of *People* magazine is nearly identical to its newsstand counterpart, which means it offers a variety of well-written, easily digestible stories about American life and culture in the late 20th century. Here you will find the Chatter section, Picks & Pans, Passages, and the patented *People* magazine featurettes. (See figure 1.4.)

FIGURE 1.4

People magazine is online. Unfortunately, you can't take most desktop computers into the bathroom with you.

Entertainment Weekly

http://www.pathfinder.com

Entertainment Weekly is a handy resource for up-to-date show-biz news and reviews, including movies, TV, music, CD-ROMs, and games. (See figure 1.5.) And unlike *People*, it won't distract you with stories about serial killers and babies with baboon hearts. The online version of *Entertainment Weekly* has the added advantage of being searchable and back-indexed.

FIGURE 1.5

An interview with Michael Stipe of R.E.M., from the online version of Entertainment Weekly.

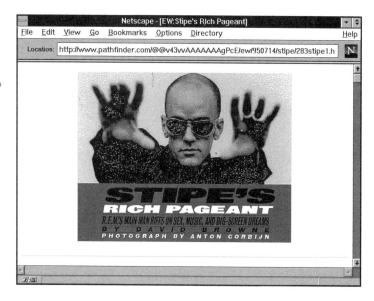

TRUE CONFESSIONS OF A *PEOPLE* CORRESPONDENT

In 1987 I was a graduate student at the University of Missouri School of Journalism. One of the visiting professors that year was a reporter from *People* magazine. During a seminar one afternoon on "celebrity journalism," he said that his proudest achievement at *People* was an article that debunked the wholesome image of singer Andy Gibb by exposing him as a pill popper and a consumer of pornography. I respectfully suggested that maybe the reporter had been a little too zealous in attacking Gibb, and he responded that I had a lot to learn about the real world.

One year later I found myself working in Los Angeles as a correspondent for *People* magazine. My first story assignment came to me in an excited late-night phone call from headquarters. Andy Gibb had just died, and all the correspondents were needed to come in the next morning to cover different angles of the story. I was assigned to call Gibb's acquaintances in the music business.

I spent the next morning at the Wilshire Blvd. office, calling some of the people who'd been closest to Andy Gibb. One by one they told me what a sweet guy he had been and how he just couldn't handle the pressures of fame. "But you know what probably hurt him the most?" asked one the them. "The article that appeared in *People* magazine a few years ago. He never got over it." This is what I reported for my portion of the story. Not a word of it was used in the magazine.

Soon after that, I ended my association with *People* magazine. I suppose I still have a lot to learn about the real world.

Newspapers

The Gate (*San Francisco Chronicle* and *Examiner*)

http://sfgate.com

This joint venture of the *San Francisco Chronicle* and the *San Francisco Examiner* is mighty handy, and it's free. Along with all the headline news and commentary you would expect from a major metropolitan daily in the coolest city on earth, you get classified ads, extensive coverage of the computer biz, and best of all, the famous "pink section" of entertainment news and reviews. (See figure 1.6.)

FIGURE 1.6

Some movie reviews, from the entertainment section of the San Francisco Chronicle, as excerpted in The Gate Web site.

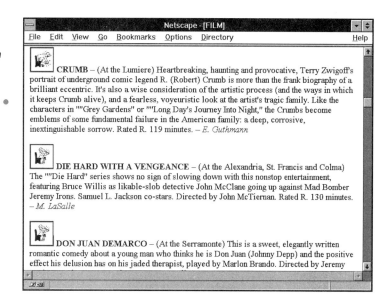

Trib.com
http://www.trib.com

From the Casper, Wyoming, *Star-Tribune* comes "The Internet's Newspaper." Trib.com provides headline news from the Associated Press, CBS News, National Public Radio, and other sources, and it combines them with an intelligent collection of Internet links (the What's On Tonite television guide, the Ultimate Band List) to provide a complete news and information resource. (And if you're one of the three or four people who actually live in Wyoming, this site will come in especially handy.)

Trib.com is connected to the Associated Press headline service, so you can use it to access the latest national and international news stories. (The list is updated every five minutes.)

San Jose Mercury News
http://www.sjmercury.com

The highly regarded Web site for the *San Jose Mercury News* claims to be the world's first completely online daily newspaper. The online *Mercury News* is fee-based, although it does offer a smattering of free features and is worth looking into. And because San Jose is home of the Silicon Valley, the paper is well-known for its computer-industry coverage.

If you are too busy to scour the Net for news, try the Mercury Center's Newshound. The Newshound is an electronic clipping service. It automatically searches articles from a range of newspapers and wire services, and selects only those articles that conform to the specs that you've provided. Information at *http://www.sjmercury.com/hound.htm*.

Electronic Telegraph
http://www.telegraph.co.uk

If you'd like a perspective from somewhere other than the U.S. of A., try the electronic version of Britain's *Telegraph* newspaper, which features news from around the world as well as entertainment reviews. It's free.

Wire Services

The following news services are available online for those who'd like an immediate fix of the latest celebrity news and hype.

ClariNet

ClariNet is a subscription-based news service that operates over the Internet. That means you have to pay extra for it (or more typically, your Internet service provider has to pay extra for it and will pass the cost along to you). I am not necessarily an advocate of paying for access to individual Internet facilities, but if up-to-the-minute news is important to you, it's worth looking into.

In addition to headline and financial news, ClariNet offers entertainment and lifestyle articles, which are parceled out to dedicated newsgroups.

ClariNet isn't affected by many of the editorial restrictions that you'd find in a typical newsroom. As a result, you can often find obscure articles in ClariNet newsgroups that would never make their way into the typical newspaper.

clari.apbl.entertain

The *clari.apbl.entertain* newsgroup is one place on the Internet to get the kind of breaking news that a newswire can offer you about "what's hot and what's not" (which, by the way, is one of the most loathsome clichés in the news business).

The *clari.apbl* (ClariNet AP Bulletin) hierarchy is the most widely distributed of the several dozen ClariNet hierarchies that exist, and it is included with a budget subscription to the ClariNet News Service. If your Internet service provider (ISP) offers ClariNet, you'll automatically have access to the AP Bulletin newsgroups.

clari.living.entertainment

The *clari.living* hierarchy is a "value-added" service offered by ClariNet, and as such, is much less widely distributed than the *.apbl* group mentioned previously.

You'll find much of the same kind of information here, but because there are newsgroups in this collection that focus specifically on movies, TV, people, and so on, the topics are somewhat more filtered than what you'd find in *clari.apbl*.

ClariNet itself recently established a home page on the World Wide Web. It has an interesting approach to access: It scans your login ID for the domain name of your ISP. Once it has that information, it can determine if your ISP is a ClariNet subscriber—and if so, at which level. If you pass muster, you can access all of the eligible newsgroups directly from ClariNet's Web site.

Reuters

The Reuters entertainment-news wire is available at several places on the Net. Recently it was added to the Yahoo menu at *http://www/yahoo.com*. After you choose the Entertainment subdirectory from the main index on the home page, the first choice is "Current Entertainment News." Clicking this will give you about a dozen single-paragraph entertainment-news items from the Reuters service.

CLARINET, THE INTERNET'S NEWS WIRE

The news that begins with AP stringers around the world goes through some interesting hoops before it hits your newsreader.

That process works as follows:

* Via satellite, ClariNet receives up-to-the-minute news from various sources, such as news syndicates, the Associated Press, and Reuters.

* Next, the raw news is processed into the format required by UseNet newsgroups, and a copy editor writes a meaningful headline. This is useful for busy readers who prefer only to read articles that are of specific interest.

* If the subject matter overlaps into various categories, articles are cross-posted to the relevant newsgroups.

* The articles are finally released into the Internet, which carries them to subscribers around the world.

Multimedia Archives

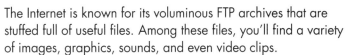

The Internet is known for its voluminous FTP archives that are stuffed full of useful files. Among these files, you'll find a variety of images, graphics, sounds, and even video clips.

The quality of the audio, video, and imagery in these files can range from excellent to awful. Many of the commercial sites maintained by film studios and record labels offer original clips from first-run movies or newly released CDs. On the other hand, many of the sounds and images you can find online are home brewed, and the quality can range widely.

At FTP sites such as *ftp.funet.fi/pub/culture*, you can also find complete movie scripts, TV episode guides, performer bios, song lyrics, and much more. Information on specific FTP sites are scattered throughout this book within the chapters devoted to that particular area of interest.

Company-Sponsored Sites

As interest in the Internet has reached critical mass, commercial organizations have figured out that having a presence on the Web offers a cheap means of reaching and maintaining customers. This is especially the case with entertainment corporations.

Film Studios

A growing number of movie studios have established Web sites in the recent past. And not coincidentally, because entertainment is their business, these sites are often excellent examples of well balanced, interesting, and often interactive, presentation.

Studios that can be found on the Web include:

* Buena Vista Pictures (See figure 1.7.)
* New Line Cinema
* MCA Universal

FIGURE 1.7

Disney's Buena Vista Movieplex looks like a hip enough site, but it's actually a front for a company that makes wholesome family-oriented motion pictures and cartoons! (http://www.disney.com)

• • • • • • • • • • • • • • • •

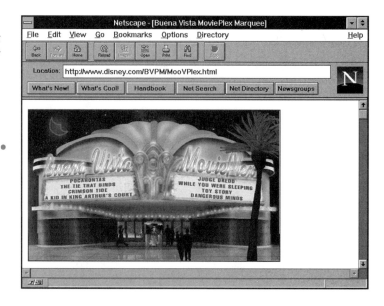

More specific information on studio sites can be found in Chapter 2, "General Movie Resources."

TV Networks

New sites sponsored by TV networks and production companies are popping up all over the Internet. Currently, there are sites for a dozen or more TV networks and cable outlets, including:

* CBS
* NBC
* The Fox Network
* The Discovery Channel
* MTV
* United Paramount Network

These are discussed in more detail in Chapter 5, "General TV Resources."

Record Companies

Among the almost 200 record labels that have a presence on the Web are such corporate heavyweights as:

* Sony (Columbia, Epic)

* Warner Bros (Reprise, Elektra, Atlantic)

* Polygram (A&M, Island)

* Geffen

* EMI/Capitol

Record-label sites are discussed in more detail in Chapter 8, "General Music Resources."

Gossip and Celebrity Sites

It's no use lamenting how weird it is that so many people are more interested in their favorite celebrity than in, say, their second-favorite family member. It's part of a larger, global phenomenon in which spiritual values have been crowded aside by bright images and primal sensations. Moses tried to warn us about this sort of thing, but a lot of us didn't listen (maybe because he didn't look enough like Charlton Heston). Today the people we're most likely to heed for our political opinions and purchasing decisions are not clergy nor teachers nor kin, but rather the celebrities we find the most pleasing.

Of course, as long as we're swimming in the bathwater of celebrity, we've got the option of sinking the battleships, of deflating our heroes when they fail to meet our needs, or creating new playthings from the nameless fish who wander into the celebrity net by accident.

Following are some sites devoted to the ebb and flow of celebrity—and to ordinary Joes who find themselves thrust into the spotlight when they have sex with bloodthirsty Long Island teenagers.

Flash (Mr. Showbiz)
http://web3.starwave.com/showbiz/flash

Flash (see figure 1.8) is the weekly celebrity section of the Mr. Showbiz site (described earlier in this chapter). It is updated with fresh features every Friday. These features include:

* J-Pegged: Mr. Showbiz's celebrity profile. This is the feature to follow if you're interested in such trivia as what kind of bed Bo Derek sleeps on, or whether or not she's ever punched or kicked anyone.

* The Watch: A unique photo feature. Recently featured were five celebrities with moles.

* Their Stories: "Revelatory" or even "educational" stories, such as Marlon Brando's thoughts during the filming of *Last Tango in Paris*.

* Tabloid Headlines: The best from around the world.

* Apocalypse Pretty Soon: News of doom and gloom.

* Terminal Chic: The latest news and commentary on trends, fashion, and the like.

* Letter from California: An inside look at the lifestyles of those deluded souls who live in Southern California.

FIGURE 1.8

A typical table of contents for Mr. Showbiz's Flash section.

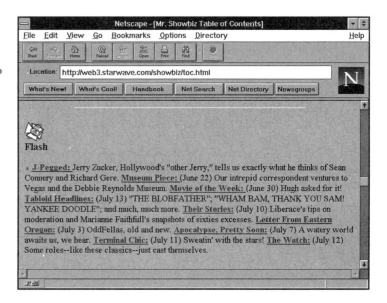

Cyber-Sleaze

http://metaverse.com/vibe/sleaze/index.html

Cyber-Sleaze is the gossip and entertainment-news section of the Metaverse, an ambitious site that was put together by former MTV veejay Adam Curry.

The gossip mostly pertains to washed-up rock & rollers, but at least it isn't lifted straight from the newspapers like you'll find at some of the other gossip sites on the Net.

You can have Cyber-Sleaze automatically e-mailed to you daily by writing *sleaze@metaverse.com* with the message **subscribe CYBERSLEAZE *yourname***.

You can learn more about the Metaverse in Chapter 9, "Rock & Roll."

Lucy Lipps
http://www.cybersim.com/lucylips

This site features Lucy Lipps' "romantic advice to the lovelorn, Web personals, Celebrity Scoop, Hollywood Hotline, and Lucy's Little Black Book." Oh, and there's also a pitch for her 900-number. (See figure 1.9.)

FIGURE 1.9
The home page for the Lucy Lipps family of fine Web services.

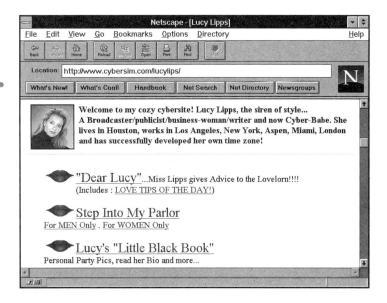

So just who is who is Lucy Lipps? "I am a radio-cable Goddess/spokeswoman/Cyber-babe/analyst/businesswoman. Through my multiple lives so far, I have had the opportunity to be Queen of the international party tornado of fun and spend time with some of the world's most amazing men and women; with years of good tips to my credit (just ask my friends) it has made me a leading authority on romance and the art of being a contemporary Sex Goddess."

Unfortunately, Lucy is spending so much time making cyber dreams come true for the lovelorn that her gossip is about two months old.

The Drudge Report

http://www.lainet.com/~drudge

This L.A.-based site is classified as "useless" by the Yahoo directory (the indispensable Web index at *http://www.yahoo.com*). But once you get past the puzzling home page, which features an up-to-the-minute snapshot of Hollywood and Vine (a corner where nothing much happens, although you should watch out for a guy named Steve), you will find an authoritative gossip and entertainment-news resource. The Drudge gossip section is amiably scattershot, jumping from the late-night rating wars, to the inside poop on the Movie Star and the Prostitute, to cranky wisecracks about politics, the weather, and the spiritual bankruptcy of modern culture. (See figure 1.10.)

FIGURE 1.10

Some observations from the Drudge Report, a well-connected Hollywood tip sheet.

● ● ● ● ● ● ● ● ● ● ● ● ● ● ●

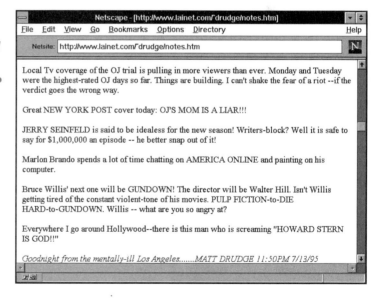

If you like the Drudge Report, you can have it sent to you via e-mail (free, and a couple times a week) by filling out a form at the home page.

Cyber Sightings
http://www.cyberpages.com/cybersightings

This is gossip in its truest and most noble form: unadulterated rumor and innuendo from anonymous Net surfers. No burden of proof is required. Thus we learn that the star of *Top Gun* and the star of *Johnny Mnemonic* are both gay (and actually share the same lover), that Cindy Crawford has no body hair, and that Madonna is actually a man from Australia. New rumors are always encouraged. (See figure 1.11.)

FIGURE 1.11

A sampling of the rumors that have been posted to Cyber Sightings. Each of these things might very well be true.

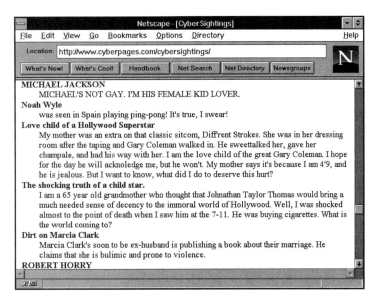

Gossip and Celebrity Newsgroups

There are scores of online fan clubs and discussion groups in UseNet, mostly in the *alt.fan* hierarchy. Not all of them are devoted to traditional entertainers. (They range from *alt.fan.dan-quayle* to *alt.fan.aspirin*.)

There are also some UseNet and Web sites that are devoted to pictures of famous people with their clothes off. I'm not here to make this sort of thing easy for you, but duty requires that I nudge you in the right direction, so here's a hint: *binaries*.

That's all you get out of me.

Celebrity Register

There are hundreds of fan-supported pages on the Web for individual actors, actresses, musicians, supermodels, and talk-show hosts. (See figures 1.12 and 1.13.)Some of these are sophisticated multimedia sites with professional-quality graphics and detailed biographical information; others are straight out of The Stalker Handbook.

FIGURE 1.12

A review of The Doors from the Val Kilmer home page at http://www.tc.cornell.edu/~cat/pages. (For the record, the author of this book was one of the "convincing extras" in the concert scenes.)

• • • • • • • • • • • • • • • • •

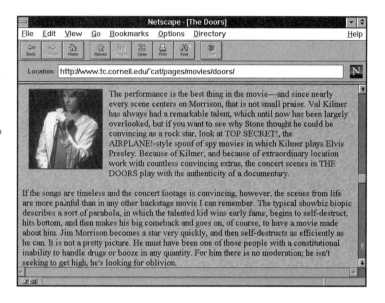

FIGURE 1.13

The Heather Locklear Home Page at http:// uptown.turnpike.net/garyfs/ index.htm includes some of Heather's beauty tips and is accessed over 40,000 times per month. (This site is not to be confused with a site called "Heather Locklear Kissed Me.")

• • • • • • • • • • • • • • • •

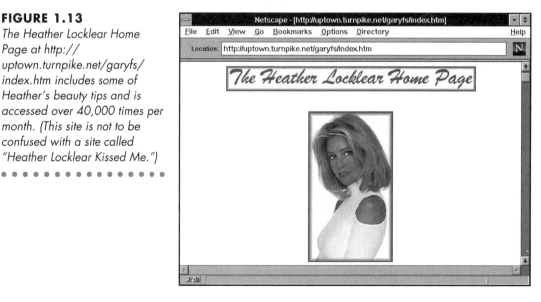

All About Supermodels

http://www.flashnet.it/models.htm

From this extensive collection of links to supermodel home pages, you can learn "all about" supermodels and hot young actresses (Sherilyn Fenn, Christina Applegate), including the following: what they look like, how well they photograph, what color their hair is, how they appear to a camera, and whether or not they're physically attractive.

The best index for cheesecake imagery on the Internet is in the Yahoo directory. Oddly it is subclassified under *Computers/Multimedia/Pictures/Supermodel_Images.*

Here you will find links to all the big name supermodels (and a few actresses who qualify as meat puppets), as well as miscellaneous collections of attractive, anonymous women frolicking in the sunshine. Not a lot of guys, though.

The Daily Babe Test

http://www.sci.kun.nl/thalia/funpage/babes

It sounds easy enough: You are shown about a dozen photographs of attractive young women and are asked to identify them from a multiple-choice list. But then all those Nikkis and Christys start to blend together and you wonder: Who *are* these people? (See figure 1.14.)

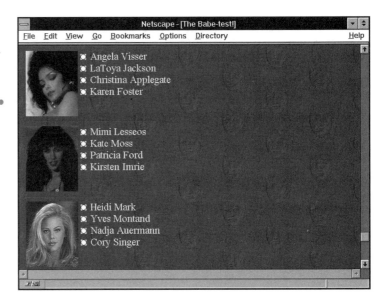

FIGURE 1.14
How well do you know your supermodels? (Can anyone ever really know a supermodel?) The Daily Babe Test.

● ● ● ● ● ● ● ● ● ● ● ● ● ● ● ● ●

The List

General Online Entertainment Sites

Mr. Showbiz
http://web3.starwave.com/showbiz

The Gigaplex
http://www.gigaplex.com/wow

The Internet Entertainment Network
http://www.hollywoodnetwork.com

The Electronic Newsstand
gopher://gopher.enews.com

Virtual Mirror
http://mirror.wwa.com/mirror

A terrific and widely varied entertainment, lifestyle, and software site.

Reuters Entertainment Wire via Nando Server
http://www2.nando.net/nt/entertainment

Entertainment Quick Link Central

http://www.dakota.net/entertainment.html

Every entertainment link that you need—and none that you don't. Set this as a bookmark.

Magazines, Newspapers, and Wire Services

Pathfinder

http://www.pathfinder.com

People

http://www.pathfinder.com

Entertainment Weekly

http://www.pathfinder.com

Entertainment Magazine On-Line

http://emol.org/emol/index.html

A Tuscon-based magazine with some coverage of national interest.

Drive-Thru

http://www.primenet.com/~joelmot/drive/index.html

An entertainment magazine from a bored teenager.

Pressure Points

http://www.ot.com/skew

For young, hip, disaffected New Yorkers over age 12.

The Muse

http://www.hyperlink.com/muse

The Gate (*San Francisco Chronicle* and *Examiner*)

http://sfgate.com

Trib.com

http://www.trib.com

San Jose Mercury News

http://www.sjmercury.com

Electronic Telegraph

http://www.telegraph.co.uk

Raleigh News and Observer

http://www.nando.net/welcome.html

ClariNet

http://www.clari.net

Also on UseNet, in the *clari.** hierarchy.

Gossip and Celebrity Sites

Flash (Mr. Showbiz)

http://web3.starwave.com/showbiz/flash

Cyber-Sleaze

http://metaverse.com/vibe/sleaze/index.html

Lucy Lipps

http://www.cybersim.com/lucylips

The Drudge Report

http://www.lainet.com/~drudge

Cyber Sightings

http://www.cyberpages.com/cybersightings

All About Supermodels

http://www.flashnet.it/models.htm

The Daily Babe Test

http://www.sci.kun.nl/thalia/funpage/babes

The Supermodel Home Page

http://www.supermodel.com

Pit's Page of Beautiful Women

http://www.cen.uiuc.edu/~morrise/girls.html

Supermodels—they're all so… beautiful.

PART II

Movies

2

General Movie Resources

IN THIS CHAPTER:

> *Movie databases, archives, and link sites*

> *Online film magazines*

> *Film history sites*

> *Movie-studio sites*

> *Resources for filmmakers*

IN OTHER CHAPTERS:

> *Movie-review sites, the latest re-
leases, and the Academy Awards
are discussed in Chapter 3.*

> *Cult movies, independent
films, fantasy, horror, and sci-fi
are discussed in Chapter 4.*

< *General entertainment resources and
gossip are discussed in Chapter 1.*

Cinema has a sanctified status among the popular media. Movies were meant to be watched in the dark, as we sit hushed and humbled before a towering screen. Until television made it acceptable to talk through a movie, the motion-picture theater was a temple, and the movies were the mouthpiece of the new gods.

Today, movies are shown in cracker-box multiplex theaters, and with the advent of video and the spread of exposé journalism, the facade of mystery had been stripped away and movies have lost much of their power over us. The movie fans of today have an iconoclastic attitude toward the medium and toward individual films that is reflected in many of the playful movie sites on the Internet. There are sites about good movies, bad movies, obscure movies, and movies that haven't even come out. And yet in most of the movie sites there is still a palpable reverence for the art form and its rich history that speaks to the part in all of us that shivers when the lights go down and really wants to believe in a Hollywood ending.

This chapter discusses some of the less glamorous (albeit more useful) film sites, including general film-information archives, studio sites, and resources for working filmmakers.

Archives and Link Sites

As with many of the larger subject areas on the Internet, it is helpful to have a good link site or general resource from which to begin your search for online information about the movies.

The Internet Movie Database
http://www.msstate.edu/Movies

This famous site, sometimes referred to as the Cardiff Movie Database (because one of its servers is in Cardiff, Wales) is one of the most useful and entertaining places on the Internet.

The Internet Movie Database is the hypertext front-end of the *rec.arts.movies* UseNet group. It has been built and maintained by Internet users as an interactive experiment in the free exchange of information. Users are welcome to update information, contribute reviews, or vote on the relative worth of the thousands of films that the site describes. (See figure 2.1.)

(See figure 2.1.)

FIGURE 2.1

A search for information about my favorite movie turned up this little surprise, which demonstrates both the flexibility of the Cardiff search engine and the inexhaustible weirdness of the filmmaking community.

• • • • • • • • • • • • • • • •

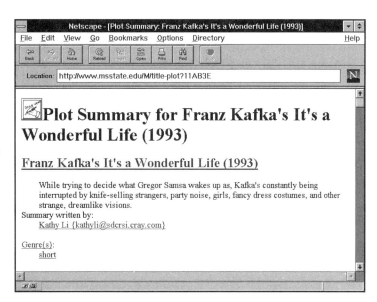

You can search the database by film title, individual actor or director, country of origin, or even by character name. The site also includes lists of such things as celebrity birthdays, famous marriages, notable movie quotes, and the best—and worst—100 movies of all time as voted by the Database users. (See figure 2.2.)

FIGURE 2.2

Some of the 100 bottom movies of all time, as voted by the users of the Internet Movie Database.

• • • • • • • • • • • • • • • •

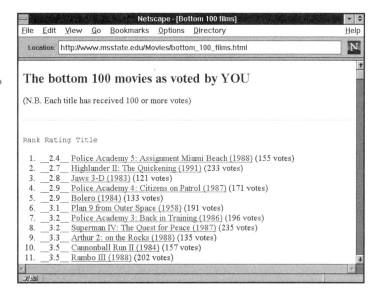

This information is mirrored (reproduced) on several servers around the world. The address listed previously is the most convenient for American users.

Cinema Sites

http://www.webcom.com/~davidaug/Movie_Sites.html

David Augsburger's Cinema Sites is an astounding and well-indexed link resource for the many cinema pages on the Internet. Of particular value are the brief descriptions of the sites, which can save you time and connect charges.

Wiretap Archive

gopher://wiretap.spies.com:70/11/Library/Media/Film

The movie section of this great pop-culture archive includes an oddly diverse listing of special-interest movies, including noir, naval-themed, railroad, and gay films. (See figure 2.3.)

FIGURE 2.3

A partial list of gay and lesbian films, from the Wiretap archive.

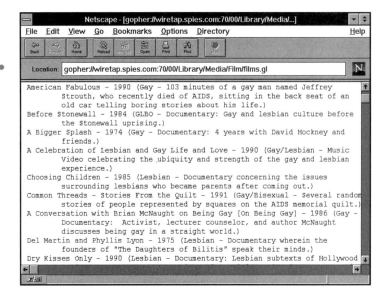

Film and Video Resources
http://http2.sils.umich.edu/Public/fvl/film.html

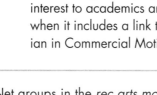

This thorough and (suspiciously tidy) site should be of special interest to academics and smarties. (It gives away its origins when it includes a link to a site called "The Image of the Librarian in Commercial Motion Pictures.")

NOTE The UseNet groups in the *rec.arts.movies* hierarchy—and their accompanying FAQ lists—are a solid place to get information about movies. A summary of the *rec.arts.movie* UseNet groups appears in The List at the end of this chapter.

Online Magazines

Some of the better film publications that are available at the newsstand have established an online presence, and there are also several Internet-specific resources that qualify under the cyber definition of a "magazine."

Film Comment
http://www.interactive.line.com/film/cover.html

Film Comment is one of the most respected film publications in the English-speaking world. It offers a somewhat highbrow perspective on offbeat, independent, and foreign films as well as the mainstream American cinema and even some television. (A recent issue contained a story about *Mystery Science Theater 3000*, the hilarious TV show where a guy and his two robot pals watch a bad movie and make wisecracks at the screen.) If you know the meaning of the terms "montage," "post-structuralism," or "honey wagon," you're ahead of the game; but nobody checks your credentials at the door.

Transient Images

http://www.cais.com/jpadgett/www/home.html

This "almost weekly e-zine" (see figure 2.4) is divided about 50-50 between film and television. It eschews highbrow analysis for low-key gossip, upcoming-release information, and box-office statistics.

FIGURE 2.4

The eye-popping home page of Transient Images.

CinemaSpace

http://remarque.berkeley.edu:8001/~xcohen

CinemaSpace is a journal from the Film Studies program at the University of California-Berkeley. The inaugural online issue includes such articles as "Narrating National Sadness: Cinematic Mapping and Hypertextual Dispersion" and "The Political Aesthetic: Nation and Narrativity on the Starship Enterprise." Sounds almost too good to be true, doesn't it?

FilmMaker

http://found.cs.nyu.edu/CAT/affiliates/filmmaker/filmmaker.html

FilmMaker is a quarterly publication from the New York University School of Film that bills itself as "The Magazine of Independent Film." The online version excerpts a couple features from the newsstand version to pique your interest. A recent issue (see figure 2.5) featured a review of the superb and disturbing documentary *Crumb* and an article on new trends in film lighting.

FIGURE 2.5
The online version of FilmMaker magazine.

Virtual Mirror
http://mirror.wwa.com/mirror

This terrific and wildly varied site features computer news, a gardening section, interesting general-interest features, and excellent movie and music and sections. The movie section focuses equally on Hollywood product and independent art films (such as the work of Akira Kurosawa and Hal Hartley).

Film History Sites

Film historians and preservationists have established a niche on the Internet, as have memorabilia collectors.

American Memory

http://lcweb2.loc.gov/papr/mpixhome.html

The American Memory Collection of historical artifacts from the Library of Congress includes an early-American film archive. The downloadable film clips cover the period from 1897 to 1916 and include footage of San Francisco at the turn of the century and scenes from the funeral of President William McKinley. There is also an interesting essay about early film genres—in particular, "actuality" films: footage of "panoramic views, civic events, parades, new buildings, new inventions, policemen and firemen in action, risqué novelties, and exotic looking immigrants."

Silent Movies

http://www.cs.monash.edu.au/~pringle/silent

There is a surprising amount of online information about silent movies, and most if it can be accessed from here. This site includes a Chaplin bio, links to home pages for Buster Keaton and Lillian Gish, the Cardiff filmography for many of the major silent stars, and a tribute to the "Silent Star of the Month." (See figure 2.6.)

FIGURE 2.6

Blanche Sweet, "Silent Star of the Month."

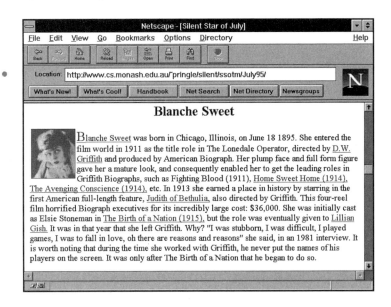

In 1988, the United States Library of Congress established the National Film Preservation Board to preserve American films that are deemed "culturally, historically, or esthetically important". Each year, the board selects 25 films to add to the National Film Registry. The complete list of the films so honored to date can be found at the Clamen's Movie Information Collection at *http://www.cs.cmu.edu/afs/cs.cmu.edu/user/clamen/misc/movies/NFR-Titles.html*.

Movie Deaths
http://catless.ncl.ac.uk/Obituary/movies.html

Obituaries and film credits of the recently departed, in reverse order of their demise. Hours of side-splitting fun.

The GRAFICS Server
http://grafics.histart.umontreal.ca/default-eng.html

GRAFICS is a Canadian site dedicated to early cinema, mostly via links. It is available in both English and French.

The Picture Palace
http://www.ids.net/picpal

This site is a middle-man resource for old movies on videotape and laserdisc, with an emphasis on horror, Western, sci-fi, and exploitation movies. Value is added to the site with a monthly "Hollywood Scriptwriter" interview and excerpts from *Psychotronic* and *Alternative Cinema* magazines.

Film Studios

Not surprisingly, the studios that make those big-budget movies have a lot of talented, visually attuned people sitting around looking for something to do between *Batman* sequels, and so most of the film companies have used these people to establish interesting—or gaudy—Web sites that promote their products.

Paramount Pictures

http://www.paramount.com

The Paramount site uses an image of its famous Melrose Avenue entrance as its user interface. (Did you know that Paramount is the only major movie studio that is actually within the boundaries of Hollywood?) Here you can click on icons representing one of the Paramount-produced TV shows or movies to get information about that particular production, or you can click on the gates themselves to get the latest Paramount studio news. (See figure 2.7.)

FIGURE 2.7

The Paramount Pictures home page.

MCA/Universal Cyberwalk

http://www.mca.com

Cyberwalk (see figure 2.8) is the big promotional site for the MCA family of fine corporate entertainment, which includes Universal Pictures, MCA Records, the Universal Studios tour, and even Spencer's Gifts (without which a mall is just a shopping center).

FIGURE 2.8

The MCA/Universal Cyberwalk home page.

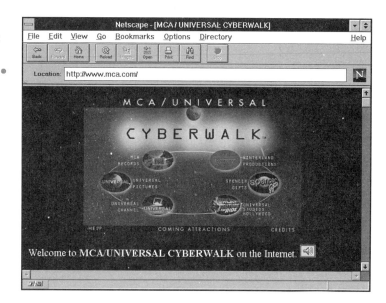

The Universal Pictures component of the site offers downloadable video clips from upcoming Universal releases. For aspiring filmmakers, this site also has a lot of good behind-the-scenes info about the film and TV production process, including actual scripts and detailed shooting schedules.

Sony Pictures Entertainment

http://www.spe.sony.com/Pictures/SonyMovies/index.html

The word "interactive" is invoked like a magic spell at this site for the Sony studios (Columbia and Tri-Star). For instance, you can use this site to "Interact with Sandra Bullock!" (This is a promotional gimmick for a movie called *The Net,* which is just the first of many ill-conceived movies we can expect about the Internet in the next couple years.) There is also a *"First Knight* Interactive Quest." (*First Knight* was a movie with Sean Connery and Richard Gere that most of us didn't get around to seeing.)

And finally there's a reminder that Sony is the company that gave us *Johnny Mnemonic* (with which not many people interacted). If I were Sony, I'd start thinking about next year's word.

Film Festivals

Film festivals often function as a bridge between aspiring film-makers and successful careers. The major studios scout for new talent at regional festivals, and many low-budget films that might otherwise get recycled for guitar picks are delivered to a receptive audience.

Cannes Film Festival

http://www.mhm.fr/cannes/eng/index.html

This elegant site offers a wealth of information about the Cannes Film Festival (as if we're actually going to *go* there), including a schedule and a description of all the films entered in the competition. (See figure 2.9.)

FIGURE 2.9

A movie that you're not likely to see at the Mallplex, from the Cannes Film Festival Web site.

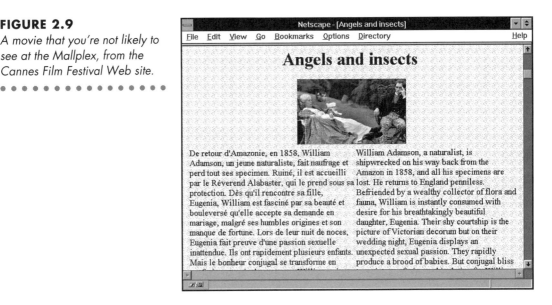

Sundance Film Festival/Sundance Institute

http://cybermart.com/sundance/institute/institute.html

The Sundance Institute was founded by Robert Redford in 1981 to promote independent American filmmakers. The Institute and the yearly film festival it sponsors have debuted such notable films as *Reservoir Dogs* and *sex, lies and videotape*. (Now there is also a Sundance cable TV service for American independent films.)

This site describes the mission and history of the Institute and provides information about next year's festival.

Resources for Filmmakers

At this very moment, aspiring filmmakers are scouring the Internet for information. Unfortunately, the information they're after is background material for hackneyed scripts about online stalkers, cybersex, and government surveillance of e-mail. I'm telling you, there are almost no good movies to be made about computers. However, computers *can* be used to access information about making movies with *people* in them.

Cyber Film School

http://www.io.org/~mbelli

A giant step beyond correspondence school, the Cyber Film School is a terrific filmmakers' resource that is equal parts entertaining and useful. It offers solid, detailed advice for the would-be filmmaker about scriptwriting, budgeting, cinematography, lighting, and career management. And it's fun: In the past it has featured a "cyber screenplay" in which participants added one line at a time to an evolving script called *Fire Alley*, and lately it has included an online game in which you direct the career of Marty, an aspiring filmmaker. ("Guide him wisely, he could be the next Quentin Tarantino; guide him badly, he'll wind up ushering at the local multiplex.") It also includes Cinema Canada Online, an online directory of Canadian film and TV resources. Plus, it looks great. (See figure 2.10.) And finally, it's got a practical and well-organized array of links.

FIGURE 2.10

The Cyber Film School, one of
the truly great sites on the Net.

● ● ● ● ● ● ● ● ● ● ● ● ● ● ● ●

The Cyber Film School is everything that the Internet ought to be: creative, educational, empowering, and fun. Moe Belli and Barbara Jones, the developers of this site, have set the standard for others to follow.

Independent Film and Video Makers Internet Resource Guide

http://www.echonyc.com/~mvidal/Indi-Film+Video.html

This is a great, politicized resource for independent filmmakers. It includes information about grants and festivals, and it has links to many sites that would be of special interest to video renegades who are strapped for cash or inspiration.

Screenwriters' Resources Pages

http://www.teleprt.com/~cdeemer/Screenwriters.html

This exhaustive site offers straightforward real-world advice about plot structure, agents, pitches, and everything else that's related to the eternal riddle of beginning-middle-and-end. (I think it was Orson Welles who said that any story with a happy ending isn't finished yet.)

The List

Archives and Link Sites

The Internet Movie Database
http://www.msstate.edu/Movies

Cinema Sites
http://www.webcom.com/~davidaug/Movie_Sites.html

Wiretap Archive
gopher://wiretap.spies.com:70/11/Library/Media/Film

Film and Video Resources
http://http2.sils.umich.edu/Public/fvl/film.html

CineMedia
http://www.gu.edu.au/gwis/cinemedia/CineMedia.cinema.html

The CineMedia link index is divided into sites for movie companies, movie history, scripts, organizations, individual films, and more.

Clamen's Movie Information Collection
http://www.cs.cmu.edu/afs/cs.cmu.edu/user/clamen/misc/movies

Contains a complete list of the films that have been added to the National Film Registry.

Cathouse Archive
http://cathouse.org/cathouse/movies

Online Magazines

Film Comment
http://www.interactive.line.com/film/cover.html

Transient Images
http://www.cais.com/jpadgett/www/home.html

CinemaSpace
http://remarque.berkeley.edu:8001/~xcohen

FilmMaker

http://found.cs.nyu.edu/CAT/affiliates/filmmaker/filmmaker.html

Virtual Mirror

http://mirror.wwa.com/mirror

Boxoffice Magazine

http://cwis.usc.edu/dept/etc/boxoffice/boxoffice.html

Film History Sites

American Memory

http://lcweb2.loc.gov/papr/mpixhome.html

Silent Movies

http://www.cs.monash.edu.au/~pringle/silent

Movie Deaths

http://catless.ncl.ac.uk/Obituary/movies.html

GRAFICS Server

http://grafics.histart.umontreal.ca/default-eng.html

The Picture Palace

http://www.ids.net/picpal

C*Stars Cinemagic Art

http://www.3i.com/cstars/cinemagic/cinemagic_top.html

A site for buying and selling movie posters.

Movie Poster Warehouse

http://www.io.org/~mpw

Movie Studios

Paramount Pictures

http://www.paramount.com

MCA/Universal Cyberwalk
http://www.mca.com

Sony Pictures Entertainment
http://www.spe.sony.com/Pictures/SonyMovies/index.html

Film Festivals

Cannes Film Festival
http://www.mhm.fr/cannes/eng/index.html

Sundance Film Festival/Sundance Institute
http://cybermart.com/sundance/institute/institute.html

Santa Clarita International Film Festival
http://www.smartlink.net/~director/scviff

The world's first and only family-oriented film festival.

Film Festival Index
http://www.film.com/film/filmfests

Sponsored by the Seattle Film Festival, this is a central site for film-festival information from around the world.

Resources For Filmmakers

Cyber Film School
http://www.io.org/~mbelli

Independent Film and Video Makers Internet Resource Guide
http://www.echonyc.com/~mvidal/Indi-Film+Video.html

Screenwriters' Resources Pages
http://www.teleport.com/~cdeemer/Screenwriters.html

Mandy's Film and Television Production Directory
http://www.mandy.com

Movie-Related UseNet Groups

rec.arts.movies

Free-form discussion of the movies.

rec.arts.movies.announce

The postings at this moderated newsgroup contain information on recent events in the world of movies, including new releases, industry developments, and recent award winners.

rec.arts.movies.current-films

This newsgroup is for discussing movies that have been released recently as well as upcoming movies.

rec.arts.movies.past-films

This newsgroup is for discussing movies that are more than two years old.

rec.arts.movies.reviews

This is a low-volume, moderated newsgroup where formal reviews of movies are regularly posted.

rec.arts.movies.people

This newsgroup discusses actors, actresses, directors, writers, composers, and other personalities within the film industry. It also contains celebrity gossip.

rec.arts.movies.movie-going

This newsgroup is about the movie-going experience itself, including theater design, ticket prices, and the *gestalt* of popcorn.

rec.arts.movies.tech

This newsgroup is for laymen who are interested in the technical aspects of movies and movie-making.

rec.arts.movies.production

The newsgroup for people who are interested in actually making films.

rec.arts.movies.misc

The catch-all group in the *rec.arts.movies* hierarchy.

CHAPTER 3

The Popular Cinema

IN THIS CHAPTER:

> *Coming attractions and publicity sites*

> *Review sites for new releases*

> *Box-office statistics*

> *Theater schedules*

> *Oscar information*

> *Individual movie sites*

IN OTHER CHAPTERS:

< *General movie archives, studio pages, and film history are discussed in Chapter 2.*

> *Fantasy films, sci-fi, horror, and movies with a cult following are discussed in Chapter 4.*

< *Entertainment news and gossip are discussed in Chapter 1.*

This is the mainstream Hollywood chapter. The organization of this chapter mirrors the life cycle of a typical big-budget movie from an American film studio.

Let's say that Universal Pictures has done extensive market research and decided to begin production on a movie that we'll call *Waterworld 2: The Deepening.* The studio's publicity department sends a press release to the *Hollywood Reporter, Daily Variety,* the *Los Angeles Times,* and *Entertainment Tonight.* Then an intern on summer break from U.S.C. suggests that the studio send the same press release to a few of the online entertainment guides and he reminds the vice president of publicity that Universal itself has a promotional Web site that could use the information. The vice president of publicity pats the kid on the back, faxes the press releases, and makes a mental note to have the ambitious little schmuck bludgeoned to death.

Production begins on the movie at a secret location in the South China Sea. Photos from the set are transmitted periodically to magazines and newspapers around the world, along with a series of press releases that downplay the budget, now estimated at half a billion dollars.

Three years later, *Waterworld 2* is 85 percent completed when suddenly the star of the movie fires the director so that the finished product will reflect his personal vision. While the star of the movie completes the shoot and begins the editing, leatherbound publicity packets are delivered to representatives of the major print, broadcast, and online news organizations during a press conference to announce that Universal is teaming up with Burger King to offer *Waterworld 2* collectors' cups. The vice president of publicity proudly announces that "Everybody's talking about *W2.*"

The movie is given an advance screening for the critics. They are unanimous in their response. Gene Siskel pronounces it "unbelievable." Roger Ebert declares, "If you liked the original, it is conceivable that you may want to see the sequel."

The online critics enter the fray, and the *rec.arts.movies.waterworld* UseNet group is overheated with activity.

On the Monday after the gala premiere, the vice president of publicity checks the box-office figures on his personal computer and makes another mental note before calling his attorney.

Two weeks later, the new vice president of publicity prepares an announcement about special pricing for the home-video release of the film.

A grade-school kid in Montana finds a copy of the movie in the used-videos bin at a Safeway store in Missoula and launches an Internet campaign to have the star of the movie nominated for an Academy Award. The Web page from the kid in Missoula gets a tongue-in-cheek mention in *Wired* magazine, and suddenly the notion of an Oscar nomination gathers critical mass. In the spirit of goodwill, members of the Academy give the star of the movie a Best Actor nomination. Three weeks later at the Dorothy Chandler Pavilion, the smiling movie star emerges from his limousine to generous applause as Leeza Gibbons announces, "Ladies and gentlemen, the star of *Waterworld 2* and a nominee tonight for Best Actor, Mr. Macauley Culkin!"

At a party hosted by *Sassy* magazine immediately after the awards ceremony, a brave but teary-eyed Culkin announces that although he's still a little shaken up from the humbling experience of the evening, he has just agreed to star in *Waterworld 3: The Musical.*

Coming Attractions

Long before a Hollywood movie lands in your neighborhood multiplex, the wheels of the publicity machine are spinning. (After all, those sneak-peek photographs don't make it into your Sunday newspaper's entertainment supplement because the paper has *spies.*) Some of the online coming-attractions sites are almost auxiliary divisions of the studio publicity apparatus, while others have a more informational and objective attitude toward the hoopla.

MovieWEB
http://movieweb.com/movie/movie.html

MovieWEB will never be confused with hard-hitting journalism, but as a *de facto* promotional tool for mainstream Hollywood releases, it is attractive, entertaining, and not too loaded with bull. (See figure 3.1.)

MovieWEB offers Quicktime video trailers, still photos, and production notes for most of the new releases from the major American movie studios and distributors. (It also offers the most recent box-office sales figures and a list of the Top 50 highest grossing movies of all time.) There is no troublesome mention of *quality* here. You'll just have to buy a ticket and decide for yourself if a movie is any good.

Hollyweb
http://www.ingress.com/users/spease/hw/hollyweb.html

Hollyweb is a plucky little one-stop movie-news site that seeks to be "an online film mecca." Although it is just as much a review site as a coming-attractions resource, it offers enough "insider" news to qualify in this category. (See figure 3.2.)

FIGURE 3.2

Hollyweb wants to be your online movie guide.

● ● ● ● ● ● ● ● ● ● ● ● ● ● ● ●

Netscape - [The Hollyweb Online Film Guide]

File   Edit   View   Go   Bookmarks   Options   Directory   Help

This main boulevard is jammed with tourists and locals! From here you can:

Read the <u>Studio Briefing</u>, a weekly report of current industry news.

Look over the <u>Production Slate</u> to find out which films have the green light.

Visit this week's <u>Box Office</u> or check the <u>All-Time Blockbusters.</u>

See what's playing at the <u>Hollyweb Cineplex</u> (a comprehensive listing of film & video reviews).

Stop by the Hollyweb <u>City Hall</u> (news, comments, and information about this site).

Hollyweb features several useful and entertaining sections. The Production Slate is a huge listing of all the films that are in development or currently shooting. (This is where you might first discover that Nancy Kerrigan has been signed to star in a Disney remake of *Some Like It Hot* or that Miramax has given a green light to a film version of the Budweiser frogs commercial.) The Production Slate listings include all the available casting and production information. (The information is gleaned from a newsletter called Electronic Hollywood.)

The section called Studio Briefing has the latest poop from the backlots and boardrooms of Tinseltown. There is also a recent box-office tally. But the best thing about Hollyweb are the movie reviews by the Webmaster, Scott Pease, who describes himself as "a bitter ex-film student." For instance, he skewers *Forrest Gump* for its "amazingly crappy metaphors" and notes that "every one of Gump's 'victories' is a result of someone else's death, disfigurement, or financial disaster." This is priceless stuff.

Hollywood Online
http://www.hollywood.com

Hollywood Online is another splashy site that offers a slew of multimedia files for upcoming films and new releases. It also offers a toolbox of software to help you use the files. (Strangely, this site also features a section of ads for pricey Los Angeles real estate, so you can buy a house from one of the movie stars you've just been reading about.)

NOTE

Before you download audio or video files from any site, you should have the necessary media-player software loaded onto your computer and placed in an appropriate directory. (Some sites offer the software directly; others offer pointers to one of the many places online where the software is freely available.) Describing how to install and use multimedia software is beyond the scope of this book, but you can get a lot of this information from a Toolkit site operated by former MTV veejay Adam Curry at *http://metaverse.com/vibe/toolkit.html.*

Note also that until you get a much better modem than the one you've got now, almost any multimedia file will take a *very* long time to download, and it will likely consume a lot of disk space.

Reviews of Current Releases

As soon as a movie is completed, it is offered to the pundits for constructive criticism. When the critics like a movie, their words are plastered all over the newspaper ads. When they don't, the studios complain that critics are irresponsible elitists who are out of touch with the general public and ought to be banned from the theaters if they're not willing to fork over $7.50 like everyone else. This love-hate relationship is really quite funny, actually (although you wouldn't know it from that unremarkable cartoon show, *The Critic*). Today, the Internet allows everyone with a computer and a phone line an equal opportunity to slag the hard work and high hopes of people who are more talented than themselves (such as the nice folks who made that ambitious cartoon show *The Critic*). The Internet is filled with movie-review sites that range from highbrow analysis to illiterate screed.

Film.com
http://www.film.com/film

Film.com is a dandy site for serious film lovers (as opposed to lovers of serious film, although often these are the same people). The brainchild of syndicated Seattle film critic Lucy Mohl, Film.com assesses the current releases, previews the coming attractions, interjects a few featurettes (up-and-coming stars, a history of zombie flicks), and sponsors a quintet of online discussion groups on subjects ranging from Quentin Tarantino to do-it-yourself filmmaking.

Generally, the reviews (which come from several critics across the country) have a droll and slightly scalded sense of humor and are aimed at a film-wise, middlebrow readership. (See figure 3.3.)

FIGURE 3.3

A review of a movie called The Net, from the Film.com site.

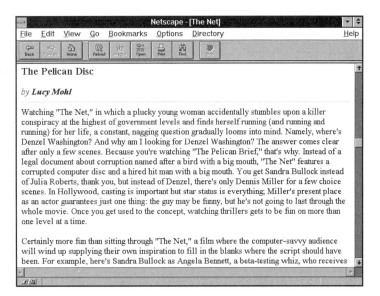

Movie Reviews by Edwin Jahiel
http://www.prairienet.org/~ejahiel/reviews.htm

Edwin Jahiel is a movie buff in Champaign, Illinois, who comes across as neither a crackpot nor an aesthete (although he's not afraid of them there *foreign* films). A nice thing about Jahiel's site is that he covers both current films and neglected oldies, and he does it with depth and an even-tempered intelligence.

Teen Movie Critic

http://www.skypoint.com/members/magic/roger/teencritic.html

Teen Movie Critic is 16 years old. "The reviews I give are not for one type of teen, but for every teen that you can possibly imagine." Teen Movie Critic is Everyman. He is my new hero. (See figure 3.4.)

FIGURE 3.4

This is Teen Movie Critic. He has come to show us The Way.

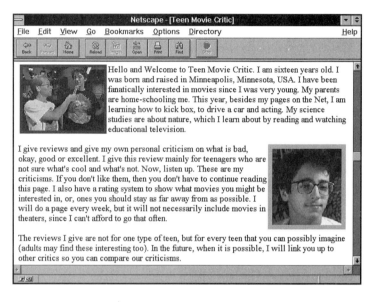

Hello and Welcome to Teen Movie Critic. I am sixteen years old. I was born and raised in Minneapolis, Minnesota, USA. I have been fanatically interested in movies since I was very young. My parents are home-schooling me. This year, besides my pages on the Net, I am learning how to kick box, to drive a car and acting. My science studies are about nature, which I learn about by reading and watching educational television.

I give reviews and give my own personal criticism on what is bad, okay, good or excellent. I give this review mainly for teenagers who are not sure what's cool and what's not. Now, listen up. These are my criticisms. If you don't like them, then you don't have to continue reading this page. I also have a rating system to show what movies you might be interested in, or, ones you should stay as far away from as possible. I will do a page every week, but it will not necessarily include movies in theaters, since I can't afford to go that often.

The reviews I give are not for one type of teen, but for every teen that you can possibly imagine (adults may find these interesting too). In the future, when it is possible, I will link you up to other critics so you can compare our criticisms.

To get a better idea of why critics are always dissing what appear to be perfectly good movies, take a gander at the Movie Cliches List at *http://www.well.com/user/vertigo/cliches.html*. After reading this massive list (which is alphabetized by category), you will realize that *everything* has been done before, and because critics see more movies than the rest of us, they quickly learn to recognize—and despise—the cliches that the rest of us mistake for originality. Example: In the movies, all computer monitors display inch-high letters.

The Movie Mom's Guide to Movies and Videos for Families

http://pages.prodigy.com/VA/rcpj55a/moviemom.html

Nell Minow, an author, movie critic, and mother, offers this service for parents who are concerned about the degenerate filth that masquerades as entertainment today. (See figure 3.5.) The good news is that she is able to find a fair number of movies that she can recommend (the occasional "damn" notwithstanding). The bad news is that the genie of moral decay is so hard to put back in the bottle. 👉

FIGURE 3.5
The Movie Mom gives a hearty "OK" to The Indian in the Cupboard and Apollo 13.

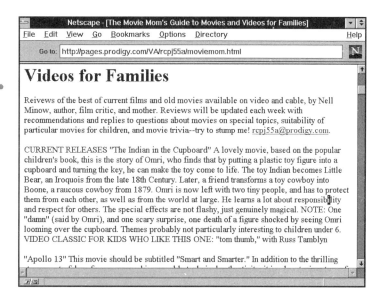

Movie Reviews by Ellis: The Art and Craft of Cultural Context

http://movie.infocom.net

Joan Ellis provides us with 100 movie reviews and an equal number of quotable quotes (suitable for extracting to newspaper ads), such as this typical one, about *The Lion King*: "This story inflicts an additional affront: it's a pure patriarchy in which Simba's mom was merely a pregnant vessel." 👉

Movie Review Query Engine

http://byron.sp.cs.cmu.edu:9086/movie

This automated index of reviews is part of Clamen's Movie Information Collection, a nice assortment of movie links and database info. (Clamen's site also contains a listing of what's playing in Pittsburgh this week, in case you're interested.)

The Movie Review Query Engine enables you to enter a movie title and receive a hypertext listing of reviews that have appeared in either the *rec.arts.movies.reviews* UseNet newsgroup or in one of the many newspapers or magazines that are available online.

Some other good places to find movie reviews are in the general-interest entertainment sites that are discussed in Chapter 1, including *Entertainment Weekly* and *People* magazines at *http://www.pathfinder.com* and the terrific Mr. Showbiz site at *http://web3.starwave.com/showbiz.*

Schedules

You've seen the commercials and read the reviews. Now nothing on earth can stop you from seeing that new film where Liza Minnelli and Pee Wee Herman are a pair of bickering ambulance drivers by day and a ballroom dance team by night. But is *Break a Leg* only showing in the sophisticated big cities? To help you solidify your entertainment timetable, the Internet has several sites that offer movie schedules for towns across America.

MovieLink

http://www.movielink.com/?TP:National

This movie-schedule and ticket-ordering service is operated by the same people as the *777-FILM* phone service. It provides movie-schedule information for theaters in about 20 cities, mostly around the rim of the U.S. (See figure 3.6.)

FIGURE 3.6

If you live in any of the cities shown on this map, not only do you enjoy a high quality of life, you can also use the MovieLink service to find out what time the newest movies are playing.

After you select a city, you learn that the site also features thumbnail movie descriptions, a parents' movie guide, downloadable multimedia, and links to the movie-related UseNet groups.

Local Movie Listings

http://www.actwin.com/movies/other.html

This handy site lists movie schedules for theaters in 20 American metropolitan areas, as well as cities in Canada, England, Ireland, South Africa, and even Slovenia.

Box Office Activity

Thanks to computers, the movie studios can learn the fate of their new films within hours of the opening; and thanks to the Internet, so can you.

Boxoffice Magazine

http://cwis.usc.edu/dept/etc/boxoffice/boxoffice.html

I don't know if *Boxoffice* is another one of those magazines that claims to be the "Bible" of its particular industry, but I do know that you will find it in the manager's office of most movie theaters.

The online version contains numerous movie reviews, box-office reports from around the world, analysis of new theater technologies, information from exhibitor conventions and film festivals, and feature stories on "bankable" movie stars. (See figure 3.7.)

FIGURE 3.7

The online version of Boxoffice magazine.

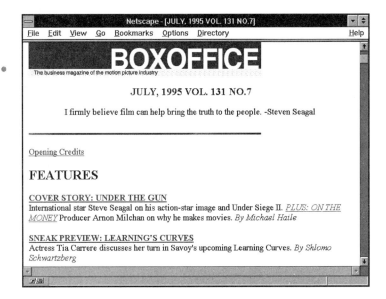

The Top 25

http://movieweb.com/movie/top25.html

The MovieWeb site (mentioned earlier in this chapter) posts the Top 25 highest-grossing movies of the preceding week. The list is updated every Thursday.

The Academy Awards

When it's Oscar Night in Los Angeles, everybody in town understands that they're in the center of the universe, and even the bums comport themselves with a little extra style. Limousines glide along Sunset Boulevard. from dusk until dawn, and each of them is carrying somebody that you've seen in the media a hundred times.

Everybody in the world (except maybe the Academy) realizes that the Oscars have little to do with art. But this spectacular awards presentation continues to fascinate us and attracts tremendous television ratings worldwide because it's a celebration of what America does best—create sensational images populated by attractive people.

The Academy of Motion Picture Arts and Sciences
http://www.oscars.org/ampas

The home page for the governing body that awards the Oscars is a sober place (unlike the backstage area at the ceremony). This site deflects the emphasis away from the Oscar celebration and focuses on the larger mission of the Academy, including its fellowships and its educational and historical activities. (See figure 3.8.)

The AMPAS home page offer press releases throughout the year on the Academy's activities, such as the recent decision to change the nominating procedure for Feature Length Documentary films. (This decision is intended to promote documentaries that actually play in commercial movie theaters and to prevent another debacle like the recent snub of *Hoop Dreams*.)

FIGURE 3.8
The home page of the Academy
of Motion Picture Arts and
Sciences.

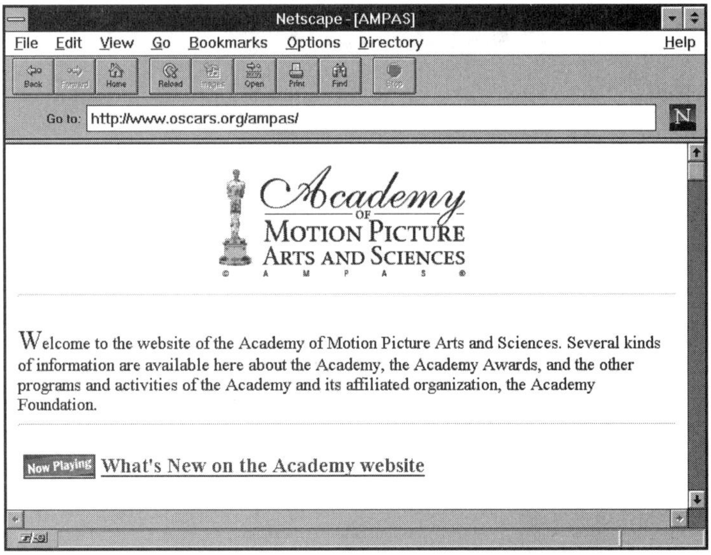

The Envelope Please
http://guide.oscars.org

This site is billed as "The Official Interactive Guide to the Academy Awards," and it is sponsored by the Academy. It offers splashy graphics, a good Oscar trivia challenge, and official information about the Oscar broadcast. In time for the next ceremony, the Academy intends to add downloadable video clips from nominated films.

OscarNet
http://ddv.com/Oscarnet

OscarNet is an unofficial Oscar site that encourages visitors to vote on the actual Academy Award nominees, to submit alternate nominees (for the so-called "Nettie" awards), and to vote on the *worst* performances of the year (coinciding with the Golden Raspberry Awards, which are held every year on the day before the Oscars—see figure 3.9.). It also features a year-by-year listing of all the Academy Award winners and nominees.

Visitors to the OscarNet site are encouraged to make donations to AIDS Project Los Angeles or the A-T Children's Foundation.

FIGURE 3.9

Recent nominees for the Golden Raspberry ("Razzie") Awards for the worst performances of the year.

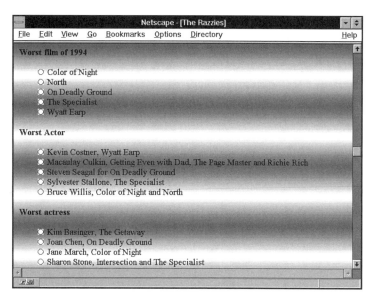

Individual Movie Sites

Because the theatrical release of a motion picture is a temporary thing, few movies have permanent Web sites dedicated to them (although many new films have short-term promotional sites provided by the studios that made them). Some of the hit movies that become cultural icons or that have a lot of toys associated with them will have Web sites that are built and maintained by fans (and some of these films are discussed in Chapter 4, "Cult Cinema and Fantasy Film"); but the life expectancy of individual movie sites such as the following is hard to determine.

Batman Forever
http://batmanforever.com

This promo site for the latest *Batman* flick is dense with memory-hogging graphics and elaborate substructures. There are sections containing clips from the movie soundtrack, production notes and storyboards, interactive riddles to solve, and a photo gallery of the stars.(See figure 3.10.)

FIGURE 3.10

Nicole Kidman co-stars as Dr. Chase Meridian in Batman Forever. She's supposed to be a renowned psychologist, but in this photo she's simply a projection from the subconscious.

The Lion King Page

http://www.clark.net/pub/lupine/www/lionking.html

There are about 10 Lion King pages on the Net (including one that argues that *The Lion King* is a rip-off of a Japanese cartoon called *The Jungle King*), but this one is the most obsessive. Phil Pollard, the guy who runs this site, is micro-fanatical about Disney animation. He claims to have found a "hidden Mickey" in one of the frames of *The Lion King* (see figure 3.11), and he includes a page about "mistakes" in some of the animal drawings—such as misplaced whiskers.

FIGURE 3.11

Can you spot the hidden Mickey
in the image on the left? I can't
either.

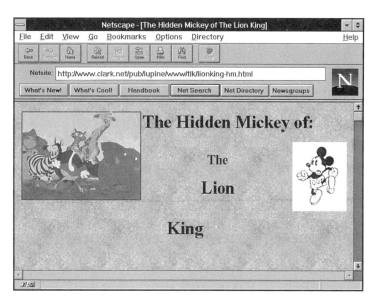

The Jeff Spicoli Home Page (*Fast Times at Ridgemont High*)
http://turtle.ncsa.uiuc.edu/spicoli

This Web site celebrates the life and legacy of Jeff Spicoli, the
pot-besotted anti-hero of Amy Heckerling's now-legendary 1982
film *Fast Times at Ridgemont High*. (See figure 3.12.) The more
you meditate on the audio and video wisdom contained here,
the less important the workaday worries of the world become.
(You might also notice that Spicoli bears an uncanny resemblance to Sean Penn.)

FIGURE 3.12
Hey, I know that dude: The Jeff
Spicoli Home Page.

The List

Coming Attractions

MovieWeb
http://movieweb.com/movie/movie.html

Hollyweb
http://www.ingress.com/users/spease/hw/hollyweb.html

Hollywood Online
http://www.hollywood.com

Movie Reviews

Film.com
http://www.film.com/film

Movie Reviews by Edwin Jahiel
http://www.prairienet.org/~ejahiel/reviews.htm

The Movie Cliches List

http://www.well.com/user/vertigo/cliches.html

Teen Movie Critic

http://www.skypoint.com/members/magic/roger/teencritic.html

The Movie Mom's Guide to Movies and Vidoes for Families

http://pages.prodigy.com/VA/rcpj55a/moviemom.html

Movie Reviews by Ellis: The Art and Craft of Cultural Context

http://movie.infocom.net

Movie Review Query Engine

http://byron.sp.cs.cmu.edu:9086/movie

Godfrey Cheshire on Film

gopher://gopher.interpath.net/11/Spectator%20Magazine/Godfrey%20Cheshire%20On%20Film

Indeed.

Cinemaven Online

http://useattle.uspan.com/maven

Reviews and features from Doug Thomas, a Seattle critic.

Movie Reviews by Matt and Kenny

http://www.primenet.com/~kennyb/reviews.htm

Because two heads are better than one.

rec.arts.movies.reviews

This is the UseNet group for do-it-yourself reviewers, many of whom are fully qualified and maybe even smarter than you.

Movie Schedules

MovieLink

http://www.movielink.com/?TP:National

Local Movie Listings

http://www.actwin.com/movies/other.html

Box-Office Activity

Boxoffice Magazine

http://cwis.usc.edu/dept/etc/boxoffice/boxoffice.html

The Top 25

http://movieweb.com/movie/top25.html

The Academy Awards

The Academy of Motion Picture Arts and Sciences

http://www.oscars.org/ampas

The Envelope Please

http://guide.oscars.org

OscarNet

http://ddv.com/Oscarnet

The Oscars

http://www.hype.com/movies/oscars/home.htm

From Hype! Online.

Individual Film Sites

Batman Forever

http://batmanforever.com

The Lion King Page

http://www.clark.net/pub/lupine/www/lionking.html

Stokowski's Disney Page

http://www.clark.net/pub/lupine/www/disney.html

Companion site to Phil Pollard's *Lion King* page, with *Beauty and the Beast* and general Disney stuff thrown in.

The Lion King

http://bvp.wdp.com/BVPM/PressRoom/LionKing/LionKing.html

This is Disney's official *Lion King* promo page, full of multimedia downloads.

The Indiana Jones WWW Page

http://dialin.ind.net/~msjohnso

Reams of *Raiders* stuff, including images, memorabilia, spoofs, a pointer to the much-needed Karen Allen page, and historical information about the Ark of the Covenant.

The Making of Citizen Kane

http://www.voyagerco.com/CC/gh/welles/p.makingkane.html

Lest we forget.

CHAPTER 4

Cult Cinema and Fantasy Film

IN THIS CHAPTER:

> *Science-fiction films*

> *Horror movies*

> *Japanese cinema*

> *James Bond*

> *Midnight movies and cult directors*

IN OTHER CHAPTERS:

< *General movie resources are discussed in Chapter 2.*

< *The popular Hollywood cinema is discussed in Chapter 3.*

> *Science fiction and fantasy on television is discussed in Chapter 7.*

The term "cult movie" refers to science fiction, horror, martial-arts, and just about any other genre outside of mainstream Hollywood "realism." Sometimes a mainstream movie that languishes in obscurity until it is rediscovered by a later generation is considered a cult movie as well. (Take the films of Jerry Lewis. Please.)

Genre movies are rarely concerned with "art"—and yet they are often the most artfully resonant movies of all, because, like opera or puppetry, they rely on timeless motifs that are recognized across cultural divisions.

This chapter introduces some of the better sites on the Internet that are devoted to cult movies and cult filmmakers. These are some of the most personal and obsessive sites on the entire Net—and they are a good indication of where our collective energy and attention is focused.

General Cult-Movie Resources

The following cult-movie resources do not pertain to a particular genre but rather to the shameless glory of fringe film in all its manifestations.

The Cult Shop
http://lasarto.cnde.iastate.edu/Movies/CultShop

This fan site is dedicated to a contemporary generation of filmmakers who have become cult figures in their own right: the Coen brothers (*Raising Arizona*), Sam Rami (*Darkman*), John Carpenter (*Halloween*), Dan O'Bannon (the *Alien* screenplay), and the ubiquitous Quentin Tarantino. (See figure 4.1.)

The cult shop is not an extensive resource, but it does offer a few video clips, publicity stills, webmaster Adam Bormann's peculiarly individual perspective on modern filmmaking (we learn that his favorite actress is Deborah Foreman of *Valley Girl* and *My Chauffeur*), and appropriate links to the Internet Movie Database.

FIGURE 4.1

Uma Thurman enjoys a five-dollar milkshake in a scene from Quentin Tarantino's Pulp Fiction. Accessed via the Cult Shop.

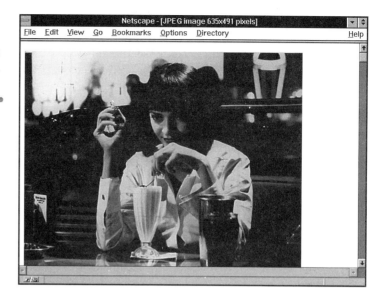

Wiretap Archives

gopher://wiretap.spies.com:70/11/Library/Media/Film

This pop-culture treasure chest contains many nuggets that will interest schlock movie buffs, including:

* Cult Movies FAQ

* Faces of Death Index

* Film Noir List

* GLBO (Alternate Sexuality) Films

* Godzilla Cast and Credits Lists

* James Bond Movie List

* Japanese Monster Guide

* Vampires in Movies

* Weird Movie List

Professor Neon's TV and Movie Mania

http://www.vortex.com/ProfNeon.html

The ambitious Professor Neon site is an amalgam of TV, film, radio, and online technology. The Professor is a maven of cult movies and television who has thrown together a bubbling stew of sci-fi sound effects, forgotten theme songs, and straightforward interviews with notables in the fantasy film and television industries. This audio stew is available on selected radio stations, on the telephone, and directly over the Internet itself through the magic of the RealAudio system.

Although Professor Neon seems to have a particular fondness for fantasy TV of the 1960s (including *The Twilight Zone*, *The Outer Limits*, and you-know-what), there's plenty here for the movie buff, including photos and reviews of recent features, such as *Ed Wood*, *The Flintstones*, and *Star Trek Generations*. (See figure 4.2.)

FIGURE 4.2

Tom Cruise and Brad Pitt in a scene from the offbeat baseball movie Interview with the Umpire. Accessed from the Professor Neon site.

Mad Prof. Mike's Headbanger Movie Reviews

http://www.dnai.com/~ochobbit

At the bottom of a page for a fantasy bookstore in Berkeley called A Change of Hobbit, you'll find a subsection called Mad Prof. Mike's Headbanger Movie Reviews. Mike Marano has a real love for schlock, as evidenced by his lengthy piece on *Teenagers From Outer Space* and its neglected director, Tom Grieff. Other reviews include *Tank Girl*, *This Island Earth* (the 1954 classic that is rumored to be used in the upcoming film version of *Mystery Science Theater 3000*) and the bloodcurdling Nancy Kerrigan ice-show production of *101 Dalmatians*.

Science-Fiction Films

Science fiction is the most generally respected of the "cult" movie genres, and it is the one most likely to produce a mainstream box-office success, such as *E.T.*, *Close Encounters*, or *Star Wars*.

The Star Wars Archive
http://www.wpi.edu/ftp/starwars

Star Wars was a phenomenon both as a film and as a marketing vehicle. In 1977, George Lucas' richly imagined fable of intergalactic rebellion and fi™lial loyalty was the highest-grossing film to date.

The Star Wars Archive (see figure 4.3) is the oldest of the two dozen *Star Wars* sites on the Internet. It is a mothership of information that includes the following:

* Lists of *Star Wars* books, videos, music, and comics
* Hints and downloadable accessories for *Star Wars*-related computer games
* Scripts for *Star Wars*, *The Empire Strikes Back*, and *Return (Revenge) of the Jedi*
* Fan-written stories and parodies
* *Star Wars* images in EPS, ASCII, and XBM formats
* Lists of *Star Wars* toys, models, and games

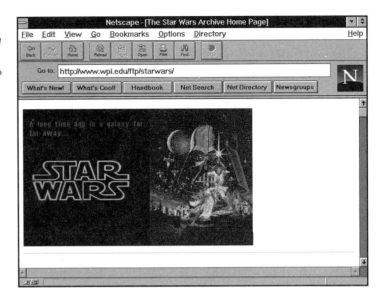

2001: A Space Odyssey

http://www.lehigh.edu/~pjl2/2001.html

For many sci-fi aficionados, Stanley Kubrick's *2001: A Space Odyssey* is the supreme achievement of science-fiction cinema. Sumptuously filmed, richly imagined, and overripe with mysterious symbols that allude to man's place in the cosmos, *2001* is sci-fi for grown-ups. Justly celebrated for its prescient speculations on human-computer interaction, the film is equally notable for its production details, such as the anti-gravity toilet and the intrusion of corporate advertising in the space environment.

This site offers a gallery of photos from one of the most beautiful films ever made. (See figure 4.4.) It also offers links to more substantive *2001* and Kubrick resources.

FIGURE 4.4

In this scene from 2001, a team of lunar flatfoots ponder the mysterious appearance of a humming monolith on the surface of the moon.

● ● ● ● ● ● ● ● ● ● ● ● ● ● ● ● ●

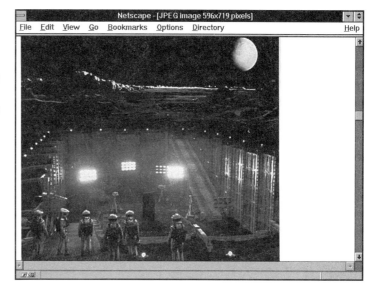

Off-World (The Blade Runner Page)
http://kzsu.stanford.edu/uwi/br/off-world.html

Blade Runner is a favorite film among the cyber set because it was adapted from a novel by a techno luminary (Philip K. Dick's *Do Androids Dream of Electric Sheep?*) and because its vision of L.A. in the year 2019 as a polyglot neon wasteland was so much smarter and less sanitized than the usual sci-fi sterility. (See figure 4.5.)

FIGURE 4.5

Somewhere in the neon fog is Harrison Ford. From a collection of Blade Runner stills at http://www.smartdocs.com:80/~migre.v/Bladerunner.

● ● ● ● ● ● ● ● ● ● ● ● ● ● ● ● ●

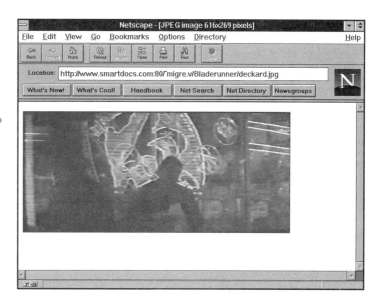

There are several *Blade Runner* and Philip K. Dick pages on the Internet. Off-World has a compilation of *Blade Runner* postings to the *rec.arts.movies* UseNet group, an index of print references to *Blade Runner,* and links to the *BR* FAQ and various versions of the *BR* script.

Harrison Ford, the star of *Blade Runner,* played Wally's friend "Chester" in several episodes of *Leave it to Beaver* under the stage name "Buddy Hart." (Honest.)

Horror Films

Psychologists tell us that the horror genre is an archetypal meditation on human mortality and the potential for violent passion that is necessarily repressed in order to fulfill our everyday responsibilities. In creating fictive "monsters," we acknowledge the monster within ourselves while keeping it safely marginalized.

The Internet Movie Database (Genre Search)

http://www.msstate.edu/M/list-genres

The Internet Movie Database is a terrific all-purpose film archive and has been mentioned elsewhere in this book. You can use it to look up cast and credit information, plot summaries, and user-submitted evaluations on a scale of 1 to 10. It also has extremely versatile search capabilities; you can search by title, year, actor, director, studio, and genre. Its horror index is especially strong, comprising about 500 films, from *The Abominable Dr. Phibes* to *Zombie High.* (See figure 4.6.)

FIGURE 4.6

An index of the horror movies for which there is cast and plot information contained in the Internet Movie Database. The numbers in parentheses represent the average rating of the movie (on a scale of 1 to 10) by users of the database.

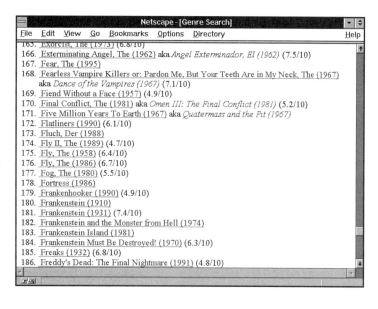

The Vampyres Movie List

http://ubu.hahnemann.edu/Misc/Vamp-Mov.html

This comprehensive list of hundreds of vampire (or "vampyre") movies from around the world is also a customized, vampire-specific front-end to the Internet Movie Database. It will link you to descriptions and reviews of most, but not all, of the films. The list includes all of the well-known films (*Dracula, Nosferatu, Love at First Bite*) as well as such obscurities as *Wanda Does Transylvania* (starring Kitty Love) and *La Vampira Indiana*.

The Cabinet of Dr. Casey (The Horror Page)

http://www.ee.pdx.edu/~caseyh/horror/html

This graphics-intensive page is devoted to horror themes in the movies, literature, and the visual arts. (Note: The graphics froze my underpowered computer on three different occasions, so don't access this site until you've saved any open documents and freed some memory.)

Japanese Cinema

Although there is a rich tradition of Japanese cinema that extends from the lyricism and stylized violence of Akira Kurosawa to the unabashed eroticism of Nagisa Oshima, most Westerners only know about two minor Japanese genres: the monster epic and the style of high-octane adult animation known as *anime*.

The Gamera Home Page
http://tswww.cc.emory.edu/~kgowen/gamera.html

Gamera is the fire-breathing turtle who starred in nine underrated Japanese monster epics. Kevin Gowen, webmaster of the Gamera page, introduces the monster thusly: "Gamera is the sole surviving member of his race of prehistoric giant turtles. He was asleep for countless centuries in the Arctic until a nuclear explosion awakened him from his slumber. Gamera was understandably cranky after just waking up, but he soon shed his bad guy image to become the friend of all children."

The Gamera Home Page features detailed synopses and credits for all the Gamera movies (most of which featured children in the leading human roles), Gamera sound clips, and high-quality Gamera art. (See figure 4.7.)

FIGURE 4.7

A folk rendering of Gamera in action. (Gamera's the turtle.)

• • • • • • • • • • • • • • • •

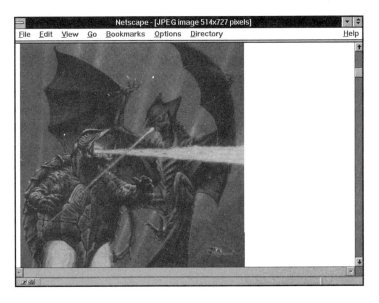

Anime Resources and Info
http://www.best.com/~gaxiola/Anime

If you've seen *Speed Racer*, you've seen anime—or at least the wide-eyed, kid-friendly face of it. This Japanese genre of adult animation can also be as lurid as any pulp fiction or underground comic book.

There's an abundance of information about anime on the Internet, and Dave Gaxiola's Anime Resources Site is a good introduction to the topic and a valuable roadmap to the labyrinthine network of anime pages available throughout the world. There are pointers to numerous FTP image and sound archives, plot synopses, anime conventions and collector sites, anime film festivals, anime-based online games, a parents' guide to anime violence and nudity, and Dave's own article comparing anime to opera.

Good Guys and Bad Guys

Ever since the ancient Greeks invented the action genre with *Oedipus 2: An Eye for an Eye*, the conflict between good and evil has been the basis of dramatic structure.

Hong Kong Movies Home Page
http://www.mdstud.chalmers.se/hkmovie

This extensive site from Sweden was dubbed "worryingly comprehensive" by *.net* magazine. It's a thorough introduction to the eye-popping glory of Hong Kong cinema, where Jackie Chan and John Woo deliver non-stop martial-arts action in a frenzied milieu of evil warlords, treacherous babes, and transdimensional wizards. This site includes a Hong Kong movie FAQ, biographies of the biggest stars, a guide to cult-video mail order, and the handy "Girls With Guns" list of female action heroines. (See figure 4.8.)

FIGURE 4.8

The Hong Kong Movies Home Page. (Careful with that crossbow. You'll put somebody's eye out.)

● ● ● ● ● ● ● ● ● ● ● ● ● ● ● ●

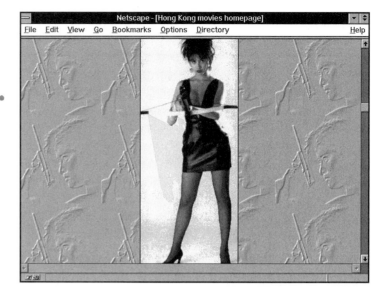

James Bond 007 on the WWW

http://www.mcs.net/~klast/www/bond.html

This extensive and well-designed site by Kimberly Last has a lot of material about *GoldenEye,* the new James Bond spy thriller starring Pierce Brosnan. (For instance, you can hear an audio clip of Brosnan intoning the famous words that are in every 007 movie: "Bond... James Bond. But, uh, you can call me Jimbo if you fancy.")

You will also find: a briefcase full of information on James Bond merchandise, old and new; descriptions and parodies of the James Bond literary source material by Ian Fleming and John Gardner; facts and figures on the Bondmobiles, including the new BMW Z3; fan club information; FAQs from the *alt.fan.james-bond* UseNet group; photos of "the Bond girls;" and biographies of all the Bond guys, including a light serving of George Lazenby and a heavy dose of Sean Connery. (See figure 4.9.)

FIGURE 4.9

Sean Connery as the quintessentially roguish James Bond. Image culled from the Internet Movie Database.

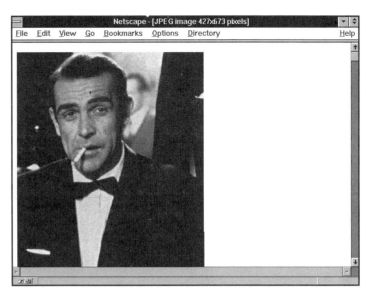

No Place for a Woman: The Family in Film Noir

http://www.ncrel.org/ncrel/jb/jb-1toc.htm

John Blaser has produced a hypertext version of his master's thesis that is a captivating read and an effective use of online technology. Blaser examines the significance of the family unit (and in particular the ambiguous role of women) in the *film noir* genre of hard-boiled post-war dramas. Blaser's work incorporates photos, movie posters, and even audio clips. (See figure 4.10.)

FIGURE 4.10

The visually arresting introductory page to John Blaser's study of "The Family in Film Noir."

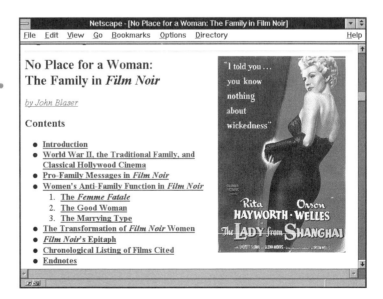

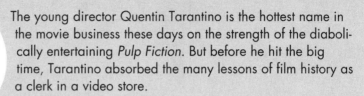

CLOSE-UP: QUENTIN TARANTINO

The young director Quentin Tarantino is the hottest name in the movie business these days on the strength of the diabolically entertaining *Pulp Fiction*. But before he hit the big time, Tarantino absorbed the many lessons of film history as a clerk in a video store.

Tarantino's first feature was the ultraviolent heist film *Reservoir Dogs*. He also wrote the screenplays for *True Romance* and *Natural Born Killers* (which he has disowned). However, it wasn't until the release of *Pulp Fiction* in late 1994 that Tarantino became a hero to millions of movie-addled misfits worldwide. This contemporary variation on the 1970s action-exploitation genre is noteworthy for its stylishly-violent imagery and dialogue that's a crazy hash of streetwise poetry and pop-culture smarts. (The movie is also completely amoral, but hipsters by definition don't care about such things.)

The fanatical devotion that Tarantino has inspired is remarkable even by cult-movie standards. There are about a dozen Tarantino sites on the Net, many with absurdly slavish names such as Tarantino Worship, The Tarantinoverse, and The Shrine. A site called Tarantino World at *http://www.ios.com/~jbonne/qt* proudly quotes a review that calls it "one of the better" Tarantino sites on the Internet, and it's certainly the one with the most visual pizzazz. (See figure 4.11.) It offers a Tarantino FAQ, numerous photos from *Pulp Fiction* and Tarantino's *Reservoir Dogs*, parodies (including something called *Gump Fiction*), links to the other QT sites, and a bit of speculation on what exactly was in Marcellus' briefcase.

Tarantino also has an acting career and seems to be making a cameo in every new film that features stylized violence and a soundtrack full of 1960s surf instrumentals (and there are lots of them). Plus he recently directed an episode of the hospital drama *E.R.* It looks like Tarantino's particular vision of the world is here to stay.

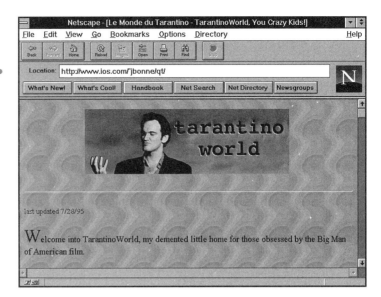

Midnight Movies

The phenomenon of midnight movies was born in the 1970s at decrepit big-city art-house movie theatres. Often, midnight movies are raunchy, inept, or special-interest films that appeal to a carousing, late-night audience.

The Rocky Horror Picture Show Page
http://chs-web.umdl.umich.edu/odd/RHPS/net1.1_index.html

There are at least 10 sites on the Internet devoted to *Rocky Horror*, the gender-bending musical that became a cult phenomenon as stately old movie theaters were besieged with flying toast and corseted merrymakers.

Almost all of the Rocky Horror sites have "Rocky Horror Picture Show" in their name. The one listed here (see figure 4.12.) is a good all-purpose site that features several versions of the film script (with and without the audience participation elements), lists of theaters that are still showing the darn thing, links to other RHPS sites, and the promise of audio and video clips in the near future.

FIGURE 4.12

*One of many Rocky Horror
home pages.*

The alt.sex.movies Page

http://www.xmission.com/~legalize/asm/asm.html

There's no use pretending that adult films are an obscure little corner of the marketplace. Without adult films, there wouldn't be a videotape industry in the first place, and a similar argument can be made for the importance of adult entertainment in the development of the Internet and online services. This page will give you a lot of the kinds of information you would expect (fan-club addresses, overly descriptive filmographies), as well as some thought-provoking material on censorship, pornography, and the law. Enter at your own risk.

The Left-Wing Film Guide·

http://ccme-mac4.bsd.uchicago.edu/DSAFilms.html

This helpful site provides thumbnail synopses for dozens of films that might come in handy if you're trying to rally the troops for various liberal causes. (Be advised that you can't charge admission without the say-so of the copyright holders, although the good-hearted people who compiled this list suggest that selling popcorn is an appropriate fund-raising idea.) The films are indexed by their suitability to a given theme—the labor movement, women's rights, environmental issues, U.S. imperialism, and so on. (See figure 4.13.)

FIGURE 4.13

A roster of films that might have come in handy for a proletariat uprising before 1989—at which time the proletariat declared that what it really wanted was a world full of scantily-clad spokesmodels.

• • • • • • • • • • • • • • • • •

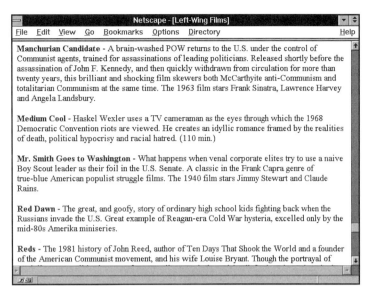

Netscape - [Left-Wing Films]

File   Edit   View   Go   Bookmarks   Options   Directory   Help

Manchurian Candidate - A brain-washed POW returns to the U.S. under the control of Communist agents, trained for assassinations of leading politicians. Released shortly before the assassination of John F. Kennedy, and then quickly withdrawn from circulation for more than twenty years, this brilliant and shocking film skewers both McCarthyite anti-Communism and totalitarian Communism at the same time. The 1963 film stars Frank Sinatra, Lawrence Harvey and Angela Landsbury.

Medium Cool - Haskel Wexler uses a TV cameraman as the eyes through which the 1968 Democratic Convention riots are viewed. He creates an idyllic romance framed by the realities of death, political hypocrisy and racial hatred. (110 min.)

Mr. Smith Goes to Washington - What happens when venal corporate elites try to use a naive Boy Scout leader as their foil in the U.S. Senate. A classic in the Frank Capra genre of true-blue American populist struggle films. The 1940 film stars Jimmy Stewart and Claude Rains.

Red Dawn - The great, and goofy, story of ordinary high school kids fighting back when the Russians invade the U.S. Great example of Reagan-era Cold War hysteria, excelled only by the mid-80s Amerika miniseries.

Reds - The 1981 history of John Reed, author of Ten Days That Shook the World and a founder of the American Communist movement, and his wife Louise Bryant. Though the portrayal of

Our Secret Century: Revelations from The Prelinger Archives

gopher.well.sf.ca.us:70/11/Art/Experimental.Film.and.Video/secret.century

This gopher site contains interesting material describing the films of the Prelinger Archives, a collection of so-called "ephemeral" or social-instruction films that were made between the 1930s and the early '60s. These were short films that provided corporate goodwill, civic boosterism, and adolescent attitude adjustment for a prosperous America that still had a stomach for such things. They were often shown in school assemblies and at club meetings. (Today these films are spliced into *Letterman* segments and *Nick at Nite* promos and are sometimes shown before the main attraction at art-house movie theaters.)

The Prelinger Archive includes such howlers as the immortal *Dating Do's and Dont's* and *Shy Guy*, starring Dick York (later of *Bewitched* and the star of over 150 instructional films, including *Combat Fatigue: Insomnia*, *How To Read a Book*, and *The Last Date*, as well as the mainstream Hollywood classic *Inherit the Wind*). The ephemeral films of the Prelinger Archive are available on a series of laserdiscs, videos, and CD-ROMs from the Voyager company.

The List

General Cult-Movie Resources

The Cult Shop
http://lasarto.cnde.iastate.edu/Movies/CultShop

Wiretap Archives
gopher://wiretap.spies.com:70/11/Library/Media/Film

Professor Neon's TV and Movie Mania
http://www.vortex.com/ProfNeon.html

Mad Prof. Mike's Headbanger Movie Reviews
http://www.dnai.com/~ochobbit

alt.movies.cult
The main UseNet newsgroup for fans of specialty cinema.

The Movie Poster Archive
http://anubis.science.unitn.it/services/movies/index.html

JPEG images of old movie posters, divided into sci-fi, horror, and the classics. A must-visit for fans.

Science-Fiction Films

The Star Wars Archive
http://www.wpi.edu/ftp/starwars

2001: A Space Odyssey
http://www.lehigh.edu/~pjl2/2001.html

The 2001 Internet Resource Archive
http://pubweb.acns.nwu.edu/~gdd816/2001.html

Links to all known sites related to *2001*, Stanley Kubrick, and Arthur C. Clarke.

Off-World (The Blade Runner Page)
http://kzsu.stanford.edu/uwi/br/off-world.html

Blade Runner GIFs
http://www.smartdocs.com:80/~migre.v/Bladerunner

Star Trek Movies (Trek Reviews Archive)
http://www.mcs.net/~forbes/trek-reviews/home.html

This is the home base for the archives of the *rec.arts.startrek.reviews* UseNet group. It contains a cargo load of information on the *Star Trek* movies and TV series.

Terminator/T2
http://www.maths.tcd.ie/pub/films/terminator

Alien, Aliens, Alien 3 (The Art of Survival)
http://dutial.twi.tudelft.nl/~alien/alien.html

Dune
http://www.princeton.edu/~cgilmore/dune/dune.html

rec.arts.sf.movies
The all-purpose UseNet group for science-fiction films.

Horror Films

The Internet Movie Database (Genre Search)
http://www.msstate.edu/M/list-genres

The Vampyres Film List
http://ubu.hahnemann.edu/Misc/Vamp-Mov.html

The Cabinet of Dr. Casey (The Horror Page)
http://www.ee.pdx.edu/~caseyh/horror/html

Japanese Cinema

The Gamera Home Page

http://tswww.cc.emory.edu/~kgowen/gamera.html

Mel's Godzilla Page

http://www.ama.caltech.edu/~mrm/godzilla.html

alt.movies.monster

UseNet group for fans of Japanese monster flicks and other movie monsters.

Anime Resources and Info

http://www.best.com/~gaxiola/Anime

MIT Anime WWW Server

http://web.mit.edu/afs/athena/user/o/m/omv/Anime/default.html

rec.arts.anime

The main UseNet group for fans of Japanese adult animation.

A Tribute to Akira Kurosawa's "Dreams"

http://www.pitt.edu/~ddj/dreams

Good Guys and Bad Guys

Hong Kong Movies Home Page

http://www.mdstud.chalmers.se/hkmovie

Hong Kong Cinema

http://egret0.stanford.edu/hk/index.html

A serious look at the state of Hong Kong cinema, including box-office reports, theater schedules, and the winners of the fabled Golden Banana Award. (I have no idea what the Golden Banana is for, so don't ask.)

James Bond 007 on the WWW

http://www.mcs.net/~klast/www/bond.html

No, Mr. Bond, i Expect You to Die

http://www.nmt.edu/~champ/bond.html

James Bond FTP Site

ftp://ftp.ainet.com/pub/plosher/007

Sounds and images.

alt.fan.james-bond

UseNet group for fans of the Ian Fleming novels and the movies they inspired.

Tarantino World

http://www.ios.com/~jbonne/qt

The Tarantinoverse

http://rmd-www.mr.ic.ac.uk/~dan/tarantino/tarantino.html

This jumbo site has lots of fun facts, images, and transcriptions (including scenes that were cut from *Pulp Fiction*, a *Saturday Night Live* parody, and the transcript of Christopher Walken's "gold watch" speech.)

alt.movies.tarantino

UseNet group for the Woody Allen of his generation.

alt.fan.woody-allen

UseNet group for the *real* Woody Allen.

alt.movies.tim-burton

UseNet group for the director of *Batman, Pee Wee's Big Adventure,* and *Ed Wood.*

alt.movies.scorsese

UseNet group for the director of *Boxcar Bertha.*

Alfred Hitchcock on the WWW

http://nextdch.mty.itesm.mx/~plopezg/Kaplan/Hitchcock.html

An utterly terrific tribute to the life and work of the master of suspense.

No Place for a Woman: The Family in Film Noir

http://www.ncrel.org/ncrel/jb/jb-1toc.htm

Midnight Movies

The Rocky Horror Picture Show Page
http://chs-web.umdl.umich.edu/odd/RHPS/net1.1_index.html

The Rocky Horror FTP Archive
ftp.best.com/pub/zenin/RHPS/text

Images, sounds, and scripts.

The alt.sex.movies Page
http://www.xmission.com/~legalize/asm/asm.html

Left-Wing Film Guide
http://ccme-mac4.bsd.uchicago.edu/DSAFilms.html

Our Secret Century: Revelations from The Prelinger Archives
gopher.well.sf.ca.us:70/11/Art/Experimental.Film.and.Video/
secret.century

Ed Wood
http://www.wdp.com/BVPM/PressRoom/EdWood/EdWood.html

Blue Velvet
http://www.iac.net/~brian/bluevelvet.html

CHAPTER 5

General TV Resources

IN THIS CHAPTER:

- > *Archives and link sites*
- > *TV schedule guides*
- > *TV ratings information*
- > *TV review sites*
- > *Television-network home sites*
- > *Academic sites*

IN OTHER CHAPTERS:

- < *General entertainment news is covered in Chapter 1.*
- > *News and talk shows are discussed in Chapter 6.*
- > *Series, sitcoms, and TV animation are discussed in Chapter 7.*

Most historians agree that the so-called Information Age began in 1875, with the invention of the television by Japanese engineer Noru Hitachi and the invention of the personal computer by American refrigerator magnate Peter Westinghouse. For 120 years, these two remarkable inventions have enlightened and entertained us, and the development of the two technologies has been inextricably linked.

In 1894, Thomas Edison used computer-generated special effects in the first-ever television series, "The Adventures of Rocket Boy." In 1927, the enigmatic inventor Nikola Tesla developed a prototype of the Macintosh from leftover television parts, and two years later he conceived of the idea for the Game Boy microcomputer system while watching an episode of the quiz show "It Doesn't Take a Genius." In 1966, it was a Univac computer with artificial-intelligence capabilities that wrote the pilot episode for the TV series "Gilligan's Island." (Upon reading the script, an excited studio executive named Marhall McLuhan declared, "The medium is the Mouse Age.")

Although television has been derided by critics as a "vast wasteland," that hasn't stopped anyone from watching it. Television is the most powerful communications medium ever invented, and in the years to come, when the visual immediacy of television is more fully combined with the utility of the Internet, we will have a global sales-and-amusement apparatus that will be virtually impervious to criticism. As you will see in this chapter, the seeds of this alliance have already been planted.

Archives and Link Sites

There are so many TV-related pages on the Internet—including home pages for various shows, fan-club sites for actors and actresses, academic forums, and information on new technologies—that the best way for a newcomer to approach the subject is through a comprehensive and well-organized link site, such as one of the following.

CineMedia Television Sites
http://www.gu.edu.au/gwis/cinemedia/CineMedia.tv.html

This exhaustive TV link resource has pointers to virtually every television-related site on the Internet, from the C-SPAN home page to the "Rocky and Bullwinkle" episode guide to "Gay and Lesbian TV Listings" to an article on "Copyright Law in Japan."

The CineMedia site is organized by the following categories: Networks & Stations, New Technologies, Individual Programs, Scripts & Episodes, and TV Lists.

It has a particularly strong collection of links to sites that address the public-policy and technological aspects of the broadcast and cable industries. But you can also use it to jump straight to the *Beavis and Butt-head* home page, if that's more your style. ☞

Tardis TV Archive
http://src.doc.ic.ac.uk/public/media/tv/collections/tardis/index.html

This insanely detailed, text-only compendium of TV information from the U.K. is an excellent resource for researchers, and it is one of the best places on the Net for information about international television. You can use it to access TV information for the U.S.A., U.K., Canada, Japan, and Sweden. It features episode guides, links to TV-show home pages, photo archives (see figure 5.1), ratings archives, information on conventions, lists of award winners, biographies of TV-related people, and the *alt.video.tape-trading* archive. ☞

FIGURE 5.1

Max Headroom, patron saint of contemporary television. From the Tardis TV archive.

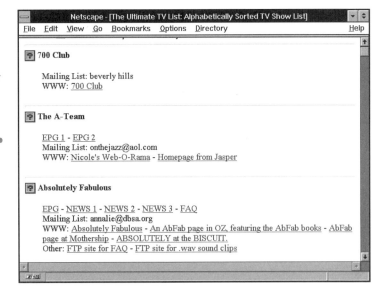

The Ultimate TV List

http://tvnet.com/UTVL/utvl.html

This site, part of the TV Net enterprise, contains more than 1,000 links to more than 300 television shows, which can be accessed alphabetically or by type of show. It includes links to home pages, episode guides, and UseNet discussion groups. (See figure 5.2.)

FIGURE 5.2

The first entries in the Ultimate TV List, which comprises more than 1,000 links to more than 300 television shows. (Question: If these three programs got into a fight, which do you think would win?)

Internet Television Resource Guide

http://www.teleport.com/~celinec/tv.htm

This easily manageable link site offers an extensive list of TV-related UseNet groups, and links to web pages of past and current shows, actors and actresses, magazines, and other TV-related sites.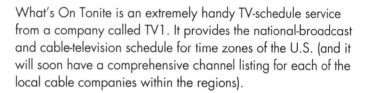

Guides and Listings

A handful of services on the Internet duplicate the function of *TV Guide* magazine or the TV-listings section of the daily newspaper. And in some cases they are easier to use and more comprehensive than their paper counterparts.

What's On Tonite

http://tv1.com

What's On Tonite is an extremely handy TV-schedule service from a company called TV1. It provides the national-broadcast and cable-television schedule for time zones of the U.S. (and it will soon have a comprehensive channel listing for each of the local cable companies within the regions).

You may view the listings in classic grid format, by time schedule (see figure 5.3), grouped by program category (movies, sports, series, talk, and so on), or by channel lineup.

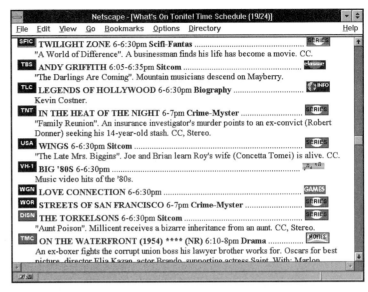

What's On Tonite is also available as a text-only gopher service at *gopher.enews.com:2100/11/entertainment/television/whatson.*

TV Tonite
http://metaverse.com/vibe/tv.html

The TV Tonite schedule service doesn't compare to What's On Tonite for technical acumen, graphic appeal, or comprehensiveness. However, it does have the advantage of some opinionated wisecracks and personal recommendations from the guy who's running the site. So if you find that you share his taste in entertainment (pro-MTV, anti-prestige—he says he's never been able to sit through *The Grapes of Wrath*), you might want to turn to this service and forget all the hassle of thinking for yourself.

Australian TV Guide
http://www.sofcom.com.au/TV/index.html

If you happen to be Down Under and you need to know the schedule for *Kangaroo Korner*, this is the place to look. (And before you jump all over me, I know there's no such thing as

Kangaroo Korner and that I'm using the most simplistic short-hand imaginable to characterize a vibrant and diverse culture that will someday take over the world.)

Reviews of Television Shows

Because television episodes, unlike movies, cannot be revisited at will, there are very few television review sites on the Internet. Perhaps this will change in the future, particularly if video-on-demand becomes a reality and includes individual episodes of TV shows.

TV Chat
http://tvnet.com/TVChat/chat.html

Since television is such a populist medium, almost everybody is qualified to pass judgment on it. The TV Chat site allows Net surfers to discuss their favorite TV shows with equally deluded people from around the globe.

TV RATINGS

Most Americans realize that the weekly television ratings are the lifeblood of our economy. The ratings determine everything from the Christmas inventories of major department stores to the cost-of-living adjustments for elderly Medicare recipients. These ratings are obtained by implanting electrodes into the foreheads of a dozen average Americans and recording their brain waves while a black-hooded researcher recites an alphabetical list of television programs that the participants have never actually seen.

You can obtain the latest Nielsen TV ratings (with apologies to Arbitron, which still isn't a household word and hasn't perfected the electrode thing) from the wonderful Mr. Showbiz entertainment site at *http://web3.starwave.com/showbiz* or from the Gigaplex site at *http://www.gigaplex.com/wow*.

Professor Neon

http://www.vortex.com/ProfNeon.html

The Professor Neon site focuses mostly on sci-fi and offbeat movies and television. From here you can download radio-format audio files in which the Professor chats with notables from the world of fantasy film and TV. ☞

Transient Images

http://www.cais.com/jpadgett/www/home.html

This "almost weekly e-zine of television and film" features gossip, TV/film news, and the occasional penetrating insight. ☞

Many general-interest online entertainment sites contain TV reviews. For instance, *People* magazine, available online at *http://www.pathfinder.com*, has a weekly section called "The Tube" (which apparently is the latest slang for "television") as part of its Picks & Pans review gallery. You can also try the online *Entertainment Weekly*, at the same address, or The Gate, which features the online entertainment section of the *San Francisco Chronicle* newspaper, at *http://sfgate.com*.

Broadcasters, Networks, and Cable Channels

Most of the television broadcast networks and cable channels have established a Web site, although there are still some broadcasters who are under one of the following misimpressions: 1.) The Internet is a fad that will soon disappear; or 2.) The Internet is the enemy. They ought to realize that by working together, everyone can make a ton of money. This Internet thing is a cash cow.

Traditional Broadcast Networks

You may notice some high-profile no-shows from the list of TV networks that have established Web sites (see the preceding explanation), specifically ABC, which has a special arrangement with America Online; however, I'd wager that the stragglers will get onboard within a few months.

CBS
http://WWW.CBS.COM

Here you can read the latest news about upcoming CBS blockbusters (the fall season is described as "different—younger and contemporary"), view the most-recent David Letterman Top Ten list (or search the archives for those timeless "Buttafuocco" references), and order "cool CBS stuff" with logos all over it. (10 percent discount for members of the "Eye On" Club!) See figure 5.4.

FIGURE 5.4
The home page for the CBS television network.

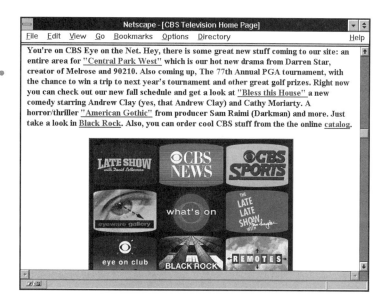

NBC
http://www.nbc-com

As this book was going to press, the NBC network unveiled a colorful and well-executed Web site. From the NBC site you can access schedule information, sports-programming news, series descriptions, and detailed biographies of the NBC stars. ☞

PBS

http://www.pbs.org

At the home site of the Public Broadcasting System, you can learn about upcoming PBS productions (including Ken Burns' 20-hour documentary on the Slinky), scan a list of all the PBS affiliates in the country (for when you're traveling and your kid needs a Barney fix), read some instructive articles about the evolving public policy toward federally subsidized broadcasting, and even check the classified ads for PBS staff positions. ☞

The BBC Networking Club

http://www.bbcnc.org.uk

At this genteel site from British Broadcasting, you can preview the schedule for BBC Television (see figure 5.5) as well as get information about BBC Radio, BBC Education, the BBC World Service (global radio news), and BBC Internet (a helpful guide to the online world, with software). ☞

FIGURE 5.5

The TV schedule page from the BBC Networking Club. (Say, mate, isn't it about time for Ready, Steady, Cook?)

• • • • • • • • • • • • • • • •

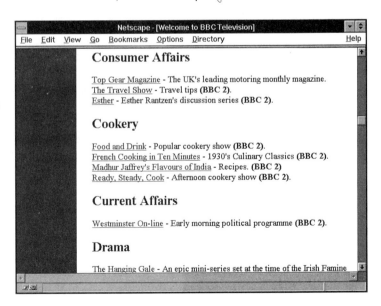

The CBC Home Page
http://www.cbc.ca

The Canadian Broadcasting Corporation operates a comprehensive and attractive home page for both its English- and French-language services, including CBC Radio.

Fox Broadcasting
http://www.foxnetwork.com

This recently upgraded site will get you information about Fox programming, Fox sports, Fox affiliates, the Fox schedule, and fan-administered sites devoted to such Fox shows as *The Simpsons* and *The X-Files*. What it *won't* get you is an opportunity to hand Rupert Murdoch your proposal for a new series about two Klingons and a Ferengi sharing a beachfront apartment on Planet Rigel 5. (See figure 5.6.)

FIGURE 5.6
This version of the Fox broadcasting home page is firm-but-fair when it comes to unsolicited material for new TV series.

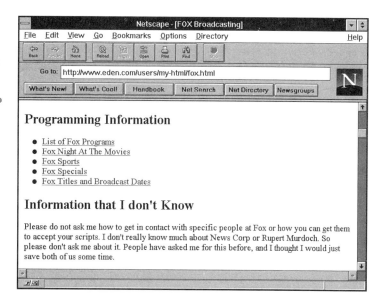

Cable Channels

On the whole, the cable channels have done a better job of utilizing the capabilities of the Web than their broadcast counterparts. No surprise there.

ESPNet
http://espnet.sportszone.com

This whopper of a site is invaluable for the sports fan who needs to know the latest scores and sports news (and can't wait for tomorrow's newspaper, because if the Giants didn't cover the spread, he might have to skip town).

Along with all the sports information, there is a corner of this site called ESPN Studios where you can get ESPN scheduling information and learn about the on-air personalities. (See figure 5.7.)

The sports-information capabilities of ESPNet are covered in detail in Chapter 15, "Sports."

FIGURE 5.7
The ESPN Studios section of ESPNet will give you the lowdown on the network's operations and its on-air personalities.

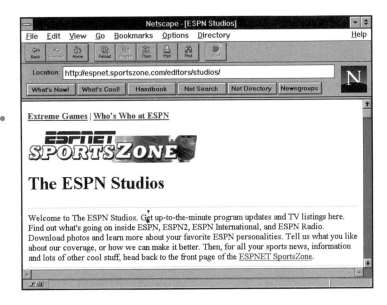

The Discovery Channel
http://www.discovery.com

The Discovery Channel home page is as fun and informative as the cable channel itself. It has a fresh and colorful look and it is loaded with breezy, human-interest articles that parallel the features on the cable channel. A recent edition included gardening tips, advice from The Computer Guy, a photo essay on Airstream trailers, a look at the life of a tugboat pilot in Pittsburgh, and Marshall Sella's letters from the road (see figure 5.8), which included a visit to the Spam Jam, a canned-meat festival in Minneapolis.

FIGURE 5.8

A report from the American road, from the Discovery Channel home site.

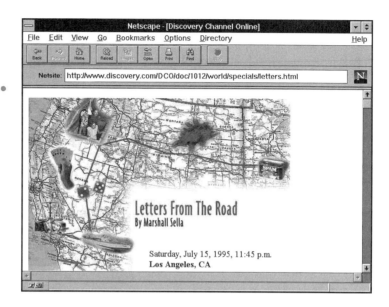

(By the way, The Discovery Channel is the home of two programs that should be of special interest to readers of this book. *Next Step* and *Beyond 2000* are layman-friendly TV series about new technologies, mostly of the handy-gadget sort.)

Nick Linx
http://cctr.umkc.edu/user/rbarrow/nicklnx.html

This site offers links to all the known Nickelodeon-related Web pages and UseNet groups on the Internet, including: fan pages for *Rugrats, Ren and Stimpy, The Monkees, The Muppets, Clarissa Explains It All*, and more; episode guides; mailing lists; and FAQs.

Local Broadcasters

Many local TV stations are now starting Web pages as a community-outreach tool and promotional apparatus. These can provide TV schedule information; offer up-to-the-minute news, weather, and sports headlines; and solicit feedback from viewers.

TV Net
http://tvnet.com/misc/abouttvnet.html

TV Net (which sponsors the Ultimate TV List, mentioned earlier in this chapter) has compiled links to all of the local TV-station pages at this site, along with a list of international broadcasters.

World Resource for Student Television (WORST)
http://www.efd.lth.se/~e91rw/WORST.html

WORST provides links to student-run TV operations around the world, so the revolutionaries of tomorrow can start coordinating their efforts today.

Miscellaneous TV Resources

There are many other kinds of TV-related sites on the Internet, including: technical information about new broadcast, cable, and satellite technologies; resources for students; media watch-dog organizations; censorship news; copyright law citations; and even a few cites that are dedicated to notable TV commercials.

Academic, Research, and Technical Resources

Television research is not a new discipline, but the Internet gives media critics and academics an audience beyond the classroom.

The WWW Virtual Library Telecommunications Index

http://www.analysys.co.uk/commslib.htm

The indispensable and ever-growing service called the World Wide Web Virtual Library has an extensive section on the technical, political, and social parameters of the ongoing telecommunications revolution (including television, radio, and the Internet itself). The site includes subsections on the following topics:

* Broadcasting

* Economics

* Education

* Finance

* International Telecommunications

* Internetworking and LANs

* Journals and Other Electronic Media

* Manufacturers and Vendors

* Mobile Communications

* Multimedia

* Operators

* Policy and Regulation

* Regulators

* Research Institutions and Programs

* Satellites

* Service Providers

* Social

* Standards, Testing, and Protocols

* United States Government Sources

* Universities

* Videoconferencing

Each of these subsections will take you to a list of appropriate links and textual material.

NEW TV SERVICES: A MODEST PROPOSAL

Television is changing rapidly (even while it remains the same), and new technologies promise to offer us hundreds of new and specialized programming services in the future. The following is a proposal for a cable service that could fit nicely into the landscape of nostalgia TV that seems to be expanding rapidly as Baby Boomers take over the controls.

Before the end of the century there could be entire networks devoted to the television of a particular year. Consider, for example, the 1972 Channel, which would only show the programs that were on the air in 1972—in the exact order that they were aired, complete with the original commercials and news broadcasts. Thus, at the stroke of midnight on January 1, 1999, you could watch the New Year's broadcast from January 1, 1972, complete with Dick Clark introducing the Grass Roots' rendition of "Midnight Confessions." The cycle would continue for a full year (perhaps with one service for each of the three networks that were operating at the time), through the episode of *The Partridge Family* where Laurie picks up radio stations on her new braces, through the Fisher-Spassky chess challenge, through the '72 Olympics, and finally concluding with the Christmas season (when "Noelco" would sponsor *Frosty the Snowman*).

If any of you actually implement this idea, I want 10 percent of the gross and a souvenir videotape of my 1980 appearance on an NBC show called *The Sunday Games,* in which I competed in "The National Collegiate Beer-Chugging Championship" with the aid of guest star O.J. Simpson.

SCREENsite
http://www.sa.ua.edu/TCF/welcome.htm

This site from the University of Alabama's Department of Telecommunications and Film contains a wealth of information related to the academic study of television and film. It includes: information on college film/TV schools; syllabi from various film and TV curricula; notices about teaching jobs; textbook samples; indexes of academic film and TV journals; archives of credits/reviews; online catalogues (such as, Library of

Congress); links to online discussion groups; and information on film studios, and television networks. And it does all this with a perceptible spirit of fun. (See figure 5.9.)

Media Watchdog
http://theory.lcs.mit.edu/~mernst/media

Today it is more important than ever that the ownership and content of the mass media are subjected to scrutiny by independent researchers.

There are "media watch" groups on both the right and the left side of the political spectrum. Those on the left observe that the media is dominated by corporate interests and advertisers, and that the news coverage of complex issues is trivialized by a reliance on sound bites and sensational images. Those on the right contend that the media is corrupting the values of youth and foisting a liberal agenda on the populace. (One could argue that the institutionalized left vs. right debate that you hear from Washington is just a family squabble between different factions within an irrevocably capitalist superstructure, so just how "liberal" can the media be? I have yet to read an editorial in the *Washington Post* that calls for collective farming and the nationalization of the banks.)

Media Watchdog is "a collection of online media-watch resources, including specific media criticism articles and information about media watch groups. The emphasis is on critiquing the accuracy and exposing the biases of the mainstream media."

Recent postings at this site include an article on welfare myths in the mainstream press; a pointer to the ACLU's censorship resources and Banned Books On-Line; an analysis of the much-ballyhooed study of "pornography on the Internet"; and Herbert I. Schiller's "Challenging the Global Cultural Factories," which notes that "the world's most powerful and sophisticated message- and image-making apparatus is almost totally in the service of selling the goods, services, and general perspectives of the dominant Fortune 500 companies." Partypooper.

TV Career and Professional Resources

The Internet can be a handy source of information for anyone contemplating a career in television or film. Often, film and television resources are lumped together, as in the following sites. (See Chapter 2, "General Movie Resources," for more information on these sites.)

Screenwriters' Resources Pages
http://www.teleport.com/~cdeemer/Screenwriters.html

This site contains terrific nuts-and-bolts advice about the craft and business of screenwriting, TV writing, and playwriting. (See Chapter 2, "General Movie Resources.")

Mandy's Film and Television Production Directory
http://www.mandy.com

A fine collection of links to technicians, producers, and technical facilities worldwide. Thus, if you find yourself filming in Iceland and you need to rent a gorilla for the day, the information is here.

Film.com
http://www.film.com/film

This site is notable for its film and video reviews; it also has a useful discussion and bulletin-board section for film buffs and aspiring filmmakers.

MCA Cyberwalk
http://www/mca.com

The excellent home site for Universal Studios and MCA offers detailed behind-the-scenes information about the making of a typical television show (*Vanishing Son*), from script to locations to a shot-by-shot breakdown of the production schedule. (See figure 5.10.)

FIGURE 5.10

A menu of publicity and production notes from the TV series Vanishing Son, from the MCA Cyberwalk site.

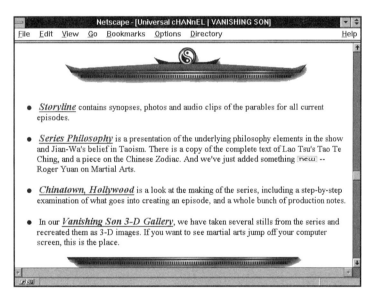

The List

Archives and Link Sites

CineMedia Television Sites
http://www.gu.edu.au/gwis/cinemedia/CineMedia.tv.html

Tardis TV Archive
http://src.doc.ic.ac.uk/public/media/tv/collections/tardis/index.html

The Ultimate TV List
http://tvnet.com/UTVL/utvl.html

or

gopher.enews.com

Internet Television Resource Guide
http://www.teleport.com/~celinec/tv.htm

English Server Film and Television
http://english.hss.cmu.edu/FilmandTV.html

A large collection of provocative articles about television and its effect on the culture.

Wiretap Archiveswiretap.spies.com/11/Library/Media/Tv

General Television-Related FTP Sites
src.doc.ic.ac.uk:/public/media/tv/collections/tardis

General TV site, very up to date.

src.doc.ic.ac.uk:/usenet/usenet-by-hierarchy/alt/tv

FAQs for the alt.tv. groups
ftp.uu.net:usenet/rec.arts.tv

"Official" guide site.

ftp.funet.fi:pub/culture/tv+film

Lots of assorted guides, plus archived images.

elbereth.rutgers.edu:/pub/sfl

Various sci-fi holdings.

cathouse.org:pub/cathouse/television

A comedy archive.

General Television-Related UseNet Groups

alt.tv.misc

Free-ranging TV discussion.

rec.arts.tv

Still more free-ranging TV discussion.

rec.arts.tv.uk

Free-ranging discussion on U.K. TV.

rec.video.satellite

Satellite TV programming.

Guides and Listings

What's On Tonite

http://tv1.com/

TV Tonite

http://metaverse.com/vibe/tv.html

Austrailian TV Guide

http://www.sofcom.com.au/TV/index.html

TV Reviews

TV Chat

http://tvnet.com/TVChat/chat.html

Professor Neon

http://www.vortex.com/ProfNeon.html

Transient Images

http://www.cais.com/jpadgett/www/home.html

Broadcasters, Networks, and Cable Channels

CBS

http://WWW.CBS.COM

NBC

http://www.nbc-com

PBS

http://www.pbs.org

The BBC Networking Club

http://www.bbcnc.org.uk

The CBC Homepage

http://www.cbc.ca

Fox Broadcasting

http://www.foxnetwork.com

ESPNet

http://espnet.sportszone.com

Discovery Channel

http://www.discovery.com

Nick Linx

http://cctr.umkc.edu/user/rbarrow/nicklnx.html

Cable News Network

http://www.cnn.com

MTV

http://www.mtv.com

MuchMusic

http://www.muchmusic.com/muchmusic.html

Canada's answer to MTV has a much better site than MTV does.

Playboy TV

http://www.playboy.com/PlayboyTV/PlayboyTV.html

For the man with that certain something.

Bravo! (Canada)

http://www.bravo.ca/bravo.html

Canada's 24-hour arts-and-entertainment channel, featuring "TV too good for TV."

TV Net

http://tvnet.com/misc/abouttvnet.html

World Resource for Student Television (WORST)

http://www.efd.lth.se/~e91rw/WORST.html

Miscellaneous Resources

The WWW Virtual Library Telecommunications Index

http://www.analysys.co.uk/commslib.htm

ScreenSite

http://www.sa.ua.edu/TCF/welcome.htm

Screenwriters' Resources Pages

http://www.teleport.com/~cdeemer/Screenwriters.html

Mandy's Film and Television Production Directory

http://www.mandy.com

Film.com

http://www.film.com/film

MCA Cyberwalk

http://www/mca.com

The Infomercial List

http://www.best.com/~dijon/tv/infomercials/info-list.html

Find out which washed-up celebrity is endorsing which useless appliance or beauty product. Fans of the Flowbee, take note.

Super Bowl TV Commercials

http://www.csua.berkeley.edu/~milesm/supercomm.html

Mentos—The Freshmaker!

http://www.best.com/~dijon/tv/mentos

A tribute to the TV ad campaign that defined an entire generation. Enjoy.

6

News and Talk

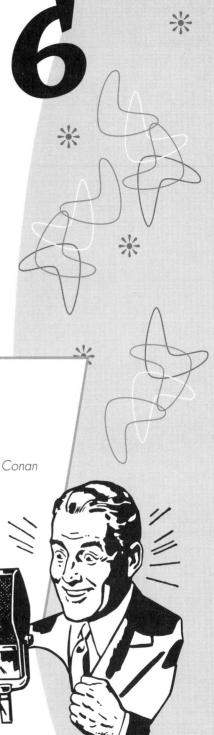

IN THIS CHAPTER:

> Network and cable news broadcasts

> Afternoon and topical talk shows

> Late-night talk shows: Letterman, Leno, and Conan

IN OTHER CHAPTERS:

< General TV resources on the Net are discussed in Chapter 5.

> Series and sitcoms are discussed in Chapter 7.

> Humor is discussed in Chapter 13.

There are probably still a few idealists left in the world who think that television is primarily an educational medium that can cultivate an informed citizenry; but such sentiments are rare among the people who actually produce and sponsor the programs that get on the air. Yes, there is some genuine news on the airwaves, but news and public-affairs programming are a minor niche within a vast, competitive medium that depends on compelling imagery to maintain the attention of the audience.

To promote the illusion of a social conscience, the major networks have staked out a middle ground where news and entertainment meet, and that's where they've pitched the carnival tent of "infotainment." Witness the proliferation of newsmagazine shows, celebrity interview specials, and featurettes that tell us which movies were big at the box office on "This Date in History." Consider that more people get their news from the monologues on *The Late Show* than read a daily newspaper. Consider that Oprah Winfrey (bless her heart) is the most influential woman in America, while not one person in 100 would recognize Coretta Scott King if they rode in the same elevator.

This is the point in the book where I'm supposed to make some tired allusion to the movie *Network*, with its nightmare vision of a news organization that annihilates everything that stands in the way of high ratings. Or maybe I should say something incisive about the murder of a gay suitor that was widely blamed on *The Jenny Jones Show*. (Have you forgotten already?) But really, if people wanted something more substantive, they'd demand it. They'd vote with their remote controls. Who can deny that Letterman's Top Ten List is a lot more fun than C-SPAN—and a lot easier to summarize at the coffee machine the next morning?

When you get right down to it, ratings won't deter the committed journalist, viewers have plenty of choices if they know where to look, and there will always be pearls of useful information and lively news among the sensational and empty images. So dig in.

TV News

Television news is not a subject that inspires a lot of passion from people who do not actually work in the industry. Most of the outsiders who care about TV news are either academics or journalism students (and academics are thus responsible for most of the news-related sites on the Internet). The rest of us just watch CNN for the pleasant background hum of a world that we can't do anything to change.

Archives, Link Sites, and General Resources

If television news isn't a particularly self-aware medium, there are plenty of academic and public-interest groups that are willing to fill in the gaps and treat television with the same scrutiny as any other power structure in our society. The following sites can help you see TV news as part of a bigger picture.

The Vanderbilt Television News Archives
http://tvnews.vanderbilt.edu

Since August 5, 1968, Vanderbilt University researchers have recorded and indexed every network television news broadcast in the United States. Users can search the indexed archived by date or by keyword.

The Institute for Propaganda Analysis
http://carmen.artsci.washington.edu/propaganda/home.htm

This is the home page for the Propaganda Analysis Project, which is dedicated to subjecting our public discourse to critical analysis. Some of the common propaganda techniques that are scrutinized include euphemism, name-calling, false extrapolation, the bandwagon technique, and wartime censorship. (And if you think that propaganda doesn't exist in a "free" society, you've already bought into it.)

Project McLuhan

http://www.vyne.com/McLuhan

Marshall McLuhan was the Canadian social scientist who coined the term "the medium is the message," which basically means that the electronic media provide a physical sensation that obliterates the need for specific content. TV is about *itself*, not about what's *on* it.

This research site applies McLuhanesque analysis to contemporary media culture, including broadcast news and the Internet itself. (For instance, one Project McLuhan researcher refers to the kind of "cybertalk" that occurs over the Internet as "a new form of intellectual violence as a quest for identity.") McLuhan's theories are vital to our understanding of the new information space we inhabit. You can subscribe to the Project McLuhan mailing list by sending e-mail to *majordomo@inforamp.net* with the message **subscribe mcluhan list**. The home page for Project McLuhan is shown in figure 6.1.

FIGURE 6.1

The home page for Project McLuhan.

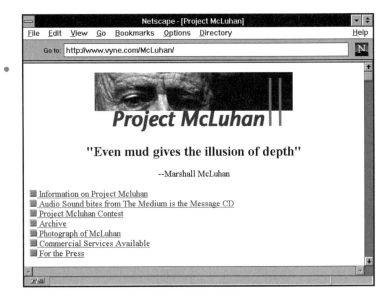

128   PART III * 𝕋𝕖𝕝𝕖𝕧𝕚𝕤𝕚𝕠𝕟

News Media Online
http://town.hall.org/places/npc/media.html

This is a collection of links and resources for professional journalists who are trying to find and gather news content online. It includes links to TV and radio news resources, as well as to print and Internet-specific news sites. (The number of Internet news sites is small but growing.)

TV News Organizations

As the public loses confidence in TV news organizations and looks to alternative sources for information (including the Internet), the networks will inevitably redefine their mission. That will probably mean a lot more fluff and a lot more stories about babies who fall into wells. In the meantime, the news organizations are not doing a lot of online crowing.

C-SPAN
http://www.c-span.org

or

gopher://c-span.org

The cable television industry created C-SPAN (Cable-Satellite Public Affairs Network) in the early 1980s to provide live, gavel-to-gavel coverage of the U.S. House of Representatives. Since then, C-SPAN has grown into a combination of networks that provide public affairs programming 24-hours-a-day. The cable industry continues to carry and fund the C-SPAN networks as a public service. C-SPAN is the only cable television network governed by the cable industry as a whole.

The C-SPAN home site is almost as much fun as the C-SPAN programming itself. It offers a program schedule, copies of important documents (such as the Republican party's "Contract With America"), resources for educators, updates on the '96 presidential campaign, and a section called the Political Resource Center, which contains addresses and biographies for all your favorite politicians.

Internet CNN Newsroom

http://www.nmis.org/NewsInteractive/CNN/Newsroom/contents.html

Until recently (with the unveiling of the headline-news service at *http://www.cnn.com*), the CNN presence on the Internet was surprisingly modest.

The Internet CNN Newsroom is a multimedia site for classroom use in conjunction with the CNN news broadcasts. From this site, students can read a breakdown of the top stories of the day (or previous days, with a search engine), answer quiz questions related to the content of the news, and download video clips that are supposed to be of interest to the average schoolkid (such as the recent video clip that was labeled thusly: "A new generation of South Koreans exercises its right...to have fun").

In the course of using the Internet CNN Newsroom, students will learn and discuss new terms, such as this list that was recently posted there: "Bill of Rights," "amendment," "desecration," "bumper sticker slogan," "demographics," "circulation," "Seoul," "demonstrations," and "Rodeo Drive." Honest.

CBS News/Up To The Minute

http://www.cbs.com:80/cgi-bin/news.cgi

Once upon a time, CBS was referred to as "the Tiffany Network" because of its high standards of quality (and possibly because it was headquartered on the same Manhattan block as the famous jewelry store). The CBS News operation was the yardstick by which all other broadcast journalism was measured. This was the network of Edward R. Murrow, Eric Severeid, Harry Reasoner, and Walter Cronkite (although it should be pointed out that CBS really dropped the ball when it sided with the Warren Report's conclusion of a lone-nut gunman in the Kennedy assassination). Today it's just another news organization groping for that extra ratings point. Even *60 Minutes* has grown flatulent, toting its ambush cameras to every corner grocery in Manhattan that dares to sell day-old muffins as fresh.

However, there must be some old guy in a closet there at corporate headquarters who gets carted out once a year to remind the News division of the glory days. CBS News is still capable of the occasional hard-hitting, unglamorous, hour-long documentary. (See figure 6.2.)

FIGURE 6.2

A CBS New press release about "Legacy of Shame," a documentary follow-up to Edward R. Murrow's "Harvest of Shame," exposing the exploitation of migrant farm workers. Accessed via the CBS home site at http://www.cbs.com.

Netscape - [Coming Soon: CBS News]

File   Edit   View   Go   Bookmarks   Options   Directory   Help

The CBS News production team for "Legacy of Shame" spent one year in the fields and groves of America and discovered that most of the misery the migrants experience is caused by a system that almost ensures that the workers will be exploited.

CBS REPORTS: "Legacy of Shame" begins in Mexico, where two men are brought across the border by a "coyote," a smuggler who brings Mexican field workers to American farms for a fee. The men move on to El Paso, Texas, where, despite well-intentioned government regulations intended to make life better for the workers, many suffer because employers find the laws too extensive and complicated to comply with.

The broadcast profiles Maria Echaveste, an undersecretary of the U.S. Department of Labor, who works to ensure compliance with minimum wage for migrants in Texas. As the child of migrant workers and a law school graduate, she is also a symbol of how much progress has been made since 1960.

CBS REPORTS: "Legacy of Shame" visits Clarendon County, S.C., where poverty and alcohol addiction keep notions of slavery alive. The broadcast also examines how the farmers' dependence on crew leaders, the go-betweens who hire workers, shields them from responsibility for the wrongs committed against migrants. "Legacy of Shame" investigates one such crew leader who allegedly holds his workers in peonage, using scare tactics and threats to keep them from running away. The investigation also uncovers how this crew leader apparently made big profits on his operation. He is currently the subject of a grand jury inquiry.

The CBS News subsection of the CBS home page has a rundown on the entire news operation. It also offers a link to a late-night news show called *CBS Up To The Minute*. This is a good place to go for news headlines, capsule movie reviews, parenting tips, and all-purpose lifestyle fodder if you don't know where else to turn. (See figure 6.3.)

FIGURE 6.3

The online interface for CBS Up To The Minute, where the news is on the lite side.

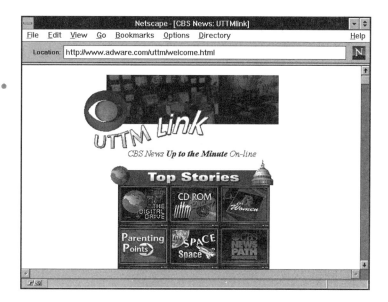

Newsmagazine Shows

As of this writing, there is not a Web site for *60 Minutes* or *20/20*, or even a Web site for the tabloid TV shows, such as *Current Affair* and *Hard Copy*. You will find sites for a couple less-well-known newsmagazines, however.

c|net

http://www.cnet.com

c|net is an interesting and useful synthesis of TV and computer: a weekly cable show about emerging technologies (it airs on the USA Network and the Sci Fi Channel) and an online adjunct that amplifies some of the topics covered on the TV show. Along with the feature stories (on subjects such as UFOs, satellite TV, virtual reality, and the latest shenanigans from Microsoft), the online version of c|net features links to related Web pages; a column by computer know-it-all and CD-ROM reviewer John Dvorak; online chat; video clips; and a linked index to 100,000 downloadable shareware files. (See figure 6.4.)

FIGURE 6.4

The table of contents of the online version of the cable TV newsmagazine c|net.

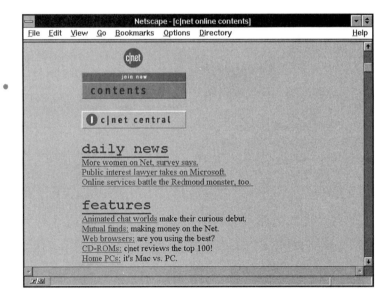

TV Nation
http://www.teleport.com/~xwinds/TVNation.html

TV Nation is the much-beloved and little-seen satirical newsmagazine from documentary wiseguy Michael Moore. After airing on NBC during the summer of 1994, the show has moved to Fox (where it will probably run for a few weeks before the Fox executives get annoyed with all the segments that feature Moore's camera crew trying to push past a flustered security guard to visit a corporate C.E.O.).

The TV Nation home page features synopses of the NBC broadcasts, excerpts from the *alt.tv.tv-nation* UseNet group, an update on Moore's ongoing attempt to hug the governors of all 50 states, and the text of the actual, this-is-not-a-joke United States House Resolution that declared August 16, 1994 as "TV Nation Day." (See sidebar.)

TV Talk

Talk shows are relatively inexpensive to produce, and when they are provocative they can attract high ratings, so they are an increasingly useful tool in the TV-programming repertoire.

Afternoon and Topical Talk

Afternoon talk shows are populated by dysfunctional people who are goaded into telling their secrets for a breathless and easily-outraged public. For some reason, the few sites on the Internet that are devoted to the afternoon talk-and-trauma shows are administered by the networks and the production companies that produce the shows rather than the fans who soak them up.

YOUR GOVERNMENT AT WORK: TV NATION DAY

BILL: House Joint Resolution 365

TITLE: To designate August 16, 1994, as 'TV Nation Day'.

MAY 10, 1994

Mr. Coble (for himself and Mr. Flake) introduced the following joint resolution; which was referred to the Committee on Post Office and Civil Service.

TEXT: JOINT RESOLUTION

"To designate August 16, 1994, as 'TV Nation Day.'

"Whereas television is one industry with which no other country can compete with America;

"Whereas American popular culture is a major United States export;

"Whereas some of the most memorable and uplifting moments in people's lives have occurred while watching television, from the Apollo moon landing to little baby Jessica's rescue from the well;

"Whereas TV Nation will air on broadcast television in the United States, making it available, free of charge, to everyone;

"Whereas TV Nation is the first American/European joint television venture, and will begin a new opportunity for similar ventures in the future;

"Whereas other news magazine programs focus on what's wrong with America, TV Nation focuses on what's right;

"Whereas TV Nation will help the United States economy by providing many new employment opportunities, particularly high-tech information ones; and

"Whereas TV Nation employs numerous Oscar, Emmy, and Cable-Ace Award nominees and winners:

"Now, therefore, be it resolved, that August 16, 1994, shall be designated as 'TV Nation Day'."

Ricki Lake

http://www.spe.sony.com/Pictures/tv/rickilake/ricki.html

The publicity for *The Ricki Lake Show* describes this afternoon talk program as "show-and-tell for the MTV generation." Lake, an actress best known for her work in John Waters movies, has been the most surprising success story of afternoon TV in the '90s, stealing a large portion of the youth market away from Oprah, Sally, and Donahue.

The home page for *The Ricki Lake Show* is part of the Sony Entertainment site (from which you can also access information about such Sony productions as *Jeopardy, Days of Our Lives,* and Tempest Bledsoe's new talk show). It offers bios of Ricki and her staff, audio clips, video clips, still photos, and a list of upcoming topics that might convince you that the world is coming to an end in a big hurry. (See figure 6.5.)

FIGURE 6.5

A list of discussion topics from The Ricki Lake Show.

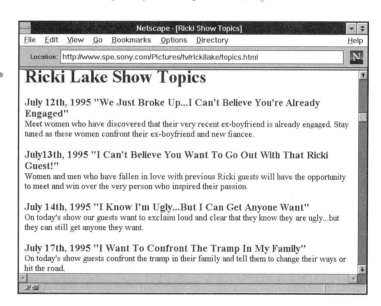

Rush Limbaugh

Radio and television commentator Rush Limbaugh is one of the most popular personalities in the online world. The CompuServe Issues Forum is dominated by his followers, and Limbaugh himself is a dedicated online habitué. (He met his wife after she sent him some argumentative e-mail.)

There is a good summary of the Limbaugh online phenomenon at a site called Aether Madness at *http://www.aether.com/ Aether/limbaugh.html.*

A fan named John Switzer writes a summary of every Limbaugh broadcast. Sixty days' worth of these summaries are collected at *ftp://ftp.aimnet.com/pub/users/jswitzer/.* A four-year archive is at *http://cathouse.org/RushLimbaugh.* (See figure 6.6.)

FIGURE 6.6

A tribute to Rush Limbaugh from an exercise in free speech called The Right Side of the Web, at http://www.clark.net/pub/ jeffd/index.html.

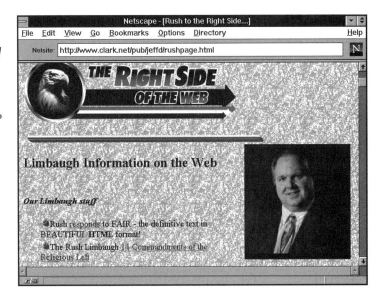

Late Night Entertainment and Talk

Back in the Stone Age (pre-Tom Snyder), the only thing that followed the Johnny Carson, Merv Griffin, and Dick Cavett shows was the national anthem. If you were a night-shift worker or a drunk on a binge, your only late-night entertainment was AM radio and the TV test pattern.

Snyder changed all that with his *Tomorrow Show* in the mid '70s. Since then, America has had late-night (and late-late-night) talk shows starring David Letterman, Joan Rivers, Arsenio Hall, Jay Leno, Dennis Miller, Alan Thicke, Pat Sajak, Rick Dees, Jon Stewart, Conan O'Brien, Greg Kinnear, and probably a few more who never made it past the test-marketing stage.

Late-night audiences can be extremely loyal, and there are many Web sites devoted to the late-night talk shows that are now on the air—including a site that surveys the late-night land-scape as a whole.

The Late Night News E-Zine

http://delphi.beckman.uiuc.edu/~jlindqui/late.news.html

or

ftp.mcs.net/mcsnet.users/barhart/late-show-news

This weekly electronic newsletter from Aaron Barnhart brings an intelligent perspective to the late-night programming and ratings competition. Late Night News analyzes the latest moves and countermoves between the networks (mostly the Jay vs. Dave stuff, but also the latest on Ted Koppel, Conan O'Brien, Howard Stern, Charles Grodin, Bill Maher, and *Saturday Night Live*), offers a schedule of this week's guests on all the major late-night shows, and tosses a bouquet when it's due. (See figure 6.7.)

FIGURE 6.7
The Late Night News e-zine says goodbye to the pretty good Jon Stewart Show.

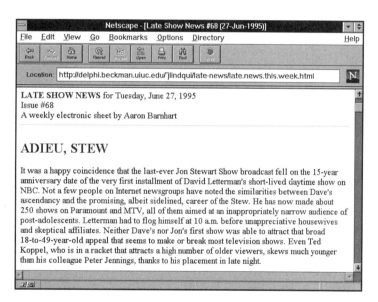

The Late Show with David Letterman

David Letterman is the king of the late-night heap (although his ratings were slipping at the time of this writing), and the profile of a Letterman viewer seems to be similar to that of the typical Internet user: a white college boy who likes a good joke, as long as it comes at someone else's expense.

Predictably, there are many Letterman sites on the Net. The Letterman page at the CBS home site (*http://www.cbs.com/lateshow/lateshow.html*) provides cast bios, ticket information, lists of upcoming guests, and the most recent Top Ten list. (See figure 6.8.)

FIGURE 6.8
The official Letterman Web site is part of the CBS network's home page.

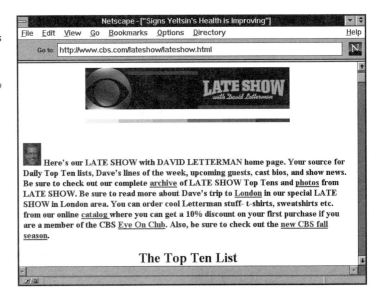

The Late Show with David Letterman Web Server at *http://bingen.cs.csbsju.edu/letterman.html* features photos, sound bites, a list of upcoming guests, a monologue browser, and a link to the Letterman Top Ten List archive and search engine at the CBS home page, which allows you to search the lists by date, subject, or keyword.

Jason Lindquist's Letterman page at *http://www.cen.uiuc.edu/~jl8287/letterman.html* features articles, culled from *alt.fan.letterman*, about the following bits of Dave-related lore:

* The Great Stevie Nicks Controversy of 1986

* The Crispin Glover incident

* Madonna

* The David Letterman song file

* Transcripts of Paul Shaffer's tirades

* An interview with Calvert DeForest (Larry "Bud" Melman)

* Late Show writer Bill Scheft's pre-taping audience warmup

* 1993 Late Night/Late Show show-by-show summaries
* Dave's closing comments from the last show at NBC

The Tonight Show with Jay Leno

http://www.nbctonightshow.com

Jay Leno is widely regarded as one of the nicest people in show business (although his monologues are typically more cutting and topical than Letterman's). Until recently he has trailed Letterman in the ratings, but as of this writing, it is a dead heat.

Leno tends to attract a slightly more mature crowd than Letterman, and he has not inspired the same kind of fan mania on the Internet. The main Leno page on the Internet is the one provided by NBC. It allows you to watch video clips from the previous night's shows, read the best of Leno's "actual headlines" bit, and visit the backstage area. (See figure 6.9.)

FIGURE 6.9

The home page for the Tonight Show with Jay Leno site.

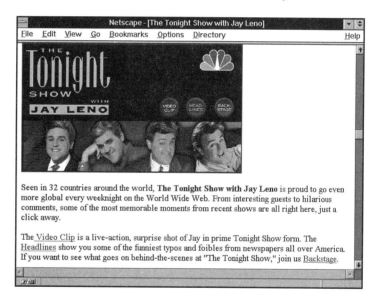

Late Night with Conan O'Brien

Call me crazy, but I think *Late Night with Conan O'Brien* is the best of the late-night talk shows. Admittedly, Conan is not the most graceful host, and he has Letterman's habit of interrupting or demeaning his guests when they're in the middle of a good anecdote; but the show aims high, it has terrific musical guests, and at its best, it has a surreal quality that is reminiscent of *The Ernie Kovacs Show.* (Conan, after all, was the producer of *The Simpsons* during its heyday.) It also has Andy Richter, the best sidekick since the days when Regis Philbin was tossing underhanded zingers into Joey Bishop's lap.

The definitive Conan fan site is The Late Night with Conan O'Brien Fan Purity Test at *http://www.rpi.edu/~nebusj/ lnfpt.html.* (See figure 6.10.) Do not attempt to take this test if you don't already know the meaning of the word "krunk."

FIGURE 6.10

The Late Night with Conan O'Brien Fan Purity Test will determine if you are a real fan or just another infiltrator.

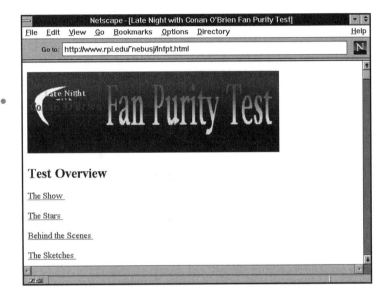

The Joyce Loves Conan page is at *http://www.rbdc.com/ ~hgambill/conan.htm.* It contains the archives of the *alt.fan.conan-obrien* UseNet group. Another good fan site is called Hereeeeeeeeee's Conan, at *http://styx.ios.com/ ~damone/gconan.html.*

The List

TV News Archives, Link Sites, and General Resources

The Vanderbilt Television News Archives
http://tvnews.vanderbilt.edu

News Media Online
http://town.hall.org/places/npc/media.html

The Institute for Propaganda Analysis
http://carmen.artsci.washington.edu/propaganda/home.htm

Project McLuhan
http://www.vyne.com/McLuhan

News Link
http://www.newslink.org

Links to most of the TV, magazine, and newspaper journalism sites on the Internet.

News Page
http://www.newspage.com

This online news service covers hundreds of topic areas, including telecominucations and news.

MediaTelevision
http://www.citytv.com/citytv/mediaTV/whatson.html

This site has information about a Toronto newsmagazine show that examines the information revolution from a post-modern perspective. I've never seen it, but it sounds great.

TV News Organizations

C-SPAN

http://www.c-span.org

or

gopher://c-span.org

Internet CNN Newsroom

http://www.nmis.org/NewsInteractive/CNN/Newsroom/contents.html

CBS News/Up to the Minute

http://www.cbs.com:80/cgi-bin/news.cgi

Newsmagazines

clnet

http://www.cnet.com

TV Nation

http://www.teleport.com/~xwinds/TVNation.html

Topical Talk

Ricki Lake

http://www.spe.sony.com/Pictures/tv/rickilake/ricki.html

Aether Madness (Limbaughmania)

http://www.aether.com/Aether/limbaugh.html

Limbaugh Summaries

ftp://ftp.aimnet.com/pub/users/jswitzer

Right Side of the Web

http://www.clark.net/pub/jeffd/index.html

Oprah Winfrey
http://www.wvec-tv13.com/wvec/releases/entry-9.html

This little page will give you the phone numbers for the Oprah Winfrey ticket line, for general Oprah information, and for ordering the book that features Oprah's favorite recipes.

King of All Media Fan's Web Page (Howard Stern)
http://krishna.cs.umd.edu/stern

Late Night Talk

The Late Night News E-Zine
http://delphi.beckman.uiuc.edu/~jlindqui/late.news.html

or

ftp://ftp.mcs.net/mcsnet.users/barhart/late-show-news

The Official Late Show With David Letterman Page (CBS)
http://www.cbs.com/lateshow/lateshow.html

The Late Show With David Letterman Web Server
http://bingen.cs.csbsju.edu/letterman.html

Jason Lindquist's Letterman Page
http://www.cen.uiuc.edu/~jl8287/letterman.html

The Tonight Show with Jay Leno
http://www.nbctonightshow.com

The Late Night With Conan O'Brien Fan Purity Test
http://www.rpi.edu/~nebusj/lnfpt.html

Joyce Loves Conan
http://www.rbdc.com/~hgambill/conan.htm

Hereeeeeeeeee's Conan
http://styx.ios.com/~damone/gconan.html

Browse the Late Night Talk Show Monologues

http://www.tns.lcs.mit.edu/cgi-bin/vs/vsjoke

At this site, the MIT Laboratory of Computer Science uses recordings of late night talk show monologues to demonstrate the VuSystem of video capture and transmission for UNIX computing systems. (My battery-operated Commodore 64 doesn't have the necessary gear, so I don't know which shows are excerpted or how often the monologues are updated.)

Talk-Related UseNet Groups

alt.tv.talkshows

alt.tv.talkshows.daytime

alt.tv.talkshows.late

There are also individual *alt.fan* sites for most of the national talk-show hosts.

Series, Sitcoms, and Animation

IN THIS CHAPTER:

> Today's TV: popular dramas and sitcoms

> Nostalgia TV: dramas and sitcoms of yesteryear

> Fantasy TV, including **Star Trek**

> TV animation for kids and grown-ups

IN OTHER CHAPTERS:

< General TV resources are discussed in Chapter 5.

Television as a form of narrative entertainment is the most effective synthesis of art and commerce that humankind has ever devised. In particular, the situation comedy (or "sitcom" as we like to call it) is as much a ritual affirmation of America's values and beliefs as Kabuki theatre is of Japan's.

What makes television comedy so great is its ability to recycle the same 13 plots (what those in The Industry call "The Canon of Comedy"), using nuance and gesture to make them seem hilariously original. For instance, Plot #6, "The Boy Who Had Two Dates for the Same Night" recently celebrated its 1,000th incarnation, edging ahead of "The Overheard Remark" and "The Woman Who Thought That Nobody Remembered Her Birthday" for the highest total number of uses.

Conversely, while sitcoms are known and loved for their predictability, TV drama is the medium of choice for contemporary artists who want to break new ground in a free-form, unregulated, and unpredictable milieu. Rarely will you see the same idea repeated on a TV drama. Just when it seems that no corner of the human experience has gone unexamined, the visionaries who run the TV networks surprise us with such new ideas as The Mobster Who Was an Undercover Cop, The Suburban Housewife Who Was an Undercover Cop, and The Attractive High School Student Who Was an Undercover Cop. And TV drama has been at the forefront of untraditional casting, giving previously excluded sectors of our society their turn in the spotlight with such shows as "Rosie Perez, Texas Ranger."

This chapter celebrates the diversity of entertainment on television—the artform that is beaming across the galaxies to give distant civilizations an uncanny snapshot of life on Earth at the end of the millennium.

Archives, Link Sites, and General Resources

There are a growing number of Internet sites, particularly in the FTP domain, that collect and index text-based information about various TV shows or genres. There are also many general-interest sites that provide a springboard to specific TV resources or home pages.

Wiretap Archives
gopher://wiretap.spies.com/11/Library/Media/Tv

The wiretap archives feature an extensive collection of episode guides and miscellaneous information for dozens of shows in a text-only format, from *Alf* to *Young Indiana Jones*, including the invaluable guide to *Twin Peaks* symbolism.

The Cathouse Archives
http://cathouse.org/cathouse/television

The Cathouse TV Archives are part of a larger archive of science-fiction and humor-related information, including a compendium of British humor, movie scripts, urban legends, and summaries of *The Rush Limbaugh Show*.

The TV archives contain episode guides, scripts, and trivia information for such shows as *Fawlty Towers, Absolutely Fabulous, Cheers, The Muppets, Seinfeld*, and *Saturday Night Live*. (See figure 7.1.)

FIGURE 7.1

An excerpt from an early Saturday Night Live news skit about celebrity palimony. From the Cathouse Archives.

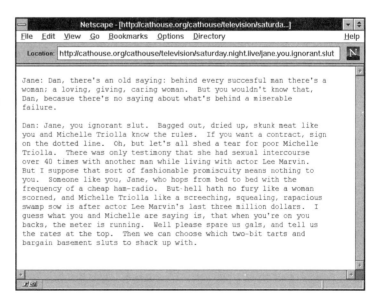

Sound Bytes: The WWW TV Themes Home Page

http://ai.eecs.umich.edu/people/kennyp/sounds.html

This remarkable site features digitized samples of the theme songs to hundreds of TV shows, past and present. Patrick Kenny has culled these themes either directly from his TV set or from the various theme-song collections that are available (such as those from TVT Records).

You will need a modicum of technical expertise to use the site properly, but it offers a bounty of downloadable software to assist you, and once you have your media player configured, there are many wonderful tunes to choose from. (See figure 7.2.)

FIGURE 7.2

A portion of the theme songs that are available from the WWW TV Themes Home Page.

Internet TV Resources

http://www.teleport.com/~celinec/tv.htm

As mentioned in Chapter 5, the Internet TV Resources page is a good general resource for TV links, particularly for links to popular TV series, past and present.

Although the Internet TV Resources Page is handy because of its limited scope, the shows can be accessed from any number of link sites on the Internet. Some of the most comprehensive include the following:

* The *Entertainment/Television/Shows* directory of the Yahoo utility at *http://www/yahoo.com*.

* CineMedia Television Sites at *http://www.gu.edu.au/gwis/ cinemedia/CineMedia.tv.html*, which also contains links to broadcasters, academic sites, technological info, and government telecom regulations.

* The Ultimate TV List at *http://tvnet.com/UTVL/utvl.html*, which contains over 1,000 links to over 300 television shows.

* The Tardis TV Archive at *http://src.doc.ic.ac.uk/ public/media/tv/collections/tardis/index.html*.

See Chapter 5 for more information on general TV resources.

Today's TV

Almost as soon as a new series or sitcom hits the airwaves, some pop-culture fanatic dedicates a Web site to it. The following are some Web sites devoted to dramatic series and situation comedies that are currently on the air (or in scheduling limbo).

Drama Series

Here's the premise of an exciting and original new series that is coming soon to the Cop Network: The show is called *St. Louis Blues*. It's the story of Michael Keenan, a tough-but-fair cop on the south side of St. Louis who is two days short of retirement and looking forward to a lifetime of watching his beloved hockey team when suddenly he is pumped full of lead in a robbery at an antique store by a punk with a distinctive blue-note tattoo on his forearm. What the punk doesn't know is that the vintage Fiesta Ware he took from the antique store is radioactive. The next day Keenan drags himself out of his hospital bed and contacts a snitch for some info on the heist. It turns out that the hold-up man is Keenan's long-lost son, and now the veteran cop has 24 hours to track the kid down and get him medicated before Keenan turns in his badge. Each episode of the series represents another hour of the search.

Until the debut of *St. Louis Blues*, you can investigate the following Web sites that are dedicated to other dramatic series, which are not at all similar.

NYPD Blue
http://src.doc.ic.ac.uk/public/media/tv/collections/tardis/us/drama/NYPDBlue/index.html

The fan page for this acclaimed *cinema verité*-style cop show on ABC includes links to two different episode guides, pictures of the characters, the FAQ list from the UseNet group *alt.tv.nypd-blue*, and, incredibly (considering one of the plot threads on the show), an *NYPD Blue* drinking game. (See figure 7.3.)

ER
http://sunsite.doc.ic.ac.uk/public/media/tv/collections/tardis/us/drama/ER

The fan page for this acclaimed *cinema verité*-style hospital show on NBC includes links to two different episode guides, pictures of the characters, the FAQ list from the UseNet group *alt.tv.er*, and an *ER* drinking game. (See figure 7.4.)

FIGURE 7.3

The NYPD Blue home page, featuring the NYPD Blue drinking game. (Every time Andy shows his bare butt, take five drinks.)

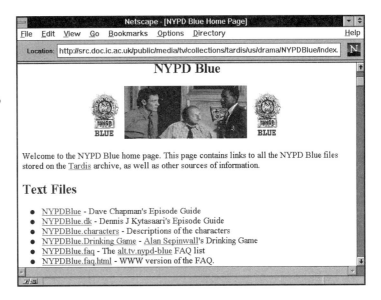

FIGURE 7.4

The ER home page, featuring the ER drinking game. (Every time George Clooney wakes up with a woman whose name he can't remember, take a drink.)

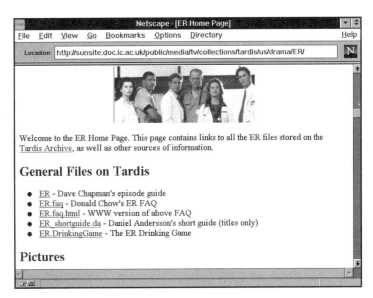

Chicago Hope

http://www-cs-students.stanford.edu/~clee/chicagohope.html

Many connoisseurs of *cinema verité*-style hospital dramas prefer *Chicago Hope* to *ER* because it substitutes sheer weirdness for the Hunk Factor.

The *Chicago Hope* fan page includes links to two different episode guides, pictures of the characters, the FAQ list from the UseNet group *alt.tv.chicago-hope*, and the *Chicago Hope* drinking game. It also has a digitized version of the theme song, and a list of the bizarre songs that are played in the background during the surgery scenes. ☞

My So-Called Life
http://www.umn.edu/nlhome/g564/lask0008/mscl.html

The fan page for this acclaimed *cinema verité*-style student drama on ABC includes links to an episode guide, pictures of the characters, the FAQ list, and, incredibly (considering one of the plot threads on the show), a *My So-Called Life* drinking game. It also includes audio and video clips, reviews, trivia, related fiction, and a lot of information about the extraordinary (and wasted) effort to keep the show from being cancelled. (See figure 7.5.)

FIGURE 7.5
The My So-Called Life home page, featuring the My So-Called Life drinking game. (Every time Angela and Jordan Catalano share a secret glance, take a sip of Dr. Pepper.)

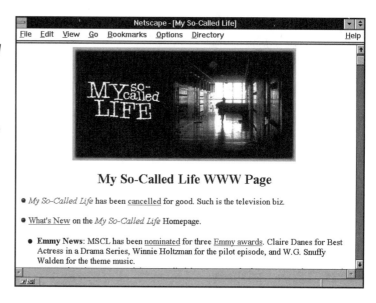

For diehard fans of this show, there are rumors of an upcoming feature-film version called *My So-Called Wonderful Life*. In the film, Angela is rescued from suicide by her guardian angel and learns that her suburban high school would have been *exactly the same* without her. ☞

The Moose's Guide to Northern Exposure

http://www.netspace.org/~moose/moose.html

Even though the show is now officially kaput, there are at least seven *Northern Exposure* sites on the Internet (probably because the show appeals to smart people, the kind who know how to use computers).

This site features a poem about moose. Among other things.

The Melrose Place Update

http://www.speakeasy.org/~dbrick/Melrose/melrose.html

Fans of the steamy nighttime soaper *Melrose Place* have several online options. The Melrose Place Update page at *http://www. speakeasy.org/~dbrick/Melrose/melrose.html* offers a good history of the show. The very popular Heather Locklear Home Page at *http://metro.turnpike.net/garyfs/index.htm* offers all the latest poop on the queen bee of *Melrose Place,* including her beauty secrets.

Melrose Place Current Synopsis at *http://www.polaris.net/ ~dayres/melrose.htm* will give you a straightforward summary of the latest happenings at the swingin' apartment complex where the show takes place, while the deceptively named Official Melrose Place Update page at *http://www.mit.edu:8001/ people/mickey/mp/melrose.html* offers a hilarious weekly spoof of the proceedings. (See figure 7.6.)

FIGURE 7.6

An episode summary for the season finale of Melrose Place. This is a joke.

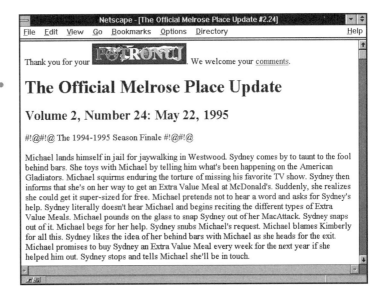

Beverly Hills 90210

http://www.prairienet.org/~rogue/homepage.html

This page, which features all the usual fan-page stuff, is worthy of mention here because of its surreal description of last season's final episode. (See figure 7.7.)

FIGURE 7.7

An episode summary for the season finale of Beverly Hills 90210. This is not a joke.

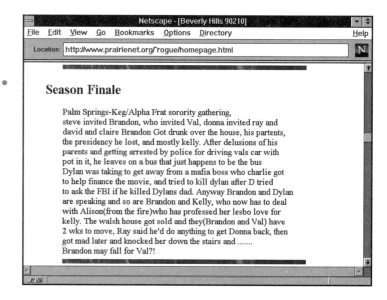

Soap Links

http://www.cts.com/~jeffmj/soaps.html

This page will jump you directly to the home sites for several soaps, both the daytime and nighttime variety. (See figure 7.8.)

FIGURE 7.8
Soap Links.

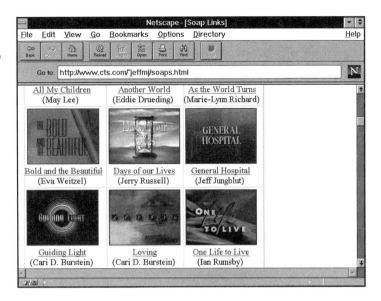

General Hospital (Port Charles Online)
http://www.cts.com/~jeffmj/GeneralHospital.html

The administrator of the Soap Links page operates this extremely comprehensive site devoted to the ABC series *General Hospital,* which stars Anthony Geary and Genie Francis as "Luke and Laura." (See sidebar.)

Days of Our Lives
http://weber.u.washington.edu/~pfloyd/days/index.html

My mother's favorite show is one of the weirder soap operas on the air. Besides all the usual character-returns-from-the-dead-with-a-different-face stuff that you see on every soap opera, *Days* has recently given us the transformation of Dr. Marlena Evans Brady (Deidre Hall) from a respected physician to a succubus (a demon that inhabits the body of a woman to fornicate men into damnation).

In 1985, I saw Anthony Geary ("Luke" from *General Hospital)* in the title role of *Jesus Christ Superstar*. About five years later I met Geary at a charity find-raiser in L.A. where my girlfriend was working. We invited him out for a drink afterwards, and he accepted.

At a corner bar I ordered a round of scotches and told him that I thought the Jesus thing was rather offbeat casting (considering that he played a lovable rapist on *General Hospital).* He didn't see my point.

After a few more drinks I got up the nerve to ask him point-blank what it was like being a celebrity. Because this was a couple years after his pop-culture zenith, he said he didn't think of himself as a celebrity and that he spent most of his nights alone, watching old *Road Runner* cartoons. But, he said, he did know a very big celebrity with some genuine insight into stardom: Elizabeth Taylor (with whom he was rumored to have had an affair). Geary said that Liz once summarized her situation thusly: "Tony, do you want to know what it's like being Elizabeth Taylor? When I [break wind], they hear it in Tokyo."

Kinda makes you think.

Sitcoms

I predict that very soon there will be a situation comedy about six attractive white people in their middle twenties who spend all of their time in a high-rise loft, wondering about the meaning of life in a gently comical way and never having sex with each other. Then one day an atomic bomb explodes, three of the people are killed, and the survivors have to decide whether to eat them. Each episode of the series represents another half-hour of the moral dilemma.

Or maybe a similar plot line can be worked into one of the following shows, which already exist.

Friends

http://geminga.dartmouth.edu/~andyjw/friends

Friends, the NBC sitcom that all the kids are talking about, is an online phenomenon. There are at least seven Internet sites devoted to the show (perhaps because it is so gently comic and true-to-life), but the site mentioned here is the Big Kahuna.

This site features extensive episode information, selected quotes from the show, stuff you can buy, links to other *Friends* sites, a photo gallery (see figure 7.9), and information about "The Friends Zone," a virtual online world of *Friends* devotees.

FIGURE 7.9
Courteney Cox of the TV series Friends, who once handed the author of this book a cup of tea in a scene from a TV movie called I'll Be Home For Christmas.

Seinfeld (The Vandelay Industries Archive)

http://www.cs.cmu.edu/afs/cs/user/vernon/www/vandelay/index.html

Seinfeld is an NBC sitcom based on a Jean-Paul Sartre play about four characters trapped in a subway where nothing ever happens. (See figure 7.10.) There are at least eight *Seinfeld* sites on the Internet, including a couple in Europe. This site is especially comprehensive, with episode guides, cast-member bios, FAQs, interviews, a summary of *Seinfeld's* "Olympic moments" ad campaign, and links to a spirited *Seinfeld* e-mail discussion group at *seinfeld-request@cpac.washington.edu.*

Location: file://ftp.doc.ic.ac.uk/../media/tv/collections/tardis/us/comedy/Seinfeld/seinsub.jpg

Married...With Children (The Bundy Page)

http://www.ifi.uio.no/~steinho/bundy.html

The Bundy Page is a Norwegian site devoted to the warmly offensive sitcom *Married...With Children*. It is one of at least nine MWC pages on the Net. Although this site was recently obliterated by a humorless administrator, it has been rebuilt. It includes *The Bundy Quarterly* newsletter, a bio of co-star Christina Applegate, and links to the episode guide and the Bundy household floor plan.

There is an archive of dozens of Christina Applegate photos at *http://baldrick.eia.brad.ac.uk/mwc/pics/christina/*. (See figure 7.11.) Various pictures of Christina—both real and fake—can be found all over the Internet, but she is actually a very sweet and down-to-earth young woman who goes bowling with her mother.

FIGURE 7.11

Christina Applegate of Married...With Children.

Netscape - [JPEG image 353x452 pixels]

File Edit View Go Bookmarks Options Directory   Help

Location: http://baldrick.eia.brad.ac.uk/mwc/pics/christina/chris.jpg

Nostalgia TV

For many of us, television was the first babysitter and caregiver we ever knew, so the TV shows of our childhood will always be precious to us. Lately the fixation with nostalgia TV has become a cultural addiction.

But a show doesn't have to be 30 years old to be dear to the memory of its fans. Many of the nostalgia-TV sites on the Internet are dedicated to shows that still exist on the periphery of prime-time, easily accessed on cable, or on your local re-run station.

NICK AT NITE 10TH ANNIVERSARY

The Nick at Nite home page at *http://nick-at-nite.viacom.com* celebrates the 10th anniversary of the cable service that changed the way we look at re-runs. (See figure 7.12.) Nick at Nite debuted in 1985 with a mission: "to preserve our TV heritage." Since then it has resurrected long-lost classics (*Dobie Gillis, Mr. Ed, The Donna Reed Show*) that even the local re-run channels wouldn't touch, and it has applied that same spirit of nostalgic reverence to newer shows (*Taxi, The Bob Newhart Show*) that no one had yet considered classic. And it has presented these shows within a snappy, retro-hip visual framework that has influenced the graphical arts beyond the TV industry.

The Nick at Nite page features a schedule of upcoming shows, a mission statement about the necessity of preserving classic TV, and a series of digitized clips of memorable Nick at Nite promo spots.

FIGURE 7.12
The Nick at Nite home page borrows from the distinctive visual style of the network.

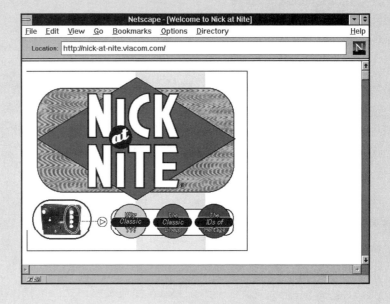

Drama Series

Classic TV drama doesn't seem to age as well as TV comedy, but there are still plenty of fans of the cop shows and family dramas of yesteryear.

Jon Yager's Ultimate Twin Peaks Reference

http://www.xmission.com/~jonyag/TP/Twin_Peaks.html

There are a whopping 10 sites devoted to this very cool but interminably baroque TV mystery series.

Jon Yager's Ultimate Twin Peaks Reference page at *http://www.xmission.com/~jonyag/TP/Twin_Peaks.html* is described as a lifelong project. It has the FAQ list from *alt.tv.twin-peaks,* an episode guide, a map of the locations used in the shooting, and the Log Lady's intros from the recent Bravo rebroadcast of the series.

The Twin Peaks Cast Table at *http://www.sal.wisc.edu/~boardman/TwinPeaks/table/* (see figure 7.13) is a quick way to learn who's who in the show and what else they've done with their lives.

FIGURE 7.13

Part of the extensive cast list of Twin Peaks.

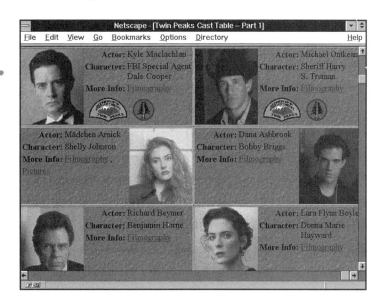

thirtysomething

http://duplox.wz-berlin.de/people/oswald/30/guide.ascii

This quintessentially '80s whine-a-thon was actually a pretty good show. Or at least the Germans still think so, because that's where you'll find the *thirtysomething* episode guide. (In German, the show is called *Die Besten Jahre*— "the best years.")

Charlie's Angels
http://www.clever.net/wiley/charliea.htm

Anyone who knows their history understands how important a show *Charlie's Angels* was. As a fable of female empowerment, it freed a generation of girls from the manacles of patriarchy and the wither of the lascivious male gaze.

The unofficial *Charlie's Angels* page (see figure 7.14) features a history of the show, a link to an e-zine called *Angel Trap,* a collectibles trading area, and an article about Shelly Hack, the forgotten Angel. ☞

FIGURE 7.14
This is the story of three little girls who went to the police academy...

The Rockford Files
http://falcon.cc.ukans.edu/~asumner/rockford

This home page celebrates the low-key private-eye series of the late '70s that updated and inverted the conventions of the gumshoe format. (Jim Rockford lived in a trailer near the beach, was always broke, and sometimes failed to solve the case.) This site is notable for its digitized collection of Rockford's phone messages. ☞

Comedy

The Internet is a goldmine for fans of forgotten sitcoms. Dig.

The Unofficial Cheers Home Page
http://s9000.furman.edu/~treu/cheers.html

Welcome to *Cheers*, the place where everybody knows your name but nobody cares enough about you to suggest that maybe you've had too much to drink. At this home page (see figure 7.15) you will find a very detailed episode guide, a *Cheers* trivia quiz, and a list of priceless "Normisms."

FIGURE 7.15

The Unofficial Cheers Home Page. B.Y.O.B.

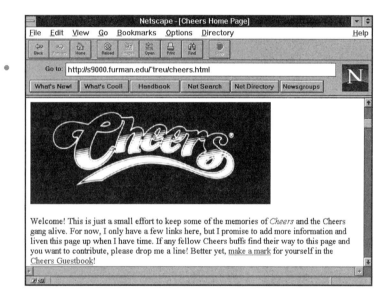

M*A*S*H Archives
http://www.best.com/~dijon/tv/mash

*M*A*S*H* was a brave and occasionally quite funny show about the survival of the human spirit in times of war. The M*A*S*H Archives have an episode guide, a cast list, photos, the theme song, and a FAQ list.

The Unofficial Brady Bunch Home Page

http://www.teleport.com/~btucker/bradys.shtml

The Brady Bunch has obliterated all considerations of taste and has become a cultural artifact of great and mysterious significance. This story (of a man named Brady) captures a particular moment in American time as shrewdly as any entertainment ever unleashed upon the public.

There are two extraordinary Brady resources on the Net. The Unofficial Brady Bunch Home Page (see figure 7.16) at *http://www.teleport.com/~btucker/bradys.shtml* contains episode guides for *The Brady Bunch, The Brady Brides,* and *The Brady Kids;* several revisions of the script for *The Brady Bunch Movie;* a Brady screensaver; an academic paper about the significance of the Bradys; and a history of the actual Brady house in the San Fernando Valley, complete with map.

FIGURE 7.16

The Unofficial Brady Bunch Home Page.

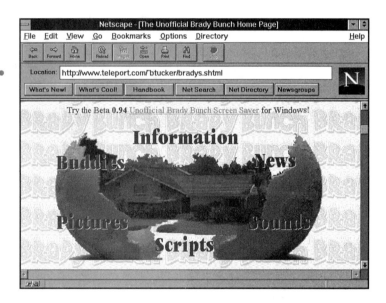

The Encyclopedia Brady site at *http://www.primenet.com/~dbrady/index.html* is the obsession of a guy named David E. Brady (no relation) who is attempting to create a hypertext A-to-Z overview of every significant character and incident in all 117 episodes of the *Brady Bunch* TV series. As a work-in-progress, it is almost Buddhistic in its mindlessness.

(Nick at Nite has a site called Buncha Brady at *http://nick-at-nite.viacom.com/menu_t.html* as a tie-in to the movie, but there's no telling how long it will stay in place. Among other things, it features the Brady Morph-a-Matic.)

Gilligan's Island Archive

http://www.best.com/~dijon/tv/gilligan

You can say what you want about *The Brady Bunch* or *I Dream of Jeannie* or *Leave It To Beaver* or *The Mary Tyler Moore Show*—*Gilligan's Island* is the prototype American sitcom, so transcendent in its stupidity that it must have come directly from the gods.

The standard Gilligan's Island Archive is at *http://www.best.com/~dijon/tv/gilligan*. It contains the requisite episode guide, cast list, and digitized theme song.

Jeff Brodrick's Gilligan's Island Home Page at *http://www.epix.net/~jabcpudr/gilligan.html* (see figure 7.17) is more devotional. It does not include an episode guide, but it features extensive credits for each of the seven cast members, a list of upcoming episodes on the TBS cable service, three versions of the theme song, information on the made-for-TV movies, and a monthly guide to production screw-ups. (In one episode, a giant bat leaves human footprints.)

FIGURE 7.17

Left to right: Willie Gilligan, Mary Ann Summers, and Jonas Grumby.

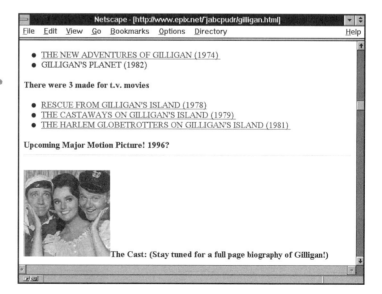

The Andy Griffith Show (Mayberry, My Home Town)

http://www.w3-design.com:80/frank/mayberry

This good-natured site features an episode guide, a cast list, a map of Mayberry, a thought for the day, and, of course, the theme song (sung, not whistled, by Andy Griffith). ☞

Fantasy TV

TV has a rich tradition of fantasy programming, from the domestic sorcery of *Bewitched* and *I Dream Jeannie*, to the space-age adventures of *Battlestar Galactica* and *Babylon 5*, to the crimefighting exploits of *Wonder Woman* and *Batman*, to the supernatural terror of the *X-Files* and *Full House*. The fantasy genre includes some of the most beloved shows on television such as the following.

Star Trek (and Related Shows)

Star Trek was an obscure mid-'60s sitcom about seven wacky space explorers who get lost in a meteor storm and find themselves stranded on a deserted planet. (Or so I've been told. I've never actually seen it.) The show has recently attracted a small cult following at some colleges in the Northeast.

Incredibly, this little-seen exercise in formulaic comedy has inspired at least three spin-off series and *hundreds* of Web sites, making it arguably the most popular subject matter on the Internet. (Whether these Web sites are all the work of a single individual is hard to tell, given the ability of today's networking systems to route information to remote servers.)

Star Trek: WWW

http://www.iwi.unisg.ch/~sambucci/scifi/startrek/st-www.html

This exhaustive index of *Star Trek* resources is the best place to start your mission "to boldly go" where a bunch of other people have already gone before you. Here you will find links to the innumerable *Star Trek*, *Next Generation;* *Voyager;* and *Deep Space Nine* sites that are scattered throughout the Internet galaxy. These include trivia quizzes, gaming information, reviews of the *Star Trek* movies, technical maps of the various Starfleet craft, episode guides to the different *Star Trek* TV programs, parodies, polls, unrepentant fan sites, and much, much more. Following are some notable *Star Trek*-related pages on the Net.

Pekka Hulkkonen's Star Trek Page
http://www.tut.fi/~pekka/trek.html

This attractive site is given the highest possible rating by the aforementioned *Star Trek*: WWW site. It includes detailed information on all the *Star Trek*-related TV series and movies, as well as such fascinating special-interest material as "Bar's Load Average (Odo's special report)," "DW9 N1.1 meta60s Battle Computer—Tactical Display," and "Quark's Holosuites." (See figure 7.18.)

FIGURE 7.18

This Finnish site is one of the best all-purpose Star Trek resources on the Net.

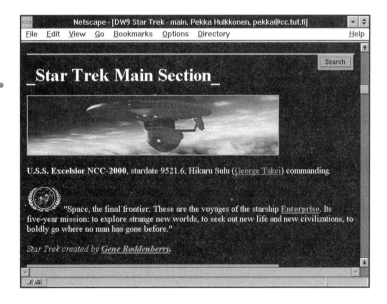

The North Star Klingon Home Page

http://web.apertus.com/~joela

There are many sites devoted to the academic study of the Klingon and Vulcan languages. This site provides handy English-Klingon and English-Vulcan translations and even offers some Bible verses in Klingon. (See figure 7.19.)

FIGURE 7.19.

A Klingon translation of a Starfleet translation of a passage from the Bible's Book of Matthew. ("And the Lord said, This is not at all what I intended.")

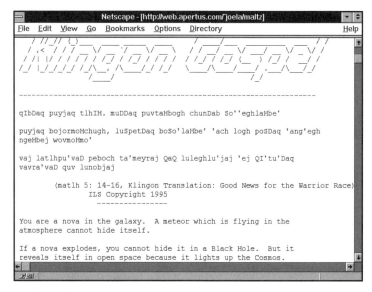

The Capt. James T. Kirk Sing-a-long Page

http://www.ama.caltech.edu/~mrm/kirk.html

You truly haven't lived until you've heard William Shatner's unique renderings of psychedelic '60s favorites from his 1968 album *The Transformed Man*. This site offers several digitized samples from that album, including Shatnerized versions of "Mr. Tambourine Man," "Lucy in the Sky With Diamonds," and something called "Spleen." Believe me, when you hear Shatner's tormented wail at the end of "Mr Tambourine Man," you will share his pain. (See figure 7.20.)

FIGURE 7.20

These William Shatner recordings will blow your mind—and
possibly your speakers.

Other Fantasy Television Programs

Star Trek might be The Franchise That Wouldn't Die, but there's
plenty of other sci-fi and fantasy TV on the airwaves and on the
Internet.

The X-Files
http://www.rutgers.edu/x-files.html

This Fox series has captured the public imagination by locating
the supernatural horror right here on earth in the 1990s.

There are an astounding 21 Internet sites devoted to this show,
and this site is one of the best. It features episode guides, FAQs,
fan-club information, audio clips, a nitpickers' guide, and a
complete set of links to related sites. (See figure 7.21.)

FIGURE 7.21

One of the many X-Files home pages that are breeding across the Internet like pod people.

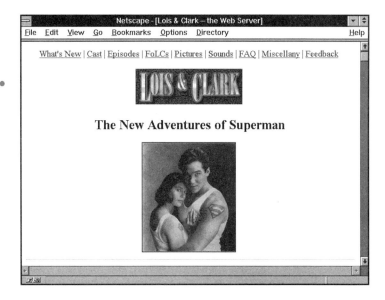

Lois & Clark

http://www.xnet.com/~creacon/LNC

Lois & Clark is the excellent new version of the Superman story on the ABC television network. It features two attractive personalities in the lead roles (Dean Cain and Teri Hatcher), a fine supporting cast, snappy writing, and a romantic subtext that is contemporary without being cynical. A *Lois & Clark* home page is shown in figure 7.22.

FIGURE 7.22

A fan page for the ABC series *Lois & Clark: The New Adventures of Superman.*

Max Headroom (Network 23)
http://www.net23.com/0/max.main.html

This nightmare vision of a post-nuclear society dominated by television was so far ahead of its time that most people thought it was a soda commercial. (Note: The Web site is unpredictable. Check *alt.tv.max-headroom* for updates.)

The Prisoner
http://itdsrv1.ul.ie/Entertainment/Prisoner/the-prisoner.html

One of the smartest and weirdest shows ever on television, *The Prisoner* was Patrick McGoohan's diabolical fairy tale of Cold War politics and social engineering circa 1967. The government surveillance capabilities that McGoohan envisioned don't seem so far-fetched anymore.

Animation and Kids' TV

If TV is good for anything (which remains an open question), it's good for entertaining children—no matter what their age.

Animation

Concurrent with the emergence of nostalgia TV is the re-emergence of TV animation, as exemplified by the following programs.

The Simpsons Archive
http://www.Digimark.net/TheSimpsons/index.html

There are many sites devoted to *The Simpsons*, but few Web sites devoted to *any* TV show are as comprehensive, funny, and popular as The Simpsons Archive. Of course, *The Simpsons* isn't just another TV show. This Matt Groening/James L. Brooks production about a dysfunctional middle-American family has single-handedly resurrected the TV-animation industry, and there are many people who would argue that the show is the wisest and funniest thing on television—animated or otherwise.

The much-celebrated Simpsons Archive was a more graphical place before the folks at Fox threatened a lawsuit over unauthorized use of images and video clips; but it is still a treasure chest for fans of *The Simpsons* TV show. It includes a floor plan of the Simpsons house, the full resume of actor Troy McClure, and hilarious speculation on where "Springfield" is actually located.

You might want to try some of the other *Simpsons* pages of note. These include:

* The Krusty the Clown Home Page at *http://zivijo.cc.columbia.edu/~mrr18/original.html.*

* The Simpsons on Geography (sound bites) at *http://everest.hunter.cuny.edu/~jlerner/simpsons.html.*

* The Simpsons in French at *http://www.unantes.univ-nantes.fr/~elek/simpson.html.*

* Jim's Simpsons Page at *http://www.tiac.net/users/jimt/simp/simpage.html,* which has a lot of the graphical stuff that some of the other pages are lacking. (See figure 7.23.)

FIGURE 7.23

Some Simpsons stuff.

Beavis and Butt-head
http://calvin.hsc.colorado.edu

B&B are another online phenomenon, with 10 sites paying homage to two cartoon characters who think "homage" is something you eat for breakfast.

This particular site is good for some guilty laughs (just like the show), such as the B&B list of 18 different kinds of...um...*evacuations*.

The Beginner's Guide to Animaniacs
http://weber.u.washington.edu/~wbwolf/Beginners.html

Animaniacs is a new carton show with a great old look to it. The premise of the *Animaniacs* is that a stable of rambunctious cartoon characters that were created in 1930 have escaped their pen and are running amok on the Warner Bros. studio lot of today. The Beginner's Guide is a detailed introduction to the show and its recurring characters. (See figure 7.24.)

FIGURE 7.24
Dot Warner, one of the Animaniacs.

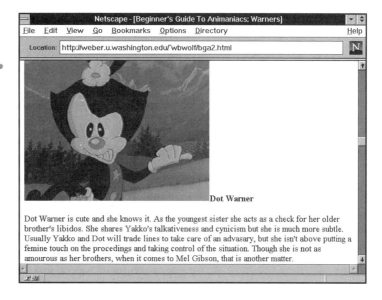

Other Kid Shows

The following are non-animated shows with a mostly kid audience.

The Muppets

http://www.ncsa.uiuc.edu/VR/BS/Muppets/muppets.html

This lollapalooza of a site has collected just about everything that is known about the Muppets' TV shows, films, and recordings (along with information and episode guides for *Fraggle Rock* and *Dinosaurs*) in a site that is thoroughly respectful of Jim Henson's legacy. (See figure 7.24.) It's almost hard to believe that this kind of sweetness still exists in the world, but that's the legacy of *Sesame Street* for ya.

Those who are interested in Muppet paraphernalia might want to take a gander at Pigs in Cyberspaaaaaaaaaace at *http://www-leland.stanford.edu/~rosesage/Muppet.html.*

FIGURE 7.25

The Muppets Home Page.

Mighty Morphin Power Rangers

http://marge.phys.washington.edu/tv/mmpr.html

Mister Rogers this ain't, but at least this site recognizes the show for the worthless cheese that it is.

Beakman's World

http://www.spe.sony.com/Pictures/tv/beakman/beakman.html

This goofball Saturday-morning science show delivers some legitimate learning along with the broad laughs.

Barney and Friends

alt.tv.barney

I think it's wonderful that children love Barney while parents just don't get it. Kids need to have a world unto themselves that parents can't recall how to enter. Unfortunately, our inability to respect the differences between parents and children has caused some of us grown-ups to treat Barney with undisguised contempt, and thus when our children get old enough to seek our intellectual approval, they repudiate Barney—and his message of love—because they think it will please us.

Barney's a guy in a purple dinosaur costume on a PBS TV show that has crummy production values and unremarkable songs about manners and hygiene. But that doesn't make him Hitler, for cryin' out loud. And yet, except for the *alt.tv.barney* UseNet group (which accepts all comers), the only Barney sites I am able to find on the Internet are violent anti-Barney sites, including Day of the Barney and The Jihad to Destroy Barney on the Worldwide Web. I guess that's what happens when you watch too much TV.

The List

Archives, Link Sites, and General Resources

Wiretap Archives
gopher://wiretap.spies.com/11/Library/Media/Tv

The Cathouse Archives
http://cathouse.org/cathouse/television

Sound Bytes: The WWW TV Themes Home Page

http://ai.eecs.umich.edu/people/kennyp/sounds.html

Internet TV Resources

http://www.teleport.com/~celinec/tv.htm

CineMedia Television Sites

http://www.gu.edu.au/gwis/cinemedia/CineMedia.tv.html

The Ultimate TV List

http://tvnet.com/UTVL/utvl.html

The Tardis TV Archive

http://src.doc.ic.ac.uk/public/media/tv/collections/tardis/
index.html

Current Dramas

NYPD Blue

http://src.doc.ic.ac.uk/public/media/tv/collections/tardis/us/
drama/NYPDBlue/index.html

ER

http://sunsite.doc.ic.ac.uk/public/media/tv/collections/tardis/us/
drama/ER

Chicago Hope

http://www-cs-students.stanford.edu/~clee/chicagohope.html

My So-Called Life

http://www.umn.edu/nlhome/g564/lask0008/mscl.html

The Moose's Guide to Northern Exposure

http://www.netspace.org/~moose/moose.html

Melrose Place Update

http://www.speakeasy.org/~dbrick/Melrose/melrose.html

Melrose Place Current Synopsis

http://www.polaris.net/~dayres/melrose.htm

Official Melrose Place Update

http://www.mit.edu:8001/people/mickey/mp/melrose.html

Beverly Hills 90210

http://www.prairienet.org/~rogue/homepage.html

Soap Links

http://www.cts.com/~jeffmj/soaps.html

General Hospital (Port Charles Online)

http://www.cts.com/~jeffmj/GeneralHospital.html

Days of Our Lives

http://weber.u.washington.edu/~pfloyd/days/index.html

Homicide, Life on the Web

http://www.gl.umbc.edu/~jlempk1/homicide.html

An interactive fiction loosely based on the *Homicide* TV series.

Current Sitcoms

Friends

http://geminga.dartmouth.edu/~andyjw/friends

Seinfeld (The Vandelay Industries Archive)

http://www.cs.cmu.edu/afs/cs/user/vernon/www/vandelay/index.html

Married...With Children (The Bundy Page)

http://www.ifi.uio.no/~steinho/bundy.html

Mad About You

http://tam2000.tamu.edu/~n020ic/may.html

Roseanne

http://pmwww.cs.vu.nl/service/sitcoms/Roseanne

Sourpuss comedy for the Heartland. Attagirl, Rosie.

Home Improvement

http://src.doc.ic.ac.uk/public/media/tv/collections/tardis/us/comedy/HomeImprovement

Nostalgia: Dramas

Nick at Nite

http://nick-at-nite.viacom.com

Jon Yager's Twin Peaks Page

http://www.xmission.com/~jonyag/TP/Twin_Peaks.html

Twin Peaks Cast Table

http://www.sal.wisc.edu/~boardman/TwinPeaks/table

(There is also a home page for David Lynch at *http://web.city.ac.uk/~cb157/Dave.html*.)

thirtysomething

http://duplox.wz-berlin.de/people/oswald/30/guide.ascii

Charlie's Angels

http://www.clever.net/wiley/charliea.htm

The Rockford Files

http://falcon.cc.ukans.edu/~asumner/rockford

MacGyver (The Phoenix Foundation)

http://www.prairienet.org/~mcnelson/mac.html

CHiPs

http://www.wpi.edu/~patrickd/CHiPs/CHiPs.html

Hawaii Five-O

http://mindlink.net/a4369/fiveo.html

Nostalgia: Comedy

The Unofficial Cheers Home Page
http://s9000.furman.edu/~treu/cheers.html

M*A*S*H Archives
http://www.best.com/~dijon/tv/mash

Unoffical Brady Bunch Home Page
http://www.teleport.com/~btucker/bradys.shtm

The Encyclopedia Brady
http://www.primenet.com/~dbrady/index.html

The standard Gilligan's Island Archive
http://www.best.com/~dijon/tv/gilligan

Gilligan's Island Home Page
http://www.epix.net/~jabcpudr/gilligan.html

Monty Python's Flying Circus
http://www.unisuper.com.au/python/monty.htm

Try this one yourself.

The Sledge Hammer! Arsenal
http://www.mit.edu:8001/people/mickey/sh/sledge.html

At least *somebody* remembers.

All in the Family
http://pmwww.cs.vu.nl/service/sitcoms/AllInTheFamily

In many ways, the most important show in the history of television.

Bewitched
http://pmwww.cs.vu.nl/service/sitcoms/Bewitched

Bosom Buddies
http://www.ozemail.com.au/~peterv/bb/index.html

Now there's an *underrated* show.

Fantasy TV

Star Trek: WWW
http://www-iwi.unisg.ch/~sambucci/scifi/startrek/st-www.html

Pekka Hulkkonen's Star Trek Page
http://www.tut.fi/~pekka/trek.html

The North Star Klingon Home Page
http://web.apertus.com/~joela

Trek Reviews Archive
http://www.mcs.net/~forbes/trek-reviews

Selected *Star Trek* UseNet Groups
rec.arts.startrek.misc

rec.arts.startrek.current

rec.arts.startrek.fandom

rec.arts.startrek.info

rec.arts.startrek.reviews

rec.arts.startrek.tech

alt.startrek.creative

alt.startrek.klingon

alt.startrek.bajoran

alt.startrek.borg

alt.startrek.romulan

alt.startrek.vulcan

Babylon 5
http://www.hyperion.com/b5

Dr. Who
http://www.phlab.missouri.edu/HOMES/ccpeace_www/Dr.Who

The Green Hornet

http://moose.uvm.edu/~glambert/green.html

Lost in Space

http://www.mgmt.purdue.edu/~vkoser/lost_in_space/lost_in_space.html

Quantum Leap

http://lumchan.ifa.hawaii.edu/ql/ql.html

seaQuest

http://www.mca.com/tv/seaquest

Twilight Zone

http://www.twilight.com/twilight-zone.guide

A text-only episode guide.

Animation and Kids' TV

The Simpsons Archive

http://www.Digimark.net/TheSimpsons/index.html

Jim's Simpsons Page

http://www.tiac.net/users/jimt/simp/simpage.html

Krusty the Clown Home Page

http://zivijo.cc.columbia.edu/~mrr18/original.html

The Simpsons on Geography

http://everest.hunter.cuny.edu/~jlerner/simpsons.html

The Simpsons in French

http://www.unantes.univ-nantes.fr/~elek/simpson.html

Beavis and Butt-head

http://calvin.hsc.colorado.edu

The Beginner's Guide to Animaniacs

http://weber.u.washington.edu/~wbwolf/Beginners.html

Ren & Stimpy

http://www.cris.com/~lkarper/rands.html

Rocky and Bullwinkle

http://www.pomona.claremont.edu//frostbite/frostbite.html

Ten Reasons Why Scooby Doo Was a Drug-Influenced Cartoon

http://www.duc.auburn.edu/~burgest/scooby.html

The Muppets

http://www.ncsa.uiuc.edu/VR/BS/Muppets/muppets.html

Pigs in Cyberspaaaaaaaaaaaace

http://www-leland.stanford.edu/~rosesage/Muppet.html

Mighty Morphin' Power Rangers

http://marge.phys.washington.edu/tv/mmpr.html

Beakman's World

http://www.spe.sony.com/Pictures/tv/beakman/beakman.html

Shining Time Station

http://www.catt.ncsu.edu/users/gkeeper/HTML/my.useless.pages/STS/index.html

You Can't Do That On Television

http://cctr.umkc.edu/user/rbarrow/ycdtotv.html

PART IV

MUSIC

CHAPTER 8

General Music Resources

IN THIS CHAPTER:

> *Music link sites*

> *Databases: reviews, discographies, and lyrics*

> *Record-label sites*

> *Mail-order services*

IN OTHER CHAPTERS:

> *Rock & roll and alternative music are covered in Chapter 9.*

> *R&B, blues, jazz, and rap are covered in Chapter 10.*

> *Country-western, folk, Christian, and ethnic music are covered in Chapter 11.*

> *Classical music is covered in Chapter 12.*

Music is truly the international language. Well, actually, you could just as easily say that laughter is the international language. Or money. Or English, for that matter. But there's no denying that music is pretty darn important to a lot of people. Indeed, some of us would go crazy if we didn't hear music 24 hours a day. That's why we insist that it be played on elevators, and if you're anything like me, you sleep with a miniature AM transceiver implanted into your cerebral cortex so you can incorporate the Top 40 into your nightmares.

Clearly, many of the people who feel that music is an indispensable part of the human experience have found a cozy home on the Internet.

You can use the Internet to find record reviews, song lyrics, artist biographies, concert schedules, academic discussions of music theory, and even classified ads for used instruments. And with the multimedia capabilities of the World Wide Web, the transmission of digitized music over the Net is now commonplace.

General Music Information and Link Sites

At this stage in the development of the Net, there is little need to memorize specific addresses or to maintain an ever-expanding list of bookmarks in order to access the resources you want. Although bookmarks are helpful, there are people out there who have already done the work for you, compiling link sites that will instantly spring you to almost every musical resource online. Some of these master sites are of general-interest, while others specialize in a particular subset of the musical domain, such as an individual genre, academic sites, or resources for practicing musicians.

Music Resources on the Internet

http://www.music.indiana.edu/misc/music_resources.html

If you want to go straight to the most comprehensive list of music sites on the Internet, point your browser to a page called Music Resources on the Internet.

Music Resources on the Internet is an extraordinary collection of links from the Indiana University School of Music. Compiling this list has probably cost a few grad students their sanity, but you, Dear Reader, are the beneficiary.

Links are all you'll get here, divided into Academic, Non-Academic, Geographically Related, and Artist sites. (See figure 8.1.)

FIGURE 8.1

Abandon hope, all ye who enter here: The deceptively mild opening to a monstrous site called Music Resources on the Internet.

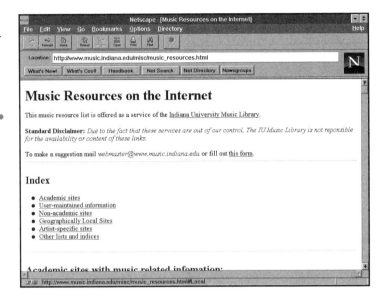

This site ain't pretty, but it's thorough, with page after page of listings. It's enough to make your eyes bleed. The following is a sample of some of the more interesting site names on the list. All of these things are just a click away.

* The Barbershop Quartet Gopher (dedicated to the indigenous American artform that changed the world)

* Bulgarian Folk Music

* The Center for Research in Computing and the Arts

* Dr. Demento FAQ site (*rec.music.dementia*)

* Drum and Percussion Page

* The Frank Sinatra WWW Page

* Gems of Compositional Wisdom

* Gregorian Chant Home Page

* Indian Classical Music by N.S.Sundar

* Indie Label List: A Partial Guide to Independent Record Labels

* The Internet Ghetto Blaster

* Jammin Reggae Archives

* Little Judy Juepa page

* Music, Mind, Machine: Computational Modeling of Musical Knowledge and Cognition

* Negativworldwidewebland

* Nadine: The Magazine that Wishes It Were a Band

* P-Funk Motherpage

* Righteous Babe Records

* SCREAM (Southern Center for Research into Electro Acoustic Music)

* SKA! SKA! SKA!

* Society for the Preservation of Film Music

* The Society for the Promotion of Indian Classical Music and Culture Amongst Youth

* Space Age Pop Music

* 37th Annual Grammy Awards (banality as an artform)

* The Totally Unofficial Rap Dictionary

* Trombone Home Page

* TweeNet

* The Unknown Composers page

The Indiana University resource also includes links to many performing-artist home pages and fan sites, which I will spare you. Take my word for it—your favorite recording artist is on this list, and yes, that does include Those Darn Accordions.

Many individual musicians and bands have mailing lists devoted to them. In a mailing list, you send a message to the site administrator, asking to subscribe and giving your e-mail address. Thereafter you will receive all the postings to this group via your e-mail account—either in real-time (as they are received at the home site) or in a periodic digest (usually weekly or monthly).

Mailing lists are discussed in Chapter 17, "Getting Connected," and some specific lists for rock and alternative performers are mentioned at the end of Chapter 9. You can access a similar and more exhaustive list from a site called simply The List of Musical Mailing Lists at *http://server.berkeley.edu/ ~ayukawa/lomml.html*.

At the end of this chapter you will find mailing lists for particular genres of music or specific instruments.

Musical Web Connections
http://lps2.esu18.k12.ne.us/inthtml/music.html

If your tastes are generally inclined toward "youth music," you might prefer to do your linking from a site called Musical Web Connections. It is nearly as ambitious as the Musical Resources site, but it dispenses with a lot of the academic (that is, Squaresville) sites that don't appeal to the Now Generation. It has a particularly good collection of techno and rave-music resources.

The links within Musical Web Connections are divided as follows:

* Broad Musical Sites

* Other Web Musical Indexes

* Individual Band Pages

* Mailing List Home Pages

* Music Review Sites

* Ambient/Techno/Trance/Rave Web Sites

* Digitized Music on the Net

* Record Labels on the Net

* Regional Links: Radio stations, local music, festivals, etc.

* Radio Program Play Lists

* Music Zines and Publications

The list of Broad Musical Sites is particularly impressive. It covers scores of one-stop "genre" pages—everything from the Death Metal Archive and Gothic Stuff to the Flamenco Server and the Disco Hut. (See figure 8.2.)

FIGURE 8.2

Home site for Rob's Gothic Pages (a.k.a. Gothic Stuff), at http://www.crg.cs.nott.ac.uk/ ~rji/Gothic/index.html. As far as I can tell, this has almost nothing to do with medieval architecture but rather is a site about gloomy, big-haired rock bands. (Accessed via the Musical Web Connections link site.)

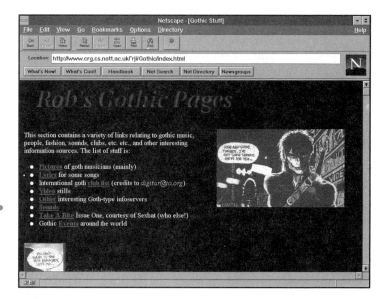

Mammoth Music Meta List

http://www.pathfinder.com/@@0mi7HQAAAAAgMn5/vibe/mmm/music.html

VIBE magazine (the real *VIBE* magazine, as discussed in the R&B chapter, and not the lifestyle e-zine from Adam Curry that is discussed in the rock & roll chapter) provides computer space for something called the Mammoth Music Meta List. The MMML is a perfect combination of link resources and nuts-and-bolts musical information.

The site has thousands of links, including what is probably the most comprehensive-yet-manageable menu of performer and band pages, as well as a good all-around collection of genre sub-sections. It also has information on music festivals, regional radio, and obscure music publications, and it is linked to archives of charts, reviews, lyrics—and the most comprehensive site in the world for barbershop-quartet information. (See figure 8.3.)

FIGURE 8.3

The Barbershop Gopher at the University of Pennsylvania, which is the home of the Fighting Quakers and the Penny Loafers singing group. (Accessed via the Mammoth Music Meta List.)

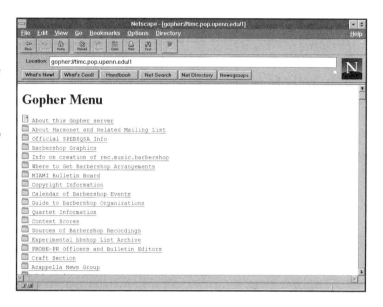

The English Server

http://english-www.hss.cmu.edu/music.html

The English Server is an oddball little collection of musical documents from a server at Carnegie Mellon University in beautiful Pittsburgh, PA.

It features an assortment of just-plain-interesting articles and links, most of which treat a seemingly banal topic as grist for a super-heated mill of intellectual activity.

FIGURE 8.4

A serious think-piece about Madonna, who has stopped selling records but seems to have become the musical equivalent of a Rorschach test. (From the English Server.)

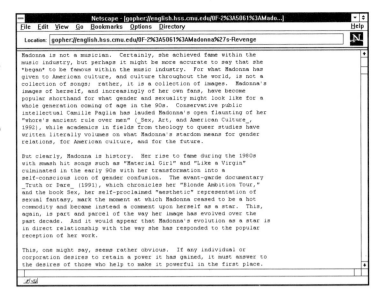

Databases: Discographies, Reviews, Lyrics, and Venues

Some sites accumulate a big pile of info and invite you to navigate on their server and dig in. Within the various Net databases you can find complete discographies for Tasmanian garage bands of the 1960s, meticulous reviews of 45-rpm singles that originally came on the back of cereal boxes, and even the real lyrics to "Louie Louie" (which apparently call for the violent overthrow of the U.S. government by an army of computer-crazed automatons. Who would've guessed?).

All-Music Guide
http://cdnow.com

The All-Music Guide is the best archive for record reviews and discographies on the Net. All-Music is an invaluable resource that lists, rates, and discusses practically every piece of popular music ever recorded—on vinyl, cassette, CD, video, and probably 8-track tape if it's still out there somewhere.

OUR FRIEND YAHOO

If you're surfing the World Wide Web, chances are you're using a browser. As of this writing, the best and most popular of the browsers is the Netscape Navigator. In Netscape you will find a pointer to the Yahoo utility, the handiest of all the Web-site indices that are currently available. (If you don't have Netscape, you can access Yahoo at *http://www.yahoo.com.*) In Yahoo, approximately 44,000 Web sites are categorized and subcategorized, and from Yahoo these sites can be accessed directly.

The *Entertainment* subdirectory of the Yahoo directory is one of the largest, and it is likely to become one of your favorite places to start exploring the Net. After you choose the *Entertainment* category, you will see a menu of subcategories, one of which is *Music*.

The *Yahoo/Entertainment/Music* directory is further subdivided into the following areas:

* Archives
* Artists
* Awards
* Books
* Charts
* Commercial Music Resources
* Composers
* Countries
* Education
* Events
* General Information
* Genres
* History
* Instruments
* Internet Underground Music Archive
* Labels
* Lyrics
* Magazines
* Mailing Lists
* Marching Bands
* Movie Soundtracks
* Musicals
* Organizations
* Promoters
* Reviews
* Sheet Music
* Software
* Sound
* Studios
* Therapy
* Trivia
* FAQ: UseNet Music
* Indices
* UseNet Groups

You can further narrow your search by choosing one of these categories. *Genres*, for instance, is divided into 27 categories, from *Ambient* to *World Music*, including *Rock and Roll, Classical, Folk, Reggae, Polka*, and so on. With enough clicking, you will eventually be presented with a catalog of Web sites pertaining to that category.

If you want to save yourself some hierarchical clicking, Yahoo also has a search engine in which you can enter a keyword to see if there is a site in the index that refers to the subject you are interested in.

To access the All-Music Guide, you first enter the virtual store of a service called CDNow! (discussed later in this chapter), and then select the AMG logo. From there you can select a musical style from a list that includes Blues, Cajun, Classical, Comedy, Country, Easy Listening, Environmental, Exercise, Folk, Gay, Gospel... well, you get the idea. If, say, you pick "Rock" (thinking that that's a pretty a self-explanatory category), then you get another menu of sub-genres, which includes Adult Alternative, Alternate Tunings, Ambient, Atonal, Avant-Garde... Eventually you dig your way to the two or three records that fit your mental picture.

AMG also offers feature articles about the different styles of popular music. Like the AMG reviews, these articles are written by qualified experts and they help to place the recordings within a larger music-historical context. (See figure 8.5.)

FIGURE 8.5

A menu of articles from the All-Music Guide.

● ● ● ● ● ● ● ● ● ● ● ● ● ● ● ●

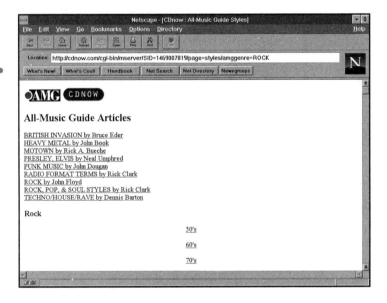

The All-Music Guide covers both out-of-print and freely available titles, and it does a good job of cross-referencing between the title you seek and those of similar artists. It also features up-to-date sales charts in most popular genres (which are probably the best charts on the entire Net), artist bios, discographies, and album-track listings. And if it helps you find what you are looking for (or something you didn't know that you were looking for but decide to explore further) you can "buy" the record, on the spot, through CDNow!.

Web Wide World of Music/The Ultimate Band List

http://american.recordings.com/WWWoM

This is one of the true gems of the Internet, an ongoing database project that aims to establish links to information on every major recording artist, including FAQs, Web pages, lyrics, and sound clips. It is dominated by rock and alternative band listings, but there are listings in other genres as well.

The parent site, the Web Wide World of Music, has a master list of e-zines, a big heap of cool links, sales charts, a chat forum, and some featurettes, such as the one in which notable alternative-music performers list their favorite new recordings.

But it is the Ultimate Band List that is the bread and butter of this site. The UBL does not provide much information of its own. Rather, it contains the accumulated Net profile of over 700 performers in most genres of popular music. It includes links to Web pages, lyric sites, UseNet newsgroups, FAQs, mailing lists, and audio clips. (See figure 8.6.)

FIGURE 8.6

These are the artists whose names start with "B" who have links within the Ultimate Band List.

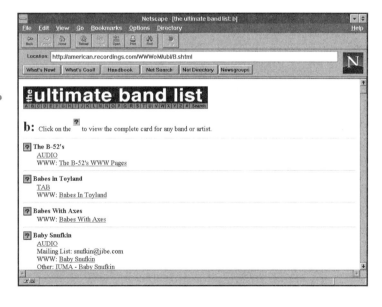

You can access band profiles alphabetically, by genre, or by the type of resource to which it points (mailing lists, Web pages, audio clips, etc.).

The most frequently accessed artists in the Ultimate Band List during a recent period were, in order, as follows:

* Pearl Jam
* Nirvana
* Pink Floyd
* Aerosmith
* R.E.M.
* Tori Amos
* Nine Inch Nails
* The Beatles
* 10,000 Maniacs
* Jimi Hendrix
* U2
* The Grateful Dead
* Led Zepplin
* Green Day
* The Doors
* The Cure
* The Cranberries
* Metallica
* Soundgarden
* Eric Clapton

It kinda makes you wonder whatever happened to Bo Donaldson and the Heywoods.

Record Collector's Web
http://www.onramp.net/RecordWeb/record.html

The Record Collector's Web is a valuable resource for obsessive seekers of bootlegs, imports, alternate pressings, and out-of-print music rarities.

Essentially a marketplace and bulletin board (the ads are free, at least for now), there are meticulously detailed for-sale listings for most of the popular musical genres and recording formats as well as memorabilia.

The Record Collector's Web also offers a handful or reviews of current releases, some features on the minutia of collecting records (especially vinyl), and lists of upcoming collectors conventions and good used-record stores throughout the country.

The Song Lyric Server/Vivarin Lyric Server
ftp.uwp.edu /pub/music/lyrics

http://vivarin.pc.cc.cmu.edu/lyrics.html

The Song Lyric Server is a repository for the lyrics to thousands of songs in several genres, with an emphasis on rock and alternative performers. Users are invited to contribute lyrics to songs that are not yet archived or to request that someone in Cyberland transcribe the lyrics to a particular song. There are also discographies, bios, and downloadable image files of some performers.

To access the Lyric Server, anonymous FTP to *ftp.uwp.edu* and then choose the following options, in order: *pub, music,* and *lyrics.* The song lyrics are indexed according to an alphabetical list of performers—so if you don't know who actually recorded "Baby I Need Your Love Tonight (And Here Comes My Great Big Euphemism)," you're out of luck.

The main site at the U. of Wisconsin-Parkside is very busy (and indeed may have shut down altogether by the time you read this), and it is often difficult to access during normal business hours, so you might want to try the Vivarin lyric server mirror site at *http://vivarin.pc.cc.cmu.edu/lyrics.html,* at least from 9-5, Mon.-Fri. The Vivarin site has all the lyrics in easily searchable form from a snazzy Web interface, but it does not have all the discographies and miscellany of the Wisconsin FTP site.

The World-wide Internet Live Music Archive (WILMA)
http://underground.net/Wilma

WILMA is an extensive resource for tour information and concert venues in the U.S. and around the world. It lists symphony halls, amphitheaters, nightclubs, and other performance spaces, which are listed by city, state, and country. (At last count, WILMA listed 11 different concert venues in Indonesia.)

This site also has an up-to-date roster of who's-touring-where, from the Allman Brothers to Yanni, as well as some amateur concert reviews. (See figure 8.7.)

FIGURE 8.7

A concert review from the WILMA site. Note the barber-shop reference.

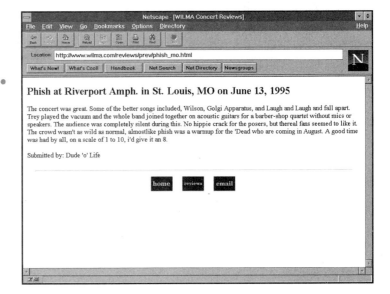

Record Labels

As of this writing, most (but not all) of the major record-label conglomerates had home pages on the Net, either for the umbrella organization (Polygram, Sony) or for their subsidiaries (Elektra, Motown).

There are also many smaller, independent labels with a Net presence. The Web has proven to be a useful way of communicating with the buying public, and with its multimedia capabilities, it can effectively sidestep the hard-to-crack radio markets as a means of getting the music directly to the listener.

Major Labels

There's a cliché among musical highbrows that the major labels are the bullies of the music industry, shoving the little independent guys off the record shelves and the airwaves, or else buying them up when the indies have something irresistible to offer. That cliché is largely true, but the line between the majors and the indies is blurring as more hipsters go to work for the big guys and more long-time hold-out musicians sign on the devil's dotted line. And you can no longer say that the majors are only interested in selling us watered-down corporate swill; they're more than happy to give us daring bands like Nirvana or Body Count if we've got money in hand. Outrage, it seems, is more marketable than ever.

ONLINE MUSIC MAGAZINES

Most of the online or online-via-print music magazines are specific to a particular genre, and these are discussed in the pertinent chapters of this book. You can find a list in the Yahoo directory under *Entertainment/Music/Magazines*. (These are mostly alternative music mags.)

The West Coast Music Review (*http://www.cyberstore.ca/WCMR*) covers the bases from Pop to Country to New Age to Kids' Music. A recent issue featured reviews of CDs that ranged from the Barenaked Ladies to Raffi.

BMI Music World at *http://bmi.com/MusicWorld/MW1994/MWSU94/index.html* is the house-organ of the BMI music-rights organization (the sworn enemy of ASCAP). It has features on a variety of artists who are no-doubt BMI signees (Ace of Base, Spin Doctors, Smashing Pumpkins, Indigo Girls), as well as industry fluff about such things as the BMI Song of the Year ("I Will Always Love You": easily the most insipid song since "The Greatest Love of All"—a quenelle for Whitney!).

There is a good all-purpose music-magazine bibliography service from Norway called RoJaRo (*http://www.notam.uio.no/rojaro/maglist.cgi*) that compiles and indexes the contents of over 250 music magazines. The RoJaRo index is quite extensive, and it claims to cover every genre of music except classical. (However, I couldn't find a word about barbershop quartets in its database. If this is an accidental omission, it's inexcusable considering the enormity of the subject matter. If it's deliberate, this is just the kind of antagonism we don't need in a world already simmering with geo-political tensions.)

Warner Bros.

http://www.iuma.com/Warner

For years, Warner Bros. has been the classiest of the major labels, and I'm not just saying that because I'm trying to get back on their mailing list of free stuff. They've got a distinguished and relatively stable roster of performers, and they market their products with care and intelligence.

The Warner home page embodies these qualities. It is part of a very fine site called the Internet Underground Music Archive (I.U.M.A.), which, among other things, gives exposure to unsigned bands (albeit for a modest fee). Warner's presence gives I.U.M.A. a big credibility boost, and makes WB seem that much hipper. (Warner also has a presence on America Online, which shows you that they're covering all the angles.)

The Warner site allows the user to access audio and video clips of some of the label's more interesting performers, such as those shown in figure 8.8.

FIGURE 8.8

From these thumbnail album covers, you can access audio and video clips of performers on the Warner Bros. record label.

MCA
http://www.mca.com/mca_records

For a long time, MCA was considered the rustiest of the majors, but at least when it comes to an online presence, MCA has the goods. The MCA online magazine, AMP, is a good-looking and effective promotional tool. A recent issue featured articles about a remastered version of The Who's epochal *Live at Leeds* album and a new release from the seemingly bottomless Jimi Hendrix estate. It also invites reader participation. (See figure 8.9.)

FIGURE 8.9

MCA's online magazine invites its readers to risk eternal damnation for the sake of music.

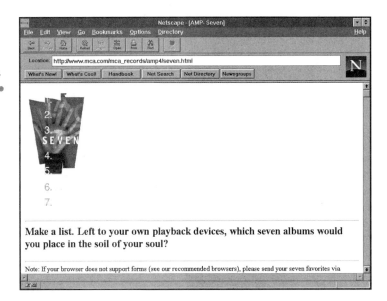

Independent Labels

Technically, an independent label is one that is not distributed by one of the six major-label conglomerates (Warner, Polygram, Capitol-EMI, Sony, MCA, BMG). But that definition gets fuzzier all the time as the majors make deals with the indies that trade street-level credibility for just a little bit of marketing juice and a percentage or two of the gross. (Would you like to hear how major-label Virgin Records acquired the rights to Smashing Pumpkins from seemingly independent Caroline Records? Clue: They all had it planned from the start. It looks better when a band comes up "the hard way.")

Nonetheless, there are still some mavericks out there (some of which are more maverick than others). Following are some indie and pseudo-indie labels (mostly of the alternative variety) that have Web pages you might want to visit if you'd like to learn about the next big thing. (These sites can be accessed from a list of record-label hot links at The Musical Web Resources site, *http://www.cc.columbia.edu/~hauben/music-index.html,* or from the Yahoo list under *Entertainment/Music/Labels.*)

* 4AD (atmospheric Anglo pop for Now people)

* American Recordings (home to the Ultimate Band List)

* Bedazzled

* Boston Skyline Records

* Breakfast Records in Boston

* Choke, Inc.

* Creation Records (the fountainhead of English indie pop)

* Go! Discs

* "God Says No!" Records ("a new direction in techno")

* Hearts of Space

* Heyday

* Mammoth Records

* Moonshine Music (Ambient, Acid Jazz, Techno, and other new forms of music)

* Moosetone Records

* Nation Records (world fusion)

* Nettwerk Records

* Quagmire

* Queenie Records ("your premiere girl-powered record label")

* Racer Records

* Rhino (misunderstood-junk collectors' paradise)

* Silent

* Schoolkids' Records

* Spill
* Sub Pop
* Taang! Records
* TeenBeat
* Transmission Communications
* TVT Records
* Underdog Records
* World Domination
* Windham Hill Records (classical-music lite)

Commercial Music-Ordering Services

If you are so sodden and flabby from years at the keyboard that you can't physically pick yourself up and drive to the record store, there are several online services from which you can order music directly. Often these services are able to locate rare and-out-of-print recordings (although the same may also be said of your neighborhood record store). If you can believe the hype, the security of credit-card transactions on the Net is not a big worry. (What worries *me* is the growing "necessity" of credit cards themselves and the gradual phasing out of cash. After cash is outlawed—and it *will* happen—how are we supposed to pay bribes to meter maids?)

CDNow!
http://cdnow.com

I give CDNow! a big thumbs-up because of their technical support for the amazing All-Music Guide (discussed earlier in this chapter), and I'll add a little pat on the head for their contribution to the brave new world of virtual commerce.

You can use AMG to browse through a virtual supermarket of recordings, putting your selections into a "cart" as you go.

There is also a warehouse of 300 magazine titles to choose from.

Purchases are made by credit card, right there online, and you can have your merch delivered within a couple days.

If you're really antsy to spend some of that virtual cyber-cash you've accumulated in your account, but you don't know quite what to spend it on, you might want to check out the HOMR Music Recommendation Service (formerly the RINGO Music Recommendation Service) at *http://jeeves.media.mit.edu/ringo.*

This dandy server is designed to fix you up with a musical blind date (that is, a band or performer you haven't heard before) based on a series of questions you answer and a statistical probability that someone liking Band "A" ought to like Band "B" as well. Thus, if you mention that you're crazy about the Beatles, HOMR will do a little cogitating and eventually tell you to run out and buy the new Posies album.

HOMR also can be used as a thumbnail record-review server. It features hundreds of synopses of recordings in most genres (except classical and barbershop).

Although HOMR is run by some smarties from M.I.T., the main page gives a copyright credit to Matt Groening, creator of *The Simpsons.* Groening is a former rock critic, but his connection to the HOMR service is not immediately apparent.

Tower Records
http://www.shopping2000.com/shopping2000/tower

Tower operates some of the best and biggest record stores in the world, and now they have brought their considerable marketing clout and inventory to the Web.

At the Tower site (see figure 8.10), you can check a list of new releases or audition a few seconds of a recording that sparks your interest. The actual ordering is then done over the phone.

FIGURE 8.10
The home page for the Tower
Records site.

When you shop at Tower Records, 1-800-ASK-TOWER, your selection of records is huge. Make your choice from the following index of Music Categories.

- **Boxed Sets**
- **Children's**
- **Classical/Opera**
- **Comedy**
- **Country**
- **Greatest Hits**
- **Jazz**
- **Rock/Pop/Hip-Hop**
- **Soundtracks/Shows**
- **Vocals**

Several other music-ordering services are cited in The List section at the end of this chapter. You may have to contact more than one if you are seeking a particularly obscure recording. You can also access these sites via Yahoo at *Entertainment/Music/CDs, Records and Tapes.*

The List

General Sites

Music Resources on the Internet
http://www.music.indiana.edu/misc/music_resources.html

Musical Web Connections
http://lps2.esu18.k12.ne.us/inthtml/music.html

Mammoth Music Meta List

http://www.pathfinder.com/@@0mi7HQAAAAAAgMn5/vibe/mmm/music.html

The English Server

http://english-www.hss.cmu.edu/music.html

Databases

All-Music Guide

http://cdnow.com

Web Wide World of Music/The Ultimate Band List

http://american.recordings.com/WWWoM

Record Collector's Web

http://www.onramp.net/RecordWeb/record.html

The Song Lyric Server/Vivarin Lyric Server

ftp.uwp.edu/pub/music/lyrics

http://vivarin.pc.cc.cmu.edu/lyrics.html

The World-wide Internet Live Music Archive (WILMA)

http://underground.net/Wilma

Major Record Labels

Warner Bros./Reprise

http://www.iuma.com/Warner

MCA

http://www.mca.com/mca_records

Capitol-EMI

http://www.riv.nl/emi/default.htm

Read all about the Beastie Boys—in Dutch!

Geffen/DGC

http://geffen.com

Polygram

http://www.polygram.com/polygram/Music.html

Dutch conglomerate. Includes A&M and Island.

Sony

http://www.music.sony.com

Japanese conglomerate. Includes Columbia and Epic.

Music-Ordering Services

CDNow! The Internet Music Store

http://cdnow.com

Tower Records

http://www.shopping2000.com/shopping2000/tower

CD Banzai

http://www.lainet.com/~cdbanzai

They claim to have the hard-to-find stuff.

CD Connection: Compact Disc Mail Order

http://ftp.cdconnection.com

CD Land

http://www.cdland.com/cdland

From beautiful San Francisco, where music fills the air.

Music Connection

http://www.inetbiz.com/music

Newbury Comics Interactive

http://www.newbury.com

The best record and comic store in Boston.

Noteworthy: CD Discount Mail Order

http://www.netmarket.com/noteworthy/bin/main/:grml:mode=text

A very sophisticated operation.

UseNet Groups

In general, the UseNet newsgroups in the *alt.music* and *alt.fan* hierarchies are slightly more adventurous and lively than those in the *rec.music* hierarchy, which tend toward reliable and complete information. The *rec.music* hierarchy contains the "music maker" newsgroups, for practicing musicians.

alt.music hierarchy

alt.music.a-cappella

Which, for our purposes here, would also include barbershop.

alt.music.alternative

Ostensibly groups with two or fewer platinum-selling albums.

alt.music.alternative.female

alt.music.big-band

alt.music.complex-arrang

alt.music.deep-purple

alt.music.dio

Dedicated to some guy who used to be in Black Sabbath.

alt.music.enya

Gaelic space music.

alt.music.fleetwood-mac

alt.music.genesis

alt.music.hardcore

alt.music.independent

alt.music.jewish

alt.music.leonard-cohen

alt.music.marillion

alt.music.midi

alt.music.nirvana

The band, not the state of mind.

alt.music.paul-simon

alt.music.pearl-jam

The band, not the breakfast food.

alt.music.pink-floyd

alt.music.prince

alt.music.progressive

alt.music.queen

alt.music.rush

alt.music.soul

alt.music

alt.music.techno

alt.music.the-doors

rec.music hierarchy

rec.music.a-cappella

Vocal music without instrumental accompaniment (which would therefore include barbershop).

rec.music.afro-latin

Music with Afro-Latin, African and Latin influences.

rec.music.ambient

rec.music.artists

rec.music.artists.beach-boys

rec.music.artists.bruce-hornsby

rec.music.beatles

rec.music.bluenote

Discussion of jazz, blues, and related types of music.

rec.music.bluenote.blues

Strictly blues.

rec.music.cd

CDs: availability and other discussions.

rec.music.celtic

Traditional and modern music with a Celtic flavor.

rec.music.christian

Christian music, both contemporary and traditional.

rec.music.classical

A series of newsgroups for fans of classical music.

rec.music.compose

For those creating musical and lyrical works.

rec.music.country

rec.music.country.old-time

rec.music.country.western

rec.music.dementia

Discussion of comedy and novelty music

rec.music.dylan

Discussion of Bobby's works and music.

rec.music.early

Discussion of pre-classical European music.

rec.music.folk

rec.music.funky

Funk, rap, hip-hop, house, soul, and R&B music.

rec.music.gaffa

Discussion of Kate Bush. Moderated.

rec.music.gdead

A group for Grateful Deadheads.

rec.music.hip-hop

rec.music.indian

rec.music.indian.classical

Hindustani and Carnatic Indian classical music.

rec.music.indian.misc

Discussing Indian music in general.

rec.music.industrial

Discussion of all industrial-related music styles.

rec.music.info

News and announcements on musical topics. Moderated.

rec.music.makers

A series of newsgroups for players of different musical instruments.

rec.music.makers

For performers and their discussions.

rec.music.makers.bagpipe

rec.music.makers.bands

rec.music.makers.bass

Upright bass and bass-guitar techniques and equipment.

rec.music.makers.bowed-strings

rec.music.makers.builders

rec.music.makers.dulcimer

rec.music.makers.french-horn

rec.music.makers.guitar

rec.music.makers.guitar

Electric and acoustic guitar techniques and equipment.

rec.music.makers.guitar.acoustic

Discussion of acoustic guitar playing.

rec.music.makers.guitar.tablature

Guitar tablature/chords. See also *alt.guitar.tabs*.

rec.music.makers.marketplace

Buying and selling used music-making equipment.

rec.music.makers.percussion

Drum and other percussion; techniques and equipment.

rec.music.makers.piano

Piano music, performing, composing, learning, styles.

rec.music.makers.songwriting

rec.music.makers.synth
Synthesizers and computer music.

rec.music.makers.trumpet

rec.music.marketplace
Records, tapes, and CDs: wanted, for sale, etc.

rec.music.misc
General music lovers' group.

rec.music.movies

rec.music.newage
"New Age" music discussions.

rec.music.opera

rec.music.phish
A forum for discussing the musical group Phish.

rec.music.progressive

rec.music.promotional

rec.music.ragtime

rec.music.reggae
Roots, rockers, dancehall reggae.

rec.music.rem

rec.music.reviews
Reviews of music of all genres and mediums. Moderated.

rec.music.video
Discussion of music videos and music-video software.

Mailing Lists

Mailing lists are often the best way for fans of a particular artist or devotees of a particular style of music to communicate with each other. Interested parties send an e-mail message to the mailing list administrator, often with a pre-set message, asking to participate. Thereafter the participant receives all of the postings to the group, either in "real time" as they are posted or in periodic digests.

The following list represents some of the musical mailing lists on the Internet that are devoted to specific instruments, technologies, and musical issues rather than to a particular performer. (Because most of the performer lists are devoted to rock musicians, they are cited at the end of Chapter 9, "Rock & Roll.")

(Note: Where the instructions ask for "your name," "yourname," "address," or "email address," you should, of course, replace those terms with your particular information.)

ACCORDIONS

accordion-request@cs.cmu.edu

BAGPIPES

bagpipe-request@cs.dartmouth.edu

BARBERSHOP

bbshop-request@cray.com

BASS (The Bottom Line)

bass-request@uwplatt.edu

BOOKS ABOUT MUSIC (Music Books Plus)

info@nor.com

Message Body: **Subscribe - Music Books Plus**

BRASS

brass-request@geomag.gly.fsu.edu

CHAPMAN STICK (Touch-Playable Musical Instrument)

sticky-request@cs.nott.ac.uk

Message Body: **subscribe stickwire-L**

CHORALIST

listproc@lists.colorado.edu

Message Body: **subscribe Choralist yourname**

Choralist is intended to be a communication mechanism for the exchange of information and ideas between practicing choral conductors. It is open to anyone, but is specifically oriented towards the choral-conducting professional.

CREATIVE MUSICIANS COALITION (CMC)

majordomo@cs.uwp.edu

Message Body: **subscribe cmc**

DIGITAL GUITAR

pvallado@waynesworld.ucsd.edu

DO-IT-YOURSELF MUSIC (Gajoob's DiY Digest)

gajoob@utw.com

DOUBLEREED-L

listserv@acc.wuacc.edu

Message Body: **subscribe doublereed-l yourname**

DRUM

drum-request@brandx.Rain.COM

drum-digest-request@brandx.Rain.COM

For discussion of anything related to drums and percussion. You can sign up for either the regular list (send to *drum-request*) or digest (send to *drum-digest-request*). In the body of the message, just type **subscribe**, or **subscribe youraddress** if you want a different address used than your return address.

EDUCATION, UNIVERSITY-LEVEL (CTI-Music)

mailbase@mailbase.ac.uk

A discussion list for people involved in university-level music education. It is run by the CTI Centre for Music, which is a UK centre working on the use of computers to assist teaching in universities. To subscribe, write **join cti-music firstname lastname**.

EPULSE

listserv@netcom.com

Message Body: **subscribe epulse-l**

EPULSE is the weekly free email zine from the editors of *PULSE!* and *CLASSICAL PULSE!* magazines, published by Tower Records.

EXOTICA

majordomo@xmission.com

Message Body: **subscribe exotica**

Or for the digest, Message Body: **subscribe exotica-digest**. Discussion of exotic and unusual recordings from the 1950s and 1960s.

FILM MUSIC

listserv@iubvm.ucs.indiana.edu

Discussion of dramatic music for film and television.

To subscribe, send a mail message that consists of only one line: **SUBSCRIBE FILMUS-L Yourfirstname Yourlastname**.

FLUTE

flute-m-request@unixg.ubc.ca

FRENCH MUSIC (Chanter)

majordomo@wimsey.com

To subscribe, send a message to *majordomo@wimsey.com*: **subscribe chanter-liste**. (Note French spelling of *liste*.)

FRENCH SINGERS, FEMALE (Chanteuse)

majordomo@wimsey.com

To subscribe, send a message to *majordomo@wimsey.com*: **subscribe chanteuse-liste**. (Note French spelling of *liste*.)

FRENCH SINGERS, MALE (Chanteur)

majordomo@wimsey.com

To subscribe, send a message to *majordomo@wimsey.com*: **subscribe chanteur-liste**. (Note French spelling of *liste*.)

HAMMER DULCIMERS

hammerd@mcs.com

HAMMOND ORGAN

hammond-request@zk3.dec.com

HANDBELLS

Handbell-L@ringer.jpl.nasa.gov

To subscribe, type the word **SUBSCRIBE** in the subject line.

HARMONICA

MXserver@WKUVX1.WKU.EDU

Message Body: **subscribe HARP-L yourname**

HARPSICHORDS AND RELATED TOPICS (HPSCHD-L)

listserv@albany.eduorLISTSERV@ALBANY.BITNET

To subscribe, send the following command in the body of your message:
SUBSCRIBE HPSCHD-L yourfirstname yourlastname

HORNS (International Horn Society maillist)

horn@merlin.nlu.edu

To subscribe, send a message to **MUGREENE@MERLIN.NLU.EDU**
saying you want to subscribe to the horn mailing list.

IMPULSE MUSIC JOURNAL

impulse@dsigroup.com

Subject: **SUBSCRIBE IMPULSE**

INDEPENDENT MUSIC (Indie-List)

grumpy@access.digex.net

LUTE

lute-request@cs.dartmouth.edu

MIDI WIND CONTROLLER

listserver@morgan.ucs.mun.ca

This is a mailing list devoted to wind controllers. To subscribe, put type the following as the body of the message:

subscribe wind your-name-not-your-email-address

MIXMASTERS

mixmasters-request@infopro.com

To join, send the command **subscribe** in the body of an e-mail message.

MORRIS DANCING

listserv@suvm.syr.edu

To subscribe, type **SUBSCRIBE your-real-name (your-team-name)**.

MUSICALS

majordomo@world.std.com

To join the list, send mail with the message: **subscribe musicals**.

MUSICALS-MAIL

majordomo@world.std.com

To join the list, send mail with the message: **subscribe musicals-mail**.

NEW RELEASES

majordomo@cs.uwp.edu or new-releases-request@cs.uwp.edu

Write **subscribe new-releases** in the body of your message.

PIPE ORGANS AND RELATED TOPICS (PIPORG-L)

listserv@albany.eduorLISTSERV@ALBANY.BITNET

To subscribe, send the following command in the body of your message:
SUBSCRIBE PIPORG-L yourfirstname yourlastname

QUADRAVERB

qv-request@incog.com

RADIO CONCERTS

radio-concerts-request@cs.albany.edu

Send the command **sub** in your message to subscribe to the digest.

Provides advance notice for upcoming special musical events on radio and TV. Typical info includes upcoming syndicated radio shows such as Westwood One's "In Concert" and "Superstars" concert series, DIR Broadcasting's King Biscuit Flower Hour and MTV's Unplugged, as well as live FM broadcasts (from satellite feeds) and musical guests on late night talk shows. Send a **help** message for details.

TROMBONE (Trombone-L)

listproc@showme.missouri.edu

To subscribe, send mail with **sub yourname** in the body.

TRUMPET

listserv@acad1.dana.edu

Message body: **subscribe trumpet**

Please do not include any other words or punctuation in this message. This list is also available in digest form (one message per day) via the following command: **subscribe trumpet-digest**.

TUBA AND EUPHONIUM (TUBAEUPH)

listserv@cmsvmb.missouri.edu

To subscribe, send mail with **sub yourname** in the body.

VOX MUSICAL INSTRUMENTS (Vox-L)

listserv@netcom.com

In message body, type **subscribe vox-l yourname**.

CHAPTER 9

Rock & Roll

IN THIS CHAPTER:

> General rock & roll and alternative music resources

> Online magazines

> Record reviews

> Legends of rock: Elvis, Beatles, The Dead, and more

> Resources for rock musicians

IN OTHER CHAPTERS:

< General music resources are discussed in Chapter 8.

Rock & roll may have started in the 1950s as a legitimate expression of youthful rebellion, but for at least 20 years it's been nothing more than an institutionalized scam to bilk teenagers out of their pocket change. The libidinous impulses that once compelled kids to "rock around the clock" have been co-opted by multinational corporations, fossilized in tourist attractions like Graceland and the Rock & Roll Hall of Fame, and sold back to the kids at a profit.

That's why punk rock (now called "alternative music" by the folks in the marketing department) had to be invented and why the most interesting music sites on the Internet belong to do-it-yourself renegades who want to stand as far as possible from the smell of rock orthodoxy. There are countless Web sites that are devoted to the honorable history of rock & roll—and these are some of the most enjoyable places on the Net—but most of the best music sites eschew the rock & roll label and confine themselves to the alternative subset.

General Rock & Roll Resources and Link Sites

Rock & roll is such a fractured category that it doesn't lend itself to the kind of "all-purpose" pages you'll find on the Net for country-western, jazz, or classical music. Nonetheless, there are a few pages that try to function as one-stop rock & roll information resources—and often they are so self-consciously hip and obviously funded by profit-seekers that no kid with an ounce of Internet know-how would spend more than ten seconds there. I'll begin the chapter with a couple of them anyway, and then I'll discuss some genuinely useful sites for record reviews, song lyrics, and performer pages.

The Internet Underground Music Archive
http://www.iuma.com

Even though it's not a charity, there's nothing phony or venal about the Internet Underground Music Archive. IUMA is one of the coolest and most useful music sites on the Internet, an admirable mix of fannish zeal and commercial enterprise.

IUMA provides a stylish and technologically sophisticated home for dozens of smaller operations, including record labels, unsigned bands, and music publications. (See figure 9.1.)

FIGURE 9.1

The basic menu of choices from the Internet Underground Music Archive includes record labels, bands, and publications.

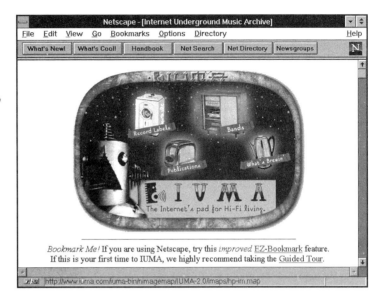

The labels that have pitched a tent here range from the mighty Warner Bros. and 4AD to such interesting indies as Teen Beat and Blue Goat. Most of the labels have artist rosters, digitized samples, and ordering information.

The unsigned-band section allows struggling artists of many categories to post a picture, bio, and audio sample on the archive (for a reasonable fee).

The IUMA publications section offers digest versions of such newsstand magazines as *Fizz*, *Seconds*, and industry tipsheet *Gavin*, as well the complete text of the excellent e-zines *Strobe* and *Addicted to Noise* (described elsewhere in this chapter).

Metaverse/The Vibe
http://metaverse.com

Adam Curry was an MTV veejay who has taken his name-brand status and applied it to Internet marketing. He and a partner started an Internet service called On Ramp. (Adam was also the first to trademark the online use of the term "MTV," beating his former employer to the punch. He subsequently got sued.)

Within this very large and seemingly successful enterprise, you will find the Metaverse, an information station for entertainment culture that revolves around mainstream rock music (although it also has a useful TV schedule service, a classical music server, and high-profile advertisers coming out of its ears). (See figure 9.2.)

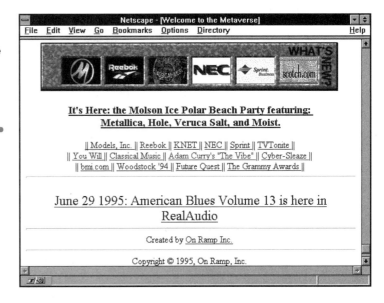

The rock music section of the Metaverse is found in something called Adam Curry's "The Vibe" at *http://metaverse.com/vibe*. (This should not be confused with VIBE magazine, an R&B publication from Time, Inc., which is also available online.) The Vibe is divided into sub-sections called "Sights" (movies and TV), "Sounds" (rock music), "Sleaze" (gossip), and "Surf" (Internet links).

The Sounds section is obviously Adam's pride and joy. It features mainstream and alternative record reviews (see figure 9.3), concert information, a site for BMI (the music copyright administrators), a site for the Grammy Awards, a showcase for unsigned bands, and an audio collection of thoughts "From the Mind of Adam Curry."

FIGURE 9.3

In The Vibe's music-review section, you can access reviews for artists ranging from Bonnie Raitt to King Missile.

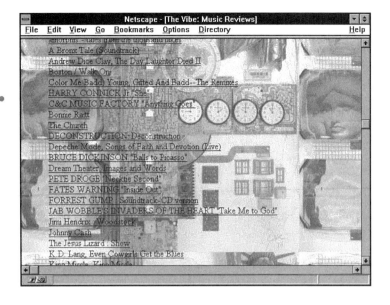

Metaverse is a flashy, high-tech site that is meant to please as many young consumers as possible. It's surely a hint of things to come on the Internet. (At the time of this writing, the Metaverse home page was touting the "new" Metaverse—which will be accessed with a password.)

Rocktropolis
http://underground.net/Rocktropolis

Another rock-music megaplex that is trying to lure young consumers is called Rocktropolis. It uses the metaphor of a neon-lit, sci-fi cityscape as the framing device for its handful of services. (See figure 9.4.) This under-construction site includes a chat room, an unsigned-band forum, and information about Sting, the Doors, and I.R.S. Records (which seems to be a sponsor of the site). It promises something called the Rocktropolis Library in the near future, "containing a 'music only' search engine, allowing you easy and direct access to every music site on the Net. The Library will also feature interviews and quotes from rock's greatest poets and lyricists." We'll see.

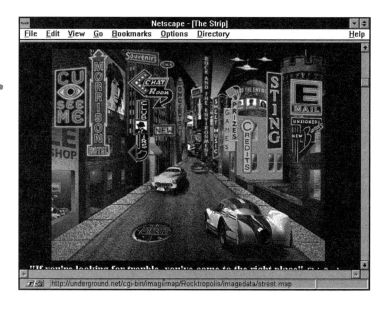

MTV

http://www.mtv.com

You would expect MTV to have as strong and innovative a place on the Net as it does on television, but the MTV site, as of this writing, is a major disappointment.

All it offers is a section on an animated series called "MTV's Oddities" and a link to information about the MTV beach house.

With all the potential advertising tie-ins, I wouldn't bet that the MTV site will stay this lame or this limited for very long. ☞

Don't forget that you can check the home pages of the major record labels for information on particular artists, upcoming releases, tour dates, movie soundtracks, compilation albums, and more. The six major-label conglomerates—WEA, Sony, Capitol, Polygram, BMG, and MCA—have home sites, and there are pages for most of their subsidiary labels as well. (For instance, Columbia is a division of Sony; A&M is a division of Polygram; Elektra is a division of WEA, and so on.) Label sites are discussed in more detail in Chapter 8.

Online Magazines

Surprisingly, as of this writing you will not find online editions of *Rolling Stone* or *Spin*, the two biggest mainstream rock publications that you can pick up at the newsstand. Most of the music magazines on the Net are oriented toward alternative rock, which suits a lot of us just fine.

Addicted to Noise

http://www.addict.com/ATN

Addicted to Noise is a tremendous new online publication that has a cutting-edge attitude but also features a posse of veteran rock critics (Greil Marcus, Dave Marsh, my buddy Bud Scoppa) who travel a little deeper into the mainstream than the writers of the average punk e-zine.

As a recent ATN cover story suggests "The (Punk) Revolution is Over"—which is to say, alternative music has obliterated the mainstream marketplace, and now every frat boy and corporate middle manager has a record collection that's "alternative." Thus, Addicted to Noise is in the right place at the right time. It could very well be the *Rolling Stone* of the cyber generation—visionary, comprehensive, and well-supported by advertisers.

Addicted to Noise is also a world-class read. The quality of the writing is unmatched by any other publication online and by few of the magazines you can purchase at the newsstand. (See the record review excerpt in figure 9.5.) It has extensive feature stories, reams of record reviews, a music-news section that is updated daily, and a menu of think-pieces by the sanctified gurus of rock journalism. It is further enhanced by color-saturated graphics and by liberal doses of downloadable audio.

FIGURE 9.5

An ATN review of Elastica's debut album by music-industry good guy Bud Scoppa (who was my partner in a disastrous record-label start-up deal we thought we had finalized with a zillionaire music-biz weasel whom I'll call "Irving A.").

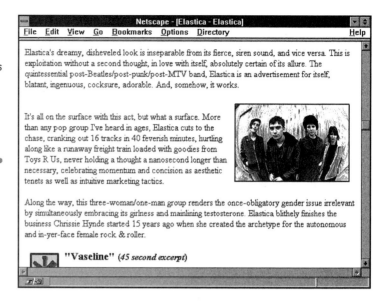

Strobe

http://www.iuma.com/strobe

Strobe is a terrific online music magazine based in Los Angeles. Befitting its hometown, Strobe is at the forefront in sniffing out the latest and coolest alternative and post-alternative sounds. It features columnists who've got the inside poop on the street-level music biz, profiles of unsigned bands, interviews with the alternative elite, and a hefty section of record reviews. (See figure 9.6.)

FIGURE 9.6

A review of the new Pooh Sticks album from Strobe, the online e-zine that shouts "L.A.!"

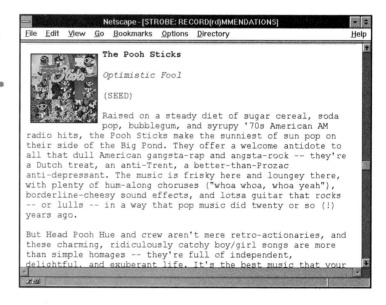

DREAMPOP

http://www.itp.tsoa.nyu.edu/~student/brendonm/dream1.html

Brendon Macaraeg's excellent e-zine is a good all-purpose guitar-pop almanac and the definitive online resource for information about what is sometime called "shoegazer" or "miasma" music—ethereal, sometimes noisy post-pop as embodied by such bands as Ride, My Bloody Valentine, and The Cocteau Twins.

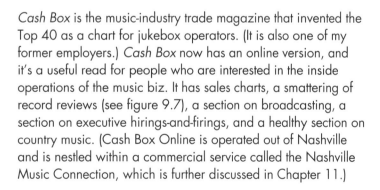

There are thousand of low-budget, special-interest music magazines or fanzines available by mail-order or at neighborhood record stores around the country. These range from such well-known punk publications as *Flipside* and *Maximumrocknroll* to such obscurities as *Oswald, Morning Toast*, and *Slugs & Lettuce*. If you're interested in the arcane world of 'zines and other fringe publications, check out the online version of *Factsheet Five*, the bible of low-fi publishing, at *ftp://etext.archive.umich.edu/pub/Factsheet.Five*, for countless 'zine reviews and contact information.

Cash Box

http://online.music-city.com/CASHBOX.HTML

Cash Box is the music-industry trade magazine that invented the Top 40 as a chart for jukebox operators. (It is also one of my former employers.) *Cash Box* now has an online version, and it's a useful read for people who are interested in the inside operations of the music biz. It has sales charts, a smattering of record reviews (see figure 9.7), a section on broadcasting, a section on executive hirings-and-firings, and a healthy section on country music. (Cash Box Online is operated out of Nashville and is nestled within a commercial service called the Nashville Music Connection, which is further discussed in Chapter 11.)

The features and reviews are pretty good, because the people who write for *Cash Box* are intelligent, underpaid music buffs who will very soon be working for better and more generous employers.

FIGURE 9.7

An excerpt from the Cash Box
record-review section.

• • • • • • • • • • • • • • • • •

```
─ Netscape - [Cash Box - <IMG ALIGN=top SRC="Redball2.gif"> <A HREF=EXECS.HTML">  ▼ ♦
File   Edit   View   Go   Bookmarks   Options   Directory                     Help
```

SUDDENLY, TAMMY!: *(We Get There When We Do.)* (Warner Bros. 45831)
The debut major-label release from this Pennsylvania trio starts off with "Hard Lesson," a very
Belly-sounding pop tune that is also the CD's first single. It's an unfortunate opening choice, as once
you get past that number, the trio's line-up of bass, drums and piano (the whole record is *sans*
guitar) gives them their own delightfully unique alternative sound. Though her roots are in jazz,
vocalist/pianist Beth Sorrentino lends a classical touch to the CD that marks *(We Get There...)* with
an air of dignity. That is never more in evidence than on "Snowman," a lovely tune that lingers with
the memory of 1920s torch songs. A pure delight. (S.B.)

NITZER EBB: *Big Hit* (Geffen 24718)
Recorded at eight different locations on two continents, the new record from the English trio appears
to have been inspired by that many different artists, as well. Because of the lineage they follow, from
Adam & The Ants on "Border Talk" to Nine Inch Nails on "I Thought," the CD's strongest track,
there is a consistency throughout that distinguishes *Big Hit* as a Nitzer Ebb recording. Credit for
intertwining the different melodies into a whole album should be shared by the band with producer
Flood, who also assists with programming and guitars. Particularly impressive is the gritty edge
Nitzer Ebb bring to "In Decline," a feat not easily accomplished in progammed music. (S.B.)

Record Reviews and Discographies

The Web is a good place to dig up record reviews and collectors' information for the latest releases and long-ago obscurities. The most fanatical, up-to-the-minute record-review sites are devoted to alternative rather than mainstream rock, although many of the reviews in the so-called review archives are just brief bursts of ill-considered opinion. (The online magazines and general-interest entertainment sites mentioned in this chapter and throughout this book might give you more in-depth reviews.)

All-Music Guide
http://cdnow.com

The best online archive for thumbnail record reviews is the All-Music Guide. All-Music is an invaluable resource that lists, rates, and discusses what seems like every piece of popular music ever recorded, in most genres, with a particular emphasis of mainstream rock and alternative releases. (See figure 9.8 for an example.) The Guide covers both out-of-print and freely available titles. It also features up-to-date sales charts, artist bios, discographies, and album-track listings.

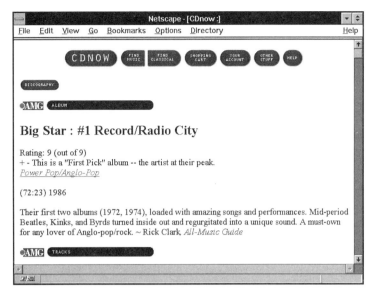

The much-traveled All-Music Guide must now be entered through the home page of a music-ordering service called CDNow! You can use CDNow! to order any in-print recording that is reviewed in AMG.

Quick Fix Music Reviews
http://www-leland.stanford.edu/~witness/qfmrl/qfmrl.html

For people with short attention spans, this site provides snap judgments on hundreds of recordings that are dear to the heart of the Alternative Nation, with nary a word of explanation. (See figure 9.9.)

Shopping 2000
http://shopping2000.com/shopping2000/1musrev.html

This review area is an adjunct to a jumbo advertising and home-shopping site. It takes a broad sampling of music releases (mostly rock and alternative, from ABBA and Foreigner to the Red House Painters and Guided By Voices) and offers a brief summary of what the critics are saying. The result is the kind of the "on the one hand/on the other hand" encapsulation that ends up telling you nothing at all. (See figure 9.10.)

FIGURE 9.9

A selection of reviews from the "B" section of the Quick Fix Music Reviews site. (He's wrong about Big Dipper's Craps album, by the way.)

● ● ● ● ● ● ● ● ● ● ● ● ● ● ● ● ●

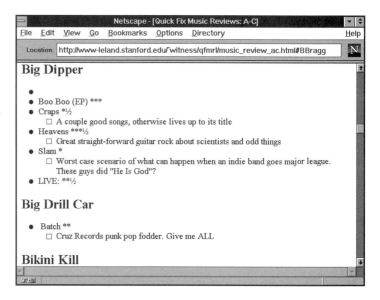

FIGURE 9.10

A record review from the Shopping 2000 service of an important new recording that might appeal to the typical Shopping 2000 customer.

● ● ● ● ● ● ● ● ● ● ● ● ● ● ● ●

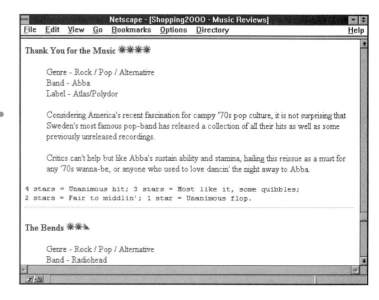

Record Collectors Web

http://www.onramp.net/RecordWeb/record.html

The Record Collectors Web is a valuable resource for obsessive compilers of bootlegs, imports, alternate pressings, and out-of-print music rarities.

This site offers for-sale listings in such categories as '50s-'60s singles and albums; psychedelic music; alternative music; rhythm & blues; Beatles recordings; and a plethora of general-interest and non-rock genres.

Especially pertinent here are the feature articles and reviews that are appended to the site. These include "Ask the Guru," in which site master George Gimarc answers questions about the recorded output of such lovable obscurities as Klaatu and the Shaggs (see figure 9.11), and a smattering of reviews of recent releases.

FIGURE 9.11

George Gimarc spreads the word about the amazing Shaggs in this excerpt from The Record Collectors Web site.

Miscellaneous Rock & Roll Databases

The following sites feature bios, discographies, or song lyrics for performers in many genres of music, with an emphasis on rock and alternative music.

The Ultimate Band List at *http://american.recordings.com/ WWWoM/ubl/ubl.shtml*, is one of the true gems of the Internet, an ongoing database project that aims to establish links to information on every major recording artist, including FAQs, Web pages, lyrics, and sound clips. It is dominated by rock and alternative band listings.

The Song Lyric Server at *ftp://ftp.uwp.edu /pub/music/lyrics* is a repository for the lyrics to literally thousands of songs in several genres, with an emphasis on rock and alternative performers. To access it, anonymous FTP to *ftp.uwp.edu* and then choose the directory path *pub/music/lyrics*. (Note: The main site at the U. of Wisconsin is very busy during normal business hours and may be difficult to access, so you might want to try the Vivarin lyric server mirror site at *http:// vivarin.pc.cc.cmu.edu/lyrics.html*. The Vivarin site has all the lyrics in easily searchable form, but it does not have all the discographies and miscellany of the Wisconsin FTP site.)

VIBE magazine (the real VIBE magazine, from Time, Inc., not from Adam Curry) provides computer space for the Mammoth Music Meta List at *http://www.pathfinder.com/ @@9uAoxwAAAAAAQNXr/vibe/mmm/music.html*. The site has thousands of links, many to artist home pages, in most genres of music. It is also linked to archives of charts, reviews, and lyrics.

The Worldwide Internet Live Music Archive (WILMA), at *http://underground.net/Wilma*, is an extensive resource for tour information and concert venues in the U.S. and around the world. It lists symphony halls, amphitheaters, nightclubs, and other performance spaces by city, state, and country, and it also has an up-to-date roster of who's-touring-where, mostly for rock and alternative bands.

More information on these general resources can be found in Chapter 8, "General Music Resources."

UseNet Newsgroups

There are too many UseNet newsgroups devoted to rock & roll to be discussed individually here. Most of the legends of rock have a newsgroup devoted to them, as do most of the genres within the broader category of "rock," from "ambient" to "zydeco."

If you're interested in posting your opinion or seeking counsel on a particular performer or genre, point your UseNet newsreader to the *alt.fan*, *alt. music*, or *rec.music* sections (or "hierarchies"), then start browsing.

History Sites

For many of us, the thing called "rock & roll" is now little more than its history, a history that will provide fodder for coffee-table books, cable-TV documentaries, and heavily advertised "re-union" tours for many decades to come. (Of course, the deification of yesterday's rockers is surely much healthier for our economy than encouraging the kids of today to take drugs, write songs, and overthrow the government. Fun is fun, but let's not get carried away. Without the federal government and the phone company, there wouldn't even *be* an Internet, you little ingrates.)

The History of Rock n Roll
http://www.hollywood.com/rocknroll/index.html

This is essentially an advertisement for a Time-Life video series called "The History of Rock 'n' Roll," which aired as a 10-hour TV special in early 1995. Either I'm getting old, or this was a pretty good show. Of course, it confined its "history" to the mega-personalities who have products to sell you (see figure 9.12); but within that corporate parameter, it was pretty honest. (For instance, it was worth 10 hours of my time just to hear Pete Townshend say that Led Zeppelin was utter rubbish.)

FIGURE 9.12

The home page for the "History of Rock 'n' Roll" video series. Let's see—that's Elvis, and Jerry Lee Lewis, and Buddy Holly, and Janis, and Jimi, and...

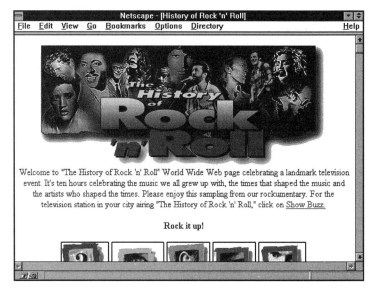

The Rock and Roll Hall of Fame

http://www.rocknroll.org

The Rock and Roll Hall of Fame is the Vatican of rock orthodoxy, and after many years as a virtual institution, it finally has a pretty building in Cleveland, Ohio, to call its own. (See figure 9.13.) The building was designed by I.M. Pei, no less, the "world's most celebrated architect."

FIGURE 9.13

The new Rock and Roll Hall of Fame building looks like it's really, really nice.

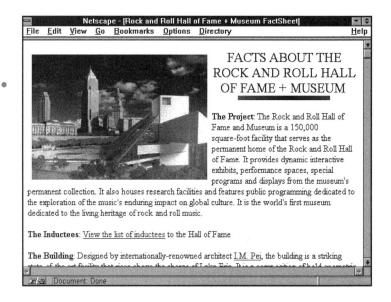

This site provides a description of the facility (which apparently does not have a vomit-encrusted, graffiti-scarred unisex bathroom) and a page that lists the inductees. ✍

The Death of Rock 'n' Roll
http://weber.u.washington.edu/~jlks/pike/DeathRR.html

When you're finished genuflecting at the Rock and Roll Hall of Fame, you might want to visit a *real* rock & roll history site—the Death of Rock 'n' Roll page. This site is a digest version of Jeff Pike's swell book by the same name, which examines "Untimely Demises, Morbid Preoccupations, and Premature Forecasts of Doom in Pop Music." (See figure 9.14.)

FIGURE 9.14

An excerpt from Jeff Pike's book "The Death of Rock 'n' Roll," from the Web site of the same name.

• • • • • • • • • • • • • • • • •

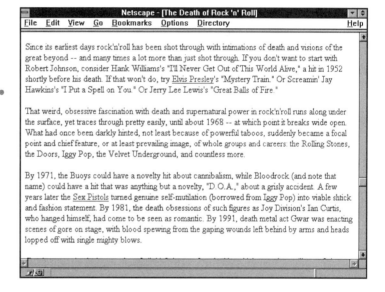

Mostly the book is an exhaustive list of rockers who died young. Pike pays particular attention to the many heroin overdoses in the rock pantheon and to the suicidal nihilism of punk. There's also a chapter on the many Beatle-related deaths, from Stu Sutcliffe and Brian Epstein to John Lennon and (maybe) Paul McCartney. ✍

Legends of Rock

With its multimedia capabilities, the World Wide Web is an excellent place for fans to build virtual shrines to whatever performer is the center of their universe, and not surprisingly there are Web sites devoted to most of the legends of rock music, from Elvis Presley to Spinal Tap to Bruce "The Employer" Springsteen.

Elvis Presley

Elvis Presley was a sharecropper's son from Tupelo, Mississippi, who bought a guitar, recorded a song for his mother, made a movie about a jitterbugging race-car driver, and died face-down in a shag carpet. (Or so I've been told.) He has since attracted a cult following.

There are about a half dozen Elvis sites on the Internet, including the *alt.elvis.king* UseNet group, as well as another handful of oddball sites that embrace the larger phenomenon of velvet paintings, long sideburns, and indiscriminate pill popping. (You can find the most extensive list of Elvis-related pages at the Elvis Home Page, described forthwith.)

The Elvis Home Page
http://sunsite.unc.edu/elvis/elvishom.html

Also known as The Elvis Aaron Presley Home Page, this is one of the great sites on the Internet, a repository for all things Elvis.

Unfortunately, the toadies at Graceland recently cracked down on this site for using copyrighted images (apparently Michael and Lisa are supposed to get a nickel every time you even say the word "Elvis"), so the scope of this site has been scaled back. (See figure 9.15.) However, that now gives it a certain outlaw quality. (The site features some interesting material about copyright infringement and the Internet culled from legal and academic resources.)

FIGURE 9.15

The Elvis Home Page, which notes its recent run-in with the King's estate.

● ● ● ● ● ● ● ● ● ● ● ● ● ● ● ● ● ●

The site includes a virtual tour of Graceland that is patched together from smuggled Polaroids, a copy of E's last will and testament, Elvis software, the cartoon adventures of Space Elvis, Elvis images (see figure 9.16), and an incredible list of Elvis-related links. ☞

FIGURE 9.16

Elvis Presley and Richard Nixon meeting in the Oval Office to discuss the threat to America's youth from the international drug conspiracy, Dec. 21, 1970. This is the most bizarre photograph ever taken.

● ● ● ● ● ● ● ● ● ● ● ● ● ● ● ● ●

The Beatles

By all indications, this Elvis fellow was a true giant; but as far as I'm concerned, you can take all that "Elvis is King" stuff and tuck it into bed. For my money, no performer(s) made a more substantial contribution to the history of rock music than The Beatles. Unlike Elvis, The Beatles wrote their own songs, played their own instruments, and occasionally sang about something other than "love." So naturally, they don't appeal to as broad a range of fans and they haven't inspired the same kind of quasi-religious devotion that "the King" has. That's fine with me. I'd rather not see the Beatles turned into side-show curiosities.

Unlike many of the Elvis-related sites, which are gloriously tacky, the many Internet sites that are devoted to the Beatles are notable for their good taste, intelligence, and graphical appeal.

There are at least 18 different Beatle pages on the Web, and there is considerable Beatles information at FTP sites, in UseNet, and within the larger rock-music archives and databases.

According to a helpful link site called The Beatles Information Page at *http://www.cs.rochester.edu/users/grads/jonas/ beatles/beatles.html*, the following are some of the Beatle resources that can be found on the Net (or accessed directly from the preceding address):

* *http://bobcat.bbn.com* has information culled over the years from the UseNet group *rec.music.beatles*, including bootleg recording info, GIF files of all the album covers, Beatle FAQs, trivia, and much more.

* The Backwards Beatles page *at http://www.cs.rochester. edu/users/grads/jonas/beatles/backwards.html* contains a collection of reversed Beatles sounds, some of which supposedly reveal hidden messages, as well as some diabolical album-cover information and a link to two lengthy articles on the "Paul is Dead" controversy. (See figure 9.17.)

* Maurizio Codogno has set up a Beatles FTP site in Italy at *ftp://beatles.cselt.stet.it/pub/beatles*. It mirrors some of the information available on bobcat and may provide faster access if you're coming from Europe.

FIGURE 9.17

A list of clues from the "Paul is Dead" controversy that erupted around the time that Abbey Road was released. (This rumor was later verified with the release of the impostor McCartney's "Silly Love Songs.") Accessed from the Backwards Beatles Page.

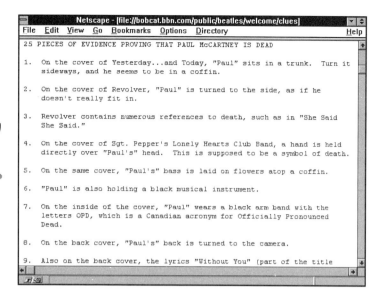

Netscape - [file://bobcat.bbn.com/public/beatles/welcome/clues]

File Edit View Go Bookmarks Options Directory Help

25 PIECES OF EVIDENCE PROVING THAT PAUL McCARTNEY IS DEAD

1. On the cover of Yesterday...and Today, "Paul" sits in a trunk. Turn it sideways, and he seems to be in a coffin.

2. On the cover of Revolver, "Paul" is turned to the side, as if he doesn't really fit in.

3. Revolver contains numerous references to death, such as in "She Said She Said."

4. On the cover of Sgt. Pepper's Lonely Hearts Club Band, a hand is held directly over "Paul's" head. This is supposed to be a symbol of death.

5. On the same cover, "Paul's" bass is laid on flowers atop a coffin.

6. "Paul" is also holding a black musical instrument.

7. On the inside of the cover, "Paul" wears a black arm band with the letters OPD, which is a Canadian acronym for Officially Pronounced Dead.

8. On the back cover, "Paul's" back is turned to the camera.

9. Also on the back cover, the lyrics "Without You" (part of the title

＊ When all else fails, there is the UseNet newsgroup *rec.music.beatles*, which is heavily traveled.

Mike Markowski's Beatles Page

http://www.eecis.udel.edu/~markowsk/beatles

Of all the Beatle pages I have found on the Web, this one is my favorite, partly because it has a sweetness to it that transcends fandom or cliche, and partly because it looks so cool. (See figure 9.18.)

The Markowski site features an extensive discography (including bootlegs), information about Beatle conventions and merchandise, individual pages for each of the Fabs (with a digitized "hello" from each), and a funny document from *rec.music.beatles* that suggests that Paul McCartney was the only Beatle who *didn't* die a mysterious death and get replaced with an impostor.

FIGURE 9.18
Mike Markowski's Beatles Page.
Dig the quote from Tim Leary.
• • • • • • • • • • • • • • • •

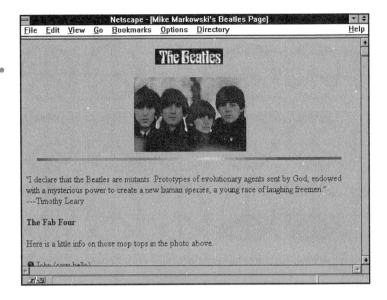

The Rolling Stones

What can you say about the Rolling Stones? That they embody the rebellious spirit of rock? That they bravely refuse to grow old gracefully? That they've milked this "World's Greatest Rock & Roll Band" nonsense like an old cow until the only people who still care are beer companies and the weekend renegades of Yupdom? You've got to admire their shamelessness, if nothing else. Make no mistake—the Stones are an astute bunch (Mick, after all, attended the London School of Economics) and they are profiting from online technology as well as any mainstream rock band. One of the shows on the "Voodoo Lounge Tour" was transmitted in quasi-real time over the Internet, and they were the first of the legends to sponsor or endorse a Web site.

There are at least nine Stones-related sites on the Internet, including the Undercover mailing list, the *alt.rock-n-roll.stones* UseNet group, and a bountiful site called Completely Stoned at *http://www.leo.org/~tromsdor/stones.html*.

The Voodoo Lounge
http://www.stones.com

This is the "official" Stones site on the Web. It is chock full of multimedia frou-frou, including photos, audio clips, video clips, and candid Polariods by Ronnie Wood. (See figure 9.19.)

FIGURE 9.19

The home page for the Rolling Stones Voodoo Lounge web site. (The tongues represent how the Rolling Stones speak the international language of music, and the devil heads symbolize their pact with Satan. I kid you not.)

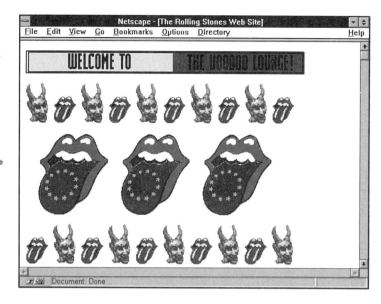

The Grateful Dead

If cyberculture has a mascot band, it's the Grateful Dead. Even with the passing of Jerry Garcia, the presence of the Dead in the online world is likely to remain strong. (See figure 9.20.)

FIGURE 9.20

The online community reacted quickly to the death of Jerry Garcia. Members of the rec.music.gdead UseNet group posted 2,000 messages within the first 48 hours of his passing.

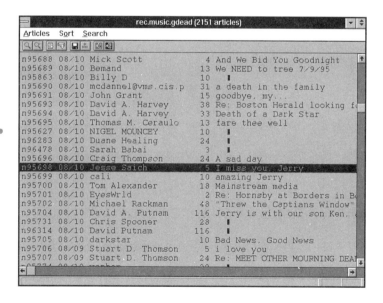

At first glance, there's nothing cyber about a hippie jug band that played the same acid-addled repertoire to a traveling circus of blissed-out ragamuffins for 30 years. But in their faithful adherence to a vision and in the do-it-yourself spirit of community that they generated, the Dead were an inspiration to a decentralized cyber culture that makes it own rules and lives by its own code. And, not incidentally, the Dead were extremely prosperous. They proved that if you stand still long enough, the ever-spinning world catches up with you again—and gives you lots of money for being so darn cute. Also not incidentally, the Dead came out of the Bay area, where much of the cyber revolution is still taking place. Many of the people who are building the hardware, writing the software, and administering the Internet sites are Dead fans, and are likely to stay that way. So there's plenty of Dead activity online.

From a helpful resource called simply The Grateful Dead Page at *http://www.cs.cmu.edu/afs/cs.cmu.edu/user/mleone/web/dead.html*, you can access the following Dead-related Web pages:

* Queer Dead Head Web Page

* The Deadhead Home Page Index

* The Ultimate Tape List

* The Tape Traders Circle

* The Pacific Northwest Dead Page

* Annotated Grateful Dead Lyrics

* Dr. Beechwood's Terrapin Station Web Page

* Highlights from the *gdead.berkeley.edu* FTP archive

* The Grateful Dead page at The Well (The Well is a S.F.-based server that is chock full of forward-thinking, left-leaning sites and is the home base for much of the Dead activity online. Check out *http://www/well.com* and go where your bliss takes you from there.)

* David Gans' home page (Gans is the host of *The Grateful Dead Hour*.)

* The Grateful Dead Almanac (the Dead newsletter, now available online in system-crashing graphic splendor)

* The DAT-heads page
* The Modulus Graphite home page (makers of Phil Lesh's and Bob Weir's instruments)
* A Dead BBS list

Because the Dead experience has always been such a family thing, there are numerous Deadhead home pages, ranging from the Queer Dead Head Home Page to Bobkirks' Deadhead Family Home Page at *http://www.primenet.com/~bobkirk/index.html*. (See figure 9.21.)

FIGURE 9.21
Bobkirk's Deadhead Family Web Page. Right on.

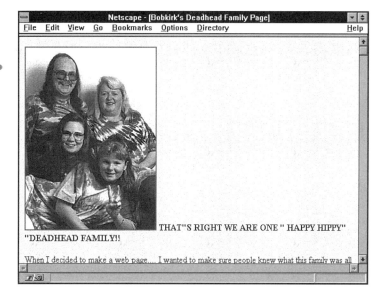

The Grateful Dead FTP Site
ftp://gdead.berkeley.edu/pub/gdead

This mammoth FTP site is the best place for authoritative Dead information, including lyrics, discographies, photos, FAQs, and much more. A list of some of the highlights of the archive is shown in figure 9.22.

FIGURE 9.22

Some of the many fun articles that can be accessed from the gdead.berkely.edu FTP site or from this hypertext version at http://www.cs.cmu.edu/ ~mleone/gdead/highlights.html, including useful tips from the tie-dye masters.

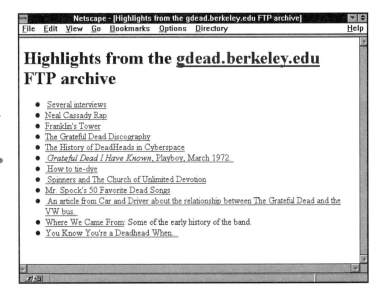

Highlights from the gdead.berkeley.edu FTP archive

- Several interviews
- Neal Cassady Rap
- Franklin's Tower
- The Grateful Dead Discography
- The History of DeadHeads in Cyberspace
- *Grateful Dead I Have Known*, Playboy, March 1972.
- How to tie-dye
- Spinners and The Church of Unlimited Devotion
- Mr. Spock's 50 Favorite Dead Songs
- An article from Car and Driver about the relationship between The Grateful Dead and the VW bus.
- Where We Came From: Some of the early history of the band.
- You Know You're a Deadhead When...

Spinal Tap

Of all the legendary bands of rock & roll, history has perhaps been the least kind to Spinal Tap. Where once they were heavy-metal hitmakers, with such mammoth albums as "Shark Sandwich" and "Intravenous DeMilo," today they've been relegated to the "Where Are They Now?" file. But the true fans do not forget.

The Spinal Tap Home Page

http://rhino.harvard.edu/elwin/SpinalTap/home.html

This site features photos of the legendary Tap, an extensive bio (see figure 9.23), reproductions of the album covers, and the script to the epic rockumentary "This is Spinal Tap."

FIGURE 9.23

Some informative background information on Spinal Tap, from the extremely informative and informational Spinal Tap Home Page, which is all about Spinal Tap.

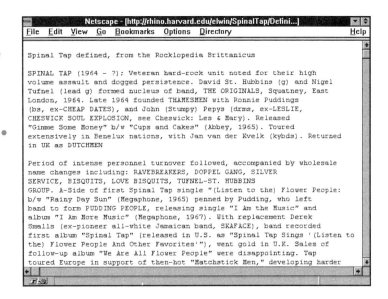

Spinal Tap defined, from the Rocklopedia Brittanicus

SPINAL TAP (1964 - ?); Veteran hard-rock unit noted for their high volume assault and dogged persistence. David St. Hubbins (g) and Nigel Tufnel (lead g) formed nucleus of band, THE ORIGINALS, Squatney, East London, 1964. Late 1964 founded THAMESMEN with Ronnie Puddings (bs, ex-CHEAP DATES), and John (Stumpy) Pepys (drms, ex-LESLIE, CHESWICK SOUL EXPLOSION, see Cheswick: Les & Mary). Released "Gimme Some Money" b/w "Cups and Cakes" (Abbey, 1965). Toured extensively in Benelux nations, with Jan van der Kvelk (kybds). Returned in UK as DUTCHMEN

Period of intense personnel turnover followed, accompanied by wholesale name changes including: RAVEBREAKERS, DOPPEL GANG, SILVER SERVICE, BISQUITS, LOVE BISQUITS, TUFNEL-ST. HUBBINS GROUP. A-Side of first Spinal Tap single "(Listen to the) Flower People: b/w "Rainy Day Sun" (Megaphone, 1965) penned by Pudding, who left band to form PUDDING PEOPLE, releasing single "I Am the Music" and album "I Am More Music" (Megaphone, 1967). With replacement Derek Smalls (ex-pioneer all-white Jamaican band, SKAFACE), band recorded first album "Spinal Tap" (released in U.S. as "Spinal Tap Sings '(Listen to the) Flower People And Other Favorites'"), went gold in U.K. Sales of follow-up album "We Are All Flower People" were disappointing. Tap toured Europe in support of then-hot "Matchstick Men," developing harder

Celebrity Register

Rock stars inspire a kind of zeal among their fans that is unequaled by our reverence for movie stars and sports heroes. From several sources, including the Yahoo directory (*http://www.yahoo.com/Entertainment/Music/Artists*) and the Musical Web Resources page at *http://lps2.esu18.k12.ne.us/inthtml/music.html,* you can access home pages for many rock and alternative music performers.

Resources for Musicians

If you're one of those dreamers who really believes you've got musical talent and a God-given right to be as famous as any of those people who have Web sites devoted to them, the Internet is a good place to gather information before you descend into a life of delusion and scorn from which there is no return.

Online Want Ads

There are now a couple services on the Internet that offer free classifieds for musicians, and there will probably be more in the future.

CLOSE-UP: TODD RUNDGREN

Todd Rundgren has never been a hitmaker—he has a single gold album to his credit, for 1972's magnificent Something/Anything, featuring "Hello It's Me" and "I Saw the Light"—but he is one of the most influential figures in contemporary music. Echoes of Rundgren's pop stylings can be heard in the work of such disparate artists as Prince and Hall & Oates, and his distinctive production technique resulted in hit records for such commercial castaways as Meat Loaf and Grand Funk Railroad. But it is as a video producer and all-around techno weenie that Rundgren has had his greatest effect on the culture.

Rundgren's "Time Heals" was the second video ever played on MTV—the first was "Video Killed the Radio Star" by the Buggles—and he remains at the forefront of this nascent artform. He also has had a long relationship with Apple computers, and his software company has produced screensavers, music software, and video applications for the Mac.

Rundgren's 1994 "No World Order" album was an interactive CD, and his new album "The Individualist" is being released on the new CD+ format. It features video and text components along with the music, and individual listeners can customize and manipulate it to their own tastes. (Rundgren is now calling himself TR-i, as both a parody of Prince's name change and as a mocking reference to software naming conventions.)

Yet despite his reputation as a technical wizard, Rundgren is essentially a humanist and even a bit of a technophobe (which I found out when I shared a smoke with him at a record-release party in 1989).

In addition to an e-mail discussion group, there is a Rundgren UseNet group (*alt.music. todd-rundgren*) and a sophisticated Web site (The TR Connection at *http://www.roadkill.com/todd/trconn*) that features lyrics, photos, video clips, audio clips (forward and *backward* audio!), a bounty of downloadable software, and even the text of a letter that John Lennon wrote Rundgren during a mid-70s tiff. (The home page for The TR Connection is shown in figure 9.24.)

FIGURE 9.24

The home page for the TR Connection, one of the most technologically sophisticated fan sites on the Net.

● ● ● ● ● ● ● ● ● ● ● ● ● ● ● ●

Netscape - [The Todd Rundgren Connection]

File Edit View Go Bookmarks Options Directory   Help

Location: http://www.roadkill.com/todd/trconn

From SacRAmento, California (via Champaign, Illinois), the only US State Capital West of the Mississippi with a Utopia album title in its name...

... the original TR/Utopia WWW info page formerly known as the TR Connection. It is constantly under revision, but should be functional. I especially want to know if things don't work as advertised. Please contact me at roger@rocemabra.antelope.ca.us with any comments.

Watch this space for the latest information!

Music Gear Marketplace

http://indyunix.iupui.edu/~badrian/list.html

This service actually delivers what it promises—a good selection of ads for guitars, drums, basses, and amps, all of which are free to the advertisers and posted for one month. (See figure 9.25.) 👈

FIGURE 9.25

The Music Gear Marketplace, featuring a picture of a beautiful old Fender with which you could become a rock star.

● ● ● ● ● ● ● ● ● ● ● ● ● ● ● ●

Netscape - [USED GEAR!!!]

File Edit View Go Bookmarks Options Directory   Help

The Big Used Gear List

Well, I've decided tackle this great undertaking. If you have anything that you wish to sell or buy, send mail to bpadrian@indyunix.iupui.edu. Ads are free, (but no businesses) and they stay up for a month (unless the item is sold earlier).

Give vital stats and a *brief* description (I don't want to type forever:))

Document: Done

Music Exchange
http://www.scsn.net/~musex

This is another free-classified service, offering both buy and sell ads, including musical instruments and recorded collectibles. This ambitious site is organized by geographic region, or you can access all the ads worldwide.

Guitar Tablature

Once you have your instrument, you've got to learn to play it (if only just barely). That's where guitar chord charts or *tablature* comes in handy. There are a growing number of FTP suites that post the tablature to hit songs and old standards, so you can learn from the experts (i.e., people who are more talented than you).

The Online Guitar Archive (OLGA)
ftp.nevada.edu/pub/guitar

The Online Guitar Archive at the University of Nevada is a real monster. It has the tablature to what seems like thousands of rock tunes, along with the lyrics. It is alphabetized by performer/writer.

Figure 9.26 illustrates the chord structure for a swell ditty called "Kiss Me on the Bus" by the Replacements.

FIGURE 9.26

The guitar tablature for the Replacements' "Kiss Me on the Bus" might convince you that you could write a pop song just as good, but you'd be wrong.

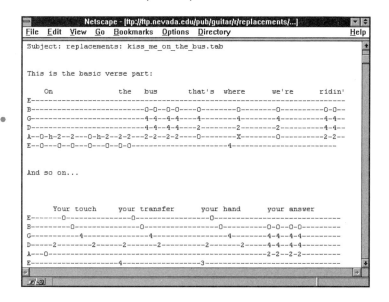

There is also an equivalent site for bass players at *ftp.nevada.edu/pub/bass.*

alt.guitar.tab

This UseNet group features guitar tabs to a wide variety of songs and is a good place to request information on songs that you aren't able to find in the OLGA archive or at *rec.musc.makers.guitar.tablature.*

Choosing A Name

Okay, so you've got a guitar, you've learned how to play it, you've recruited a neighborhood bassist and drummer with poofy hairdos, and you've perfected a sneer that would make Billy Idol run screaming. But you're missing one last thing: a band name. That's where the following site comes in handy.

The Band Name Server

http://ugweb.cs.ualberta.ca/~aaron/band_names.html

A Canadian college kid named Aaron Humphrey has collected over 3,000 possible band names, either from his own fevered imagination or from fellow Web surfers (who are welcome to contribute to the list). Wanna-be rockers can press a button on the home page and receive a name from the list at random.

I've taken the trouble of pressing the button for you. Your new band's name is shown in figure 9.27.

If you don't like the name that was selected for you, you can rack your brain for another one. Just don't try using Pineapple 69, Left-Handed Tomorrow, or Righteous Broccoli, because they're all mine.

FIGURE 9.27

A randomly selected band name
from the Band Name Server.
Actually, I think that's a pretty
cool name.

• • • • • • • • • • • • • • • •

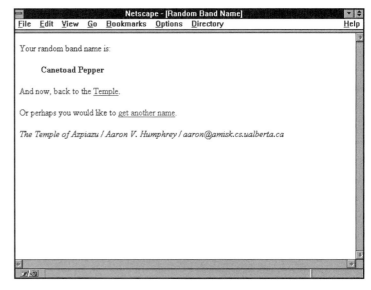

The List

General Resources and Link Sites

Internet Underground Music Archive
http://www.iuma.com

Metaverse/The Vibe
http://metaverse.com

Rocktropolis
http://underground.net/Rocktropolis

MTV
http://www.mtv.com

SonicNet
http://www.sonicnet.com

An ambitious music site and chat forum based in New York. It features
"The Loser's Guide to N.Y.C" as well as online discussion with alternative
luminaries like Laurie Andreson.

Music Kitchen
http://www.nando.net/music/gm

Online Magazines

Addicted to Noise

http://www.addict.com/ATN

Strobe

http://www.iuma.com/strobe

Dreampop

http://www.itp.tsoa.nyu.edu/~student/brendonm/dream1.html

Cash Box

http://online.music-city.com/CASHBOX.HTML

Factsheet Five

FTP address: etext.archive.umich.edu/pub/Factsheet.Five

The premiere resource for information about fanzines and other fringe publications.

Intrrr Nrrrd

http://www.etext.org/Zines/Intrrr.Nrrrd/text.html

A hip, flip e-zine for the post-grunge generation. Recommended.

Buzznet

http://www.hooked.net/buzznet/index.html

This is a punchy, counter-cultural entertainment e-zine with a mostly alt music section.

TOTAL: Substance

http://www.totalny.com

This stylish, New York-based entertainment and culture mag features mainstream and alternative record news and reviews.

Spontaneous Combustion

http://www.interaccess.com/scol

The online version of a long-standing fanzine that is punk rock wthout apologies.

Record Reviews

All-Music Guide
http://cdnow.com

Quick Fix Music Reviews
http://www-leland.stanford.edu/~witness/qfmrl/qfmrl.html

Shopping 2000
http://shopping2000.com/shopping2000/1musrev.html

Record Collectors Web
http://www.onramp.net/RecordWeb/record.html

Hype! Reviews
http://www.hype.com/music/rock/rock.htm

Strictly mainstream and corporate hard-rock reviews

Mike Wasson's Record Reviews
http://www.io.com/~wasson/records.html

Reviews of mostly obscure and noisy bands from around the world, including a lot of experimental Japanese music.

Al's Review Archive
http://www.access.digex.net/~awrc/review

Mostly synth-pop and industrial music reviews from an inveterate scribbler.

Real Cool Rain
http://www.primenet.com/~tripmon

Give this one a try.

Rock History

The History of Rock n Roll
http://www.hollywood.com/rocknroll/index.html

The Rock and Roll Hall of Fame
http://www.rocknroll.org

The Death of Rock & Roll

http://weber.u.washington.edu/~jlks/pike/DeathRR.html

Legends of Rock

The Elvis Home Page

http://sunsite.unc.edu/elvis/elvishom.html

The Beatles Information Page

http://www.cs.rochester.edu/users/grads/jonas/beatlesbeatles.html

Mike Markowski's Beatles Page

http://www.eecis.udel.edu/~markowsk/beatles

Completely Stoned

http://www.leo.org/~tromsdor/stones.html

The Voodoo Lounge

http://www.stones.com/

The Monkees Home page

http://www.primenet.com/~flex/monkees.html

The Jimi Hendrix Server

http://www.parks.tas.gov.au/jimi/jimi.html

Electric Ladyland

http://www.univ-pau.fr/~minfo002/Jimi

For the record, there's never been a better rock & roll band than The Who. (And yes, I *am* the person who decides these things.)

The Hypertext Who

http://www-scf.usc.edu/~wbiggs/who.html

The Lifehouse

http://www.interport.net/~scottj/who/Lifehouse.html

The Grateful Dead Page

http://www.cs.cmu.edu/afs/cs.cmu.edu/user/mleone/web/dead.html

FTP address: gdead.berkeley.edu/pub/gdead
The big FTP archive of all things Deadly

Suzy Shaw's Bruce Page
http://e-street.eastlib.ufl.edu/bruce.html

Cecil's Springsteen Page
http://www.stpt.usf.edu/~greek/bruce.html

The Spinal Tap Home Page
http://rhino.harvard.edu/elwin/SpinalTap/home.html

Selected Artist Mailing Lists

Mailing lists are discussion groups for which interested parties subscribe, usually by sending a brief e-mail message to the group administrator or to an automated LISTSERV facility. Often there is a specific message that must be included in the body of the subscription request, as specified herein. You will then receive the postings of the other list members, either as soon as they are posted or in a periodic digest of collected messages. (Mailing list procedures are discussed in more detail in Chapter 17, "Getting Connected.")

Mailing lists are available for the following rock and alternative-music performers. (These are the performers who the author of this book happens to like or whose importance and popularity cannot be denied. There are hundreds more—and there are thousands of mailing lists on other subjects as well. For a full list, try the directory at *http://www.neosoft.com/internet/paml*.) The following list includes the performer's name, the cutesy name of the group (in parentheses, if any), the address of the group, and the required subscription message, if any. (Where a group asks you to specify "email address" or "yourname," that means *your* e-mail address and *your* name. Got it?)

10CC

capnbizr@interaccess.com

Message Body: **subscribe Minestrone** *email-address yourname*

The list discusses the artsy British pop band 10cc, who gave the world "I'm Not In Love" and never have to do another thing to gain a place of honor in this book.

10,000 MANIACS

majordomo@egr.uri.edu

Message Body: **subscribe 10k_maniacs** *your_email_address*

AEROSMITH

aerosmith-fans-request@dartmouth.edu

Message Body: **subscribe aerosmith-fans**

TORI AMOS (really-deep-thoughts)

really-deep-thoughts-request@gradient.cis.upenn.edu

The list is available in a 24-hour digest format only. The purpose of the list is to discuss and disseminate information on Tori Amos and her scary music.

THE BEACH BOYS

smile-approval@smile.sbi.com

BEASTIE BOYS

majordomo@world.std.com

Message Body: **subscribe beastielist**

BEE GEES

listproc@cc.umanitoba.ca

Message Body: **subscribe Bee-Gees** *yourname*

A worldwide forum for the exchange of discussion and information concerning the music of Barry, Robin, and Maurice Gibb and their heavy-metal funk band the Bee Gees.

BLONDIE/DEBORAHHARRY

lab@indirect.com

BLUES TRAVELER

blues-traveler-request@cs.umd.edu

BON JOVI (The Jersey Syndicate)

BJLISTSUB@aol.com

Discussion list for the timeless and heavily symbolic music of Bon Jovi. Currently available as a daily digest. (Fun fact: Jon Bon Jovi and I were married by the same minister in Las Vegas, the Rev. George Cotton. I don't know about Jon's wedding, but my pal and I weren't completely serious about ours. Hello, Ashley.)

BILLY BRAGG

majordomo@fish.com

Message Body: **subscribe billy-bragg**

For the discussion of all things billy.

THE BYRDS

richruss@gate.net

Subject: **Subscribe**

CAMPER VAN BEETHOVEN (Campervan-Etc)

majordomo@list.stanford.edu

Message Body: **subscribe campervan-etc**

THE CARPENTERS

schmidt_r@swosu.edu

Subject: **subscribe**

Message Body: **subscribe Newville Ave** (and include a short personal bio)

A new list for fans of The Carpenters, the most underrated band in the history of pop music. Anyone who could listen to the guitar solo in "Goodbye to Love" and not swoon in delirium ought to be shot.

NICK CAVE (goodson)

goodson-request@geog.leeds.ac.uk

BRUCE COCKBURN (humans)

majordomo@fish.com

Message Body: **subscribe humans**

Bruce Cockburn is a Canadian singer-songwriter who's trying to make the world a better place.

THE CONNELLS (Boylan Heights)

jipson_art@msmail.muohio.edu

For discussion of the fine North Carolina pop band The Connells. This is a digest.

ELVIS COSTELLO

majordomo@rain.org

Message Body: **subscribe costello-l**

The greatest songwriter of the last 20 years.

COUNTING CROWS

counting-crows-request@ariel.com

THE CRANBERRIES

majordomo@ocf.berkeley.edu

Message Body: **subscribe cranberry-saw-us** *your-email-address*

CROWDED HOUSE

listproc@listproc.wsu.edu

Message Body: **subscribe ch-digest** *yourname*

THE CURE (Babble)

babble-request@anthrax.ecst.csuchico.edu

DEEE-LITE

Majordomo@world.std.com

Message Body: **subscribe deee-lite**

THE DENTISTS

mail@dentists.demon.co.uk

DEPECHE MODE (bong)

bong-request@fletch.earthlink.net

Message Body: **subscribe bong** or **subscribe bong-digest**

This group is for the discussion of the mostly-electronic band Depeche Mode and related projects such as Recoil. Depeche Mode incorporate synth-pop, industrial dance, Kraftwerkian electro, ambient, techno, and rock influences into a dark blend. Somebody must really like this stuff, because they play in football stadiums.

BOB DYLAN (HWY61-L)

LISTSERV@UBVM.CC.BUFFALO.EDU

Subject: **Subscribe**

Message Body: **SUBSCRIBE HWY61-L** *yourname*

ECHO & THE BUNNYMEN

seven-seas-request@dfw.net

Message Body: **subscribe seven-seas**

BRIAN ENO

Eno-L-Request@noc.pue.udlap.mx

ERIC'S TRIP

majordomo@winston.interlog.com

Message Body: **subscribe ET_etc** *your-email-address*

Discussion of Canadian Independent music and the band Eric's Trip.

MELISSA ETHERIDGE

Etheridge-request@cnd.mcgill.ca

This list is available in bounce, digest, and moderated info-only formats. Please specify which format you wish to receive when you ask to sub-scribe. Also specify your full name. (It need not be publicly available, though.

FAITH NO MORE/MR. BUNGLE (Caca Volante)

majordomo@tower.techwood.org

Message Body: **subscribe cv**

Digest Message Body: **subscribe cv-digest**

My band Pineapple 69 blew these guys away at the Blue Note in Colum-bia, Mo, in 1987, and they haven't been the same since.

DAN FOGELBERG

ai411@yfn.ysu.edu

The list is an electronic discussion of Dan Fogelberg and his music. Come on, admit it—you like some of his stuff.

PETER GABRIEL

majordomo@ccsdec1.ufsia.ac.be

Message Body: **subscribe gabriel email_address end**

GRATEFUL DEAD (High Volume)

Dead-Flames-Request@gdead.berkeley.edu

Message Body: **subscribe dead-flames**

The mail volume is high on this list. For a more concise and informative-oriented list, see GRATEFUL DEAD (Low Volume).

GRATEFUL DEAD (Low Volume)

Dead-Heads-Request@gdead.berkeley.edu

This list provides a lower mail volume ratio and more informative information. For more in-depth discussion, see GRATEFUL DEAD (High Volume).

JIMI HENDRIX

hey-joe-request@ms.uky.edu

JOHN HIATT (Shot of Rhythm)

shot-of-rhythm-request@chinacat.unicom.com

ROBYN HITCHCOCK/SOFT BOYS (Fegmaniax)

fegmaniax-request@nsmx.rutgers.edu

INDIGO GIRLS

listserv@geko.com.au

Message Body: **subscribe indigo-girls** *yourname*

JOE JACKSON

majordomo@primenet.com

Message Body: **subscribe joe-jackson end**

MICHAEL JACKSON

Thriller-request@umich.edu

Subject: **subscribe**

The unofficial Michael Jackson Internet Fan Club. No age restrictions.

JANE'S ADDICTION

janes-addiction-request@ms.uky.edu

This list is for discussing anything related to the defunct band Jane's Addiction and the former members' current projects (Porno for Pyros, Deconstruction, and yes, even the Red Hot Chili Peppers).

The JESUS & MARY CHAIN

majordomo@macel.st.hmc.edu

Message Body: **subscribe jamc**

k.d.LANG

majordomo@world.std.com

Message Body: **subscribe k-d-lang**

PAUL KELLY (oph)

majordomo@fox-in.socs.uts.edu.au

Message Body: **SUBSCRIBE OPH**

OPH is a list for discussion of the cool Australian singer/songwriter Paul Kelly and related topics.

THE KINKS

otten@quark.umd.edu

Subject: **SUBSCRIBE**

Discussion about the criminally underappreciated Kinks and related subjects.

KRAFTWERK

kraftwerk-request@cs.uwp.edu

A forum for discussions about the German band Kraftwerk and other related German electronic artists. The discussions are not moderated. The list is available as a daily digest and reflector.

CYNDI LAUPER (she bop)

shebop-request@law.emory.edu

Cyndi Lauper deserves to sell more records than Madonna.

LED ZEPPELIN (Digital Grafitti)

listserv@cornell.edu

Message Body: **subscribe zeppelin-l yourname**

How many parties have been ruined by a Led Zeppelin album played at full volume? It boggles the mind.

LEMONHEADS (Hate Your Friends)

hyf-request@acca.nmsu.edu

Message Body: **subscribe** *your_email_address*

The Lemonheads are cool.

LIGHTHOUSE (Beacon)

lighthouse@qmusic.com

The mailing list provides information about the latest goings-on of the Canadian band "Lighthouse," who were popular in the late 60's and early 70's and will be rewarded in heaven for their song "Pretty Lady."

+LIVE+ (Straight Outta York)

live-request@mediafive.yyz.com

The official Live mailing list. Please send your name with your request.

THE LOUD FAMILY

loud-fans-request@primenet.com

Message Body: **subscribe**

This list is for fans of The Loud Family and Scott Miller's previous band, the amazing Game Theory. (If you've ever bought a Game Theory album, you're my friend.)

MADONNA

madonna-request@umich.edu

madonna-digest-request@umich.edu

I really can't stand her music, but I like that she messes with our collective head and that she did a book full of naked pictures.

ROGER McGUINN

richruss@gate.net

Subject: **Subscribe**

MARIA McKEE/LONE JUSTICE (Little Diva)

mckeefan@kbourbeau.Kenmoto1.sai.com

For discussion of Maria McKee, her former band Lone Justice, and related subjects. (If you ask me, mandolin player Marvin Etzioni was the best thing about Lone Justice.)

SARAH McLACHLAN

listserv@yoyo.cc.monash.edu.au

Message Body: **SUB fumbling-towards-ecstasy** *yourname*

JOHN MELLENCAMP (Human Wheels)

da2x+request@andrew.cmu.edu

Dedicated to the patron saint of Indiana, the digest comes out weekly, on Monday nights. Just send a short message to subscribe.

METALLICA (Metallica Digest)

metallica-request@thinkage.on.ca

Processed manually by human; do not expect instant gratification. Only available in digest format. This is not the official fan-club.

MIDNIGHT OIL (Powderworks)

majordomo@cs.colorado.edu

Message Body: **subscribe powderworks**

Discussion of the music, politics, and hairstyles of Midnight Oil.

THE MOODY BLUES

lost-chords-request@mit.edu

Here's my Moody Blues story: In 1991, I met a fellow at Ye Coach & Horses bar in Hollywood who claimed to be John Lodge of the Moody Blues. Even though he looked nothing like John Lodge and had a teenage runaway girlfriend and a bad jailhouse tattoo on his arm, I believed him because of his accent. My friend Matt and I bought him several drinks. After we'd become such great friends, he asked for our address, so he could send us a copy of his new album and put us on the guest list for the next big Moody Blues concert. When I got home, I looked at a picture of John Lodge on an album cover and realized I'd been scammed. If my roommates hadn't been home that evening, I could have been burglarized by one of John's accomplices when he relayed the address of our presumably empty house. Let that be a lesson to everyone: Never give your address to anybody claiming to be a member of the Moody Blues.

MY BLOODY VALENTINE

majordomo@sunshine.io.com

Message Body: **subscribe mbv**

This band *shreds*.

NEW ORDER (ceremony)

ceremony-request@niagara.edu

The place to be for New Order, Joy Division, and its various offshoots. Group maintains large ftp area with pix, lyrics, discographies, etc.

PEARL JAM (Gardens Of Stone)

listserv@cornell.edu

Somebody's going to have to explain the popularity of this band to me. Eddie's cool and all, but the music is so **bombastic**.

LIZ PHAIR

listproc@phantom.com

SAM PHILLIPS

p9490086@qub.ac.uk

Message Body: **Subscribe SAM**

For discussion of the remarkable singer-songwriter Sam Phillips (ex Leslie Phillips) as well as her husband T-Bone Burnett, and other related artists.

PINK FLOYD (Echoes)

echoes-request@fawnya.tcs.com

For and about things related to Pink Floyd, including present and past members. Religious arguments, e.g. Dave vs. Roger, strongly discouraged.

PJ HARVEY

majordomo@langmuir.eecs.berkeley.edu

Message Body: **subscribe pjharvey**

THE POLICE

majordomo@xmission.com

Message Body: **subscribe police**

Digest Message Body: **subscribe police-digest**

POSIES, THE (Dear 23)

dear23-request@seanet.com

Dear 23, the Posies mailing list, also supports discussion of Big Star, the Minus Five, and all things power pop. The Posies are the greatest American pop band of the last 10 years. Buy their albums, make them rich, and give them complicated lives.

QUEENSRYCHE (Screaming in Digital)

Qryche@ios.com

A hand-edited weekly digest about all things Queensryche, the smarter-than-average metal band.

THE REPLACEMENTS (The //Skyway\\)

lists@phoenix.creighton.edu

Message Body: **subscribe skyway-l**

The list comes out roughly every month in digest format. (I've got plenty of Replacements stories, if you're interested. For instance, there was the concert where I handed my backstage passes to a struggling L.A. band called the Mutts, who considered the Replacements to be several notches above the Beatles in the pantheon of rock gods. They get backstage, pop a couple brews, and are promptly asked to leave because they're behaving "too drunk." Too drunk for the Replacements? You gotta be kidding.)

ROLLING STONES (Undercover)

undercover-request@tempest.cis.voguelph.ca

A daily digest of Stones info, crossposted to *alt.rock-n-roll.stones*.

ROXY MUSIC/BRIAN FERRY (avalon)

avalon-request@dfw.net

Message Body: **subscribe avalon**

TODD RUNDGREN

awizard-request@planning.EBay.Sun.COM

SLADE

slade-request@gnu.ai.mit.edu OR slade-request@a3.xs4all.nl

Message Body: **subscribe slade** *yourname your-email-address*

Slade is the greatest of all the British glamrock bands.

THE SMITHEREENS

Smithereens-request@hookup.net

For discussion of the dreamboat American rock quartet the Smithereens (Pat DiNizio, Dennis Diken, Mike Mesaros, Jim Babjak). Any aspect of the band's music, videos, performance, graphic design, interests, fandom, hairstyles, and wardrobe is fair game, particularly Pat's incredible resemblance to the author of this book.

THE SMITHS/MORRISSEY (Bigmouth)

majordomo@langmuir.EECS.Berkeley.EDU

Message Body: **subscribe bigmouth**

For humorless, misunderstood boys everywhere.

SUBBACULTCHA

listserv@cs.mcgill.ca

Message Body: **subscribe subbacultcha** *your-email-address*

Mailing list for Belly, The Breeders, Frank Black, The Pixies, Throwing Muses, Kristen Hersh.

SUGAR/BOB MOULD/HUSKER DU

majordomo@csua.berkeley.edu

Message Body: **subscribe sugar** *your-email-address*

I saw the last ever Husker Du show, which was in Columbia, Mo, in Dec. 1987. I'd heisted my parents' car for the occasion and driven the hundred miles from St. Louis. On the way home, the engine blew. It was quite an amusing phone call that I had to make at that point.

THE SUNDAYS (Arithmetic)

arithmetic-request@uclink.berkeley.edu

Subject: **SUBSCRIBE**

If you want the digest version, also put **DIGEST ME** in the subject. Arithmetic is the electronic mailing list dedicated to discussion of the British band The Sundays.

MATTHEW SWEET (Inside)

matthew-sweet-request@acca.nmsu.edu

Message Body: **subscribe** *your-email-address*

TALKING HEADS

listproc@ukanaix.cc.ukans.edu

Message Body: **subscribe talking-heads** *yourname*

THEY MIGHT BE GIANTS

they-might-be@super.org OR majordom@super.org

Message Body: **subscribe they-might-be** *your-email-address*

Send a "Help" message for instructions. (John and John stayed at my house on two separate occasions when they were touring the Midwest in the mid '80s. Now they're big stars. God bless you, boys. Don't forget to write.)

TOAD THE WET SPROCKET

listproc@sprocket.silverplatter.com

Message Body: **subscribe Toad** *yourname*

TOO MUCH JOY

tmj-request@emu.con.wesleyan.edu

Too Much Joy is one of the smartest pop bands in the world, and they're my sworn buddies for life. They deserve your money a lot more than White Zombie. If they come to your town, buy them drinks, find them dates, and let them sleep on your couch. Okay?

THE TRAGICALLY HIP

listmanager@hookup.net

Message Body: **subscribe tragically-hip** *yourname*

U2 (Wire)

u2-list-request@ms.uky.edu

Is this the most self-important band on the planet, or just a group of Irish lads who dig the American mythos a little too much?

SUZANNE VEGA (Undertow)

undertow-request@law.emory.edu

TOM WAITS (Rain Dogs)

listserv@ucsd.edu

Discussion of Tom Waits' music and other pursuits (including his new chain of haberdasheries).

PAUL WELLER/STYLE COUNCIL/THE JAM

kosmos-request@mit.edu

I couldn't have gotten through my twenties without Paul Weller and The Jam.

THE WHO

majordomo@cisco.com

Message Body: **subscribe thewho**

I couldn't have gotten through my teens without Pete Townshend and The Who.

WIRE (Wire Service)

lubertdas@delphi.com

Current information on WIR/WIRE and the Colin Newman, Bruce Gilbert, and Graham Lewis solo projects. (If I remember correctly, it was Wire's "Two Girl Rhumba" that was playing on my girlfriend's stereo when I found her entertaining one of her coworkers, Labor Day 1990. No hard feelings.)

XTC (Chalkhills)

chalkhills-request@presto.ig.com

Chalkhills is a mailing list for the discussion of the music and recordings of XTC. Chalkhills is moderated and is distributed in a digest format.

NEIL YOUNG

majordomo@fish.com

Message Body: **SUBSCRIBE RUST**

Resources for Musicians

Music Gear Marketplace
http://indyunix.iupui.edu/~badrian/list.html

Music Exchange
http://www.scsn.net/~musex

The Online Guitar Archive (OLGA)
ftp.nevada.edu/pub/guitar

The Band Name Server
http://ugweb.cs.ualberta.ca/~aaron/band_names.html

R&B, Rap, Blues, and Jazz

IN THIS CHAPTER:

> *General resources for R&B, rap, blues, and jazz*

> *Online magazines and e-zines*

> *Charts, reviews, lyrics, and discographies*

> *History sites*

> *UseNet Groups*

> *Festivals*

IN OTHER CHAPTERS:

< *General music information resources are discussed in Chapter 8.*

< *Rock & Roll is covered in Chapter 9.*

R&B, blues, and jazz are indigenous American art forms.

The origins of the blues and jazz are familiar to almost every American schoolkid: The blues were born in Clarksdale, Mississippi, on July 23, 1921, when a barber named Madison Blue inadvertently dropped a razor on his foot. His customer at that moment was a young composer named Edward "Duke" Ellington, who leapt out of the chair and rushed back to his hotel room with a face full of lather. That afternoon, in a burst of inspiration and manual dexterity, Ellington combined the basic song structure of the blues with the sounds of the glockenspiel, the harpsichord, and the Indian sitar to create what we now call jazz.

But there's more to blues and jazz than just these timeworn (and perhaps debatable) facts—much more.

This chapter will examine Internet resources for modern R&B and rap, traditional jazz, and the root source of almost all popular American music, from rock to rave to disco: the thing called the blues.

R&B

R&B—that's rhythm & blues—is the direct descendent of the field chants, hollers, and Negro spirituals that united the African American community in the darkest days of American history. In the 20th Century, it evolved through the boogie-woogie swing of Louis Jordan; the gospel crooning of Sam Cooke and the Soul Stirrers; the doo-wop sounds of the Penguins and the Moonglows; the acid funk of George Clinton and Parliament; and the mixmaster hip-hop stylings of Grandmaster Flash, Run-DMC, and Public Enemy.

Although the R&B of today is a highly polished and commercial sound that is popular throughout the world, you can still hear the soul of the Old South in the tender love songs of Luther Vandross or the dance beat of Bobby Brown.

General R&B and Hip Hop Resources

General R&B/rap resourceson the Internet are relatively scarce (compared to, say, alternative rock and roll sites), but the numbers are growing as Internet technology becomes more accessible. Some of the best sites are composed of archives, link resources, and record reviews that were put together by the street-level fans—both in the U.S. and around the world.

The R&B Music Page
http://www.ocf.berkeley.edu/~lingo/music.html

This site was created by a student named Lingo Leung at the University of California at Berkeley. "The only reason why I created this page is to keep people updated on the latest happenings in the R&B music industry," he says in his preface to the site, "and because there is no one out there who's doing it."

The R&B Music Page is a good-looking general-interest site with a handful of useful links; some brief record-industry news ("The R&B Rap Sheet"); and up-to-date chart and "what's new" information from Billboard magazine. (See figure 10.1.)

FIGURE 10.1

Tidbits of R&B news, from the R&B Music Page.

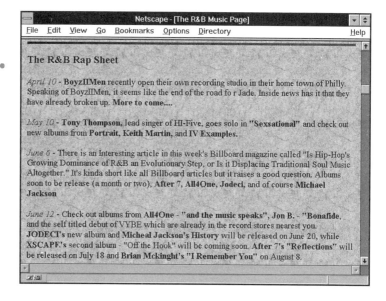

The R&B Page

http://www.dsi.unimi.it/Users/Students/barbieri/home.html

Oddly, one of the best R&B sites on the Internet is administered by a lad named Matteo Barbieri in far-away, sun-drenched Italy. Matt offers the usual chart information, although it is a couple weeks old by the time it gets posted. But what makes this a useful site is the collection of links—to record companies, lyric sites, VIBE magazine, MIDI software resources, an "unofficial rap dictionary," and a George Clinton/P-Funk site. Plus, you can read Matteo's home page—which, unlike the R&B info, is in Italian. ☞

Hip-Hop Links

http://www.cs.tut.fi/~p116711/hiphop.html

This is a comprehensive link source for hip-hop related sites online—and naturally it comes from Finland, the birthplace of rap. Here you will find links to 16 hip-hop and rap magazines online, 71 R&B and hip-hop artists pages, 21 record labels, and numerous home pages with a hip-hop flavor.

Some of the artists whose fan pages can be accessed from this site include Big Daddy Kane, Cypress Hill, Ice Cube, MC 900-Foot Jesus, Sly and the Family Stone, and the Sugar Hill Gang. ☞

Online Magazines and E-Zines

Some of the popular R&B and rap publications that are available at the newsstand have an online version, and there are a number of good Internet-only R&B zines as well.

VIBE Online

http://www.pathfinder.com/@@tSh8*QAAAAAAI*w/vibe/VibeOnline!.html

VIBE is a glossy general-interest R&B/rap monthly from producer Quincy Jones (by way of Time, Inc.). VIBE may be corporate, but it's a pretty decent read, as evidenced by the R&B articles index shown in figure 10.2.

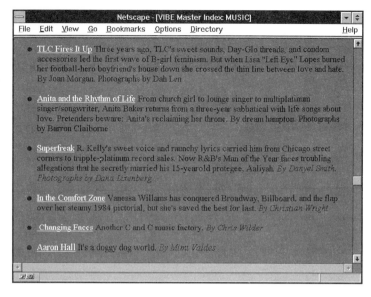

Like the newsstand version, VIBE Online is divided into sections called Urban Life (politics, fashion, culture) and Entertainment (film, sports, music). The magazine operates at the level of journalistic quality and intellectual comprehensiveness you'd expect from Time, Inc.—which is to say, enough to flatter the reader and not enough to alienate the advertisers.

Electronic Urban Report
http://www.trib.com/bbs/eur.html

Here's a good idea: a daily digest of R&B news and reviews, delivered free by e-mail to subscribers around the world. The promo blurb for this service promises the daily dope on Whitney, Janet, Snoop, and all the gang. The Electronic Urban Report is produced by Bailey Broadcasting, which distributes the Radio-Scope R&B news show to radio stations around the country.

The first issue of EUR that I accessed featured a frank review of Michael Jackson's multimillion-dollar tantrum called *HIStory*. Subsequent editions have reported on the hit record that badboy Tupac Shakur released from his jail cell and the death of singer Phyllis Hyman. (See figure 10.3.)

FIGURE 10.3

An excerpt from the Electronic Urban Report, a daily R&B newsletter that is sent to subscribers via e-mail.

● ● ● ● ● ● ● ● ● ● ● ● ● ● ●

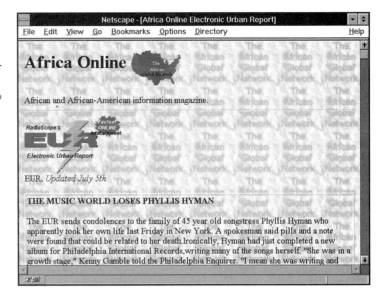

To get EUR, you simply type your e-mail address into a form and submit it electronically. (It may take a week or more to start rolling in, but it will.)

EUR is part of Africa Online, an interesting and much-needed electronic almanac of information for (and about) continental Africans and African-Americans. Africa Online includes news headlines from several African nations, and political and business news of interest to the global black community.

Streetsound Online

http://www.phantom.com/~street

This e-zine covers "techno/rap/house/reggae/dancehall/acid jazz/industrial/bhangra/freestyle/soul/funk/r&b/alternative/latin/hi-nrg/hip hop/jungle/ambient" and probably a few other things as well. It's colorful and has a refreshingly unserious attitude. For instance, its "Handy Guide to Alternative Music" defines the "experimental" genre as "any guy with a foreign name who composes music that's difficult to dance to."

The Source

gopher://gopher.enews.com:70/11/magazines/alphabetic/su/source

The Source is a widely respected hip-hop publication that was started by some smarties from Harvard. Although it's the furthest thing imaginable from ivory-tower stuffiness, it does cover the wider issues of politics and culture that influence hip-hop music. This gopher site features archives of past issues.

4080 Online

http://www.hooked.net/buzznet/4080/index.html

The online digest of *4080* has the uncensored lowdown on such rap renegades as The Alkaholiks, Da Brat, and Closed Caption.

Databases, Lyrics, and Discographies

As of this writing, the best databases for R&B lyric and discography information are contained within the larger general-interest music databases on the Net.

The All-Music Guide at *http://cdnow.com* is a just-plain-awesome resource that lists, rates, and discusses practically every piece of music every recorded in any genre, including R&B. Although it is newly affiliated with the CDNow! music-ordering service (from which the Guide is accessed), the Guide covers both out-of-print and freely available titles.

The Ultimate Band List at *http://american.recordings.com/ WWWoM/ubl/ubl.shtml*, is one of the true gems of the Internet, an ongoing database project that aims to establish links to information on every major recording artist, including FAQs, Web pages, lyrics, and sound clips. Although it is dominated by rock and alternative band listings, this site's R&B linkages are extensive (albeit loosely defined—*Debbie Harry* under R&B?).

The Song Lyric Server at *http://vivarin.pc.cc.cmu.edu/ lyrics.html* has lyrics to thousands of songs in several genres.

VIBE magazine provides the computer space for the Mammoth Music Meta List at *http://www.pathfinder.com/ @@9uAoxwAAAAAAQNXr/vibe/mmm/music.html*. The site has thousands of links, many to artist home pages, in most genres of music. It is also linked to archives of charts, reviews, and lyrics. Ironically, despite its affiliation with VIBE, its R&B holdings are not extensive.

Record-Label Sites

Very few record labels with mass distribution are dedicated exclusively to R&B or rap, but that number may grow as the Internet creates alternative means of marketing music to selected audiences.

The Motown Labels

http://www.musicbase.co.uk/music/motown

You'd think that Motown would have a way-cool site, with a stylish home page and plenty of audio and video clips to re-create the sheer joy of the music that rocked the '60s and the sheer genius of the most successful black-owned business in world history.

Nope.

Motown hasn't been Motown for quite some time now. It was bought by a multinational corporation and splintered into Motown proper (home of Boyz II Men), MoJazz, Motown Classics (a ceaseless spigot of cut-rate anthologies), and a rap label called Mad Sounds (home of some "scary" hip-hop hoodlums called the Rottin Razcals).

The Motown home site (see figure 10.4) is a visually unimaginative, multimedia-deprived waste of bandwidth. And it's operated out of England!

FIGURE 10.4

The Motown home page.

Grand Royal

http://www.nando.net/music/gm/GrandRoyal/index2.html

This is the eye-popping, state-of-the-art Web site for the label whose roster includes wiseguy rappers The Beastie Boys, funky femmes Luscious Jackson, and helium rockers Ween. It is also where you will find the Beastie's hilarious Tour Zine.

Tommy Boy

http://www.cldc.howard.edu/~aja/tommyboy

This is a small, unofficial archive of sounds, photos, and publicity information about Tommy Boy Records, the label that brought you Naughty By Nature, Coolio, and Queen Latifah.

UseNet Newsgroups

As with other forms of music, R&B and rap are well-represented on UseNet. These newsgroup are the best place on the Internet to discuss R&B and rap, both past and present, with knowledgeable peers.

alt. rap

The activity at this busy newsgroup can get downright ferocious. Racism and police brutality are not off-limits topics; the surprise is the amount of pro-and-con that such topics can generate. If you're going to post here, it helps to do it in the obligatory rap dialect, where almost every word is misspelled, to show that U R "down" wit da hood. (Word to my houseboy! I have the correct time!)

rec.music.funky

While this newsgroup sometimes serves as an all-purpose site for R&B information and discussion, it is a particularly fat place for fans of the booty-swingin' 'sounds of the '70s, such as the music of James Brown, Isaac Hayes, and Parliament/Funkadelic. (See figure 10.5.)

FIGURE 10.5

Denizens of rec.music.funky get down and dirty.

● ● ● ● ● ● ● ● ● ● ● ● ● ● ● ●

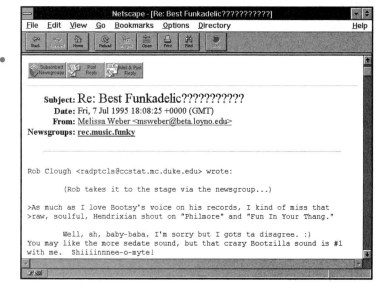

CLOSE-UP: THE ARTIST FORMERLY KNOWN AS PRINCE

If there's anyone in R&B today that understands the history of the music while propelling it joyfully towards its cyber future, it's my main man T.A.F.K.A.P.

Prince (I'm the only person alive who's allowed to call him that) is the quintessence of modern R&B. He's a rocker, a rapper, a funkmaster supreme, a love machine, a dancing dream, a superstar on the movie screen. (Okay, he's not a superstar on the movie screen, but remember, he does have an Oscar—for the soundtrack to *Purple Rain*—which is more than most people can say.)

He may have borrowed a lot of ideas from Sly Stone when he first started out, but by adding a dash of androgyny and temperamental genius to the standard funk vocabulary, he created a persona that was equal parts black/white, straight/gay, and visionary/ridiculous—and was able to sell about a billion records to every hot-blooded, misunderstood so-and-so on the planet.

In addition to producing records (and sometimes not releasing them) T.A.F.K.A.P. has collaborated on a ballet with the Joffrey and released an interactive CD-ROM.

The marketplace may have cooled to his music in the last few years, but Formerly still maintains a fanatical following. There are no less than eight Web sites devoted to Purple Boy, and several of them are very good. He's even got his own smilie/glyph: O(+>.

Steve Hammer, a writer for the Indianapolis newsweekly *Nuvo*, maintains a great-looking Prince page at *http://www.inetdirect.net/hammer/prince.html* that is full of bootleg info, obscure lyrics, and information about other sites. (I'm happy to give Mr. Hammer a plug, even though his newspaper discarded the article I sent it about my former life as a homeless rock critic and pocketed my S.A.S.E postage—twice.)

The most weird Prince stuff per square inch is at Norbert Marrale's Paisley Pages at *http://www.cyberspace.org/u/nmarrale/www/tafkap.html*. It includes a random quote generator, essays on Prince's place in the predictions of Nostradamus, and theories as to why he changed his name.

(continues)

The big-daddy of Prince-info sites is called Prince's New Power Network at *http://130.161.8:80/npn.* Unfortunately, it's in Holland and it takes us while for us Yanks to access it.

There is also a heavily traveled Prince UseNet group at *alt.music.prince*, where participants discuss such things as backwards messages in his songs.

Figure 10.6 is an image from a Prince portrait gallery at *ftp://morra.et.tudelft.nl/pub/prince/jpg/portraits.*

FIGURE 10.6
The Artist Formerly Known as Prince holding a bunch of "things," formerly known as flowers.

alt.music.soul

This is home base for discussion of the loosely defined genre called soul music, a term that embraces such greats of yesterday as Aretha Franklin and Otis Redding, as well as such contemporary artists as Terence Trent D'Arby and Barrence Whitfield.

rec.music a-cappella

This good-natured site is the Internet hangout for the plaid people —and anyone else who enjoys the keen sounds of collegiate *a cappella* and streetcorner doo-wop music. (Also see *http://www.princeton.edu/~grweiss/acappella.html* for a list of *a cappella*, barbershop, and doo-wop links. I'm telling you, this stuff is more "with it" than you kids seem to realize.)

UseNet is also a good place to find information on some of R&B's cousins: reggae, ska, world-beat, and Caribbean music. Try *alt.music.ska*, *rec.music.reggae*, or *rec.music.afro-latin*.

Jazz

On the Internet, archivists and academics are keeping the rich history of jazz alive, and fans of both contemporary and traditional jazz are spreading the word through comprehensive and innovative Web sites.

General Jazz Resources and Link Sites

The term "jazz" encompasses everything from the great Louis Armstrong to the abysmal Kenny G. It is Fats Waller and Chick Corea, Billie Holliday, and Benny Goodman. It is Dixieland, bebop, free jazz, and boogie woogie. You can even hear the influence of jazz in the Broadway pop of Cole Porter and the western swing of Bob Wills and His Texas Playboys.

The best of the general jazz resources on the Internet pay homage to this diversity. Jazz, like rock & roll, has transcended its origins to become an international medium. (Indeed, some of the best jazz in the world comes from Japan.) Therefore, the best jazz sites have both a sense of history and a far-flung collection of pointers to other sites.

JazzWeb Information Server

http://www.nwu.edu/WNUR/jazzbase

WNUR-FM (89.3) is Northwestern University's campus radio station. It is also the home of the JazzWeb Information Server, arguably the best of the jazz servers on the Internet.

JazzWeb offers album charts, discographies, artist bios, reviews, archives of the newsgroup *rec.music.bluenote*, articles of related interest (such as the influence of jazz on the beat-generation writers), and a spectacular collection of links to commercial and academic jazz sites throughout the world. (See figure 10.7.)

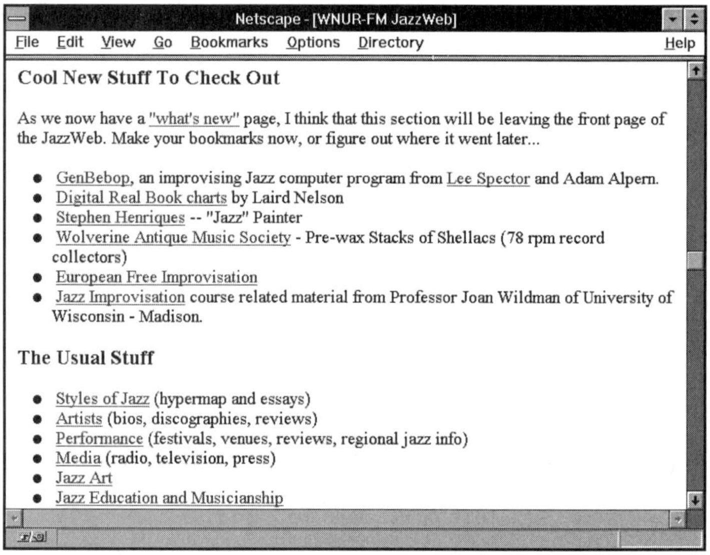

FIGURE 10.7

An excerpt from the Table of Contents for the JazzWeb.

● ● ● ● ● ● ● ● ● ● ● ● ● ● ● ● ●

For those of you who need a little schooling, JazzWeb offers a hypermap called "Styles of Jazz" that shows how, when, and where the different styles of jazz and blues evolved. (See figure 10.8.)

FIGURE 10.8

The knee bone's connected to the shin bone... JazzWeb's "Styles of Jazz" hypermap shows the evolution of the various styles of jazz and blues. Note the conspicuous absence of "barbershop" in this chart.

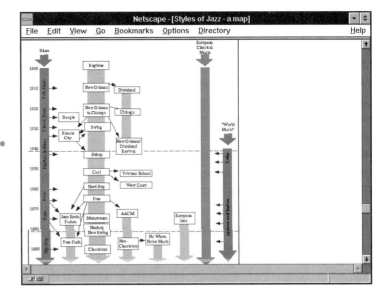

Jazz Online

http://www.jazzonln.com/JAZZ

Although it appears unfinished, JAZZ Online is a good general resource for contemporary jazz information, including record reviews, jazz festival info, feature stories, label notes, and more. See figure 10.9.

FIGURE 10.9

A list of resources from the JAZZ Online server.

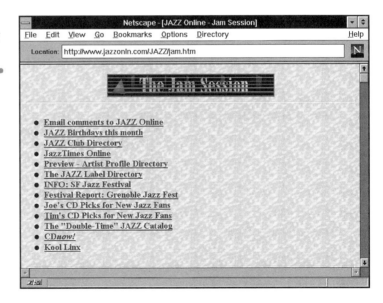

JAZZNet

http://www.dnai.com/~lmcohen

JazzNet offers an array of San Francisco Bay-area club information as well as links to commercial entities that deal in the extended jazz marketplace, including Da Capo Press, the Blue Note and Verve records labels, radio-station KJAZ, and *Jazz In Flight* magazine. (See figure 10.10.)

FIGURE 10.10

Two recent editions of JazzNow Interactive Magazine, which calls JazzNet home.

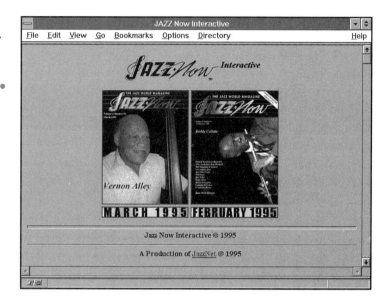

JazzNet also offers a jumping-off-point to numerous other Internet jazz and blues pages.

UseNet

The UseNet *rec.music* newsgroups are the best source of general music information across the board, and this holds true in the *rec.music.bluenote* hierarchy, as well. (There is inevitably a lot of crossover between jazz and blues discussions, and the *rec.music.bluenote* hierarchy embraces both.) The best sources of blues and jazz discussion and general information on the Net can be found in the following newsgroups:

rec.music.bluenote

The granddaddy of the bluenote newsgroups, *rec.music.bluenote* is an unmoderated newsgroup that was formed in late 1987 to provide a forum for discussion of both jazz and blues music—past, present, and future. (Yes, that includes alien space jazz.)

Over time, however, the primary focus of this group began to shift—with a predominant bent toward jazz. As a result, in late 1994, those readers interested primarily in blues split off into another newsgroup, known as *rec.music.bluenote.blues*. There's still plenty of overlap and cross-posting that goes on here, though. The two artforms are so intricately woven together that it's sometimes hard to figure out where one ends and the other begins. (See figure 10.11.)

FIGURE 10.11
This is the type of freeflowing rhetoric you will sometimes find in the rec.music.bluenote hierarchy.

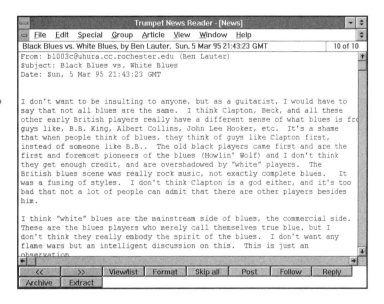

History and Archives

The history of jazz is best told in the music; however, the following sites demonstrate that jazz has had a distinctive *visual* style as well.

The Jazz Photography of Ray Avery

http://bookweb.cwis.uci.edu:8042/Jazz/JPRA1.html

Photographer Ray Avery was the unofficial archivist of West Coast jazz in its 1950s heyday (when Chet Baker was still beautiful and when Jack Kerouac and Neal Cassady were smoking tea and listening to Coltrane records for hours at a stretch). This Web page, sponsored by Jazz on the Web, focuses on a recent exhibition of his work at the University of California at Irvine. The photos are nicely complemented by a history of jazz, which traces the growing popularity of so-called cool jazz, bebop, and hard bop through magazine articles of the era and dozens of sound files. The following three figures are representative of Avery's work.

FIGURE 10.12

The original Lighthouse Cafe in Hermosa Beach. It's still there today (unlike almost everything else in the L.A. area that was hep in the '40s and '50s). Photo by Ray Avery.

FIGURE 10.13

Billie Holiday, 1955. Photo by Ray Avery.

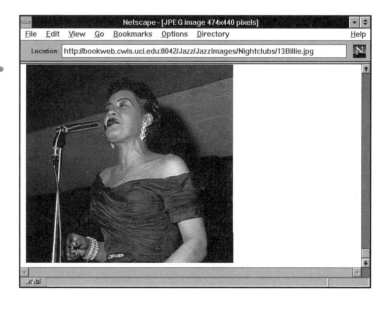

FIGURE 10.14

Chet Baker, Miles Davis, and Rolf Ericson, 1953. Photo by Ray Avery.

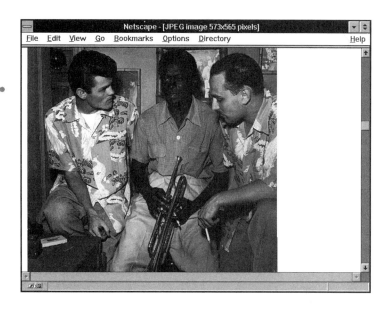

CLOSE UP: RAY AVERY, A MASTER OF JAZZ PHOTOGRAPHY

The undisputed master of jazz photography traces his interest in photography back to 1945, when his father gave him an Argus C3 camera as a going-away gift when he joined the Army.

Late in the '40s, Ray turned his attention to the jazz he loved so well and opened his first record shop, Ray Avery's Rare Records, which soon became a haven for the serious collector.

The retail record business gave Ray the opportunity he'd never had before to pursue his interest in jazz photography, and before long, friendships developed that led to the photo opportunities he documented so well.

Ray traces his first jazz photos to the early 1950s. Since that time, his photos have appeared on the covers of over 100 vinyl albums and 50 CDs.

All of the photographs in the current exhibition are available for purchase as signed fine prints. For information, contact:

Ray Avery's Jazz Archives
1800 North Beverly Glen Blvd.
Los Angeles, California 90077

The NJIT Blues/Jazz FTP Archive

ftp://ftp/njit.edu/pub

The New Jersey Institute of Technology is home to a fabulous FTP archive that is stuffed full of images of blues and jazz singers. These images are stored in various formats, including .gif, and have all been released into the public domain. If you crave a picture of Howlin' Wolf, Thelonious Monk, or Fats Domino, this archive is a swell place to visit.

A great image archive of jazz album covers can be found at *http://bookweb.cwis.uci.edu:8042/Jazz/JPRA5.html*.

Festival Information

If you're a workin' Joe with responsibilities or morals that keep you away from the nightclubs, a good way to meet your annual requirement for jazz intake is to attend a festival. There are prestigious jazz festivals in Newport (Rhode Island) and Montreux (Switzerland); but the biggest and best is in the Southern town that claims to be the birthplace of jazz.

The New Orleans Jazz and Heritage Festival

http://www.yatcom.com/neworl/jfest/jfesttop.html

Since its inception in 1970, New Orleans Jazz and Heritage Festival has attracted millions of people from around the world to participate in a 10-day celebration of American roots music. (See figure 10.15.) This annual event brings together scores of artists from the worlds of jazz, R&B, gospel, Cajun, zydeco, and other genres.

Whether or not you can get to the Crescent City to be part of the fun, you can visit Virtual New Orleans on the Web. VNO is the definitive Net location for above-board information about where to stay, what to eat, and what to do when you do get to New Orleans. (Here's a couple free pointers: Head straight for the French Quarter. Ignore everything else in New Orleans. Drink indiscriminately in public. Ask the locals where they keep those cool beads. Visit an after-hours adult-entertainment center. Get arrested. Tell your cellmate that you're a tourist.)

FIGURE 10.15

Vintage New Orleans Jazz Festival posters, from the Virtual New Orleans' Web page.

Celebrity Register

From the JazzWeb site mentioned previously (*http://www.nwu.edu/WNUR/jazzbase*) or the Yahoo directory of jazz artists (*http://www.yahoo.com/entertainment/music/genres/jazz/artists*), you can access bios and discographies for most of the giants of jazz, including the following:

Louis Armstrong	Keith Jarrett
Dave Brubeck	Stan Kenton
Ornette Coleman	Rahsaan Roland Kirk
John Coltrane	Pat Metheny
Miles Davis	Charles Mingus
Duke Ellington	Thelonious Monk
Bill Evans	Charlie Parker
Bela Fleck	James Blood Ulmer
Herbie Hancock	John Zorn

The Blues

There are those who will tell you that all modern music derives from the blues. I've got some reservations about that kind of reductionism (the Beatles probably owe as much to British folk and vaudeville as they do to Blind Lemon Jefferson), but it's impossible to disregard the stylistic and emotional connection between the blues and the R&B, jazz, and rock music of today.

General Resources and Link Sites

Unlike, say, the Net sites that are dedicated to punk and alternative music, the blues sites on the Internet are often created by people who are both chronologically and geographically removed from the source material. There are, for instance, not a lot of blues performers with fan clubs or home pages on the Net (excepting such rock/blues performers as Eric Clapton).

There is an "online museum" quality to many of the Net sites that are dedicated to the blues, which demonstrates that the Internet is more than just a glorified TV—it is an invaluable means of preserving our cultural heritage.

The Blue Highway
http://www.magicnet.net/~curtis/page1.html

This elegant Web site is both a comprehensive history of the blues and an invaluable link source for the best blues-related sites on the Net. As a history site, The Blue Highway offers a fascinating (and nearly comprehensive) collection of vignettes, photos, and sound files on the lives and music of such artists as Robert Johnson, Bessie Smith, and Muddy Waters.

The Blue Highway opens, fittingly, with the tale of Robert Johnson and the midnight deal he struck with the Devil at a country crossroads (the deal that gave the blues pioneer the gift of music in exchange for his soul). (See figure 10.16.)

FIGURE 10.16

This figure depicts Robert Johnson (one of only two photographs of him that are known to exist) and tells the story of the midnight deal he made with the Devil.

● ● ● ● ● ● ● ● ● ● ● ● ● ● ● ●

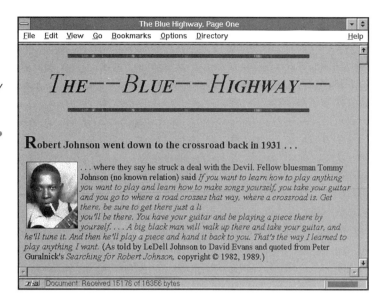

The Blue Highway moves briskly yet thoughtfully through a chronology of the blues while providing pointers to related pages, academic works, and artist bios.

BluesNet

http://dragon.acadiau.ca/~rob/blues/blues.html

BluesNet, "the Internet's Blues Resource Centre," may still be under construction, but it holds plenty of promise. As a repository for freely-distributable information on blues performers, it evolved out of a discussion on the Blues-L mailing list (discussed later in this chapter.) The BluesNet home page is shown in figure 10.17.

There's an ample collection of original material on this site. Biographies of such well-known artists as Sonny Boy Williamson, Little Walter, and Blind Willie Johnson are nicely opinionated and offer perspectives that you aren't likely to find in published blues histories or reference books. One of the most interesting things about BluesNet is its Mentor Program—a system of matching experts on certain artists or categories with folks who have questions that need to be answered.

FIGURE 10.17

*BluesNet offers an array of artist
bios, a picture archive, and
blues-related documents.*

```
┌─────────────────────────────────────────────────────────────┐
│                     BluesNet home page                  ▼ ▲ │
├─────────────────────────────────────────────────────────────┤
│ File   Edit   View   Go   Bookmarks   Options   Directory  Help│
├─────────────────────────────────────────────────────────────┤
│  ┌──────────┐                                                 │
│  │ [guitar] │   BluesNet                                      │
│  │          │   The Internet's                                │
│  └──────────┘   Blues Resource Centre                         │
│                                                               │
│  NOTE - This is under construction. Everything needs work and │
│  there's not a whole lot of data here yet. Comments,          │
│  suggestions and contributions are more than welcome.         │
│                                                               │
│    • Introduction to BluesNet                                 │
│    • BluesNet Artist Summaries                                │
│    • BluesNet Picture Archive                                 │
│    • Mentors                                                  │
│    • Blues-related Documents                                  │
│                                                               │
│  Leave your comments in the Guestbook !                       │
│                                                               │
│  Other Blues-related stuff:                                   │
│                                                               │
│      The Blue Highway                                         │
└─────────────────────────────────────────────────────────────┘
```

Delta Snake Blues News

http://www.portal.com/~mojohand/delta_snake.html

The Delta Snake Blues News is an online blues newsletter that
derives from a San Francisco newsletter that disappeared a
number of years ago. (See figure 10.18.)

FIGURE 10.18

*The main page of the Delta
Snake Blues News, an online
blues newsletter.*

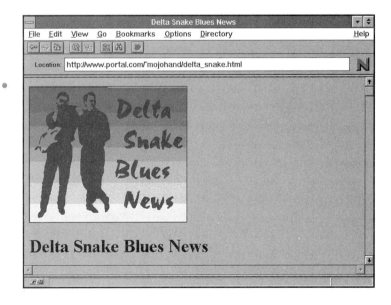

An archive of previous online editions is available for browsing, along with reviews of both new releases and classics in the delta blues genre.

UseNet Groups and Mailing Lists

If you'd like to trade views and information with other fans of the blues, a mailing list or UseNet newsgroup is the place to do it.

rec.music.bluenote.blues

The second of the newsgroups that make up the *rec.music.bluenote* hierarchy, this group split off from *rec.music.bluenote* in late 1994—a reaction to the low ratio of blues-to-jazz discussion in the main group. This unmoderated group is intended as a forum for all aspects of the blues, from the Delta to Chicago, including artists that range from Howlin' Wolf to Ali Farka Toure.

You can also obtain blues FAQs from the following addresses:

* *http://dragon.acadiau.ca/~rob/blues/blues-l.faq.html* (FAQ for Blues-L)

* *ftp://ftp.netcom.com/pub/gi/gilles/rmbb/rmbbfaq.html* (FAQ for *rec.music.bluenote.blues*)

Blues-L Mailing List

LISTSERV@brownvm.brown.edu

The Blues-L mailing list requires interested parties to subscribe to it (in the message body you simply type **SUB Blues-L**, followed by your name), and as a result, there's relatively little of the off-topic noise that tends to pop up in UseNet newsgroups. The quality and reliability of the information you'll find in Blues-L is high.

Related Music Resources

A selection of mailing lists and other Internet resources that aren't strictly geared toward blues and jazz, but which are related.

78-L
LISTSERV: 78-l@cornell.edu

78-L is a discussion group devoted to music and recordings of the pre-LP era. The list is open to lovers of all kinds of music of the era, including early jazz and blues. Discussion of recording history, discography, the collectors market, and other related topics are welcomed.

HarmoniGopher
gopher:// gopher.wku.edu/00gopher%5Froot%3A%5Bharp%5Dwelcome%2Etxt

The HarmoniGopher was established to provide easy access to information about harmonicas to the Internet community.

Festival Information

There are numerous blues festivals from Chicago to Long Beach where you can spend a pleasant afternoon enjoying the transformation of human misery into art.

San Francisco Blues Festival
http://www.dnai.com/~lmcohen/sfest94.html

This two-day festival is held in the late summer at a park overlooking the Golden Gate Bridge and San Francisco Bay. (It makes a terrific date.)

The festival features some of the biggest names in traditional blues. For instance, when I went to the festival in 1988, I witnessed The Edge (from that well-known Irish blues band U2) talking shop with John Lee Hooker over a plate of red beans and rice. (Personally, I recommend the Cajun corn.)

Guiness Temple Bar Blues Festival
http://www.eeng.dcu.ie/~stdcu/blues/

This thoroughly Irish genuflection at the altar of American music seems like a lot of fun and another perfect fit for those wholesome lads from U2—except for the beer-company sponsorship, of course.

The List

R&B General Resources

The R&B Music Page
http://www.ocf.berkeley.edu/~lingo/music.html

The R&B Page
http://www.dsi.unimi.it/Users/Students/barbieri/home.html

Home of Soul
http://mosaic.echonyc.com/%7Espingo/Soul

Hip Hop Links
http://www.cs.tut.fi/~p116711/hiphop.html

Online Magazines and E-Zines

VIBE Online
http://www.pathfinder.com/@@tSh8*QAAAAAAI*w/vibe/VibeOnline!.html

Electronic Urban Report
http://www.trib.com/bbs/eur.html

Streetsound Online
http://www.phantom.com/~street

The Source

gopher://gopher.enews.com:70/11/magazines/alphabetic/su/source

4080 Online

http://www.hooked.net/buzznet/4080/index.html

Record-Label Sites

The Motown Labels

http://www.musicbase.co.uk/music/motown

Grand Royal

http://www.nando.net/music/gm/GrandRoyal/index2.html

Tommy Boy

http://www.cldc.howard.edu/~aja/tommyboy

UseNet Groups

alt.rap

rec.music.funky

rec.music.a-cappella

alt.music.rap

alt.music.soul

Prince

Hammer's Prince Page

http://www.inetdirect.net/hammer/prince.html

Paisley Pages

http://www.cyberspace.org/u/nmarrale/www/tafkap.html

New Power Network

http://130.161.8:80/npn

Prince Portraits

ftp://morra.et.tudelft.nl/pub/prince/jpg/portraits

Jazz

General Jazz Resources and Link Sites

JazzWeb Information Server
http://www.nwu.edu:80/wnur/jazzbase

Jazz Resources on the Net
http://www.acns.nwu.edu/jazz/internet.html

Jazz NET
http://www.dnai.com/~lmcohen

JazzBase
http://www.nwu.edu/jazz/scope.html

Center for the Study of Southern Culture Home Page
http://imp.cssc.olemiss.edu

St. Louis Home Page
http://www.st-louis.mo.us

My home town (and the home town of Miles Davis, Chuck Berry, and Tina Turner) has made a significant contribution to the history of jazz, blues, and R&B.

J. Feinstein's House O' Jazz
http://sccs.swarthmore.edu/~jbf/jazz.html

Jazz and Blues
http://www.timeinc.com/vibe/mmm/music_jazz.html

JAZZ Now Interactive
http://www.dnai.com/~lmcohen/jazznow.html

Other Points of Interest along the Jazz Info-Bahn
http://www.dnai.com/~lmcohen/webidx.html

Original Jazz Charts

http://hokin.physics.wisc.edu/jazz/charts.html

A place for artists to post images of charts of their original tunes. MIDI files and files generated by musical notation software are also welcome.

UseNet Group

rec.music.bluenote

History and Archives

The Jazz Photography of Ray Avery

http://bookweb.cwis.uci.edu:8042/Jazz/JPRA1.html

The NJIT Blues/Jazz FTP Archive

ftp://ftp/njit.edu/pub

Beyond Category: The Musical Genius of Duke Ellington

http://www.magibox.net/~ncrm/duke.html

Festival Information

The New Orleans Jazz and Heritage Festival

http://www.yatcom.com/neworl/jfest/jfesttop.html

Jacksonville Jazz Festival

http://www.gttw.com/jax/events/jazzfest/index.html

Lionel Hampton Jazz Festival

http://www.cs.uidaho.edu/~vern/jazz

Monterey Jazz Festival

http://www.dnai.com/~lmcohen/montery.html

The Blues

General Resources and Link Sites

Blue Highway
http://www.magicnet.net/~curtis/page1.html

BluesNet
http://dragon.acadiau.ca:1677/~rob/blues/blues.html

Delta Snake Blues News
http://www.portal.com/~mojohand/delta_snake.html

Blues-L Shed
http://dragon.acadiau.ca:1667/@rob/blues/shed/shed.html

UseNet Groups and Mailing Lists
http://dragon.acadiau.ca/~rob/blues/blues-l.faq.html
FAQ for Blues-L.

ftp://ftp.netcom.com/pub/gi/gilles/rmbb/rmbbfaq.html
FAQ for *rec.music.bluenote.blues*.

rec.music.bluenote.blues
Also: *ftp://ftp.netcom.com/pub/gi/gilles/rmbb/rmbbfaq.html*.
FAQ for *rec.music.bluenote.blues*.

Blues-L Mailing List
LISTSERV: listserv@brownvm.brown.edu

Related Music Resources

78-L
LISTSERV: 78-l@cornell.edu

HarmoniGopher
gopher:// gopher.wku.edu/
00gopher%5Froot%3A%5Bharp%5Dwelcome%2Etxt

Festival Information

San Francisco Blues Festival
http://www.dnai.com/~lmcohen/sfest94.html

Guiness Temple Bar Blues Festival
http://www.eeng.dcu.ie/~stdcu/blues

For Further Reading (Hepcats Only)

The Influence of Jazz on the Beat Generation
http://www.charm.net/~brooklyn/Topics/JanssenOnJazz.html

CHAPTER 11

Country-Western and Folk Music

IN THIS CHAPTER:

> General resources on country, folk, and contemporary Christian music

> Online magazines

> Artist pages and fan-club information

IN OTHER CHAPTERS:

< General music resource pointers can be found in Chapter 8.

< Popular cross-over artists such as Elvis Presley are spotlighted in Chapter 9, "Rock & Roll."

At present, the country-western and folk-music communities have not embraced the Internet with the same fervor as alternative-music fans, cult-movie buffs, or computer gamers. Maybe it's because the simple folk of the heartland who constitute a large portion of the country and folk audience are suspicious of the technology. (Some of them might argue that the Internet represents a fundamental change in human behavior that is almost Biblical in its implications.) Or maybe it's because country fans actually spend time away from their keyboards, living their lives.

Nonetheless, there are plenty of resources on the Internet for fans of country-western, folk, contemporary Christian, and other indigenous American musical forms—if you know where to look.

Like country music itself, the high ground on the Internet is being seized by the innovators. Although many of the sites are created and maintained by the kind of down-home people who have traditionally given American music its strength and longevity, there is a definite focus on emerging new artists and a redefinition of the musical forms away from the taint of "showbiz."

Country

Country-western music is the sound of rural America— specifically the music of the South and the West. It bears a familial connection to the folk music of the British Isles, the region from which many of the white settlers of the American south were descended. Over time, new instrumentation was added as folk music was married to bluegrass, boogie woogie, blues, and mainstream pop to give us the plaintive hybrid sound we know today as "country." Through it's many mutations, from Western swing to honky-tonk to "Vegas" country, country-western music has maintained a consistent foundation in the honest emotions of a simple, hard-working, and largely disenfranchised people.

General Country-Western Music Resources

Almost all of the country-music resources on the Internet are built and maintained by grass-roots fans.

Wayne's Country Pages

http://galaxy.einet.net/EINet/staff/wayne/country/country.html

Wayne's Country Pages is one of several excellent, fan-administered C&W sites you can find on the Net. This one specializes in news and information about three hunky cowpokes—Alan Jackson, Dwight Yoakam, and Clint Black (see figure 11.1)—and has links to about a dozen other artist sites of the "no bull" variety.

FIGURE 11.1

The cover of Clint Black's Killin' Time album, accessed via Wayne's Country Pages. (It's hard to tell what Clint is doing in this picture. I do know that he is married to actress Lisa Hartman, so maybe that has something to do with it.)

The distinctive thing about Wayne's Country Pages is the larger worldview it invokes: the cowboy experience, from A (armadillos) to Z (zippered blue jeans: pro and con). The "Culture" subpage of the site features links on the following topics:

* American Cowboy Magazine
* Cowboy Poetry
* Cowboy Art
* Cowboy Wisdom
* Western Art
* The Cowboy Trail
* Cowgal's Home On The Web
* Sheplers Western Wear

* The *rec.autos.4x4* UseNet group (dedicated to the modern "horse")

* Western Square Dancing

It also features honky-tonk music reviews by Theresa, "the first cowgirl of cyberspace."

Wayne's site also has a list of the Top 100 Country Songs of All Time (see figure 11.2), and a funny piece called "The Do-It-Yourself C&W Song Kit" (see figure 11.3) 👈

FIGURE 11.2

This is the beginning of what purports to be a list of the Top 100 Country Songs of All Time. I don't know how this list was compiled, but I would like to know what Vince Gill is doing ahead of Patsy Cline and Hank, Sr..

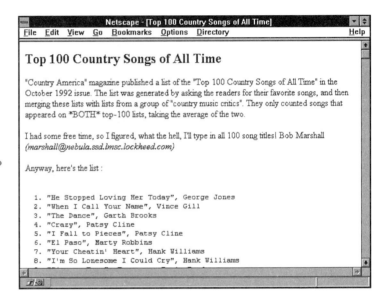

FIGURE 11.3

The "Do-It-Yourself C&W Song Kit" from Wayne's Country Pages.

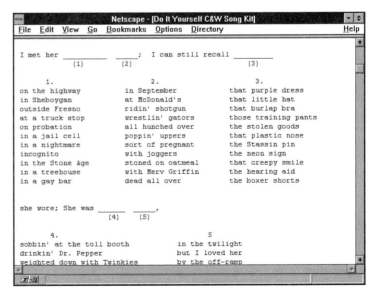

Country Connection

http://metro.turnpike.net/C/country

This site is typical of the country sites you will find on the Net. It is administered by a fan and is heavy with links to other fan-club pages and the few commercial sites that exist.

Country Connection was recently spanked for calling themselves "The Nashville Network," because the cable TV service of the same name was worried that people might confuse them with this homey little country-music site. Apparently Mike Blanche, the guy who runs this site, had a lot more to offer here before the letter came from the attorneys.

Now the site comprises links to 110 artist pages, some of which are pretty sketchy (nothing more than a fan-club address), and some of which have lyrics, photos, and sound clips.

Dawn's Country Fan Pages

http://204.96.208.1/services/staff/dawn/cfans.htm

This one is really sweet, because it's administered by a li'l filly named Dawn Banks in Tampa, Fla., who is just dying to make new friends through the shared love of country music, cowboy culture, and line-dancing.

Dawn includes information about her latest CD purchases and favorite new artists, and she invites the visitors to her site to sign the electronic guestbook so she can trade country news and reviews with her new pals.

Perhaps because of her many connections, Dawn maintains an extensive "What's New in Country?" page. She is an astute collector of links, and even has a link to "Fujita Fusayuki's Country Page from Japan."

The home page for Dawn's Country Fan Pages is shown in figure 11.4.

FIGURE 11.4

The home page for Dawn's
Country Fan Pages. Is that
adorable, or what?

Country fans...By Dawn Banks

Updated on Monday, July 10, 1995 - 8:03:48 PM

Several of my pages are Netscape enhanced, to see my pages at best use Netscape 1.1N.

Country Fans... is featured in the Cyberguide of *Netguide's* July Issue.

Online Country Magazines and E-Zines

The following country-western publications can be accessed
directly through the Internet.

Cash Box Online

http://online.music-city.com/CASHBOX.HTML

As I mentioned in chapter 9, I used to be an editor for the *Cash Box* bureau in Hollywood (where I earned a princely $6.00 an hour), and it was a favorite pastime of the staffers there to speculate on when this venerable old circus would finally fold up the tent.

Fifty years ago, *Cash Box* invented the now-familiar Top 40 music charts and the magazine was popular and influential throughout the era of Elvis and the Beatles. But even in the lean times, the magazine's Nashville operations were relatively profitable and respected, and it is country-western music that gets much of the attention in the online version of *Cash Box*.

As in many industry trade magazines, you have to skim over a lot of self-serving promotional fluff about corporate bigwigs to find anything of more universal interest, but it's here: record reviews, band news, and chart information for both major-label and independent-label performers. The Cash Box home page is shown in figure 11.5.

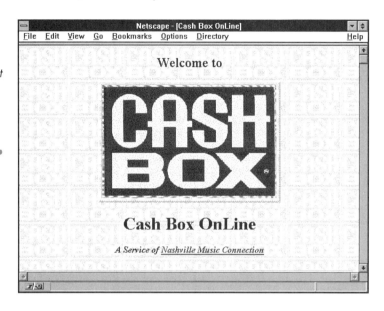

Twangin'!
http://galaxy.einet.net/EINet/staff/wayne/country/twangin1.txt

As Cheryl Cline, the editor or *Twangin'!* stated it in the inaugural online issue of this magazine, "*Twangin'!* is a monthly e-zine about country western music, covering what some people call 'real country,' others 'western beat,' and still others 'alternative country.' I usually call it 'Real country, western beat, alternative country, whatever.' If the names Tim O'Brien, Rosie Flores, Jimmie Dale Gilmore or Shaver mean something to you, then you're in the right place. If you're curious about bands with names like Hank McCoy & the Dead Ringers, Dry Branch Fire Squad, Voodoo Swing, or the Bad Livers, keep an eye on this space. Twangin's focus is country music, but it's a wide focus, since we see American music as more interwoven than the purists in any one camp like to allow. When it comes to musical purity, *Twangin'!* is slutsville. We love country music, but we're unfaithful and ramblin'; we've got roving ears. So *Twangin'!*

strays constantly into the arms of the blues, folk, and rock, and we review, interview, and otherwise promote bands that do the same."

I accessed this fine, committed e-zine through Wayne's Country pages (mentioned previously). The editor's e-mail address is *cline@well.sf.ca.us.* ✍

Nash!
LISTSERV@vm.temple.edu

According to editor Paul Erwin, *Nash!* is a new e-zine "covering American Roots Music and people who make it. Since all forms of American music have impacted each other at some point, *Nash!*'s mission is to cover everything from blues to roots-rock to progressive country to rockabilly. While *Nash!* keeps one foot firmly in the past, it looks to the future where the traditions still live." Issue #1 includes reviews of records by Lyle Lovett and the Hix, and an essay about the self-induced fall of Steve Earle. (To subscribe to *Nash!*, send e-mail to the above address; leave the subject line blank, and type **SUBSCRIBE NASH** as the body of the note.) ✍

Cybergrass (formerly Electronic Bluegrass Magazine)
http://www.info.net/BG/bg_home.html

This comprehensive and well-done e-zine could just as easily have been placed under the "Folk" subheading, but Cybergrass defines bluegrass as "virtuoso country music," and that's okay with me.

The magazine has just about every conceivable resource for the online bluegrass aficionado, including: artist profiles; articles; reviews and editorials; events, festivals, and calendar; clubs and associations; magazines and newsletters; comments; other Net links; files and archives; want-ads; and a library. The Cybergrass home page is shown in figure 11.6. ✍

Databases

There are a few comprehensive music database sites that offer discographies, artist information, and song lyrics for several styles of music, including country-western and folk.

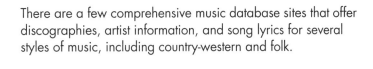

More detailed information on these databases can be found in Chapter 8, "General Music Resources."

NOTE

The All-Music Guide at *http://cdnow.com* is a just-plain-awesome resource that lists, rates, and discusses almost every piece of music every recorded, including country-western and folk music. Although it is newly affiliated with the CDNow! music-ordering service (the address will take you to the CDNow! home page, from which you click into the All Music Guide), the Guide covers both out-of-print and freely available titles. If your Web browser can place bookmarks, this should be one of them.

The Song Lyric Server at *http://vivarin.pc.cc.cmu.edu/ lyrics.html* has lyrics to thousands of songs in several genres.

Vibe magazine's Mammoth Music Meta List at the impossibly long address of *http://www.pathfinder.com/ @@9uAoxwAAAAAAQNXr/vibe/mmm/music.html* has thousands of links, many to artist home pages, in most genres of music. It is also linked to archives of charts, reviews, and lyrics. (Its country holdings are limited or difficult to access, but it is worth consulting, nonetheless.)

History

The history of country music, like the history of the blues, is the story of the rural American underclass. It is a story of ordinary people with extraordinary talents who never got rich from their music and are only now being recognized as pioneers.

The History of Country Music

http://orathost.cfa.ilstu.edu/public/OratClasses/ORAT389.88Seminar/Exhibits/JohnWalker/0home.html

This fine site is an attempt to provide some background and context for a style of music that has not been given sufficient attention by academics and intellectuals.

This general overview is roughly divided by decades and covers the period from the '20s to the '60s. It concentrates on such pioneers as Roy Acuff, Bob Wills, Hank Williams, Jimmie Rodgers, the Carter Family (see figure 11.7), Lefty Firzzell, Patsy Cline, and bluegrass legend Bill Monroe.

The History of Country Music incorporates sound and video clips with straightforward, informative text. ☞

FIGURE 11.7

This section of the History of Country Music discusses the influence of Jimmie Rodgers and the Carter Family in the 1920s and 30s.

● ● ● ● ● ● ● ● ● ● ● ● ● ● ● ●

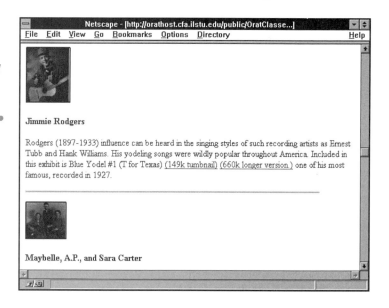

Resources for Country Musicians

There are some good nuts-and-bolts resources on the Internet for aspiring musicians, especially for pickers and pluckers.

COWPIE NEWS

gopher://gopher.ttu.edu:70/11/Pubs/Mailing-Lists/Professional/cowpie

The name of this e-zine stands for Country and Western Pickers of the Internet Electronic Newsletter. According to editor Greg Vaughn, "Its purpose in life is to allow guitar players who enjoy country music (and it's many substyles) to contact one another and swap songs, techniques, and information without wading through all the mixture of musical styles covered in the UseNet groups."

The plain ASCII-text magazine is filled with song lyrics and guitar chords for traditional and modern country songs.

Nashville Online

http://www.nol.com/nol/NOL_Home.html

This slowly evolving service aims to provide a forum for C&W songwriters, song publishers, promoters, recording engineers, and record-company executives to meet and greet. Nashville is a town full of hopefuls and bluffers and small-time back-slappers, so a service such as this fills a definite need (and can probably make a few bucks).

THE BRANSON BEAT

You can say what you want about Nashville and Austin; to me, the true capital of country music is Branson, Mo. In just a few years, this little hilltop burg outside of Springfield has mushroomed from a quaintly tacky lakeside getaway for Midwestern Christian families into the second most-visited tourist destination in America. (Destination Number One is Mouseland, Fla.)

The secret to Branson's success is that many of the biggest (and oldest) names in "Hollywood" country music have established permanent theaters there, corrugated aluminum palaces where they can perform to thousands of similarly aging fans before tottering off to their lakeside villas.

Not even in Vegas could you see Wayne Newton, Glen Campbell, Tony Orlando, Roy Clark, Mel Tillis, Andy Williams, Kenny Rogers, and Anita Bryant on the same stretch of traffic-choked two-lane highway on the same night. In Branson, you can worship at the temple of John Davidson or join the beloved Yakov Smirnoff for an authentic Russian meal before enjoying his cross-cultural comedy at the Osmond Family Theatre. And afterward you can load up on authentic Ozark handicrafts at any one of the more than 37,000 corn-cob-pipe emporiums that line the main road. (You cannot, however, get a stiff drink anywhere within miles of the place.)

Online, you can get the lowdown on Branson's family-oriented dining establishments, resorts, amusement parks, and miniature golf courses by visiting BransonNet at *http://digimark.net/branson/bransonet.html* or BransonWeb at *http://www.woodtech.com/bransonw/muscthtr.html*. (Evidently there are competing Branson information servers. Now that's the Show Me spirit!)

UseNet

If you'd like to discuss the latest trends in country music without risking an invitation to step outside and settle this thing like a man, the UseNet domain is a good place to do it.

rec.music.country.western

This trusty UseNet site is as good a resource as any for general-interest country-western music info and fan discussions. Figure 11.8 illustrates how active this site is and the kinds of general inquiries it handles. Discussion topics on this particular day ranged from "Best Songs About Texas" (my nominee is the version of "Yellow Rose of Texas" by Stan Freberg) to "Dolly's Talent" (about which there are two opinions) to "Why Are There No Black Country Singers?" (a surprisingly rich and theoretical discussion, which is not uncommon here).

FIGURE 11.8

A recent postings list for the newsgroup rec.music.country-western.

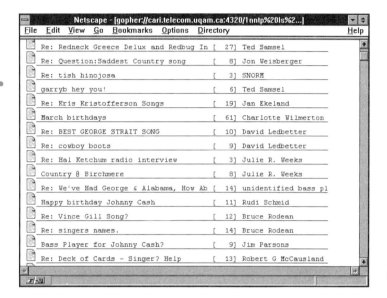

Interestingly, there were no *alt.fan* newsgoups devoted to country-music performers at the time of this writing.

Celebrity Register

The typical fan page for a country artist will feature publicity photos, album covers, discographies, tour information, and the breathless news that this particular artist will never let his or her fame distract her from being a regular guy or gal.

Reba McEntire

http://ruby.ph.utexas.edu/RebaWWW/Reba.html

Country superstar Reba McEntire seems like a genuinely likable gal, and the fan site that is devoted to her oozes the same wholesome, down-home spirit. This site includes:

* Reba's International Fan Club: how to join

* Reba Reviews: reviews of her music, acting, or appearances (moderated)

* Schedule of Appearances: when and where she will be appearing

* Reba's Albums

* List of Reba's Music Videos

* Reba's Special Events: including movies, TV appearances, and other special events

* Reba in Print: where to find recent articles about Reba

* Reba Fans Picture Page: a place for Reba Fans to put those special pictures

See figure 11.9 for a wholesome, likable, computer-reproduced image of Reba from this wholesome and likable site.

FIGURE 11.9

Reba McEntire, from a fan site at http://ruby.ph.utexas.edu/ RebaWWW/Reba.html. How could you not like her?

Other Artist Pages

Scores of country-western musicians, from established (or dead) superstars to hungry newcomers, now have home pages or fan-club sites on the Internet, and most of them can be accessed with a good search tool such as Lycos.

Another easy way to access the sites is through a comprehensive link source. From the Country Connection site (*http://metro.turnpike.net/C/country*) you can access pages for most artists.

Folk Music

The term "folk music" refers generally to song-based acoustic music (which is why Bob Dylan was considered a traitor when he picked up an electric guitar at the Newport Folk Festival way-back-when). For our purposes here, it embraces not just American hoedown music and plaintive ballads about fair maidens, but also the indigenous acoustic music of all nations. Thus, "folk music" includes everyone from Suzanne Vega and James Taylor to Ravi Shankar and The Chieftains.

General Resources

Although one of the best places to look for online information about particular geographic or stylistic subsets of the folk domain is UseNet, the Internet has several good general resources that cover the world of acoustic music in its entirety.

FolkBook
http://www.cgrg.ohio-state.edu/folkbook

FolkBook should be stop #1 for anyone interested in online information about folk, acoustic, and world-beat music—whether as a fan or as a participant.

According to site administrator Steve Spencer's description of the site: "For the fan, there are artist biographies, discographies, pictures, sound bites, lyrics, guitar tablature, tour schedules, and more! For the performing songwriter, we include lists of 'folk friendly' venues, record distributors, radio station/program information, related publications, and festival and concert listings and information organized by date and by region."

You can see how much effort goes into maintaining this site by looking at a recent "What's New" page of site improvements.(See figure 11.10.)

```
┌──────────────────────────────────────────────────────────────┐
│ ─           Netscape - [FolkBook: What's New]          ▼ ▲    │
│ File  Edit  View  Go  Bookmarks  Options  Directory     Help  │
├──────────────────────────────────────────────────────────────┤
│ 22 June 1995                                                   │
│     Added new biographies for Boneheads, Jem Moore and Ariane  │
│     Lydon, and Stan Moeller and T.S. Baker.                    │
│ 07 June 1995                                                   │
│     Reorganization of the Acoustic Music on the Web page into  │
│     four separate pages: Artist & Fan Pages, Folk Venues       │
│     Online, Record Labels & Stores, and Other Online           │
│     Resources.                                                 │
│ 05 June 1995                                                   │
│     Added six sound clips for Catie Curtis.                    │
│ 31 May 1995                                                    │
│     A biography for Dana Mase.                                 │
│ 25 May 1995                                                    │
│     A brand-new Nields home page.                             │
│ 17 May 1995                                                    │
│     A biography for Sandy Ross.                               │
│ 16 May 1995                                                    │
│     Biographies of Jim Henry and Michael Jerling.             │
│ 12 May 1995                                                    │
│     All tour itinerary information has been moved to the       │
│     wonderful Musi-Cal service. Each artist's biography        │
│     contains a link to Musi-Cal for up-to-date touring info.  │
│ 11 May 1995                                                    │
└──────────────────────────────────────────────────────────────┘
```

Folk Music Home Page
http://www.eit.com/web/folk/folkhome.html

Jay Glicksman's nice link resource has information on:

* Folk album reviews

* Folk artist home pages

* Commercial resources (venues, stores, periodicals, promoters, catalogs)

* Folk concert/folk festival schedules

* Folk-related FTP sites

* A folk radio list

* UseNet newsgroups

Online Magazines and E-Zines

There are several online folk music magazines, and they are among the best-looking and most comprehensive music resources on the Net.

Dirty Linen
http://www.dirtynelson.com/linen

The online version of this established folk magazine is a thorough, thoughtful, and entertaining guide to folk, electric folk, traditional, and world music. It features record and concert reviews, interviews, a children's music column, and considerable coverage of the international scene.

Dirty Linen also maintains an extensive and up-to-date listing of folk-festival and concert schedules.

A recent home page for Dirty Linen, showing Doc Watson tooling down the open road in his self-advertising convertible, is shown in figure 11.11.

FIGURE 11.11
The home page for the online version of the folk magazine Dirty Linen.

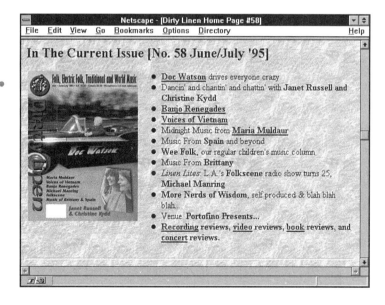

Folk Roots

http://www.cityscape.co.uk/froots

This excellent magazine covers the folk scene from Albania to Zimbabwe (with plenty for the English speaker and country tunesmith as well). Recent issues have covered such diverse topics as Hindustani raga master Ali Akbar Khan, the Band's Robbie Robertson, and the roots music of Madagascar. Visit the Table of Contents for a recent issue (see figure 11.12) and you'll return with a backpack full of incense and contraband.

FIGURE 11.12

A recent issue of Folk Roots, the magazine for armchair exotics.

Databases

Some folk-music information and song lyrics can be accessed through the general music databases that were mentioned in the country section of this chapter as well as from the following sites.

Digital Tradition Folk Songs Full Text Search

http://pubweb.parc.xerox.com/digitrad

This jumbo database contains the lyrics to thousands of songs, mostly of the traditional folk variety, collected over a six-year period by Dick Greenhaus and friends. Songs can be accessed by title or by particular lyrics. On some systems, you can even obtain audio clips of the songs. For a lyric search, the user can enter a keyword or two, and the database will regurgitate a list of any songs that contain the words. Figure 11.13 shows the list I obtained when I entered my favorite word into the search engine.

FIGURE 11.13
Keyword search results for the word "groovy" in the Digital Tradition folk songs database.

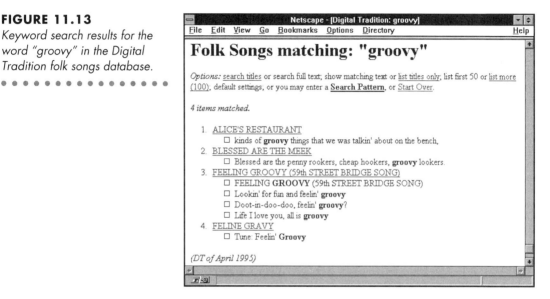

Richard Robinson's Tune Book
http://www.leeds.ac.uk/music/Info/RRTuneBk/tunebook.html

A collection of traditional tunes from Ireland, England, Scotland and the Northern Isles, Scandinavia, and further afield (jigs and reels, polkas and schottisches, waltzes, bourrees, horos, and more).

Resources for Folk Musicians

Because of its relatively limited commercial viability (and because the word "folk" means "common people"), folk music is not primarily a star-driven medium, but rather a do-it-yourself means of expression for ordinary Janes and Joes. Thus there are many resources on the Net that offer help and resources to aspiring folk musicians.

Acoustic Musician

http://www.netinterior.com/acoustic

Acoustic Musician magazine is dedicated to bluegrass and folk music. The online version is a sampler of articles from the print version. The magazine is of special interest to mandolin, dobro, banjo, and slide players.

A nice feature of *Acoustic Musician* is the monthly instruction section, as shown in figure 11.14.

FIGURE 11.14

Helpful instruction from the pages of the online edition of Acoustic Musician.

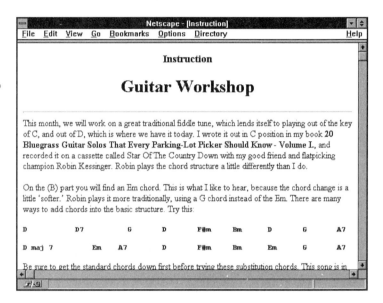

Folk Stuff

http://www.lm.com/~dshu/folkstuff.html

Folk Stuff describes itself as "a Web site dedicated to providing 'how to' and 'where to' information for folk musicians and those designing and building folk and experimental musical instruments; including dulcimers, autoharps, kalimbas, theremins, didjeridus, pennywhistles, and flutes." (A *didjeridu* is an Australian instrument made from a long, hollowed root. A *theremin* is an electronic instrument that resembles a stationary wand; as you move your hands in the vicinity of the wand, an eerie, oscillating pitch is produced, as heard in monster movies or the fade-out of The Beach Boys' "Good Vibrations." Sorry for patronizing you if you already knew that.)

UseNet

The UseNet newsgroups in the *alt.music* and *rec.music* domains are among the best places to find information and lively discussion about particular facets of the folk-music experience that may not be covered on the World Wide Web.

The following sites should be of interest to folk musicians and fans:

rec.music.folk—The general-interest folk-music site. Heavily visited from around the world.

rec.music.dylan—He was so much older then; he's younger than that now.

alt.exotic-music—This site is a little left-of-field, but it's a good place to visit for news about lesser known "unclassifiable" artists such as Esquivel and Urban Turban.

rec.music.indian.misc—For players and fans of sitars, tablas, and the like.

rec.music.makers.guitar.acoustic—Technical talk for acoustic guitar players.

Celebrity Register

There are sites for several dozen well-known folkies on the Web, and most of then are smart and even irreverent.

Bob Dylan (Expecting Rain)
http://bob.nbr.no

Some people (including Zimmy himself) may have forgotten that Dylan was the most influential folksinger since Woody Guthrie, but that's what he was, and that's where he made his lasting contribution to the culture.

Considering how he's degenerated into a mumble-mouthed curiosity trapped by his own legend, true fans would prefer to remember him as the outlaw bard of Greenwich Village, 1963. The Dylan who burst into the national consciousness was a black-clad jokerman with a six-string and a harmonica brace who sported long-haired beatnik groupie chicks on each arm as he strode the nighttime streets.

Of the many Dylan sites on the Net, Expecting Rain is the most comprehensive. (The name of the site comes from an early Dylan lyric, something like: "It is my contention that a rather nasty rainfall is imminent.")

Along with the usual discographies and lyrics, the site offers a Dylan "Who's Who" (of people alluded to in Dylan's cryptic lyrics) and a Dylan Atlas (of places alluded to in Dylan's cryptic lyrics).

Pictures of the hep young Dylan, taken from the Expecting Rain site, are shown in figure 11.15.

FIGURE 11.15
The hep young Bob Dylan, before his motorcycle (and his credibility) took a spill. (From the Expecting Rain web site)

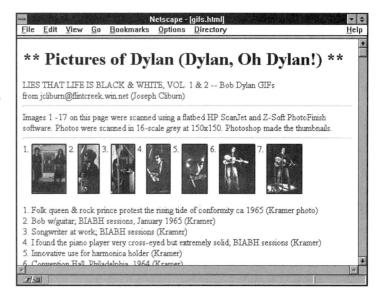

Other Artist Pages

Many folk musicians now have home pages or fan-club sites on the Internet. Most of them can be accessed with a good search tool such as Lycos.

Another easy way to access the sites is through a comprehensive link source. From the FolkBook site (*http://www.cgrg.ohio-state.edu/folkbook*) you can access pages or general information for dozens of artists.

Christian Music

Christian music is a vague term that applies to everyone from Ethel Waters and Sam Cooke to Stryper and Pat Boone, we are generally referring here to "contemporary Christian music" as exemplified by Amy Grant, Michael W. Smith, and 4 Runner. (A new term that the marketing people are trying out for this kind of music is "positive country.") But there is also a considerable amount of Christian-oriented "rock" music that is attracting young people to the church. Combined with computer savvy and public-relations smarts, today's evangelicals are using music to spread their faith to every corner of the planet.

General Christian Music Resources

As with any genre, the world of Christian music has news, awards, personalities, tour info, and new releases that are covered in "overview" Web sites.

Christian Music Online

http://www.cmo.com/cmo

Music Online is Information Central for mainstream Christian contemporary music fans. This is where you will find extensive information on the Dove Awards (the Christian Grammys) and concert schedules and bios for the artists on the Star Song and Word record labels (including the Newsboys, Sandi Patti, and wacky Christian comedian Mark Lowry). You will also find nice pictures of Amy G. at this site.

You can get a sense of where they're at from the home page shown in figure 11.16.

FIGURE 11.16

The home page for Christian Music Online.

• • • • • • • • • • • • • • • •

The Lighthouse
http://www.netcentral.net/lighthouse/index.html

If Christian Music Online is the *Entertainment Weekly* of Christian info sites, *The Lighthouse* is like a Christian *Rolling Stone*. This is an exceedingly well-done site, featuring "Christian rock" album reviews (by such artists as Beatlesque guitar virtuoso Phil Keaggy) and plenty of industry news.

Interestingly, you could spend a long time reading *The Lighthouse* and never see a mention of The Big Guy. I don't know if that's a deliberate strategy or not, but the pricey post-punk graphics and quasi-hip tone of the record reviews combine to make this a very effective outreach tool. (As with some of the high-profile sites in the secular entertainment world, you have to register at the welcome page to enter *The Lighthouse* site, although it's free and the keepers of *The Lighthouse* promise not to use your information for anything inappropriate.)

Compare the tone and target audience of the record review in figure 11.17 with the Christian Music Online page shown previously in figure 11.16. ☞

FIGURE 11.17

Review of an album by Fell
Venus, from the Web site called
The Lighthouse.

Netscape - [@ Review]

File   Edit   View   Go   Bookmarks   Options   Directory   Help

Style-wise, it's industrial. Beyond that, it's hard to draw comparisons. Fell Venus quite simply sounds unlike anything that's crossed my plate in a while. The best I can do is to say that sometimes it sounds like *Pretty Hate Machine* era **Nine inch Nails**. At other times, Venus' vocal wail scratches my **Pixies** itch. I've been waiting a long time to find a band that can do that.

Now, the more observant among you will be saying, "He just compared this band to the **Pixies**." Yes, I did. And I did so knowing full well that the **Pixies** are not an industrial act at all. This is part of why this band is so hard to describe. Fell Venus just plain doesn't seem to care what industrial bands are and are not supposed to do. Songs like "Shaped by Fear" are filled with sequencing and computer generated noise. Others--"Hate Disease" and "Nice Guy" come to mind--have virtually none. This album is incredibly diverse--but the consistent, driving guitars and Venus' wailing voice hold it all together.

Lyrically, this is pretty standard fare for the style. The majority of the songs stare in the face of human weakness and unflinchingly report what they see. The lyrical highlight of the ride is the back-to-back combination of "Hate Disease" and "Let Me Go." The first calls out in the chorus, "I've got it, don't want it. Hate Disease." The second is based around the repeating sequence of "Let me go. Let me go. Let me go. I'm all tied up." Simple, but it makes the point quite nicely. I've been saying for a while now that **Scott Albert** was the best of what was left in the Christian industrial world since the demise of **Mortal**. I don't know what he has planned for **Argyle Park**, but he's got some catching up to do.

LiNeNoIsE
http://www.catalog.com/lionsden/linenoise

If *The Lighthouse* is the *Rolling Stone* of Christian music, LiNeNoIsE wants to be its *Spin* or *Raygun*. Its focus is on the real cutting edge of Christian rock: Christian industrial, Christian punk, Christian metal (which, if you can believe what you read, is really thriving), and so on. I particularly like the helpful chart where sonic equivalencies are established between "secular" alternative bands and their sound-alike Christian counterparts. (If you like Black Flag, you'll love The Crucified.)

Editor Ryan Sager gives this e-zine a sheen of do-it-yourself credibility, and he is not afraid to lard the pages with friendly homilies like the one in figure 11.18. It's quite entertaining on a number of levels.

UseNet

Within the UseNet domain, music buffs will find spirited discussions that could be of interest to believers and skeptics alike.

rec.music.christian

This heavily visited site is ample evidence that Christian music has expanded far beyond the churches. The posts are thought-provoking and sometimes even irreverent (see figure 11.19), and most of the participants come armed with scriptural smarts.

FIGURE 11.19

Recent postings to the rec.music.christian newsgroup.

● ● ● ● ● ● ● ● ● ● ● ● ● ● ●

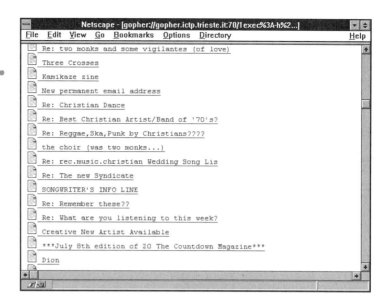

Celebrity Register

There aren't many crossover celebrities in the Christian music world, although there are plenty of artists who are well-known within their community, with fans who are truly "devoted."

The Amy Grant Archive

http://www.ipc.uni-tuebingen.de/art

Amy Grant is unquestionably the biggest star in contemporary Christian music, and she is the only one to have had a real impact on the mainstream pop music charts. (Not too surprisingly, she did it with a bouncy and undeniably *secular* tune called "Baby, Baby" that was reportedly written in 15 minutes and which was promoted with a semi-steamy video.) Amy has parlayed her wholesome beauty and seemingly incorruptible goodness into a major-label recording contract with A&M and a gig as the spokesperson for Target stores.

The Amy Grant Archive is a shrine of devotion to Miss G. that features lyrics, a bio, the FAQ sheet from *alt.music.amy-grant*, numerous pictures (see figure 11.20), tour itineraries, sound clips, fan-club information, and a nice collection of quotes called "Amy the Philosopher."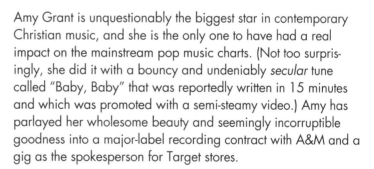

FIGURE 11.20

Amy Grant, the International Poster Child for Being Nice. (From the Amy Grant Archive)

Other Artist Pages

The Yahoo directory at *http://www.yahoo.com/ Society_and_Culture/Religion/Christianity/Music/Artists* has links to several Christian artists' home pages.

Many of the sites that are mentioned in this chapter, as well as several other sites that are related to country-western, folk, and Christian music, can easily be accessed through the Yahoo utility, which can be accessed directly from Netscape or at *http://www.yahoo.com*. From the Yahoo subject directory, select the category *Entertainment/Music/Genres* followed by the subcategories *Country and Western, Folk, Bluegrass, Cajun, Ethnic,* or *Christian*.

The List

General Country-Western Music Resources

Wayne's Country Pages
http://galaxy.einet.net/EINet/staff/wayne/country/country.html

Country Connection
http://metro.turnpike.net/C/country

Dawn's Country Fan Pages
http://204.96.208.1/services/staff/dawn/cfans.htm

Dr. Mellow's Country Music Fan Page
http://www.catt.ncsu.edu/users/drmellow/public/www/country.html

Greg Cohoon's site includes links to a dozen artist home pages and extensive information about Johnny Cash and the Highwaymen (country's answer to the Travelling Wilburys, comprising Cash, Kris Kristofferson, Waylon Jennings, and Willie Nelson).

Country Online/Nashville Music Connection
http://online.music-city.com

A commercial enterprise that aspires to being a one-stop info and advertising site for country-music resources. Affiliated with Cash Box Online.

Online Country Magazines

Cash Box Online
http://online.music-city.com/Cashbox/html

Nash!
LISTSERV@vm.temple.edu

Leave subject line blank and type **SUBSCRIBE NASH** as the body of the note.

Cybergrass (formerly Electronic Bluegrass Magazine)
http://www.info.net/BG/bg_home.html

Resources for Country Musicians

COWPIE NEWS
gopher://gopher.ttu.edu:70/11/Pubs/Mailing-Lists/Professional/cowpie

Nashville Online
http://www.nol.com/nol/NOL_Home.html

Music Exchange
http://www.scsn.net/~musex

Online music-related classified ads.

UseNet Groups
rec.music.country.western

rec.music.country.old-time

Artist Pages

Reba McEntire
http://ruby.ph.utexas.edu/RebaWWW/Reba.html

General Folk Music Resources

FolkBook
http://www.cgrg.ohio-state.edu/folkbook

Folk Music Home Page
http://www.eit.com/web/folk/folkhome.html

Online magazines

Dirty Linen
http://www.dirtynelson.com/linen

Folk Roots
http://www.cityscape.co.uk/froots

Databases

Digital Tradition Folk Songs Full Text Search

http://pubweb.parc.xerox.com/digitrad

Richard Robinson's Tune Book

http://www.leeds.ac.uk/music/Info/RRTuneBk/tunebook.html

TuneWeb

http://www.ece.ucdavis.edu/~darsie/tunebook.html

An archive of mostly Celtic and Irish folk tunes.

Record-label Sites

Oh Boy Records/Red Pajama Records/Blue Plate Music

http://www.nashville.net/ohboy/ohboy.html

Home to John Prine and Steve Goodman.

Resouces for Folk Musicians

Acoustic Musican

http://www.netinterior.com/acoustic

Folk Stuff

http://www.lm.com/~dshu/folkstuff.html

Music Exchange

http://www.scsn.net/~musex

Online music-related classified ads.

UseNet Groups

rec.music.folk

rec.music.dylan

alt.exotic-music

rec.music.indian.misc.

rec.music.makers.guitar.acoustic.

Artist Pages

Bob Dylan (Expecting Rain)
http://bob.nbr.no

General Christian Music Resources

Christian Music Online
http://www.cmo.com/cmo

The Lighthouse
http://www.netcentral.net/lighthouse/index.html

LiNeNoIsE
http://www.catalog.com/lionsden/linenoise

UseNet Groups
rec.music.christian

Artist Pages

The Amy Grant Archive
http://www.ipc.uni-tuebingen.de/art

Classical Music

IN THIS CHAPTER:

> *General classical music resources and archives*

> *Record reviews and recommendations*

> *UseNet newsgroups*

> *Record-label sites*

> *Symphonies, ensembles, and performers*

IN OTHER CHAPTERS:

< *General music-related resources and databases are discussed in Chapter 8.*

Aficionados of classical music are often stereotyped as affluent, educated, and sober people, and like most stereotypes, this one is largely correct. That's why multinational corporations pump so much money into sponsoring classical-music broadcasts on radio and television. Despite the fact that the audience for classical music is small compared to that for rock & roll or other forms of popular music, the people who listen to classical music have a disproportionate amount of money to spend.

This general affluence and high education level is reflected in the quality of the Internet sites that are devoted to classical music. Just as the classical-music community provided a market for high-end audio equipment in the 1950s, '60s, and '70s, the classical buffs of today are fueling the development of real-time audio transmission, high-resolution graphic images, and speedier access to archives. To cater to this small but affluent market, multimedia publishers and hardware developers are continually upgrading sound and storage devices for personal computers. These same advances are affecting the quality of the Web sites that are devoted to classical music. Classical-music sites are among the cleanest, most thorough, and most technologically advanced repositories of sound, text, and image that you will find on the Net.

General Classical Music Resources

As with many useful Web sites, some of the best online resources for classical music are merely composed of links to other facilities. In some cases, a musicologist, grad student, or fanatical buff has assembled pointers to the most trustworthy or comprehensive information. In other cases, the site administrator may add his or her own information (such as a list of recommended recordings) to the list of links. In either case, such sites make finding useful information considerably easier than browsing through a card catalog at the public library or asking questions to a gum-chewing clerk at a record store.

rec.music.classical FAQ Document

http://www.cis.ohio-state.edu/hypertext/faq/usenet/music/classical-faq/faq.html

As with any subject matter so intimidating to outsiders, the best place to start gathering information on classical music is probably the FAQ document of the relevant newsgroup. It ain't sexy—just a text-only format—but it's the best resource for knuckleheads and newcomers.

The *rec.music.classical* FAQ addresses the following questions:

* What are the major periods of "classical" music?

* I'm new to classical music and don't have any classical recordings. What should I listen to so that I can learn more?

* I heard this melody on the radio. How do I figure out what it is?

* When I went to the record store to buy a CD of [insert piece], I found dozens of versions. How do I know which one to buy?

* Why are there so many recordings of the same piece?

* How do I find out if [insert-piece] has ever been recorded?

* What is that music from [insert TV-show/movie] called?

* What distinguishes classical music from popular music?

* What is the difference between an opera and a musical?

* How do you pronounce all those conductors' and composers' names?

* What's the point of having a conductor?

WWW Virtual Library of Classical Music

http://www.maths.ed.ac.uk/classical

This giant site is a subsection of a true whopper among Web resources: the WWW Virtual Library.

The Virtual Library is a project from some dedicated folks in Britain who are slowly linking together *everything on every known subject.* (And of course, I applaud their ambition.)

The people at the Virtual Library have a long way to go before they corner the market on classical-music info, but they do have a good collection of links to academic and institutional sites, as illustrated by the excerpt from the index in figure 12.1.

The site also features schedules for opera companies world-wide, periodicals such as Music Theory On-Line, and a library of downloadable music software.

Especially quaint is the link to a whole section of jokes about music, divided by instrument. (Example: "What is the difference between a French horn section and a '57 Chevy? You can tune a '57 Chevy.")

FIGURE 12.1

The "C" section of the index of the Virtual Library's section on Classical Music. (One question: What does "coping with performance anxiety" have to do with music?)

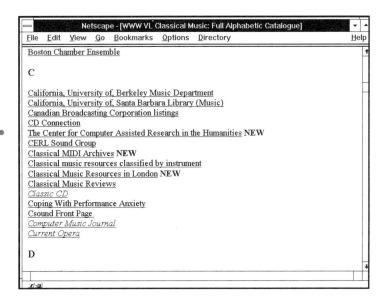

Classical Music on the Net

http://www.einet.net/galaxy/Leisure-and-Recreation/Music/douglas-bell/Index.html

This link-rich site is the personal project of a Dr. Douglas Bell, and it is a well-organized introduction to the entirety of classical-music resources on the Net.

The site is divided into three main areas: an extensive index of resources and general-interest music links; copies of and instructions for the most popular and useful search tools (Lycos, Yahoo, et al); and a section of "classical music topics."

The "topics" subsection is divided into the following pages or indexes:

* Composers and Compositions

* Computers, Midi, Software, and Universities

* Instrumental and Vocal

* Festivals and Institutes

* Organizations and Corporations

* Record Labels and Distributors

* Music Theory and History

* Other Classical Links

* Shopping for Music and Instruments

Classical Music Online
http://www.crl.com/~virtualv/cmo

This newly-formed site looks to me like a tree from which advertisers can hang their wares.

Although the site is divided into sections for Music News, CD Titles, Composers, and more, a couple things stand out on the home page (figure 12.2): Classified Ads, Membership (hmmm), and the trademark-registration symbol after the words "Classical Music Online." This tells me the site is for-profit. I don't begrudge anyone making an honest buck, but there are so many places where one can get *more* and *better* information—and get it *free*—that you wonder why anyone would bother.

In any event, at the time of this writing the site had a smattering of CD-title information along with a lot of "under-construction" pages.

FIGURE 12.2
The home page for Classical
Music Online.

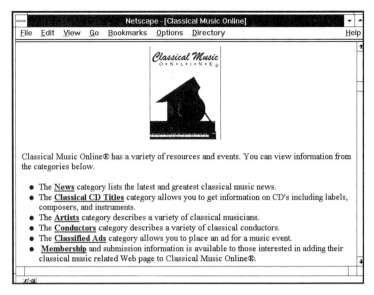

Contemporary Music Info-Junction

http://WWW.ThoughtPort.COM/thoughtport/gallery/resident/CMIJ

Now this is one *hip* site. When it comes to classical music, the contemporary variety is a strictly us-versus-them proposition. Twentieth-century composers (Arnold Schoenberg, John Cage, Philip Glass, Glenn Gould) and their fans are the renegades of classical music, and that spirit comes through in this dense, genuinely informative site. (See figure 12.3.)

If terms such as "dissonance," "atonality," and "psychoacoustics" mean anything to you, I suggest you rush to the Contemporary Music Info-Junction and see what the egg-heads on the cutting edge of symphonic and electronic music are up to. (And be prepared to ditch all that moldy Mozart.)

FIGURE 12.3

The "Table o' Contents" of the iconoclastic Contemporary Music Info-Junction.

● ● ● ● ● ● ● ● ● ● ● ● ● ● ● ● ●

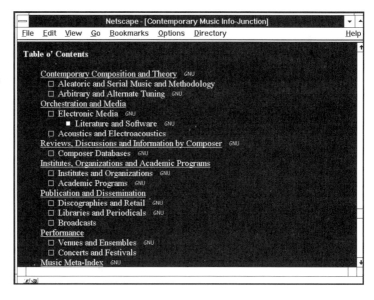

Indiana University School of Music
http://www.music.indiana.edu

Indiana University, the largest institution of higher education in the state where this book is being written, is renowned for two things. One of them is the bully who coaches the basketball team. The other is the quality of its arts programs.

The I.U. Music Department has a Web site that is a good resource for mostly bibliographic information on all types of music, with a particular emphasis on classical. (Question: Is academia inherently prejudiced against popular music? Does any university's music department specialize in, say, lumberjack songs of the 1920s, with only a cursory nod to classical music in the upper-level electives?)

The most interesting thing on the site is the information about the school's VARIATIONS Project, which is described as follows: "The Indiana University Music Library VARIATIONS Project addresses continuous, compact-disc quality digital audio over a network without audio break-up. It is a testbed for real-time multimedia networking at Indiana University." In other words, they're

working on sending high-end audio and video across phone lines, through browsers such as Netscape. Currently the project is being installed on workstations around the I.U. campus in Bloomington. A catalog of available music resources can be searched from outside the campus, but the audio cannot be transmitted to the non-Bloomington universe. (I entered two names into the search engine. "Beethoven" produced 5,000 matches of available recordings and texts; "Beatles" produced 66. "Lumberjack" produced nine matches, including a collection of songs with titles such as "Who Feeds Us Beans?," "I Am a Jolly Shanty Boy," and "When We A-Lumbering Go.")

The Indiana University Music Library also offers the most colossal list of general-interest music links that you will find anywhere (*http://www.music.indiana.edu/misc/music_resources.html*). This list, called Music Resources on the Internet, is discussed in detail in Chapter 8.

Leeds University Archives
http://www.leeds.ac.uk/music.html

This hodgepodge of links, software, and European music-festival information from Leeds University in England is useful and a lot of fun. You can use it to search for information about music by genre, period, artist, instrument, or geographic area. You'll also find an InterStudio Electronic Music Archive at *http://www.in terstudio.co.uk/isl/emusic32.htm*. (See figure 12.4)

My favorite part of this site was a recent feature called "Please help this Leeds student with his research." Here you filled out a survey on your physical reactions to a favorite piece of music. In my case, the piece of music was Gilbert O'Sullivan's 1972 masterpiece "Alone Again (Naturally)." Ostensibly this information was going into somebody's thesis. However, I imagine it could also be good material for blackmail.

FIGURE 12.4

The InterStudio Electronic Music Archive reviews electronic music at the Berlin Radio Show 1932.

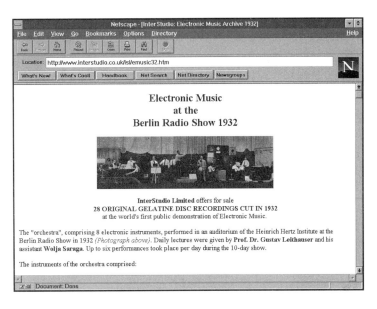

Reviews and Recommendations

There is a particularly civil tone to what classical-music buffs call "reviews." Rather than telling you what stinks, the premise seems to be that *nothing* in classical music stinks; therefore, the purpose of a record review is twofold: 1.) to assess the quality of the sound engineering for a particular recording; and 2.) to inform you of yet another CD that you must add to "the essential library." (Classical music fans are big on "essential libraries.") The following are sites that gather classical reviews or point you to a list of recordings that you simply *must have* in order to be considered musically literate.

Classic CD Beginner's Guide
http://www.futurenet.co.uk/music/classiccd/Beginners/Beginners.html

Now this is my idea of a good classical-music site: a crib sheet of composers, a guide to classical music in advertisements, a history of classical music that could fit on the back of an envelope, and a list of 100 recommended classical CDs. (See figure 12.5.)

This site from the good folks at FutureNet gives the busy dilettante exactly the info that he or she needs in order to impress that snooty new lad or lassie at the club—and not a word more. ☞

FIGURE 12.5

Take it from one who knows: If you memorize the information contained at this site, your chances on Jeopardy are doubled. (Home page of the Classic CD Beginner's Guide)

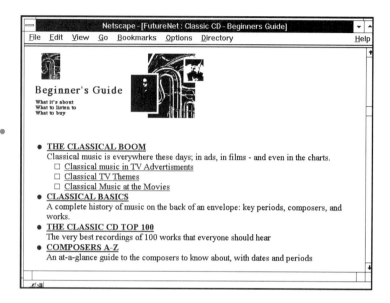

Classical Music Reviews

http://ww.ncsa.uiuc.edu/SDG/People/marca/music-reviews.html

Classical Music Reviews is a small collection of articles and reviews that were culled from other sources and organized by historical period. Within this site, under the Classical period, you'll find a lengthy article by a radio host named Deryk Baker called "Building a Library: A Collector's Guide." This article is a review of the best recordings of Beethoven. Under the Romantic period, you'll find Baker's analysis of Gustav Mahler. You'll see that Baker is a bit opinionated and surly. Personally I like that in a critic. (See figure 12.6.) ☞

FIGURE 12.6

An excerpt about Beethoven
recordings from *Building a
Library: A Collector's Guide.* So
what's this rot about Karajan's
bass being "perhaps a little
diffuse"? The gall!

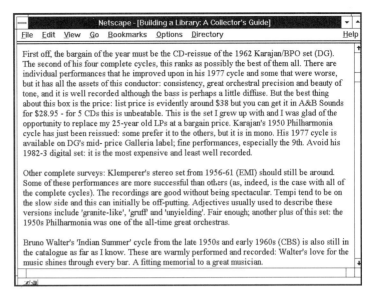

> Netscape - [Building a Library: A Collector's Guide]
>
> File   Edit   View   Go   Bookmarks   Options   Directory   Help
>
> First off, the bargain of the year must be the CD-reissue of the 1962 Karajan/BPO set (DG). The second of his four complete cycles, this ranks as possibly the best of them all. There are individual performances that he improved upon in his 1977 cycle and some that were worse, but it has all the assets of this conductor: consistency, great orchestral precision and beauty of tone, and it is well recorded although the bass is perhaps a little diffuse. But the best thing about this box is the price: list price is evidently around $38 but you can get it in A&B Sounds for $28.95 - for 5 CDs this is unbeatable. This is the set I grew up with and I was glad of the opportunity to replace my 25-year old LPs at a bargain price. Karajan's 1950 Philharmonia cycle has just been reissued: some prefer it to the others, but it is in mono. His 1977 cycle is available on DG's mid- price Galleria label; fine performances, especially the 9th. Avoid his 1982-3 digital set: it is the most expensive and least well recorded.
>
> Other complete surveys: Klemperer's stereo set from 1956-61 (EMI) should still be around. Some of these performances are more successful than others (as, indeed, is the case with all of the complete cycles). The recordings are good without being spectacular. Tempi tend to be on the slow side and this can initially be off-putting. Adjectives usually used to describe these versions include 'granite-like', 'gruff' and 'unyielding'. Fair enough; another plus of this set: the 1950s Philharmonia was one of the all-time great orchestras.
>
> Bruno Walter's 'Indian Summer' cycle from the late 1950s and early 1960s (CBS) is also still in the catalogue as far as I know. These are warmly performed and recorded: Walter's love for the music shines through every bar. A fitting memorial to a great musician.

Dave Lampson's Classical Music Home Page

http://www.webcom.com/~music

This amazing site is one of the most staggering achievements on the Net, and I don't know if that's good or bad. This fellow Lampson presents us with a list of recommended CDs for a good personal library of classical music—and if you follow his recommendations, you'll be in the poorhouse before you get past the Bs. He's got thousands—I mean *many* thousands—of recordings on his must-have list, which is broken down by period and meticulously cross-referenced to an encyclopedic assemblage of composer profiles. He also offers us page after page of intelligent hand-holding on the art and science of record collecting (and the record *keeping* that goes along with it).

Who would guess that from the benevolent home page in figure 12.7 one could be lured into the labyrinth of obsessive completism that is illustrated in figure 12.8?

FIGURE 12.7

This looks friendly enough. (Dave Lampson's Classical Music Home Page)

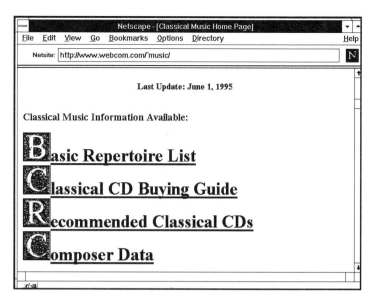

FIGURE 12.8

Dave wants you to know that you need several recordings by each of these composers (as well as the composers from the other 25 letters of the alphabet). You got a problem with that?

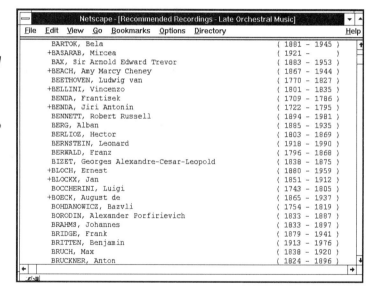

Databases

The history of classical music and the number of available recordings is so extensive compared to other genres that computerized databases are especially helpful for classical fans.

Library of Congress Gopher (MARVEL)
gopher://marvel.loc.gov

Never forget that the world's largest library is accessible from your desktop. The Library of Congress not only contains more books than any other institution on the planet, many of its holding are also available online.

The Library of Congress gopher, called MARVEL, has connections to countless musical databases, archives, and online publications, from the CANTUS database of Gregorian chants to the Endangered Music Project of Grateful Dead drummer Mickey Hart.

After accessing the address, select "Search LC MARVEL menus using Jughead." You will be presented with a keyword search engine. If you type the word **music**, you will have access to dozens of music sites at libraries and universities across the U.S.

University of Wisconsin Sheet Music Collection
gopher://gopher.adp.wisc.edu:70/11/.browse/.METAMMLSM

The eclectic assemblage of sheet music in the Wisconsin collection includes both classical music and traditional folk songs—all of which were either written in Wisconsin, published in Wisconsin, or mention Wisconsin in the lyrics. This gopher site is a catalog of the holdings and might come in handy if you're passing through Madison when suddenly your car breaks down and you're forced to entertain on a streetcorner to get the money for a new flywheel, but you left your sheet music back in Cambridge. Hey, it could happen.

Other Databases

There are a few comprehensive musicdatabase sites that offer discographies, artist information, and song lyrics for several styles of music, including classical and so-called early music.

The All-Music Guide at *http://cdnow.com* is a just-plain-awesome resource that lists, rates, and discusses what seems like every piece of music ever recorded in every genre, including classical. Although it is newly affiliated with the CDNow! music-ordering service (from which you click your way into the Guide), the Guide covers both out-of-print and freely available titles.

Vibe magazine's Mammoth Music Meta List at *http://www.pathfinder.com/@@9uAoxwAAAAAAQNXr/vibe/mmm/music.html* has thousands of links, many to artist home pages, in most genres of music, including classical.

More detailed information on general music databases can be found in Chapter 8, "General Music Resources."

UseNet Newsgroups

There are several UseNet groups devoted to classical music, as follows:

rec.music.classical carries a large volume of discussion pertaining to classical music. Concert reviews and announcements appear here, as well as discussions of the merits and demerits of various composers. A lengthy FAQ (frequently-asked-questions) list is maintained here.

rec.music.early is the place for discussion of pre-Baroque music. It is otherwise similar to *rec.music.classical*, with somewhat lighter traffic.

rec.music.classical.performing carries articles of interest to the performing classical musician. Topics include instrumental and vocal technique, performance anxiety, musical interpretation, and principles of conducting. A FAQ is available.

rec.music.classical.recordings is a newsgroup for the discussion of recorded music. General principles of recording are discussed here along with recommendations and observations about specific recordings. This is the classical newsgroup where people will ask which Beethoven CD to buy (and are likely to be told that Beethoven should only be played on vinyl).

Record-Label Sites

The following record labels maintain Web sites to promote their classical-music offerings.

Classical Music World (RCA/BMG)

http://classicalmus.com

The name of this site and a first glance at its contents might suggest that it is a comprehensive A-to-Z guide to all things classical. But a little more digging reveals that it is just a posh advertisement and online ordering service for the products of a few particular record labels. RCA Victor Red Seal, Deutsche

Harmonia Mundia, and the Russian Melodiya label are the classical labels of the German corporation BMG, and together they embrace many of the most prestigious performers and composers in classical music.

The main page of Classical Music World, shown in figure 12.9, illustrates what a fun site it is (and illustrates BMG's strategy of reaching beyond the traditional classical-music audience with a package that is deliberately lighthearted and "young").

FIGURE 12.9

The main index page of Classical Music World, an advertising and direct-ordering service of the BMG classical labels.

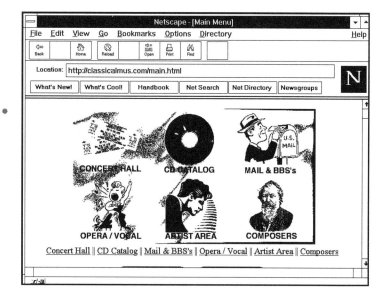

The section of the site called "Concert Hall" contains audio and video clips of selected artists. "Opera/Vocal" contains, among other things, synopses of 40 well-known librettos. The "Composers" and "Artist" areas have bios and discographies. "Mail and BBSs" is a discussion area.

All the in-depth information in the Artist Area pertains to performers on BMG-affiliated labels; but that does include some of the superstars of classical music, including Itzhak Perlman, Van Cliburn, James Galway, and Placido Domingo, and the information on such people is extensive.

Sony Classical

http://www.music.sony.com/Music/MusicIndex.html (Sony Music home page)

The Sony Classical label has its share of high-profile artists, including cellist Yo-Yo Ma and composer Philip Glass. Brief bios and sound clips of the Sony artists can be accessed by following the appropriate links from the Sony Music main page at the URL. You can also go to the alphabetical artist list at *http://www.music.sony.com/Music/ArtistInfo/ArtistInfo_Classical* or the Sony Classical Hot Links page (for short, pre-release style info) at *http://www.music.sony.com/Music/WireTap/Classical.*

NOTE

Perhaps the most prestigious label for classical music is Deutsche Gramophone, which is now a division of Polygram. The Polygram home page (*http://www.polygram.com/polygram/Music.html*) makes mention of Deutsche Gramophone, but as of this writing, the home pages for individual Polygram labels were still under construction.

Symphonies, Ensembles, and Performers

It doesn't automatically follow that the biggest names in classical music have the biggest or best sites devoted to them—or even that they have a site at all. Many of the most popular symphony orchestras and soloists haven't yet jumped aboard the cyber-wagon. Well, the way I see it, the Chicago Symphony's loss is the Nittany Valley Symphony's gain.

Symphony Home Pages

The following symphony orchestras are hip enough to have a presence on the World Wide Web at the time of this writing:

* Atlanta Symphony Orchestra

* Austin Symphonic Band

* Austin Symphony Orchestra

* Boston Chamber Ensemble

* CBC Vancouver Orchestra

* Colorado Springs Symphony Orchestra

* Het Brabants Orkest (Dutch symphony orchestra known for its "silent film with live music" projects)

* Imperial College Symphony Orchestra

* Indianapolis Symphony Orchestra

* Longwood Symphony Orchestra (an orchestra composed of professionals working in Boston's medical community)

* New England Philharmonic

* New Zealand Symphony Orchestra

* Nittany Valley Symphony (State College, PA, USA)

* Orchestra London

* Prometheus Symphony (Oakland)

* Redwood Symphony

* San Jose Symphony Orchestra

* Sinfonia Lahti

* Stanford Symphony Orchestra

* Symphony Nova Scotia

* The San Diego Young Artists' Symphony Orchestra

* University of Oslo Symphony Orchestra

* Winnipeg Symphony Orchestra

Celebrity Register: Artist and Small Ensemble Pages

Few of the classical artist pages on the Net are the work of rabid fan clubs. Rather they are the kind of sober, informational sites that are put together by record companies (indeed, almost all of them come from the two record-company sites referenced previously in this chapter).

From the *Artists* subpage of the *Classical Music* page of the Yahoo *Entertainment* search directory (*http://www.yahoo.com/ Entertainment/Music/Genres/Classical_Music/Artists*), you can access pages for classical performers and conductors.

Celebrity Register: Composer Pages

Because classical music is so dependent on the classics—that is, the work of dead guys—the composers are the real stars. Even today, a cat like Beethoven has as dedicated a fan base as your average rock star.

Many composers have home pages or biographies on the Net. (Most are from BMG's World of Classical Music.) Links to these sites can be found in the Yahoo *Entertainment* directory, under the subsections *Music/Genres/Classical/Composers*.

There is also a set of thumbnail bios for the true biggies of classical music at *http://www.cl.cam.ac.uk/users/mn200/music/ composers.html*. And there is a site in praise of "Unknown Composers" at *http://www.seas.upenn.edu/~jimmosk/TOC.html*.

CLOSE-UP: THE KRONOS QUARTET

Those of us who regularly check the barometer of culture have noticed a miniature trend in classical music: artists whose style or repertoire appeals to an avant-garde rock & roll audience. The Kronos Quartet is easily the most popular of these performers.

The four members of this San Francisco-based ensemble are David Harrington (violin), John Sherba (violin), Hank Dutt (viola), and Joan Jeanrenaud (cello). Since 1973, they have challenged the hidebound classical-music establishment with a repertoire that is almost exclusively 20th Century neo-classical, including works by Frank Zappa, Steve Reich, and John Zorn.

One afternoon in the early '80s, I almost literally stumbled on the Kronos Quartet as they were playing beneath a shade tree on the University of Southern California campus. Although they had the usual chamber-music complement of stringed instruments, what they were coaxing out of the instruments was something altogether untraditional: Jimi Hendrix' "Purple Haze." For me, it was love at first sight.

The unofficial Kronos Quartet home page is at *http://www.nwu.edu/music/kronos/kronos.html*. (There is also an "official" Kronos page from the Warner Classics record label at *http://www.foresight.co.uk/warnerclassics/kronos*) Figure 12.10 shows a graphic image of the Kronos Quartet that I accessed from this home page.

FIGURE 12.10
The Kronos Quartet.

The List

General Resources

rec.music.classical FAQ Document
http://www.cis.ohio-state.edu/hypertext/faq/usenet/music/classical-faq/faq.html

WWW Virtual Library of Classical Music
http://www.maths.ed.ac.uk/classical

Classical Music on the Net
http://www.einet.net/galaxy/Leisure-and-Recreation/Music/douglas-bell/Index.html

Classical Music Online
http://www.crl.com/~virtualv/cmo

Contemporary Music Info-Junction
http://WWW.ThoughtPort.COM/thoughtport/gallery/resident/CMIJ

Indiana University School of Music
http://www.music.indiana.edu

Leeds University Archives
http://www.leeds.ac.uk/music.html

Reviews and Recommendations

Classic CD Beginner's Guide
http://www.futurenet.co.uk/music/classiccd/Beginners/Beginners.html

Building a Library: A Collector's Guide
http://www.ncsa.uiuc.edu/SDG/People/marca/barker-beethoven.html

Dave Lampson's Classical Music Home Page

http://www.webcom.com/~music

Classical Music Reviews

http://www.ncsa.uiuc.edu/SDG/People/marca/music-reviews.html

Databases

Library of Congress Gopher (MARVEL)

gopher://marvel.loc.gov

U. of Wisconsin Sheet Music Collection

gopher://gopher.adp.wisc.edu:70/11/.browse/.METAMMLSM

UseNet Groups

rec.music.classical

rec.music.classical.performing

rec.music.classical.recordings

rec.music.early

Record-Label Sites

Classical Music World (RCA/BMG)

http://classicalmus.com

Sony Classical (via Sony home page)

http://www.music.sony.com/Music/MusicIndex.html

Deutsche Gramophone (via Polygram)

http://www.polygram.com/polygram/Music.html

Mailing Lists

Classical Music

listserv@brownvm.brown.edu

An unmoderated list for the discussion of classical music.

Classical Music Mailing List (Moderated)

classical-request@webcom.com

The Moderated Classical Music Mailing List has been set up to be a place where classical music enthusiasts can discuss music, musicians, composers, composition, instruments, performance, music history, recordings, and all topics even remotely related to classical music from all periods. (Type **subscribe** in the body of the message.)

PART **V**

FUN AND GAMES

Humor

IN THIS CHAPTER:

> *Humor archives and resources*

> *Canonical lists*

> *Comics and cartoons on the Net*

> *Online humor magazines*

> *UseNet humor sites*

IN OTHER CHAPTERS:

< *TV humor is discussed in Chapter 7, "Series, Sitcoms, and Animation."*

< *Film humor is discussed in Chapter 3, "The Popular Cinema," and Chapter 4, "Cult Cinema and Fantasy Film."*

> *Peculiar and unclassifiable Internet sites are discussed in Chapter 16, "Internet Oddities."*

Almost everybody in the world thinks that they have a good sense of humor, and of course, almost everybody is wrong. But because the Internet is so fundamentally democratic, there's a place on the Net for practically every kind of humor, from sophomoric gross-out jokes to sophisticated editorial cartoons to time-release satire that will bust your gut an hour after you read it.

The chapter will examine the rich resources of humor on the Net, including some general archives of humor, canonical lists of jokes, cartoons and comics on the Net, graphical online humor magazines, and UseNet groups that are devoted to various subcategories of the humor domain.

Humor Archives

A good place to start exploring the humor on the Net is in the various humor archives that are scattered throughout the World Wide Web and FTP-space. A typical humor archive represents the work of one individual in compiling his or her favorite jokes, scripts, parodies, and puns. Much of the material in the bigger archives is simply culled from other sites. Thus, the archives serve as a kind of global bulletin board for the reposting of material (rather than as places where new humor is invented or published).

Like inebriated college kids, some archives are merely an amusing waste of your time, and many of the same jokes inevitably will be found at several different sites. (Barney jokes seem to be especially popular as a shorthand for "I have an irreverent sense of humor.")

However, the best of the archives are impressive in their scope and in the diligent bookkeeping they represent. And they can be quite funny, too (which is always a plus when you're dealing with humor). Several of the superior archives are profiled herein.

The Cathouse Humor Archive
http://www.cathouse.org/cathouse/humor

The Cathouse archive is a large collection of material administered by a fellow named Jason Heimbaugh. It includes complete movie scripts (including some of the Monty Python films), episode guides to such TV shows as *Seinfeld, Married...With Children*, a compendium of British humor, and quotes from such stalwarts of stand-up as Stephen Wright and Lenny Bruce. (Quoth Lenny: "There's nothing sadder than an aging hipster." Ouch!) And because the Cathouse site is affiliated with the *alt.folklore.urban* UseNet group, there's a terrific section on urban legends. (No, there aren't any alligators in the sewers of New York City from people flushing away their unwanted "pets.")

The Cathouse archive has an extensive joke list, organized by subject, that is consistently clever (albeit occasionally racy). There are also longer humorous pieces some of which might qualify as "highbrow." Figure 13.1 shows four notable entries from the annual Bulwer-Lytton contest for the worst opening sentence to an imaginary novel. (This contest is named for the British author who penned the immortal opening line, "It was a dark and stormy night.")

FIGURE 13.1

Entries from the annual Bulwer-Lytton contest, from the Cathouse humor archive.

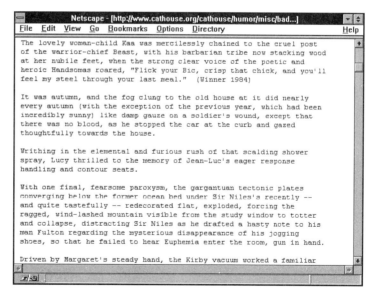

LaughWEB

http://WWW.Misty.com/laughweb

LaughWEB is a massive archive that includes an impressive list of canonical jokes, complete scripts for *The Blues Brothers* and *Airplane!,* an extensive parody section ("Just Say NO to Books," "The Hair Kit for Men"), one-liners by the boatload, and an affectionate tribute to the wit and wisdom of America's favorite young comedian, Newt "Shecky" Gingrich.

> **NOTE**
>
> *Canonical* joke lists are large compilations of the best jokes within a given category: blonde jokes, lightbulb jokes, mother-in-law jokes, and so forth. A detailed introduction to canonical joke lists is provided later in this chapter.

As with many of the hipper sites on the Internet, there is a section of LaughWEB devoted to Spam, including a tasty menu of Spam poetry and haikus. (See figure 13.2.)

FIGURE 13.2

A tempting menu of Spam haikus from LaughWEB.

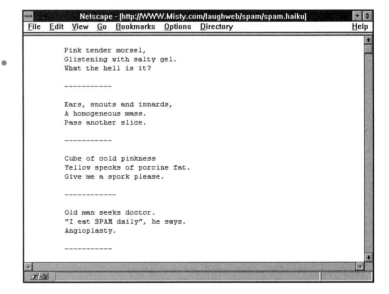

The Mother of All Humor Archives

http://www.tc.cornell.edu/~ckline/humor/maillist.html

This aptly named collection from Cornell University is the grandest repository of genuinely funny stuff on the entire Internet. It contains almost *300* documents that administrator Christopher Kline has culled over the years—enough to keep you in stitches until the millennium. The following is a representative sample of the document titles:

* Worst Country-Western Song Titles
* Sigmund Freud on Dr. Suess
* Baked Beans
* Prison versus Work
* Pleasing Your Man the '50s Way
* The Heuristic Squelch Dating Guide
* Spontaneous Head Explosion
* MICROSOFT Bids to Acquire Catholic Church
* How to Swear in French
* Gluing a Coin to the Floor
* Top Ten Sexually Tilted Lines in Star Wars
* The Coolest Hostnames on the Net
* The Chain Letter of Paul the Apostle to the Corinthians
* 20 Ways to Confuse Santa Claus
* Love

If there's anyone who could resist such a treasure-trove of funny material, they've got a promising future in the civil service.

The documents are in text-only format. (A document that is pertinent to the subject matter of this book—Roger Ebert's Movie Laws—is shown in figure 13.3.)

FIGURE 13.3

Some of the imutable laws of movie illogic, as compiled by Roger Ebert and included in the Mother of All Humor Archives.

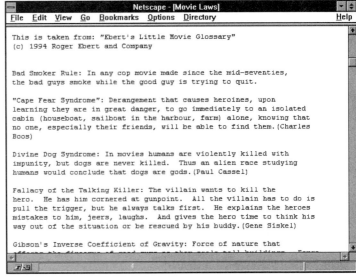

This is taken from: "Ebert's Little Movie Glossary"
(c) 1994 Roger Ebert and Company

Bad Smoker Rule: In any cop movie made since the mid-seventies,
the bad guys smoke while the good guy is trying to quit.

"Cape Fear Syndrome": Derangement that causes heroines, upon
learning they are in great danger, to go immediately to an isolated
cabin (houseboat, sailboat in the harbour, farm) alone, knowing that
no one, especially their friends, will be able to find them.(Charles
Boos)

Divine Dog Syndrome: In movies humans are violently killed with
impunity, but dogs are never killed. Thus an alien race studying
humans would conclude that dogs are gods.(Paul Cassel)

Fallacy of the Talking Killer: The villain wants to kill the
hero. He has him cornered at gunpoint. All the villain has to do is
pull the trigger, but he always talks first. He explains the heroes
mistakes to him, jeers, laughs. And gives the hero time to think his
way out of the situation or be rescued by his buddy.(Gene Siskel)

Gibson's Inverse Coefficient of Gravity: Force of nature that

The Funny Pages
http://uvacs.cs.virginia.edu/~bah6f/funnies

The Funny Pages is a good archive of the kinds of humorous odds 'n' ends that might come in handy if you're a wacky deejay from the Morning Zoo Crew in Anytown, USA. It includes a list of misheard song lyrics, physical proof that there is no Santa Claus, and the words to all the Schoolhouse Rock songs. (Remember "Conjunction Junction?")

Canonical Lists

As mentioned earlier, a canon is a collection of the "best" or most representative things within a genre. In the case of online humor, "canonical lists" refer to the best jokes in a given category (although one can also speak of the canon of Western literature, the canon of spiritual laws, and the Cannon of overweight TV detectives).

The Wrecked Humor Collection

http://www.infi.net/~cashman/humor

The best source of canonical lists that I have found on the Net is in a humor archive called the Wrecked Humor Collection. Although the archive also features the usual collection of one-liners, parodies, and Top Ten lists (as well as the official *rec.humor* FAQ document), its collection of canonical jokes is singularly impressive.

Derek Cashman's Wrecked Humor Collection started out as a repository of O.J. Simpson jokes and has grown into the definitive site for special-occasion, special-interest humor. In addition to the usual blonde jokes, lightbulb jokes, lawyer jokes, and ethnic slurs, this "list of lists" includes the following:

* Canonical List of Answering Machine Messages

* Canonical List of Computer Viruses

* Canonical List of Funny Accident Explanations

* Canonical List of Great Mysteries in Life

* Canonical List of Odd Bands

* Canonical List of Pentium Jokes

* Canonical List of Puking Terms

* Canonical List of the Shortest Books Ever Written (e.g., "The Book of Honest Lawyers")

* Canonical List of Smilies

* Canonical List of Sorority Jokes

A typical canonical list—for redneck jokes—is illustrated in figure 13.4.

FIGURE 13.4

The canonical list of redneck jokes, accessed from the Wrecked Humor Collection.

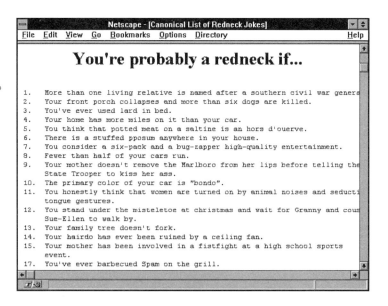

Netscape - [Canonical List of Redneck Jokes]

File   Edit   View   Go   Bookmarks   Options   Directory   Help

You're probably a redneck if...

1.   More than one living relative is named after a southern civil war genera
2.   Your front porch collapses and more than six dogs are killed.
3.   You've ever used lard in bed.
4.   Your home has more miles on it than your car.
5.   You think that potted meat on a saltine is an hors d'ouerve.
6.   There is a stuffed pposum anywhere in your house.
7.   You consider a six-pack and a bug-zapper high-quality entertainment.
8.   Fewer than half of your cars run.
9.   Your mother doesn't remove the Marlboro from her lips before telling the
     State Trooper to kiss her ass.
10. The primary color of your car is "bondo".
11. You honestly think that women are turned on by animal noises and seducti
     tongue gestures.
12. You stand under the mistletoe at christmas and wait for Granny and cous
     Sue-Ellen to walk by.
13. Your family tree doesn't fork.
14. Your hairdo has ever been ruined by a ceiling fan.
15. Your mother has been involved in a fistfight at a high school sports
     event.
17. You've ever barbecued Spam on the grill.

Comics and Cartoons on the Net

Many of the humor archives and link sites on the Net point to one or more of the cartoons and comic strips that can now be found online. Some of these comics are the same as the strips that can be found in your daily newspaper, although often these are a few days behind their printed-version counterparts (for copyright reasons).

The Comics 'n Stuff Archive

http://www.phlab.missouri.edu/c617145_www/comix.html

An incredible site called Comics 'n Stuff has links to almost every known comic strip and one-panel comic on the Internet, whether the strips are available in newspapers (*Calvin & Hobbes* in several languages), through online subscription (*Nina's Adventures*), or as Internet freebies (*NetBoy*). Because of its popularity, the site is mirrored on a second server.

The massive Comics 'n Stuff site is supported by a search form. Thus, if you're looking for something in particular, you can enter a keyword—and if that item exists on Comics 'n Stuff, the system will locate it for you.

This site is administered by Christian Cosas, who is a cartoonist himself. (His comic, *CultuRe Trap*, appears in the *Maneater*, the student newspaper of my alma mater, the University of Missouri.) Comics 'n Stuff is linked to literally hundreds of comic sites around the world.

FIGURE 13.5
The Comics 'n Stuff home page.

The Comic Strip
http://www.unitedmedia.com/comics

United Media is one of the largest syndicators of cartoon art in the United States—and now it's opened up a presence on the Web. This new site is free to the public and offers some of the best-known feature cartoons just one week after its original appearances in newspapers. (See figure 13.6.)

United Media's site houses the Web's largest collection of nationally syndicated feature comics and a major collection of editorial cartoons. Here's where you'll find the official home pages of the following "mainstream" cartoons:

* 9 Chickweed Lane
* Alley Oop
* Arlo & Janis
* Committed
* Dilbert

* Jump Start
* Marmaduke
* Robotman
* Rose Is Rose

FIGURE 13.6

United Media's Comic Strip page, home of lovable canine Marmaduke, lovable caveman Alley Oop, and lovable corporate everyman Dilbert.

• • • • • • • • • • • • • • • • •

Through these home pages, you can view previous installments of the comic strip, read a bio of the strip's creator, and obtain a list of newspapers that print the comic on a daily basis.

United Media also offers a special spotlight section, in which it features new cartoons, or those ready to roll out to national distribution.

There are many comic and cartoon-related sites among the UseNet discussion groups. *alt.comic.peanuts* discusses the psychological significance of Charles Schulz' perennial favorite; *alt.comics.batman* discusses the psychological significance of the Caped Crusader; and *alt.comics.superman* discusses the psychological significance of men in red elastic tights.

Also of interest to comic-strip and comic-book fans are the many groups within the *rec.arts.comics* hierarchy, which includes information about comic-book collecting and production, and *alt.comics.alternative*, which discusses the growing comic underground.

CLOSE-UP: VICE PRESIDENT AL GORE

http://www.whitehouse.gov/White_House/EOP/OVP/html/Cartoon.html

Despite his humorless reputation (and apparent inability to dance), Vice President Al Gore is an undeniably interesting and even somewhat funny individual. A graduate of Harvard (where he roomed with actor Tommy Lee Jones), Gore is the Clinton administration's point-man on emerging technologies, including the so-called Information Superhighway.

Gore also collects political cartoons. Over the years, his caricature has appeared in many cartoons—and many have made their way to his private collection. Along with his 1993 appearance on David Letterman's show, this collection of cartoons is evidence that the widely lampooned Mr. Gore has a healthy lack of self-importance.

The White House Web site now offers access to this collection of cartoons at *http://www.whitehouse.gov/White_House/EOP/OVP/html/Cartoon.html*. This is further proof that the world is getting stranger as it's getting cozier.

FIGURE 13.7

From the White House to Your House: An excerpt from Vice President Al Gore's collection of editorial cartoons. (In today's episode, Al ruptures his Archilles Tendon.)

CartooNet

http://prinny.pavilion.co.uk/cartoonet/cartoon.htm

CartooNet is a gateway to the world of European cartoon art—from commercially syndicated work to museum pieces, and from festival entrants to featured cartoonists.

Here you'll find excerpts of cartoons as they appear in European newspapers, information about competitions, links to many cartoon-related sites around the world, and much more.

Tool User Comics WWW Comics Project

http://www.tooluser.com

This is an archive of subscription-based comics that is keeping several starving cartoonists in beer money. (There are also public-domain comics and a free sample of each of the fee-based strips.) Many of the comics are high-quality Internet originals, although you will also find such well-known syndicated strips as *This Modern World* and *Stan Mack's Real-Life Funnies*. The in-house comic of this site is *Little Failure*, about an existentially troubled angle bracket.

Internet Published Comics

http://www.reed.edu/~rseymour/home/comics/comics.html

This Web page offers quick links to some cartoons and comic strips that you won't find easily elsewhere on the Net, including *The Far Side*, *Doonesbury*, and comics that have developed a fan base through the Internet itself, including *Borderline* and *Doctor Fun*. Figure 13.8 shows one of the more popular links available from this site: the home page for *Dilbert*.

FIGURE 13.8

This is the home page for Dilbert, the ongoing saga of a faceless information processor whose spirit is crushed beneath the jackboot of corporate fascism. (Accessed via the Internet Published Comics archive.)

Internet-Exclusive Comics

Many of the comic strips contained in the Internet Published Comics archives are an example of Internet-only or *Internet-exclusive* comics. This paperless medium of cartooning has sprung up over the past two years—an outgrowth of the World Wide Web's ability to present graphic images. The following are some of the better cartoons that can only be found online.

NetBoy
http://www.intelli.com/netboy

NetBoy, "The Choice of an Online Generation," is perhaps the best known of the Internet-only genre of cartoons and comics. The Net's response has been so overwhelming that *NetBoy* lost his home on the cartoon's original Web server.

Back now on a new server sponsored by Intelli.com, the crudely drawn, computer-savvy *NetBoy* is updated on a weekly basis. (See figure 13.9.)

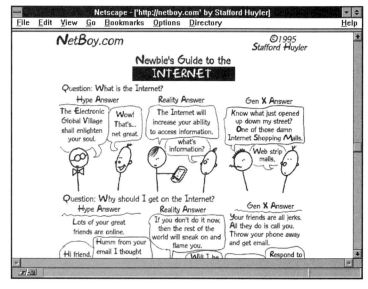

Doctor Fun

http://www.unitedmedia.com/comics/drfun

Doctor Fun, by David Farley, has a cult following not unlike that enjoyed by Gary Larson's *The Far Side*—which is not surprising, considering the similarity of the two strips (lots of dinosaur humor) and the fact that Gary Larson isn't producing any new material. (See figure 13.10.)

FIGURE 13.10

An excerpt from an archive of the one-panel comic Doctor Fun by David Farley at http:// sunsite.unc.edu/Dave/Dr-Fun.

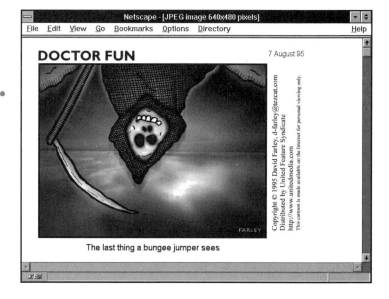

Virtually Reality

http://www.onramp.net/~scroger/vreality.html

Of all the online cartoons I have seen, Eric Scroger's *Virtually Reality* goes the furthest in utilizing the emerging graphics capabilities of the Net.

Virtually Reality is a droll one-panel cartoon of the *Far Side* ilk. What makes it unique is that it is carefully rendered with 3D Studio software, giving the characters a distinctive puppets-on-a-stage look. It looks especially good on a so-called true-color (16-million color) computer monitor. It does not look so good on paper, so for now you'll have to look at figure 13.11 and use your imagination.

FIGURE 13.11

A sample of Virtually Reality, a comic panel rendered with 3D Studio software by Eric Scroger.

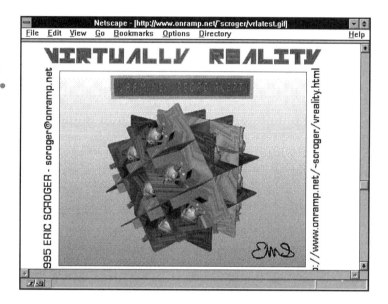

Online Humor Magazines

Along with the advent of Internet-only cartoon strips, the growth of the Web has facilitated the creation of entire magazine-style humor sites. These sites owe as much to the vintage *National Lampoon* as they do to *Wired*.

Some of the better online humor magazines are profiled here.

Melvin

http://www.melvin.com

Melvin could be the prototype for the online magazine of the future. It is a visually clever and bitterly funny arts-and-entertainment magazine that bears favorable comparison to *Spy*.

Published by the staff of *THE ONION* at the University of Illinois, Melvin features bold, entertaining graphics and attitude-drenched reviews of movies, music, and current events.

A sample page from a recent issue of Melvin is shown in figure 13.12.

FIGURE 13.12

A sample page from the trenchantly funny online humor magazine called Melvin.

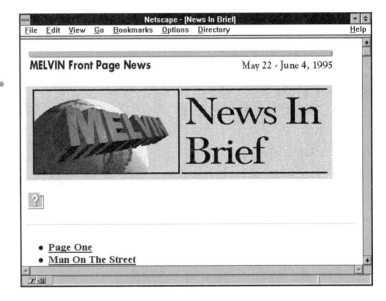

X Magazine

http://www.msen.com/~xmag

This post-ironic, neo-innocent, music-and-humor 'zine is published by a group of self-described "junk culture magpies" in Detroit.

Past issues have discussed the metaphorical significance of Fisher-Price Little People toys (the Fisher-Price version of *Catcher in the Rye* is shown in figure 13.13) and the history of bowling.

FIGURE 13.13
The opening page of the Fisher-Price version of J.D. Salinger's Catcher in the Rye, from X Magazine.

Your MoM
http://www.cc.columbia.edu/~emj5/yourmom/ymhome.html

Your MoM is a graphically superior, smarty-pants slacker magazine that was started at a high school in Evanston, Ill., and has now followed one of its founders to Columbia University in New York. Its home page is shown in figure 13.14.

One of the outstanding features of Your MoM is the movie-review section, in which the reviewer assesses a movie based on what he can figure out from its ad campaigns rather than by actually seeing it.

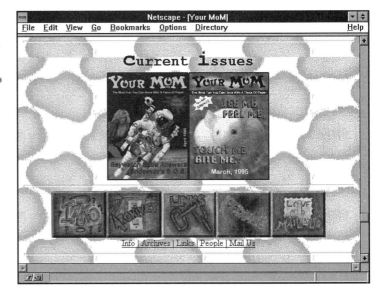

Crank
http://www.btf.com/crank.htm

Crank is a vile and hilarious magazine put out by a lad named Jeff Koyen in Philadelphia. The online version of Crank can be accessed through the Web site for a BBS called Burn This Flag, and it's the most appallingly funny thing that I've found on the entire Net.

Crank is a gargantuan stinkbomb of low-life rant. It festers with tortured tales of crummy roommates, unpaid utility bills, drunken binges, and confrontations with authority.

One of the few excerpts I could get way with printing here is figure 13.15, from a how-to article titled "The Lost Art of the Drunken Drive."

FIGURE 13.15

An excerpt from "The Lost Art of the Drunken Drive" in Jeff Koyen's hilariously offensive Crank magazine. (Note: This is not an endorsement of reckless behavior. It's a joke. Take a cab.)

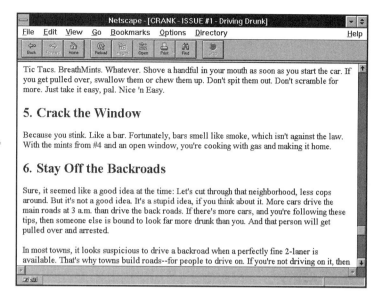

Netscape - [CRANK - ISSUE #1 - Driving Drunk]

Tic Tacs. BreathMints. Whatever. Shove a handful in your mouth as soon as you start the car. If you get pulled over, swallow them or chew them up. Don't spit them out. Don't scramble for more. Just take it easy, pal. Nice 'n Easy.

5. Crack the Window

Because you stink. Like a bar. Fortunately, bars smell like smoke, which isn't against the law. With the mints from #4 and an open window, you're cooking with gas and making it home.

6. Stay Off the Backroads

Sure, it seemed like a good idea at the time: Let's cut through that neighborhood, less cops around. But it's not a good idea. It's a stupid idea, if you think about it. More cars drive the main roads at 3 a.m. than drive the back roads. If there's more cars, and you're following these tips, then someone else is bound to look far more drunk than you. And that person will get pulled over and arrested.

In most towns, it looks suspicious to drive a backroad when a perfectly fine 2-laner is available. That's why towns build roads--for people to drive on. If you're not driving on it, then

UseNet Humor Sites

If the fundamental building block of humor is the joke, then UseNet is the industrial heartland of Internet humor.

Almost every discussion group in the *alt* and *rec* hierarchies is riddled with amateur puns, insults, one-liners, and parodies, and it's an inevitable hazard of surfing in UseNet that you will have to wade through gallons of sophomoric swill to find something that's genuinely entertaining or informative. For some people, that's part of the fun. For the rest of us, there are UseNet groups that are specifically dedicated to humor and its various subcategories. These humor groups keep some of the worst jokers out of the rest of the sites, and occasionally they even produce something witty in their own right.

The *rec.humor* hierarchy within UseNet is very popular—and generally pretty safe for the easily offended.

rec.humor

The *rec.humor* hierarchy begins with *rec.humor*. In this heavily traveled newsgroup, you'll find the kinds of jokes that eventually wind up in canonical lists (Mommy jokes, lightbulb jokes, blonde jokes, and so on.). This is not the place to ask for joke assistance, although plenty of that goes on.

Hundreds of postings arrive here every week. (Don't these people have work to do?)

rec.humor.funny

The next group in this hierarchy is *rec.humor.funny*. Here you will often find humorous narratives or jokes in story form.

You will immediately note that *rec.humor.funny* is considerably smaller than *rec.humor*. That's because *rec.humor.funny* is moderated, which means that somebody (or a team of somebodies) is actually deciding which of the jokes that the newsgroup receives is actually funny enough to post (while adhering to the committee's standards of decency). Very few of the jokes pass the rigorous screening process (which is described in the site's FAQ document), but those that do qualify have a chance to travel the global community in a matter of hours to become part of our shared cultural heritage. Or something like that.

The screeners rate the jokes for their smirkability and chucklitude, as shown under "Keywords" in the introductory gibberish that precedes the joke. See figure 13.16 for an example of the kind of thing that passes muster here.

FIGURE 13.16

This is one of the jokes that was recently approved by the committee at rec.humor.funny. (Notice the helpful keywords in the introduction, which classify the joke.) Quite a rib-tickler, eh? And not a dirty word in the bunch!

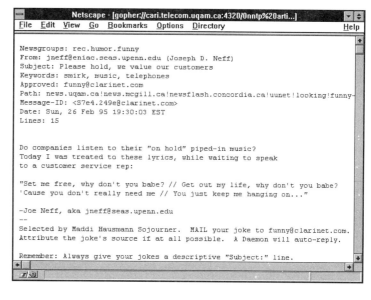

```
Netscape - [gopher://cari.telecom.uqam.ca:4320/0nntp%20arti...]
File   Edit   View   Go   Bookmarks   Options   Directory                    Help

Newsgroups: rec.humor.funny
From: jneff@eniac.seas.upenn.edu (Joseph D. Neff)
Subject: Please hold, we value our customers
Keywords: smirk, music, telephones
Approved: funny@clarinet.com
Path: news.uqam.ca!news.mcgill.ca!newsflash.concordia.ca!uunet!looking!funny-
Message-ID: <S7e4.249e@clarinet.com>
Date: Sun, 26 Feb 95 19:30:03 EST
Lines: 15


Do companies listen to their "on hold" piped-in music?
Today I was treated to these lyrics, while waiting to speak
to a customer service rep:

"Set me free, why don't you babe? // Get out my life, why don't you babe?
'Cause you don't really need me // You just keep me hanging on..."

-Joe Neff, aka jneff@seas.upenn.edu
--
Selected by Maddi Hausmann Sojourner.  MAIL your joke to funny@clarinet.com.
Attribute the joke's source if at all possible.  A Daemon will auto-reply.

Remember: Always give your jokes a descriptive "Subject:" line.
```

It's always wise to lurk for a bit before participating actively in any newsgroup, so you can become accustomed to the tone of the discourse and will be less likely to offend (which will get you flamed—that is, attacked with military-issue flamethrowers by Net surfers who extract your home address from the files of your service provider).

When it comes to offending others, however, the *rec.humor* groups can be extreme—and so can the flame wars that erupt.

Do yourself a favor and read the FAQs beforehand. (FTP to *rtfm.mit.edu/ pub/usenet/rec.humor.funny*.)

rec.humor.d

This is the discussion adjunct of the *rec.humor* hierarchy. Ostensibly it exists for the serious discussion of humor, but on my visits there, I haven't encountered a lot of academics.

Other Internet Humor Resources

If you still haven't found anything funny on the Internet, you either aren't looking hard enough or you're suffering a crisis of spirit that no amount of computing can resolve for you. As a last resort before joining the Foreign Legion, you might want to visit one of the following sites.

Imagine Publishing's Joke Board
http://www.best.com/~imagine/jokes

Imagine Publishing offers a Joke Board that is a compilation of over 200 one-liners and story jokes culled from the Internet—and it comes with a sophisticated voting/tabulation/sorting system in which you can rate the jokes on a scale of 1 (not funny) to 10 (herniatingly funny).

Here's an example of the kind of thing you might find there:

"Q: What makes men chase women they have no intention of marrying?

A: The same urge that makes dogs chase cars they have no intention of driving."

This service might save you some trouble on those days when you need to be funny but you just don't have the time to write your own material. It is available in four languages, so you French people have no excuse for remaining so dour.

The Joke Board home page is shown in figure 13.17.

FIGURE 13.17

The home page for Imagine
Publishing's nicely done Joke
Board.

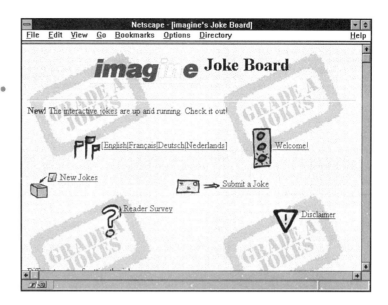

Syndicated Humor Features from ClariNet

The fee-based ClariNet News Service offers a nice selection of
nationally syndicated humor columns, including those by the
very witty Dave Barry (*clari.feature.dave barry*), the very proper
Miss Manners (*clari.feature.miss manners*), and the very cranky
Mike Royko (*clari.feature. mike_royko*).

If your service provider does not offer them, ClariNet's feature
columns—like its extensive online news service—are available
by subscription.

ClariNet features are also available via subscription e-mail. For information,
drop an e-mail message to *info@clarinet.com*.

The Comedy Central Home Page

http://comcentral.com

Comedy Central is my favorite cable TV network, the home of *Mystery Science Theater 3000* (and the disembodied voice of Penn Jillette). The home page of the Comedy Central cable TV network was under construction at the time of this writing, but it promises to be an indispensable part of your daily life in the near future. For now, you can use it to download clips from *The Benny Hill Show*—anything after that is gravy.

Many of the sites that are mentioned in this chapter, as well as several other sites that are related to humor, can easily be accessed through the Yahoo utility, which can be accessed at *http://www.yahoo.com* or directly from the Netscape browser (by clicking on the "Net Directory" button). Simply choose the category *Entertainment*, followed by the subcategory *Humor*. It's so easy, a feminist/redneck/mother-in-law/Aggie/Eskimo/Albanian/lawyer/Kato Kaelin could do it.

The List

Humor Archives

The Cathouse Humor Archive
http://www.cathouse/org/cathouse/humor

LaughWEB
http://WWW.Misty.com/laughweb

The Mother of All Humor Archives
http://www.tc.cornell.edu/~ckline/humor/maillist.html

The Funny Pages
http://uvacs.cs.virginia.edu/~bah6f/funnies

Canonical Lists

The Wrecked Humor Collection

http://www.infi.net/~cashman/humor

The definitive collection of definitive jokes.

Comics and Cartoon on the Net

The Comics 'n Stuff Archive

http://www.phlab.missouri.edu/c617145_www/comix.html

An immense collection of links to almost every cartoon and comic strip on the Net.

Al Gore's Cartoon Gallery

http://www.whitehouse.gov/White_House/EOP/OVP/html/Cartoon.html

The personal collection of the Vice President of the United States.

The Comic Strip

http://www.unitedmedia.com/comics

CartooNet

http://prinny.pavilion.co.uk/cartoonet/cartoon.htm

Dedicated to British and European cartoon art.

Tool User Comics WWW Comics Project

http://www.tooluser.com

Internet Published Comics

http://www.reed.edu/~rseymour/home/comics/comics.html

Internet Exclusives

Net Boy

http://www.intelli.com/netboy

Doctor Fun

http://www.unitedmedia.com/comics/drfun

Online Humor Magazines

Melvin

http://www.melvin.com

Hysterically funny and easy on the eyes.

X Magazine

http://www.msen.com/'xmag

Your MoM

http://www.cc.columbia.edu/~emj5/yourmom/ymhome.html

A slacker's answer to *Esquire*.

Crank

http://www.btf.com/crank.htm

Go ahead, I dare ya.

The rec.humor Hierarchy

rec.humor

The jumbo feed-trough of Internet humor.

rec.humor.funny

The invitation-only dinner party of Internet humor.

rec.humor.d

This is the discussion adjunct of the *rec.humor* hierarchy.

Other UseNet Humor Sites

alt.humor.puns

alt.tasteless.jokes

This is not about food.

alt.flame

Dedicated to the fine art of the insult.

alt.shenanigans
Practical jokes and pranks: described, discussed, and bragged about.

alt.comedy.slapstick

alt.comedy.standup

alt.comedy.improvisation

alt.comedy.british
Includes discussion of *Monty Python* and *Fawlty Towers*.

alt.comedy.firesign-thtre

alt.fan.lemurs

alt.best.of.internet
That's what it's called, but that's not what it is.

Other Internet Humor Resources

Imagine Publishing's Joke Board
http://www.best.com/~imagine/jokes

Syndicated Humor Features from ClariNet
clari.feature.dave_barry

clari.feature.miss_manners

clari.feature. mike_royko

The Comedy Central Home Page
http://comcentral.com

C H A P T E R

14

Games

IN THIS CHAPTER:

> *Computer and Video Games*

> *MUDs, MOOS, and MUSHs*

> *Fantasy Role-Playing Games*

> *Online Games*

> *Traditional Board and Strategy Games*

IN OTHER CHAPTERS:

> *Sports are covered in Chapter 15.*

Games include everything from pinball to ping-pong to Pac Man to poker. Some are physical and some are mental. Some are team-based and some are solitary. But all games have one thing in common: Games are a tool we use when we can't bear to face our workday responsibilities but we still need to act out the underlying pathology of aggression. Playing a round of Donkey Kong might seem like a harmless exercise in hand-eye coordination, but it's actually a way for you to pop your boss in the nose without either of you knowing about it. Don't believe me? That's because you're in denial. Maybe if you drop a quarter in this slot here, you'll see what I mean. Or at least you'll feel better.

General Resources

For general info about the broad spectrum of human recreational activities or the deeper meaning of the gaming impulse, try one of the following sites—or consult your health-care professional.

The World-Wide Web Virtual Library: Games and Recreation
http://www.cis.ufl.edu/~thoth/library/recreation.html

The consistently excellent resource called the World-Wide Web Virtual Library (also known as the W3 Virtual Library) has a nice "Games and Recreation" section that provides information on the whole spectrum of leisure-time activities, from computer-game sites to role-playing newsgroups to the home page of the Scottish Tiddlywinks Association. See figure 14.1.

FIGURE 14.1

An excerpt from the WWW
Virtual Library page on games
and recreation.

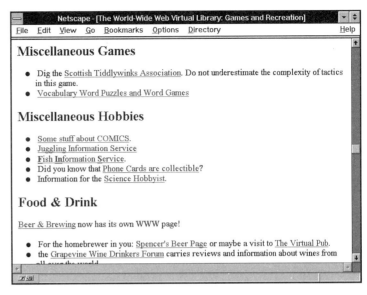

If your idea of "recreation" extends a little further than blasting aliens or donning a wizard's cloak, this page is the best place to start looking for a Web site that matches your interests.

The Virtual Playground of Dr. Fun

http://www.omix.com/zine/DeKoven

In this collection of short articles, a guy named Bernie (Dr. Fun) DeKoven answers questions and otherwise pontificates on the deeper meanings of fun, games, and recreation.

The Dr. Fun articles include "Is Fun a Four Letter Word?," "Toy Horses," "Road Games," "Elder Fun," "War Games Teach Peace, Too," some strategies for playing checkers in prison (see figure 14.2), and the following thoughts on why getting killed in video games can be a learning experience: "In kids' computer games, every little death brings a little more information. For kids on the virtual playground, death is temporary, and reincarnation is guaranteed. The trick is not to die the same way twice. To die, to be reborn to a longer life, to die again. In the most successful of the "Nintendo" games (like Sonic the Hedgehog, though Sonic was designed for a completely different game machine), death is a way of life. In fact, you usually start out with a guaranteed number of lives (and an unspecified number of implicitly guaranteed deaths). To get a longer life, you have to remember exactly what you did that led to your death the last time. You have to have actually learned something—maybe something not directly related to social or intellectual growth, but something, definitely something."

Now perhaps the good doctor could tell us what it means when players shoot a raygun full of plasma energy into the gaping mouth of a hideous dragon that is stalking them through a dark and slimy tunnel.

FIGURE 14.2

Dr. Fun explains it all for you. (Maybe if more of us played checkers in the first place, there wouldn't be so many people in prison.)

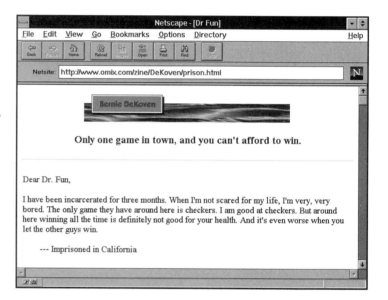

Computer and Video Games

Many of the people who are surfing the Net are of a generation that equates the word "game" with computer and video games. And indeed it can be argued that without computer and video games, the computer industry would be deprived of most of the brain power and revenues that make it tick. It's no secret that computer gamers become computer developers, and gamers have been the tail that wags the dog of the computer industry ever since Pong was slapped together in a California garage.

General Resources

There are many sites on the Internet that review, index, and sell a wide assortment of computer and video games.

The Games Domain

http://wcl-rs.bham.ac.uk/GamesDomain

The Games Domain is a large and invaluable resource for anyone who is interested in the world of computer and video games.

The main area of the Domain contains hundreds of links to FAQs, walkthroughs, FTP sites, home pages, electronic magazines, commercial sites, and much more—"everything from Doom to Darts; MUDs to Mortal Kombat; PBMs to PiD; Electronic Arts to Epic." It is also home to the Universal Hint System, which provides hints and cheat codes for dozens of popular games.

Other sections include: a site devoted to game programming (The Nexus), with links and downloadable files, texture map resources, sound files, and more; access to over 2,000 downloadable shareware and freeware games for the Mac, PCs, and Amiga; and an online gaming magazine called GD Review that features industry news and dozens of indexed game reviews. (See figure 14.3.)

FIGURE 14.3

A review of a game called Gadget, from the Gaming Review online magazine of the Game Domain. (This game is compared to a '40s noir thriller as art-directed by Frank Lloyd Wright.)

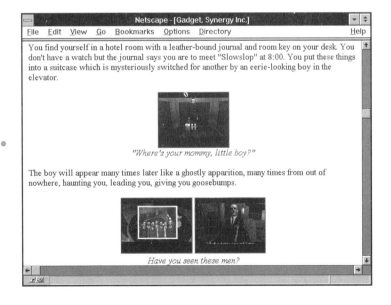

Much of the information in the Games Domain is mirrored at a site called Games on the Internet, at *http://www.power.net/games/lordsoth*. That address might provide faster access for those in the U.S.

If the Game Boy hand-held format is your thing, you'll want to check out the Game Boy Page at *http://www.cs.umd.edu/users/fms/GameBoy*. It has FAQs, news, reviews, and plenty of cheats and passwords for Game Boy-compatible games.

Console World

http://arachnid.cm.cf.ac.uk/Games

The folks at Cardiff University in Wales maintain a fabulous movie database that is well-known on the Internet and is mentioned in several places in this book. They also offer a similarly comprehensive database on video games, called Console World.

Console World's searchable holdings contain information on 1,956 different video-game titles for all of the major gaming systems. For each game it lists the year of release, the format, the number of players, and cheat codes.

The site also includes FAQs for many different games, newsgroup information, and archives of articles from gaming magazines.

NOTE

Many of the popular newsstand gaming magazines, such as *Computer Gaming World* and *PC Gamer*, have established a Web presence, while other gaming magazines exist purely online. See The List at the end of this chapter for their Net addresses. (These magazines can also be accessed directly from the Games Domain, the Game Page of the Universe, and other general gaming-resource sites.)

THE IMAGINATION NETWORK

Leave it up to the forward-thinking folks at AT&T to jump aboard the gaming bandwagon a mere 20 years after every kid in the Industrial World had chained themselves to a game box.

The ImagiNation Network is a new gaming service that will allow customers to compete via computer against players from around the country in 30 different games, from traditional casino games to shoot-em-ups to sword-and-sorcery games. All this takes place across the phone lines (natch). Players will also be able to "chat" with each other. (See figure 14.4.)

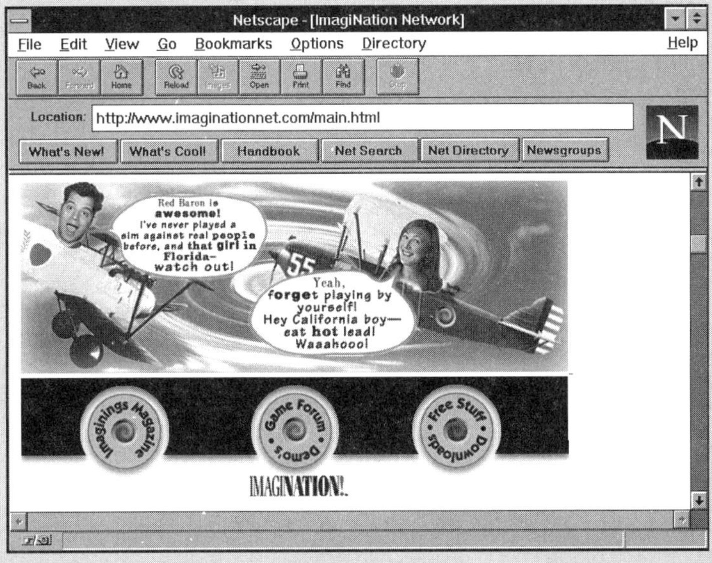

FIGURE 14.4

The ImagiNation Network offers participants a chance to play 30 different online games against real opponents—and maybe even a chance to find true love.

If making new friends in this manner sounds like something you'd enjoy, it'll cost you two to six bucks an hour. That's cheaper than a lot of other ways you can make friends. Of course, actually using your "imagination" (the mental faculty after which this service is named) is free; but who's got the time or the energy?

Game Page of the Universe

http://www.pht.com/games.html

Pacific HiTech is a distributor of CD-ROM games that maintains this excellent game resource. A highlight is its list of hundreds of freeware and shareware games that can be downloaded directly from its Web-accessible FTP site. It also has an extensive and useful list of game-related links.

Popular Computer and Video Games

There are several computer and video games that are so popular that they have inspired game-specific Web sites, mailing lists, UseNet groups, and even feature-film adaptations.

DOOM

DOOM is a true phenomenon among computer games. Episode One of this grisly and hyper-real monster hunt from id Software was made freely available through BBSs and commercial shareware compilations. After players got a taste of how advanced and effective the graphics were, the demand for further episodes was immense. And that's when id Software started raking in the dough.

It is to id Software's credit that it has allowed programmers to customize the basic DOOM engine and to distribute these variations (called WAD files) online. There are now several books and CD-ROMs that contain DOOM variations (including *Tricks of the DOOM Programming Gurus*, which yours truly edited while disguised as a mild-mannered flunky for a major metropolitan book publisher). Some of these variations include versions where the bloodthirsty monsters are all Barneys or characters from *The Simpsons*.

Because interest in DOOM is so high and the game is so interactive, there are many Internet sites devoted to DOOM in both its original form and in its many variations.

The id Software home page is at *http://www.idsoftware.com*. From there you can download the shareware version of the game, order the registered version, and learn about Heretic, a related game.

There is also an id Software ftp site at *ftp.idsoftware.com* that contains levels, patches, technical stuff, and more.

DOOM Gate at *http://doomgate.cs.buffalo.edu* is probably the biggest and most thorough of the DOOM-related pages, featuring utilities, add-ons, information about DOOM forums, and downloadable versions of DOOM, DOOM II, and Heretic (as well as the latest craze, the space-flight game Descent). See figure 14.5.

FIGURE 14.5

The main page for DOOM Gate, the best source for DOOM information on the Web.

● ● ● ● ● ● ● ● ● ● ● ● ● ● ● ● ●

A fun general-interest Web site called Squidly's Reef contains a page of DOOM-related links (and other worthwhile gaming information) at *http://linet02.li.net/~dsquid/gaming.html*. Squidly's home page is shown in figure 14.6 simply because it looks so cool and I want you to go there.

FIGURE 14.6

There is plenty of DOOM activity in the UseNet domain. Much of the authoritative info has moved from the *alt* hierarchy to the *rec* hierarchy. According to DOOM Gate, the relevant newsgroups are now as follows:

rec.games.computer.doom.announce

This moderated group replaces *alt.games.doom.announce* (general announcements).

rec.games.computer.doom.help

This moderated group replaces *alt.games.doom.newplayers*, and is used to provide general help for questions by new players.

rec.games.computer.doom.misc

This should cover all conversations that are not covered by one of the other groups.

rec.games.computer.doom.editing

This should be used to discuss editing of wads, patches for the .EXE of DOOM and DOOM II, and other issues dealing with the creation of third-party add-ons for DOOM.

rec.games.computer.doom.playing

This should replace *alt.games.doom* and *alt.games.doom.ii* for all conversations relating to the playing of either game.

Descent

Where DOOM ended, Descent begins. Descent is a fast-paced game of space combat. The action resembles the Death Star battle sequence in *Star Wars.* It is notable for allowing players a full 360-degree range of movement (which requires a fast computer with plenty of RAM). The game can be played solo, but you can also compete across a local-area network (like the kids in my office) or across the Internet itself.

The Official Descent Page from the people at Interplay is at *http://www.interplay.com/website/descent.html.* (See figure 14.7.)

FIGURE 14.7
The Official Descent Page.

Myst

Myst is a graphically sophisticated clue-and-puzzle game that involves a ghost ship, time travel, ancient manuscripts, and that sort of thing. It is very popular, which heartens those of us who are troubled by the disproportionate number of games that involve colorful acts of butchery.

The Myst Page can be found at *http://www.best.com/~rdc/ roger/myst.html*. As you can see from figure 14.8, this is a cut-to-the-chase approach to a game that ordinary requires an awful lot of digging and exploring. (There are actually people who consider the leisurely exploration of the Myst environment to be part of the "fun.")

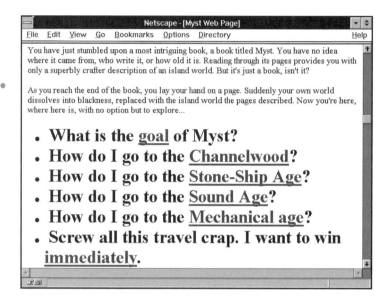

Similar information can be found at the Myst Walkthrough at *http://wcl-rs.bham.ac.uk/~djh/walkthru/myst.html* and Doug's Myst Help Page at *http://www.astro.washington.edu/ingram/ myst/index.html.*

Mortal Kombat

At its core, Mortal Kombat is a fairly simple kung-fu-and-fisticuffs game; but it's also the most appallingly violent of the big-name arcade games, and the people at Williams/Bally/Midway seem to like it that way. There's an exaggerated quality to the violence—such as when a fighter pulls the bloody spinal cord from a defeated foe and holds it aloft in triumph—that is almost too brazen to criticize. And of course, the kids dig it, which is the only social consideration that matters to a capitalist enterprise.

The Yahoo *Entertainment/Games/Video* directory lists nine different Mortal Kombat sites.

The Mortal Kombat WWW Pages at *http://www.cs.ucl.ac.uk/ students/zcacaes/mk/mk.html* has a bounty of MK information, including news on the Mortal Kombat movie, an MK animation, sound clips, screen shots (real and fake), and the latest MK gossip.

Kombat Kraft (also called the New College Video Gaming Home Page) at *http://www.sar.usf.edu/~paulino/html/ kombat.html* has a lot of Mortal Kombat stuff, including the latest on Mortal Kombat 3, as well as many general-interest gaming links. (See figure 14.9.)

FIGURE 14.9

Kombat Kraft, a page dedicated to video/computer gaming in general and to Mortal Kombat in particular.

GAME COMPANY AND PUBLISHER INFO

Nintendo is the 600-pound gorilla of the computer-gaming industry. Its home page, at *http://www.nintendo.com*, offers the usual corporate press-release stuff, product information, and a chance to talk to other Nintendo fanatics in real time. It also features links to cool sites that have nothing to do with Nintendo.

The Sega of America Home Page at *http://www.segaoa.com* has product info, some Sonic the Hedgehog animation clips, lots of promotional merchandise for sale, press releases, and information about the Sega Channel.

The most fun home page I found for a computer-gaming system was the 3DO page at *http://www.3do.com* (see figure 14.10), which uses a Communist-propaganda theme to promote its line-up of offbeat game titles.

FIGURE 14.10.
The 3DO game-system home page is not just a corporate promotional tool—it's a sophisticated art-historical lesson in the elasticity of symbols.

The Software Creations BBS, now Web-accessible at *http://www.swcbbs.com* is a semi-official hang-out for many of the biggest names in game publishing, including Apogee and id Software. Many popular games are initially released in this forum as shareware versions.

MUDs

The acronym MUD stands for *multi-user dungeon* (a.k.a. *multi-user domain* or *multi-user dimension*), and you're going to be seeing and hearing a lot about it.

A MUD is a text-based virtual environment comprising different rooms or areas in which players can examine objects and interact. Some MUDs are used for collaborative writing projects or even scientific research, but they are most popular as gaming environments. In a MUD game, each player on the network has a different persona, which usually includes a physical description, personality traits, and a history. The different characters can chat, form alliances, solve puzzles, battle demons, fight each other to the death, or even mate—all in real time.

Most MUDs have specific themes. Not surprisingly, many of them are based on science-fiction or medieval sorcery; however, there are also numerous contemporary-themed MUDs, educational MUDs, humorous MUDs, and countless MUDs that are dedicated to simulating sex between adorable furry creatures. (I kid you not.)

MUDding is done via a Telnet connection, although there are now some Web-based MUD connections to these Telnet sites. Web capability promises to add audio and graphics to a pastime that has been largely text-based. However, until that becomes more common, MUDding will continue to involve a lot of arcane text-based gobbledygook, an extensive menu of commands, and considerable knowledge about what's going on (which is why some initial lurking and fact-gathering is essential for new participants).

In MOOs (*MUDs, object-oriented),* players can effectively program and extend the environments as they participate. The most massive and famous of the MOOs is the LambaMOO, which has over 8,000 participants, its own government, virtual hotels, hot tubs, a heliport—and, not surprisingly, a waiting list to get in.

It has been estimated that an astonishing 10 percent of Internet bandwidth is consumed by MUDding.

MUDdom

http://www.shef.ac.uk/uni/academic/I-M/is/studwork/groupe/home.html

For those who are curious about MUDs (and the related games called MUSHs, MOOs, MUCKs, and so forth), this is a good introduction. It details the history, mores, and social implications of MUDding, and it gives an in-depth technical description of the MUD experience. (See figure 14.11.)

FIGURE 14.11

This screen from the MUDdom site explains some of the fantasy that goes into developing a MUD persona. (Is it any surprise that "female players are rare on MUDs"?)

• • • • • • • • • • • • • • • • • • •

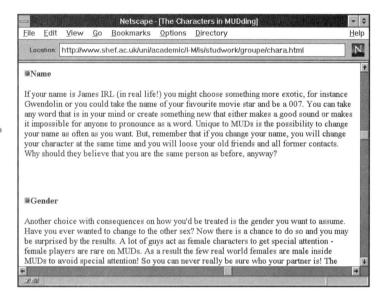

You can use the MUDdom server as a springboard to more specific MUD information, or you can simply use it learn more about the phenomenon (before you commit the next 10 years of your life to lurking around a computer environment as "Lola, the Creole seductress of old New Orleans").

The MUDdom site even gives due attention to the psychological implications and potential downside of the MUDding experience: "It is true that most people feel the freedom of anonymity [when they are playing a MUD]. They are more able to express themselves than in real life. People see MUDs as a place to experiment with various kinds of behavior before applying it in the real world.

"The danger with MUDding is, as a form of escapism it can be addictive to those who find life easier in their 'wired world.' There are known cases of people spending up to 17 hours a day MUDding and having to resort to counseling to reduce their connect times."

The MUD Resource Guide
http://www.cis.upenn.edu/~lwl/mudinfo.html

This might be the best place to visit for specific, hard-core MUD information, such as addresses, FAQs, Web pages, FTP sites, and so on. It has a particular emphasis on MUSHs (*multi-user shared hallucinations*, such as the Trippy Mush). The Resource Guide has a solid academic foundation (it comes from the University of Pennsylvania), and it features links to ethical discussions, a site about aesthetic considerations in MUD design, and lists of education-related MUDs—all of which might lead you to believe that this phenomenon is something other than just creepy and addictive.

Role-Playing Games

MUD addiction might become a trendy disease in the years ahead, but there is already a well-established history of obsessive behavior among people who participate in such role-playing games as Dungeons & Dragons. I'm not here to pass judgment on anybody's lifestyle; I only know what I've seen on the made-for-TV movies. That's where I learned that role-playing games involve a considerable investment of time in an activity that blurs the line between reality and fantasy, where your fellow participants are likely to pass you critical information about a wizard's spell or a dragon's lair in a whispered rendezvous behind the old schoolhouse.

It's actually kind of sweet that ordinarily misunderstood people can turn themselves into heroes in the context of a fantasy game, and as long as nobody gets hurt (again, like in those made-for-TV movies), I say, "Go for it."

Dungeons & Dragons

D&D (or AD&D, for Advanced Dungeons & Dragons, a commercial trademark) is the granddaddy of fantasy/role-playing games. It is a complicated, long-term role-playing game with a medieval wizards-and-warriors theme. (If you don't already know this by now, you've probably missed the boat and you'll have to find some other long-term project—like a relationship with a flesh-and-blood human.) There are many D&D resources on the Net, including FAQs, mailing lists, chat forums, spell books, and numerous online variations of the game itself. For a complete list, try the *Yahoo/Entertainment/Games/Role-Playing* directory.

The Role-Playing Games Web Page
http://www.acm.uiuc.edu/duff/index.html

This long-standing Web page is the Mecca for role-playing-game information on the WWW. It mostly concentrates on AD&D, but there is plenty of information here about other role-playing games, as well as MUDs, MUSHs, and MOOs. (See figure 14.12.)

FIGURE 14.12
The Role-Playing Games Web Page.

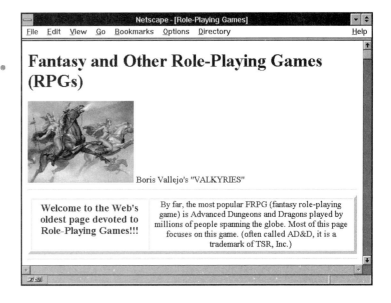

This site features utilities (a plot book for those times when your game is in a rut; a "random village generator;" a virtual mortuary for dead players), an index to FTP sites and mailing lists, a collection of fantasy art (more large-breasted space vixens astride fire-breathing dragons), and links to gaming companies.

The RPG Page

http://www.edu.isy.liu.se/~d91johol/rpg.html

This is another all-purpose role-playing page that concentrates on Dungeons & Dragons. It is notable for the fine graphic representations of AD&D characters and for something called the AD&D Book of Sex, which tells you everything you need to know about the sexual component of the Dungeons & Dragons experience. (Fact #1: It's pure fantasy.) Here is where you will learn such things as the potency of the average gnome and the mysteries of The Bitch Rule. (See figure 14.13.)

FIGURE 14.13

In this excerpt form the AD&D Book of Sex, we learn that seduction is a matter of charisma, intelligence, and dumb luck.

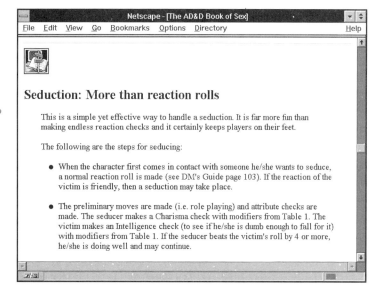

Magic—The Gathering

There are at least 26 sites devoted to this card-based role-playing game, which is a kind of D&D Lite for a mostly younger audience with a shorter attention span. The game involves accumulating (i.e., *buying*) game cards that give you various powers, and then matching your cards against other players'. (A similar game is called Jyhad, in which "you and your opponents play ancient vampires who use political manipulation and force to dominate other vampires and drain each others' blood pools.")

Wizards of the Coast at *http://www.itis.com/deckmaster* is a good general resource for information on Magic: The Gathering and Jyhad. It has rules, card information, a glossary, Magic fiction, UseNet info (*rec.games.trading-cards*), and links to many player home pages (which is helpful for traders).

Third Planet's Magic Trading Post at *http:// www.thirdplanet.com/Magic* is a free service for buying, selling, and trading cards over the Net.

Strategy Games

Before there were computers, there were strategy board games, and before there were strategy board games, there were playing cards. I have heard reports that there are still people in the hinterlands who pull out the old Parcheesi board or Canasta deck on a cold winter's night, and in honor of this hopelessly quaint behavior, this section is devoted to traditional strategy and playing-card games.

The Game Cabinet
http://web.kaleida.com/u/tidwell/GameCabinet.html

As the name implies, this is a sprawling mess of game-related stuff, the Web equivalent of a rumpus-room closet that is overflowing with disorganized game pieces and crumpled rule books. It covers "family, beer-and-pretzel, and strategy games."

It includes *extremely* detailed rules, descriptions, and reviews (see figure 14.14) for board games from around the world, as well as information from game publishers who are seeking new titles.

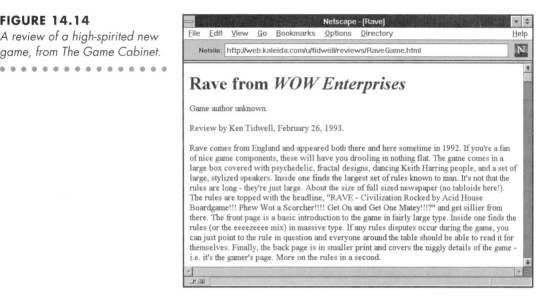

The Game Cabinet is also well-linked to gaming magazines, board-game manufacturers, collectors sites, game clubs, and mail-order merchants.

The Web Games Terminal
http://web.kaleida.com/u/tidwell/deeperDrawers/GamesOnTheNet.html

The Web Games Terminal is a front-end link site that can connect you to online competition (versus humans or computers) in chess, bridge, Go, Othello, Scrabble, and numerous other strategy games.

Chess

Chess is royalty among board games. It's played by smart people on an elegant surface with game-pieces that are often works of art. Let's not kid ourselves—it's still a metaphorical slaughterhouse where peasants are forced to lay down their lives for an arrogant axis of church and monarchy—but the bloodletting is so abstract that the players tend to think of it as pure and playful geometry.

There are many chess sites on the Net, including several chess computers that will play you for the sheer pleasure of watching you bleed.

The Chess Connection WWW Magazine

http://www.easynet.co.uk/pages/worldchess/home.htm

This is described as "a bi-weekly electronic magazine/ cybermall with chess-related articles from Grandmasters and International Masters. There are also excerpts from chess newspaper columns."

The Internet Chess Club

http://www.hydra.com/icc

What would the Internet be without a cyberspace equivalent of the Chess Club that was the target of so many thoughtless jokes in high school?

The Internet Chess Club charges a yearly membership, but it does offer a wealth of downloadable programs, 24-hours a day of online competition, and visits from actual Grandmasters who will kick your butt.

tkChess

http://pine.cs.yale.edu:4201/cgi-bin/chessplayer

This is a new chess server with a big, good-looking interface. (See figure 14.15.)

FIGURE 14.15

In tkChess, you select your move by mouse clicking, or else Mr. Smarty-Pants Computer will pick a move for you.

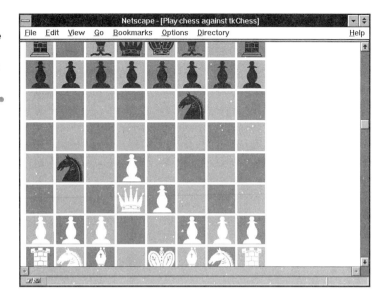

GNUCHESS

http://www.delorie.com/game-room/chess

The GNUCHESS server is another Web-compliant chess server. It's just you versus the computer. You set the time variable and the depth (the number of potential moves the computer will ponder) and thus the skill level. Moves are entered as text commands.

The Chess Server

http://www.willamette.edu/~tjones/chessmain.html

This under-construction site pits two human players against each other across the Web. I think it's some kind of magic trick.

Bridge

Bridge, if you can believe the hype, is "the most popular card game in the world," and it's pleasant to imagine a universe where sophisticates get together for regular bridge parties. I'm sure it must be happening somewhere.

Bridge on the Web

http://www.cs.vu.nl/~sater/bridge/bridge-on-the-web.html

The Bridge on the Web supersite has links to two online bridge servers, tournament info, rules, and more.

OKBridge Server

http://www.cts.com/~okbridge

This server allows swingin' sophisticates from around the world to play bridge against each other over the Internet. No more will you have to travel to tournaments in exotic lands and have to worry about Omar Sharif bumming spare change. (See figure 14.16.)

FIGURE 14.16

The OKBridge online bridge server.

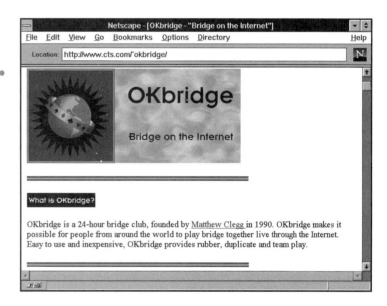

Go

Go is an ancient Chinese board game that entails the gradual accumulation of space on the playing field through the strategic placement of stone-shaped pieces. For the uninitiated, it's something like a combination of Chess and that Minesweeper game that comes with Windows.

Introduction to Go

http://www.well.com/user/mmcadams/gointro.html

This site is a fine introduction to the game of Go. It features a detailed history (which goes back at least 3,000 years), information on Go tournaments, rules, links, and extensive information about playing Go over the Internet through the ICS server. And it looks good, too. (See figure 14.17.)

FIGURE 14.17

The Introduction to Go home page.

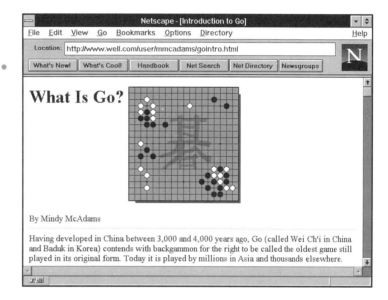

Online Games and Diversions

There are many games you can play online against an opponent who will never gloat: the computer itself. Many of these online games are harmless diversions to which you can turn for a quick bit of whimsy or intellectual stimulation when you're tired of actually working. They range from traditional time-wasters such as tic-tac-toe and hangman to interactive fictive environments and a virtual snowball fight.

Zarf's Online Interactive Games List

http://www.cs.cmu.edu/afs/andrew/org/kgb/www/zarf/games.html

www.leftfoot.com/ realgames.html

Zarf's List of Online Interactive Games is a phenomenal compilation of online games, time-wasters, and wry commentary from Andrew Plotkin at Carnegie-Mellon University in Pittsburgh.

From the Zarf list, you can instantly jump to any of dozens—nay, hundreds—of interactive games and online toys. The list is continually updated, with typically two or three new sites added per week. As of this writing, some of the highlights of the list included the following:

✳ System's Twilight, a shareware Mac game by Andrew Plotkin himself, the keeper of this fine list.

✳ The Barney Fun Page, which is not very kindly disposed towards our Purple pal.

✳ The Pub Crawl, a text-based choose-your-own adventure game, in which typically you either engage in bar chat or get into fights (http://www.webnet.com.au/pubcrawl). (See figure 14.18.)

FIGURE 14.18

One of many story openings available in an interactive, ever-unspooling text-based game called The Pub Crawl.

● ● ● ● ● ● ● ● ● ● ● ● ● ● ● ●

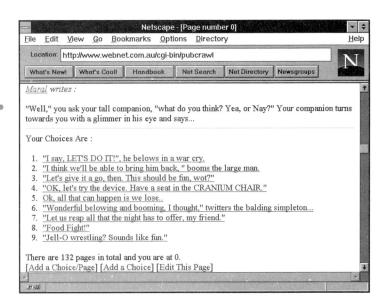

* Crime Scene Evidence, a simulated murder investigation.

* Sabacc, a card game from the Star Wars universe.

* Nowwhere, an interactive adventure by Brian Casey.

* Zbouby Burger, a fast-food game in which you try to keep up with an ever-expanding backlog of customers. (In easily-digestible French.)

* Cindy Crawford Concentration. The memory game "Concentration" played with pictures of Cindy Crawford. See figure 14.19.

FIGURE 14.19

For those of you who are in a hurry, here is the solution to the Cindy Crawford Concentration game. This took me four hours to complete. (http:// cad.ucla.edu:8001/concentration)

* Idea Futures, a stock-market system in which people trade on claims about the future. The money is play money.

* The Contact Project, a cryptogram puzzle in which you try to decipher a message received from the star Tau Ceti. From the Lunar Institute of Technology (lunar@sunsite.unc.edu). The site maintains a discussion list of people working on the messages as they appear; or, you can work by yourself and check your solutions against the group's.

* Rome Lab Snowball Camera at U.S. Air Force Rome Lab. Toss virtual snowballs at real people in their computer lab. (You'll just have to check this one out for yourself.)

* An assortment of games from Gene Cutler at Berkeley, including:

    * Guess the Macromolecule.

    * Find-The-Spam: While looking at a big picture of a can of Spam, see if you can locate the can of Spam. Yeah, that's all there is to it. (See figure 14.20.)

FIGURE 14.20

Can you find the Spam? Maybe it's not as easy as it looks. (http://sp1.berkeley.edu/findthespam.html)

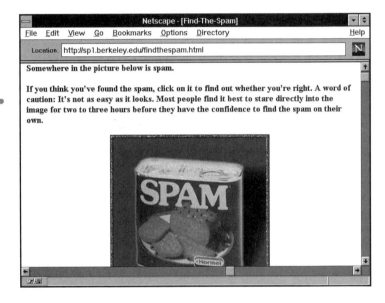

* ChibaMOO, a MUD that can be browsed from the Web. You walk around a series of text-based environments and examine things.

* A Web-based ESP test using the standard Rhine cards.

* A page in which you shoot the spy who's disguised as a member of ABBA. (See figure 14.21.)

* Games from Dr. Fellowbug's Laboratory of Fun and Horror, including:

    * Daily Noise (a new obnoxious sound each day).

FIGURE 14.21

Shoot (by clicking on) the spy who is pretending to be a member of ABBA. Another example of the strange ABBA love/hate thing that has permeated the Internet. (http://www.studentservices.com:3001/cgi-bin/sneaky-sharp.cgi)

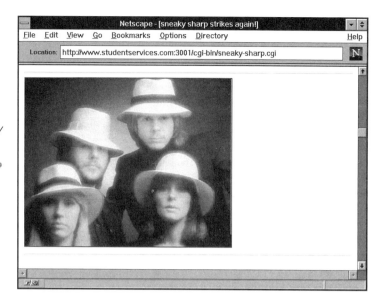

* Letter R.I.P., a version of Hangman with appropriate art. (Every time you get a letter wrong, an animated ghoul has a limb chopped off.)

* Excuse Generator, a Mad-Libs system for writing excuse letters.

* Penny's Skulls of Fate. (See figure 14.22.)

FIGURE 14.22

Penny's Skulls of Fate is about to split open your destiny. (http://www.dtd.com/skulls/)

* WWW Spirograph by Jeffrey Cohen. (Did you ever hear about the kid who was killed by a Spirograph? I swear it's true.)

* Complaint Letter Generator by Scott Pakin.

* Frog Dissection Kit at Lawrence Berkeley Laboratory (http://george.lbl.gov/ITG.hm.pg.docs/dissect/info.html). A woman of my acquaintance almost flunked her high-school biology class because of her reluctance to slice open a froggie. If this Web site had been around in those days, she could have been spared a lot of needless humiliation. In the Frog Dissection Kit, you pick an organ to cut away, and the computer does the work for you. (See figure 14.23.)

FIGURE 14.23

The Online Frog Dissection Kit. (This one's for you, Susan.)

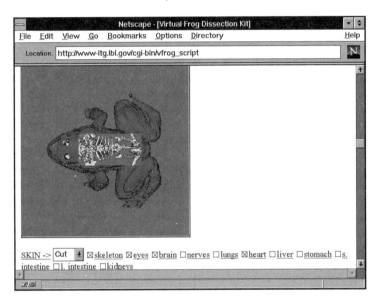

Online Trivia

I carry around a lot of trivia. I can, for instance, tell you the names of all six of Charlie's Angels (the actresses *and* the characters they played), as well as the full names of the Skipper and the Professor. I once memorized the value of *pi* to a hundred decimal places. I can list you the entire American Top 40 for the first week of September 1972. What I can't do is remember my phone number or use this wealth of information to attract new friends. But at least there's online trivia, where insufferable know-it-alls like myself can delude themselves that raw information is the same thing as knowledge.

Risky Business (formerly Jeopardy)

http://calypso.cs.uregina.ca/Games/riskybus.html

At one time this IRC-based online trivia challenge was called Jeopardy. I don't know why it changed its name, although it does occur to me that there's some kind of radio or TV game show called *Jeopardy*, so maybe that has something to do with it.

In Risky Business, up to 20 people from around the world compete in a board-based trivia game at the same time. (See figure 14.24.) The game is moderated by a computerized host or, *bot*, whose name used to be—but is no longer—Alex.

FIGURE 14.24

The home page and FAQ site for Risky Business, an online trivia challenge.

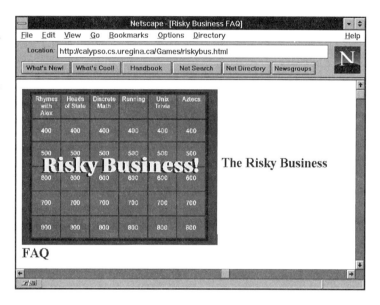

There are over 700 categories and 30,000 questions in Risky Business. A spin-off game called Music Risky Business has 300 categories.

To participate in Risky Business, you have to have IRC capability and the appropriate software. The Risky Business FAQ site will instruct you on acquiring the software and the IRC connection and will direct you to three different servers where you can play. It's free, and there is no prize money, but if you win a round you'll feel like a million virtual bucks.

Other Trivia Sites

A site called Trivia Hot Spots at *http://cybersight.com/cgi-bin/cs/s?trivia.gmml* has general trivia, trivia for liberal arts majors, and trivia for mathematics buffs.

The Osiris Online Trivia Quiz at *http://osiris.sund.ac.uk/on-line/quiz/quiztime.html* is a weekly general-interest quiz comprising 25 questions, one of which will always be about Bob Dylan. The same folks (at Sunderland University in the U.K.) also sponsor a weekly rock-music quiz at *http://osiris.sund.ac.uk/music_quiz/quiztime.html,* of which one question will always be about the British art-rock band Hawkwind (?!), and a sports quiz at *http://osiris.sund.ac.uk/online/sport_quiz/quiztime.html.*

A site called The Baby Jocko Joint at *http://www.mindspring.com/~goodson/jocko1.html* has challenging quizzes in politics and sports. ("Who was the first president to fly in an airplane?")

World Wide Trivia, at *http://www.mindspring.com/~kmims/wwt1.html,* has a new set of 15 medium-to-tough questions every month.

Two-Minute Warning is an NFL football trivia site at *http://www.dtd.com/tmw.*

A site called The Riddler at *http://www.riddler.com* combines trivia and a scavenger hunt across the Web. It claims to offer cash prizes, which should make you think twice.

The Multimedia Newsstand Interactive Quiz at *http://mmnewsstand.comhearst/features2.html* is a part of the Hearst Publishing home page and features a single question every day, from which you can win a T-shirt. ("What is the only U.S. state that a foreign flag has never flown over?" My answer: "Hawaii." I was contestant number 3,000-something.)

There is also a Sex Trivia site on the Web somewhere; but really, what could be more dreary?

Online Gambling

For the real swingers among us, the word "game" means only one thing: gambling, Vegas-style. Oh, to run with the Rat Pack in 1963! To place your last chip on red #12 and spin the wheel while Frank and Sammy and Dean and Peter Lawford cheer you on like blood brothers! That's the life!

If you're anything like me, you'd gladly spend your last peso on a game of chance, even if it means you come up snake eyes, even if it means you go hungry, even if it means that your girl-friend gets traded to a biker gang from Sacramento to settle a fifty-dollar bet that you would never have made in the first place if you weren't so caught up in the fever. Hey, if you can't take the heat...

The Internet Casinos

http://www.casino.org

Well, if you can't take the heat of Las Vegas, you can always play at The Internet Casinos, a new online service that operates out of the Turks & Caicos Islands in the beautiful blue Caribbean. (See figure 14.25.) The fun-filled interface promises that The Internet Casinos can provide you all the pleasure of a real gambling experience—entertainment, atmosphere, the thrill of a big-money payoff—while you are sitting at home in your PJs.

Yes, this is actual gambling—blackjack, slots, even sports betting—with real money involved. Not that it will *feel* like real money, because the Internet Casinos accept all manner of non-cash payments for those rare occasions when you lose.

It's obvious that the folks at the Internet Casinos have done their homework, because all of the necessary legal disclaimers are in place and there's even an article about first-amendment rights on the Internet to make it clear that what they are doing is a legitimate enterprise that is as morally defensible as R-rated movies.

It is also one of the most twisted and depressing developments in the history of civilization.

FIGURE 14.25

By the way, your friends at the Internet Casinos are happy to accommodate you with a variety of payment methods, including this new thing called virtual money.

Digital Vegas
http://spidey.usc.edu:80/ken-bin/digitalvegas.pl

There's only one place on earth where you should gamble real money, and that's Las Vegas, Nevada (and maybe Whisky Pete's at the California/Nevada border, home of the Bonnie and Clyde Death Car). Forget Atlantic City, forget the Midwestern riverboats, forget the Native-American reservations (unless you're sure that the house profits are going to The People and not to Asian gangsters, which they often are), and for Pete's sake, forget about spending your virtual money at some online sink-hole while you're sitting at home in your pajamas and your kids are wondering why they haven't had a hot meal in three weeks.

If you really need to gamble from home, try Digital Vegas, which won't cost you a nickel to play slots, blackjack, or poker. (See figure 14.26.) You start with a stake of $500 you get when you register with the Digital Bank, and you can squander it as you please.

FIGURE 14.26
Digital Vegas.

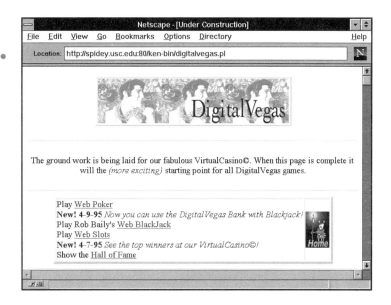

The ground work is being laid for our fabulous VirtualCasino©. When this page is complete it will the *(more exciting)* starting point for all DigitalVegas games.

Play Web Poker
New! 4-9-95 *Now you can use the DigitalVegas Bank with Blackjack!*
Play Rob Baily's Web BlackJack
Play Web Slots
New! 4-7-95 *See the top winners at our VirtualCasino©!*
Show the Hall of Fame

The Virtual Slot Machine
http://www.kaiwan.com/~smakk/cgi-bin/slots.cgi

This site is pretty self-explanatory and also pretty low-tech compared to some of the competition, but it merits inclusion here because, among other things, one of the slot-machine symbols is a chocolate donut. (See figure 14.28.)

FIGURE 14.28
The Virtual Slot Machine passes judgment.

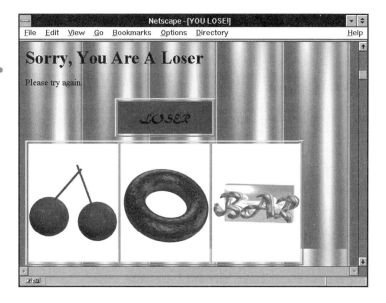

Sorry, You Are A Loser

Please try again.

VEGAS.COM

If you've got a special interest in Las Vegas—the *real* Vegas, not the online variety—check out Vegas.Com at *http://www.vegas.com*. In addition to the usual tourist come-on (including hotel reservations and gambling tips), this commercial site does a nice job of trying to present "the other side" of Vegas, with info on the Vegas art scene (such as it is), offbeat Vegas hang-outs (although all the original off-beat hang-outs are being bulldozed for "family-oriented" casino monstrosities and even Downtown is being put under a glass canopy!) and the Vegas teen scene. (See figure 14.27.)

FIGURE 14.27

Brittany and Leslie introduce you to the Teen Scene of Las Vegas in this page from Vegas.Com.

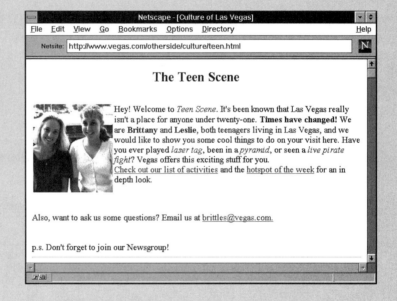

Other Games

The Web has a site for practically every pastime, from LEGOS to juggling to bingo. A representative sample follows. (If you still can't find the thing you're looking for, try pointing your browser to the *Yahoo/Entertainment/Games* directory.)

Word Puzzles

Crossword puzzles are the most rigorous intellectual exercise that average Americans will subject themselves to, and it's nice that this vestige of pre-digital humanity still flourishes. There are many sites on the Net for crossword puzzles, anagrams, and vocabulary games. Most are free. Anything that mentions "cash prizes" should be carefully scrutinized before you participate. (My friend Stephanie H. used to work for a game company in L.A. that would hook people into a seemingly innocuous word-puzzle contest via magazine ads. [Example: "Synonym for feline: C-A-_"] Then the company would extract additional money from contestants who wanted to advance to the endless series of "tie-breaker" rounds.)

The Crossword Archive
ftp://gatekeeper.dec.com/pub/micro/msdos/misc/crossword-archive

This plain-text FTP archive features tons of crossword-related stuff, including the *rec.puzzles.crosswords* FAQ, crossword software (puzzle generators), and various crossword dictionaries.

Syndicate.Com
http://syndicate.com/

This is a commercial site that offers kid-oriented word-puzzle contests along with its educational software packages and vocabulary builders. (See figure 14.29.)

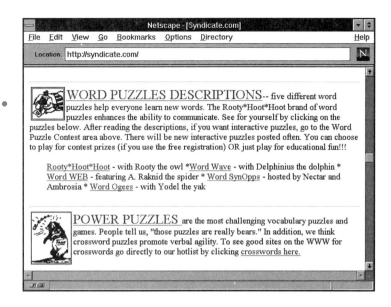

WORD PUZZLES DESCRIPTIONS-- five different word puzzles help everyone learn new words. The Rooty*Hoot*Hoot brand of word puzzles enhances the ability to communicate. See for yourself by clicking on the puzzles below. After reading the descriptions, if you want interactive puzzles, go to the Word Puzzle Contest area above. There will be new interactive puzzles posted often. You can choose to play for contest prizes (if you use the free registration) OR just play for educational fun!!!

Rooty*Hoot*Hoot - with Rooty the owl *Word Wave - with Delphinius the dolphin * Word WEB - featuring A. Raknid the spider * Word SynOpps - hosted by Nectar and Ambrosia * Word Ogees - with Yodel the yak

POWER PUZZLES are the most challenging vocabulary puzzles and games. People tell us, "those puzzles are really bears." In addition, we think crossword puzzles promote verbal agility. To see good sites on the WWW for crosswords go directly to our hotlist by clicking crosswords here.

The Puzzle Post
http://iquest.com/~pinnacle/index.html

This site covers crossword puzzles as well as trivia games, word games, Scrabble, and board games. It offers a weekly cryptic, weekly crossword, weekly teasers, information about contests, and links to online puzzles, dictionaries, and more. It is the home page for the Pinnacle Solutions puzzle software company, which offers shareware puzzle and teaser games.

Jumble and Crossword Solver
http://odin.chemistry.uakron.edu/cbower/jumble.html

If you are a crossword player—but not a very good or honest one—you'll want to acquaint yourself with this site. With this handy program, you type can solve both crossword puzzles and jumbled word puzzles. For jumbles, you type in the jumbled letters and the computer sorts through all the possible combinations until it comes up with a real word. For crosswords, you type in the letters you already know in a word, with question marks in place of the unknown letters, and the computers gives you all the possible solutions. Very handy.

Internet Anagram Server

http://lrdc5.lrdc.pitt.edu/awad-cgibin/anagram

Give it a word, it will give you an anagram. (Dormitory = Dirty Room.)

Pinball

In the '80s, because of the popularity of video arcade games, many of us feared that pinball machines were going the way of the 8-track tape player. But pinball has come back (and so has the 8-track, for that matter; see the UseNet group *alt.collecting.8-track-tapes*). Maybe it's because in pinball, unlike a video game, you are manipulating physical matter and can actually affect the outcome of the game with a little body english. Or maybe it's because they look so much cooler than those big video contraptions.

The Pinball Archive

http://pinball.cc.cmu.edu/

This is a mammoth (albeit under-construction) site that contains:

* Search and browse capability for the entire text of *rec.games.pinball*.

* Machine-specific pages that cross-reference everything known in the archive about selected machines.

* Rule sheets, tip sheets, and tech notes.

* Pinball-related images, animations, sounds, and other binaries.

* Computer pinball simulation software (freeware or shareware only).

* Links to every other known pinball-related resource on the Net.

Drinking Games

Yes, there's actually a *Yahoo/Entertainment/Games* subcategory for *Drinking Games*. Before you explore it, however, remember that these drinking games are for amusement only.

Yes, alcohol is a legal substance that can be bought and consumed by people who are over 21. But you should do some serious soul searching before you drink to excess (or at least *while* you are doing it), and you should never drink before operating a motor vehicle or heavy machinery (such as your computer).

The Unofficial Guide to Drinking Games
http://silver.ucs.indiana.edu/~bquick/drgames.html

This is a colossal (and possibly definitive) list of drinking games—as well as a barometer of how close we are to the end of civilization as we know it.

The games are classified by basis (TV, strength, skill, luck, coins, cards, ping-pong) and by buzz factor (low, medium, high, deadly, and insane). The games, described in detail, include the following:

* Barfly
* Beer Blow
* Beer Bomb
* Beers for Cheers
* Brain Damage
* Buzz
* Caps
* Chutes and Ladders
* Dazed and Confused
* Death Ring
* Fuzzy Duck
* Go Fish
* Hi Bob
* I Never
* James Bond
* Kill the Keg
* One Big Chicken

* Peuchre
* Postmodernism
* Pub Crawl
* Quarters
* Queens
* Robo-slam
* Screw Your Neighbor
* Shotgun
* Sink the Battleship
* S-M-A-S-H
* Super Quarters
* Threshold
* Thumper
* Viking
* Whales Tales
* Witch
* Wuss

My favorite drinking game goes something like this: Get drunk, oversleep, and lose your job. Argue with your friends when they say you have a problem. Then move to a new town with money you've borrowed from your parents and do it all over again. It's a riot!

Chris Ring's TV Links

http://www.rain.org/~uring/tv.html

Chris Ring has done a good job of consolidating all the drinking games that are related to TV shows, as well as providing links to the shows' home pages and audio clips of the shows' theme songs. As a bonus he throws in a drinking game based on the annual Jerry Lewis/MDA Telethon, which is a good cause and thoroughly surreal TV. (See figure 14.30.)

FIGURE 14.30

A drinking game called Tympani, based on Jerry Lewis' endlessly entertaining Labor Day telethon.

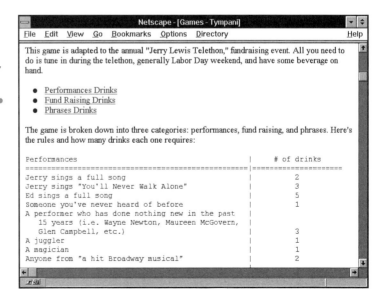

The List

Games: General Resources

The World-Wide Web Virtual Library: Games and Recreation

http://www.cis.ufl.edu/~thoth/library/recreation.html

The Virtual Playground of Dr. Fun

http://www.omix.com/zine/DeKoven

Game-Related UseNet Groups

(Note: * indicates an extended hierarchy.)

alt.cd-rom

alt.chess

alt.games*

alt.games.tiddlywinks

Potentially bigger than soccer.

alt.games.xpilot

comp.sys.amiga.games

comp.sys.mac.games

comp.sys.ibm.pc.games.*

rec.aviation.simulators

rec.games.*

rec.games.backgammon

rec.games.board

rec.games.bridge

rec.games.chess

rec.games.computer.*

rec.games.computer.doom.*

rec.games.corewar

rec.games.design

rec.games.diplomacy

rec.games.empire

rec.games.go

rec.games.hack

rec.games.int-fiction

rec.games.mud.*

rec.games.pinball

rec.games.rpg.* (role-playing games)

rec.games.video.*

rec.games.video.arcade.*

rec.puzzles.*

Computer and Video Games

The Games Domain
http://wcl-rs.bham.ac.uk/GamesDomain

Console World
http://arachnid.cm.cf.ac.uk/Games

Game Page of the Universe
http://www.pht.com/games.html

ElNet's Gaming Resources
http://galaxy.einet.net/galaxy/Leisure-and-Recreation/Games/
chris-loggins/Gaming.html

Game Zero
http://www.gamezero.com/team-0/

For a cyber-punk perspective on gaming.

Internet PC Games Chart
http://www.xs4all.nl/~jojo

A list of the The Top 100 best commercially available PC games, as voted on by the gaming public and updated weekly. Also has a list of the Top 40 best downloadable games.

Spacetec JumpGate

http://web.spacetec.com/Hard%20Disk/WEB_SITE/CED/
CEDjump.html

This is one of the best link sites on the Net for gaming information (3-D and otherwise) and the related worlds of sci-fi, virtual reality, cyberzines, and technical what-not.

The Game Boy Page

http://www.cs.umd.edu/users/fms/GameBoy

Online Gaming Magazines

Computer Gaming World

http://www.ziff.com:8017/~gaming

Digitale

http://www.umn.edu/nlhome/m447/reinb001/digi/digitale.html

Game Bytes

http://sunsite.unc.edu/GameBytes

NewType Gaming Magazine

http://www.actwin.com:80/NewType

PC Gamer

http://www.futurenet.co.uk/computing/pcgamer.html

Doom

DOOM Gate

http://doomgate.cs.buffalo.edu

Squidly's Reef

http://linet02.li.net/~dsquid/gaming.html

UseNet Group

rec.games.doom (extended hierarchy)

The Official Descent Page

http://www.interplay.com/website/descent.html

The Myst Page

http://www.best.com/~rdc/roger/myst.html

The Myst Walkthrough

http://wcl-rs.bham.ac.uk/~djh/walkthru/myst.html

Doug's Myst Help Page

http://www.astro.washington.edu/ingram/myst/index.html

The Mortal Kombat WWW Pages

http://www.cs.ucl.ac.uk/students/zcacaes/mk/mk.html

Kombat Kraft

http://www.sar.usf.edu/~paulino/html/kombat.html

MUDs, MUSHs, and MOOs

General Resources

An Introduction to MU*s

http://www.vuw.ac.nz/who/Jamie.Norrish/mud/mud.html

MUD Connector

http://www.magicnet.net/~cowana/mud.html

You can connect from this Web site directly to hundreds of MUDs.

Multi User Dungeons

http://draco.centerline.com:8080/~franl/mud.html#faq

Another good all-purpose MUD resource and link site

MUD-related UseNet Groups

rec.games.mud (extended hierarchy)

Fantasy/Role-Playing Games

The Role-Playing Games Web Page
http://www.acm.uiuc.edu/duff/index.html

The RPG Page
http://www.edu.isy.liu.se/~d91johol/rpg.html

The Great Net Spellbook/Prayerbook Page
http://hagar.arts.kuleuven.ac.be/students/Ezra.Van.Everbroeck/gnb.html

UseNet Group
rec.games.rpg

Strategy Games

General

The Game Cabinet
http://web.kaleida.com/u/tidwell/GameCabinet.html

Chess

The Chess Connection WWW Magazine
http://www.easynet.co.uk/pages/worldchess/home.htm

The Internet Chess Club
http://www.hydra.com/icc

tkChess
http://pine.cs.yale.edu:4201/cgi-bin/chessplayer

GNUCHESS
http://www.delorie.com/game-room/chess

The Chess Server

http://www.willamette.edu/~tjones/chessmain.html

UseNet Group

rec.games.chess

Bridge

Bridge on the Web

http://www.cs.vu.nl/~sater/bridge/bridge-on-the-web.html

OKBridge

http://www.cts.com/~okbridge

Bridge FAQ

ftp://ftp.cs.jhu.edu/pub/Bridge/FAQ

An extensive FTP site of bridge information, mirrored from the Australian bridge archives.

UseNet Groups

rec.games.bridge

rec.games.go

Introduction to Go

http://www.well.com/user/mmcadams/gointro.html

Irish Go Association

http://www.cs.tcd.ie/www/sflinter/iga/iga.html

I just love the name of this group, which proudly claims to be "one of the smallest national Go organisations in Europe, and probably the world."

Word Puzzles

Syndicate.Com

http://syndicate.com

The Puzzle Post
http://iquest.com/~pinnacle/index.html

The Crossword Archive
ftp://gatekeeper.dec.com/pub/micro/msdos/misc/crossword-archive

Jumble and Crossword Solver
http://odin.chemistry.uakron.edu/cbower/jumble.html

A Crossword Puzzle
http://www.linc.or.jp/~hamano/game/crossword.html

UseNet
rec.puzzles

rec.puzzles.crosswords

Pinball

The Pinball Archive
http://pinball.cc.cmu.edu

Drinking Games

The UnOfficial Guide to Drinking Games
http://silver.ucs.indiana.edu/~bquick/drgames.html

Chris Ring's TV Links
http://www.rain.org/~uring/tv.html

The Real Beer Page
http://realbeer.com/realbeer/rbp.games.html

More drinking games, nicely organized, with sane disclaimers that no one will heed.

CHAPTER 15

Sports

IN THIS CHAPTER:

> *Information on the massive servers that cover many sports*

> *A look at the top sites for coverage of football, baseball, basketball, and hockey*

> *Sites that cover other professional sports*

> *Specialty sites that concentrate on one sport or topic*

> *Recreational sports sites*

IN OTHER CHAPTERS:

< *Online and computer games are covered in Chapter 14.*

You're desperate. It's 3 a.m., and even ESPN isn't carrying the scores from last night's games on the West Coast.

You've got to find out who won that NHL game you were watching before you dozed off. You want to know how many free throws Shaquille O'Neal missed in that Sacramento game. And you've still got to fill out your lineup card for this coming weekend's fantasy golf round. Where can you go for a quick fix of information?

Or maybe you're not as hard-core as this. Maybe you just like sports and you like to appear well-informed in the presence of potential bullies.

Whatever your level of interest in sports, the Internet has a place that will satisfy you. As with the rest of the Net, the number of sports offerings online have mushroomed in the last year. Just when you think every possible area has been covered by a site on the World Wide Web, it seems another one pops up that surprises you with a new level of detail.

Sports sites on the Internet typically fall into one of two categories: large, all-purpose sites that include servers on many different sports; and smaller, independent sites that usually are narrow in focus.

For example, the large sites will include servers on all the major professional sports, which, in turn, link to sites on each of the teams in that league. Each of these links, however, leads to a site that is run by the same operator that runs the larger server. The smaller, independent sites are often operated by individuals and can be as specific as a site that covers only a single team.

NOTE There is enough information about sports on the Internet that a person could devote an entire book to it. In fact, there is an entire book devoted to it—*Sports on the Net*, also published by Que.

This chapter serves as an abridged version.

Leading All-Purpose Sports Servers

There are thousands of sports sites on the Internet. The sites covered in this section are the biggies—the ones that provide the most information for sports fans.

ESPNET SportsZone

http://espnet.sportszone.com

ESPN, the cable television sports juggernaut that years ago was scoffed at for bringing Australian Rules Football into millions of homes across the country, is a pioneer not only in the world of television but also on the Internet.

ESPN took root in the landscape of American television when it secured the rights to live broadcasts of Major League Baseball, National Football League, and National Hockey League games in the last 10 years. That added to an already strong lineup that featured auto racing, golf, and other events, and allowed the network to move away from the fringe-type sports.

ESPN made its online debut in a relationship with the Prodigy commercial service when it launched ESPNET. In early 1995, ESPNET found a home on the Internet in a partnership with Starwave, which previously operated the Satchel Sports sites on the Internet.

The result is ESPNET SportsZone. (See figure 15.1.)

It covers all of the most-popular sports more thoroughly than any other site on the Internet, and it adds solid coverage of the rest of the professional sports world.

Throw in strong coverage of college football and men's and women's basketball, a few minor league sports, and special sites that pop up for special events like the Indianapolis 500, and ESPNET SportsZone provides more information than any other sports source online.

FIGURE 15.1

ESPNET SportsZone's home page links to a world of online sports not available anywhere else.

● ● ● ● ● ● ● ● ● ● ● ● ● ● ● ●

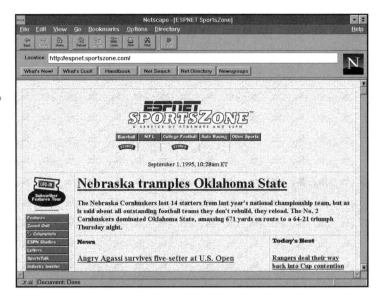

The main home page includes a link to "The Wire," which provides the news of the day as offered by major wire services. Here you'll find the day's top stories, plus game recaps, previews, injury updates, and more.

To get a more detailed look at the day's sports news, you need only to look beneath the ESPNET SportsZone logo on the home page. There, you'll find four buttons.

The first button, "Select Sport" leads you down the path toward the area of your interest. (See figure 15.2.)

FIGURE 15.2

Sports fans can pick their favorite sport in ESPNET SportsZone's "Select Sport" area.

● ● ● ● ● ● ● ● ● ● ● ● ● ● ● ●

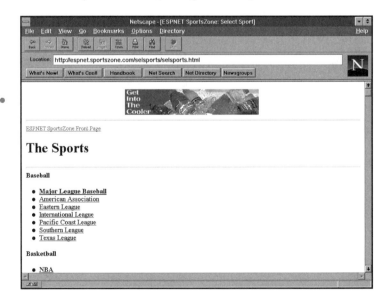

You won't find a link to Australian Rules Football here (which tells you something about corporate loyalty), but you will find links to servers dedicated to all the "major" team sports.

Servers that are available include:

* Major League Baseball

* National Basketball Association

* National Hockey League

* National Football League

* Men's College Basketball

* Women's College Basketball

* College Football

* Professional Golf Association

* Tennis

* Auto Racing

* American Hockey League

* International Hockey League

* Horse Racing

Within each of these areas is a list of the top stories of the day and a link back to "The Wire," a more complete source of stories related to that sport.

For baseball, basketball, hockey, and football, there are links to even more specific information, including:

* The Teams. A home page on each of the teams in these sports, including statistics, recaps of recent games, injury updates, notes, and more.

* The Numbers. Complete league-wide statistics for every player.

* Sportstalk. This area is for chatting with fans from around the country and worldwide.

Once you've exhausted the basics of sports—the news, statistics, standings, and so on—check out the "Zoned Out" area, which is accessed from a button at the main home page.

This area covers the more quirky end of sports, the little tidbits that keep diehard fans happy.

Included are:

* Who's Hot and Who's Not. Athletes who are involved in current streaks or slumps.

* Quotes. Timely, pointed quotes from sports personalities. (See figure 15.3.)

* Birthdays. A list of sports figures who are celebrating birthdays today.

* Notes. Tidbits from around the world of sports.

* Daily List. Offbeat lists are available every day. For example, one day Seattle Seahawks quarterback Rick Mirer offered a list of his favorite rock bands.

* This Date in Sports History. Major events that have occurred on this date.

* Trivia Questions. Where fans can test their knowledge of things that don't ultimately matter very much.

* Milestones Soon to be Reached. Lists athletes nearing records or other milestones.

* Quick Facts. Statistical notes from all sports.

FIGURE 15.3
ESPNET SportsZone's "Zoned Out" area includes top quotes from around the world of sports.

The "SportsTalk" button (on the main ESPNET SportsZone home page) leads to an online talk area that includes live chat on the four major sports, plus college football, and auto racing.

You can also send questions to ESPN that may be used on the television shows "Up Close" on ESPN and "Talk2" on ESPN2.

From time to time, users are invited to post questions to a particular sports personality, who then answers selected queries within a couple of days. ("Dear Mr. Jordan: Just between you and me, was there more to this whole retirement thing than we were led to believe?")

The final button on the main home page is "ESPN Studios," an area that includes program updates and television listings, columns written by ESPN reporters and studio hosts, and press releases from the cable network.

The NandoX Sports Server
http://www.nando.net/sptsserv.html

The Charlotte, North Carolina-based News & Observer Publishing Company offers this site, which links to servers on a wide variety of sports and sports competitions around the world.

Like ESPNET SportsZone, Nando offers complete servers on all the major sports, including links to home pages for each of the teams in each league.

It also goes beyond ESPNET in a few ways and falls short in others. The two servers, used in combination, will give sports fans just about everything they could want.

Nando's "The Sports Page" (see figure 15.4) is the primary link from the main home page, leading to a list of the main servers that Nando offers.

The most-used servers are those for the four major team sports: professional football, baseball, hockey, and basketball. In Nando, any of those servers can be accessed from just about any other page on the network.

FIGURE 15.4

The NandoX Sports Server's "Sports Page" links to the servers on each of the major sports.

Nando has an advantage over ESPNET in auto racing and soccer, to name two, in part because those sports are very popular in North Carolina. But the coverage of these and other sports on the Nando network is nationwide (and global, in some cases) in focus. Other servers offered by Nando include:

* The Racing Circuit. News and views from the world of auto racing, including NASCAR, Indy Car, Formula One, and more.

* Corner Kicks. Soccer's much-rumored popularity in the U.S. is fed by this server, which covers the sport around the world, not just in America.

* Aces. The pro tennis circuits of both men and women are covered in detail.

* Fairways. The PGA (men's), LPGA (women's), and Senior Tour are all covered in this area.

* Olympics. Naturally, the coverage improves in Olympic years, but Olympic updates are available year-round here.

* In the Ring. Not devoted to bullfighting, as you might expect, this area covers boxing news from around the world.

"Nando Sports Chat" offers online, live chat through the servers of each of the four major professional sports.

CLOSE-UP: BASEBALL STRIKES OUT

When Major League Baseball players called a strike on Aug. 12, 1994, it resulted in the premature end of the season and the cancellation of the World Series.

This left frustrated baseball fans with no sense of closure for what had been one of the most enjoyable and exciting seasons in recent history.

Then Nando offered some solace.

Four new links sprang up on Nando's baseball server. One provided the latest updates on negotiations; another took a comedic look at the strike by offering a downloadable graphic of the two chief negotiators, Donald Fehr and Richard Ravitch, superimposed over makeshift dartboards; another offered information on a fans group that was planning to boycott baseball once the players returned.

But the best of the four sites offered something that didn't really exist: major-league baseball itself.

The Second Season

http://www.nando.net/baseball/strike/recreate/recreate.html

Each day during the strike, simulated games were played by computer and the results were posted to this site. Even the playoffs were played, wherein the cyber-Chicago White Sox defeated the cyber-Atlanta Braves (four games to two) to claim their first World Series title since 1917.

Part of what made the 1994 season so interesting were the individual records that were being pursued, and in the Nando universe, the simulated Matt Williams of the San Francisco Giants completed his real-life counterpart's dream by hitting his 62nd home run on the season's final day, breaking Roger Maris' 33-year-old record. San Diego's Tony Gwynn, however, fell short of .400, hitting .382.

Sites that demonstrate creativity while meeting the needs of the user are what make sports on the Internet great.

Other All-Purpose Sports Servers

The next level of major servers on the Internet are those listed in the following sections. These sites generally cover a large number of sports, but don't have the breadth of coverage of the sites discussed earlier.

WWW Sports Information Service

http://www.netgen.com/sis/sports.html

This server won the Best of the Web '94 Contest. It does a good job of covering three of the four major team sports, and links to coverage of international sports that other servers don't have.

The main home page (see figure 15.5) links to servers covering professional hockey, basketball, and football.

FIGURE 15.5

The WWW Sports Information Service links to international sports sites.

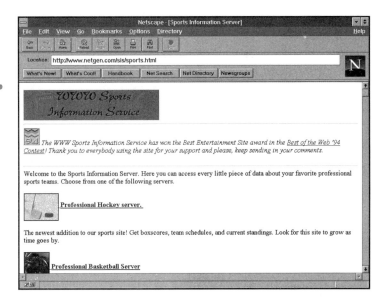

Each of those servers offer scores, schedules, player statistics, standings, and other news.

The international sports coverage is really an index of sites offered by other operators, but it is the most complete list available, making this the site of choice for those who want a more global sports perspective.

The Gate Sports
http://sfgate.com/sports

The "Gate" refers to the Golden Gate Bridge in San Francisco, the delightful city from whence this site originates. It is produced by the San Francisco Chronicle and San Francisco Examiner newspapers.

Although The Gate covers all of the major sports, it focuses on teams in the San Francisco Bay Area, and it doesn't offer servers on other sports such as auto racing, tennis, golf, bocce ball, and so on.

It features the columnists for the two newspapers (see figure 15.6), plus regularly updated reports on Bay Area teams from the sportswriters who cover them.

FIGURE 15.6

The Gate Sports has a decidedly Bay Area focus.

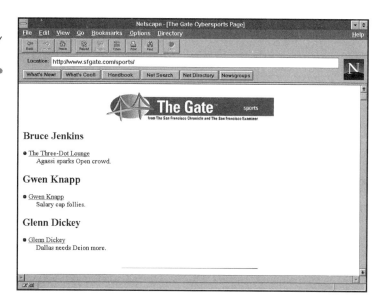

There are also links to game recaps and box scores, but those links lead directly to ESPNET SportsZone.

Specialized Sites

The sites listed in this section are specialized—that is, they cover one sport exclusively or one competition, such as the Olympics. There are way too many sports to cover a site from each one; these are the leaders.

NASCAR News (Auto Racing)

http://www.acpub.duke.edu/~jwcarp/nascarhome.html

The NASCAR circuit continues to gain in popularity in the United States, growing from a largely regional (read: Southern) phenomenon into a nationwide interest.

This site (see figure 15.7) covers the gamut of NASCAR topics. Primary links are to Winston Cup news, Busch Grand National news, Winston Racing Series news, and Winston Cup points standings.

FIGURE 15.7

The NASCAR News site offers up-to-date information for racing fans.

For fans new to the sport, there is also a link to an explanation of how Winston Cup points are awarded.

This section covers sites that aren't part of the major servers mentioned previously in this chapter.

These sites are typically run by smaller groups or individuals, and cover a specific sport or topic.

Still, this is far from a complete outline of such sites. Many more are included in the list at the end of this chapter, and a little exploration on the Internet will lead you to even more.

The 19th Hole (Golf)

http://zodiac.tr-riscs/panam.edu/golf/19thhole.html

Partly because of the sport it covers and partly because of the way it covers it, this is one of the most outstanding specialized sports sites on the Internet.

Golf's immense popularity is due in part to the fact that after watching a PGA, LPGA, or Senior Tour event, a fan can tee it up and play the same game, albeit not as well. Golf has grown markedly as both a spectator sport and a recreational sport in the last decade, and this site captures both aspects of the game.

From the main home page (see figure 15.8), golf enthusiasts can link to the latest headlines from the professional tours, including the so-called minor leagues of golf, such as the Nike Tour.

FIGURE 15.8

The 19th Hole is comfortably atop the leaderboard of Internet golf sites.

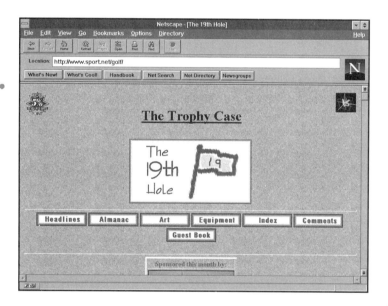

There is also an almanac section that includes links to such items as the complete rules of golf, the Golf Digest record book, frequently asked questions, and a listing of state and local golf associations.

There are a number of golf-related sites on the Internet that offer tips on improving your game or other information on such things as equipment, courses, etc. Check The List at the end of this chapter for some suggestions.

There is also a large section of downloadable golf art, including pictures of some of the game's great players, plus suggestions and information about golf equipment. (For instance, when do you employ the mashy niblick? What exactly is a wedgie?)

The Tennis Server Home Page

http://arganet.tenagra.com/Racquet_Workshop/Tennis.html

The Tennis Server does for its sport what the 19th Hole does for golf. It is a solid combination of news about the professional tennis circuit and information for those who play the sport recreationally. It includes the ATP Tour Weekly Electronic Newsletter and links to other tennis news sources. A second newsletter, called Daily News Postings, offers magazine-style coverage of both the men's and women's tours.

The site also makes tennis merchandise available and claims to be the first tennis store to operate on the World Wide Web. And finally, it provides information about tennis games for the SEGA home entertainment system.

General Horse Racing Site

http://www.inslab.uky.edu/~stevem/horses

If you're a regular at the track in your area and you can spare a few minutes before you rush to the ATM, this is the site for you.

It's no real surprise that the top horse racing site on the Internet originates from the state of Kentucky. This site covers the Kentucky Derby and the rest of the Triple Crown, plus links to sites that cover the Breeders' Cup and other horse racing sites.

On the Kentucky Derby, the site offers results of previous runnings of what is often called "the greatest 120 seconds in animal-based sporting events in North America," and it gives updates on horses that are potential participants in the next Derby.

The Atlanta Games (Olympics)

http://www.mindspring.com/~royal/olympic.html

The next Olympic Games—the Summer Games of 1996—take place in Atlanta, Georgia, USA, and this site is ready for it. (Atlanta in late summertime? Now there's a refreshing idea.)

This site (see figure 15.9) is primarily designed for people who plan to attend the Games, but it should also be of value to those who are interested in the behind-the-scenes details of how Atlanta is staging the events.

FIGURE. 15.9
Everything from ticket information to maps of venues are available at The Atlanta Games site.

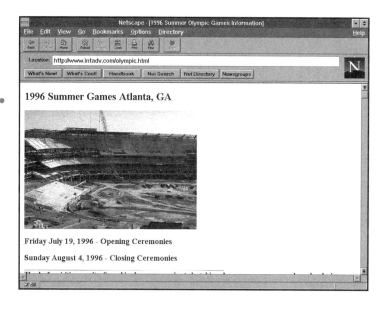

The site includes maps of the Olympic venues, hot night spots to visit while you're in Atlanta, information about tickets for events, hotel accommodations, sightseeing, transportation, and Olympic merchandise.

The Nagano Games (Olympics)

http://www.linc.or.jp/Nagano/index.html

The next Winter Games are in Nagano, Japan, in 1998, and the organizers there have wasted little time in getting an Internet site up and running.

It's similar to the Atlanta Games site in that it includes ticket information and other notices for those who plan to attend the Games.

Because some of the plans are still taking shape, there is also an Announcements page.

Try THIS

If suspense isn't a factor for you, there are also a number of sites devoted to past Olympic Games, including statistics, records, and the like. These sites are included in The List at the end of this chapter.

International Soccer Site

http://iamwww.unibe.ch/~ftiwww/Sonstiges/Tabellen/Eindex.html

You've probably heard of soccer. It's that low-scoring sport that Americans are all supposed to really like someday. (The rest of the world calls it "football," so maybe that's part of the problem.)

Fans (or "hooligans") of international soccer, particularly of the World Cup, will find a home at the International Soccer Site.

It includes a link to the latest league standings in 18 countries, including the United States. (Many of these sites are in the language of the country in which the league exists.)

There are also links to World Cup '94 sites originating out of six different countries, although these sites may soon disappear as the '94 Cup fades into memory.

An archive link leads you to the following historical information:

* World Cups from 1930–94

* European Championships from 1960–92

* The 1993–94 European Cup

* The Continental Cup from 1960–94

* The Champion's Cup from 1958–93

* National championships in six countries

* Worldwide soccer mailing list archive

* List of main pages from various European countries

The List at the end of this chapter includes more international soccer sites, and a little surfing on the Internet will lead you to home pages for most of the teams in European leagues.

The Global Cycling Network (Cycling)
http://www.cycling.org

The Global Cycling Network, VeloNet, operates this site (see figure 15.10) for the cyclist, not just the cycling fan.

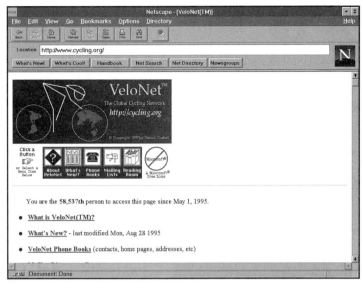

It includes links to everything from equipment manufacturers to race information to how to make your own repairs.

It requires a fair amount of cycling knowledge and is not generally for the person with a more casual interest in the sport.

Mountain biking is the hottest thing in the bicycle trade (supplanting the short-lived water-biking craze of the early '90s), and there are several good mountain biking sites on the Net. Check the list at the end of the chapter for more information.

Some of VeloNet's many links are to information on professional cycling, including the Tour de France. You would be hard pressed to discover a better cycling site on the Internet.

The Internet Ski Guide (Snow Skiing)
http://cybil.kplus.bc.ca/www/ski_net/ski_na.htm

The Internet Ski Guide is a good place to begin planning your winter sports adventure. It covers skiing throughout North America and is designed to help you find a place to go. (Hint: Choose a place in a snowy climate.)

Ski resorts around the world are stepping into the chute with their own Web sites, but this site helps you narrow your focus before you check out the individual sites to make your choice. ☞

The List

It would be impossible to list every sports-related Internet site here. Still, this is a very complete list of sites that are currently available to sports fans.

Auto Racing

The Formula One Pick 6
http://essi.cerisi.fr/Pick6/pick6.html
A fantasy sports challenge.

Formula One Racing news and information
http://www.abekrd.co.uk/Formula1

Motorsport News International Index
http://www.metrics.com/MNI/index.html

Speedway News
http://www.amg.gda.pl/speedway/speedway.html

UseNet Groups
rec.sport.autos

rec.sport.f1

rec.sport.indy

rec.sport.info

rec.sport.nascar

rec.sport.tech

ESPNET SportsZone Server
http://espnet.sportszone.com/car

Formula SAE Racing

http://www.me.mtu.edu/loew

NandoX Server

http://www.nando.net/newsroom/car/car/feat/car.html

Nascar News Home Page

http://www.acpub.duke.edu/~jwcarp/nascarhome.html

Pete Fenelow's Motor Racing Page

http://dcpu1.cs.york.ac.uk:6666/pete/racing/index.html

r.a.s. Racer Archive

http://www.eng.hawaii.edu/Contribs/carina/ra.home.page.html

Time-Speed-Distance Road Rallying Information

http://www.contrib.andrew.cmu.edu/usr/ef1c/plug.html

Baseball-Pro

FTP Baseball Archive

ftp://etext.archive.umich.edu/pub/Sports/Baseball

Includes weekly stats updates.

Swarthmore Baseball Archives

http://eucalyptus.cc.swarthmore.edu/pub/baseball

World Wide Web (WWW) Virtual Library

http://www.atm.ch.cam.ac.uk/sports/baseball.html

UseNet Groups

rec.sport.baseball

rec.sport baseball.analysis

rec.sport.baseball.data

The Internet Baseball Information Center

http://www.gems.com/ibic

Highlights of the previous day's games

http://tns-www.lcs.mit.edu/cgi-bin/sports/mlb/highlights

NandoX Minor League Baseball Server

http://www.nando.net/baseball/bbminor.html

The Baseball FTP Site

ftp://eucalyptus.cc.swarthmore.edu/pub/baseball/fanta-roto

Interactive Schedule

http://www.cs.rochester.edu/cgi-bin/ferguson/mlb

Regular-Season Schedules

telnet://culine.colorado.edu:862

gopher://umslvma.umsl.edu:71/11/BASEBALL

ESPNET SportsZone Server

http://espnet.sportszone.com/mlb

Jason Kint's Baseball Page

http://pear.wustl.edu/~jekint/baseball.html

NandoX Server

http://www.nando.net/baseball/bbmain.html

Basketball—Pro

Eric Richard's Professional Basketball Server

http://www.mit.edu:8001/services/sis/NBA/NBA.html

ESPNET SportsZone Server

http://espnet.sportszone.com/nba

Gate Cybersports Home Page

http://sfgate.com:80/sports/sports/nba/index.html

Links to NBA Team Home Pages

http://tns-www.lcs.mit.edu/cgi-bin/sports/nba/teams

NandoX Server

http://www.nando.net/sports/bkb/1994/bkbserv.html

NBA Draft Coverage

http://www.mit.edu:8001/services/sis/NBAdraft_results

NBA Statistics

FTP: ftp://wuarchive.wustl.edu/doc/misc/nbastats/facts

NBA Fantasy Pool

http://www.hal.com/~markg/NBA

Interactive NBA Schedule

http://wintermute.unh.edu/cgi.bin/nba-page.pl

NBA Schedules

telnet://culine.colorado.edu:859

Boxing

ESPNET SportsZone Server

http://espnet.sportszone.com/box

NandoX Server

http://www.nando.net/newsroom/sports/box/feat/box.html

UseNet Group

rec.sport.boxing

Collegiate Sports—Baseball

UseNet Group

rec.sport.baseball.college

Collegiate Sports—Men's Basketball

Atlantic Coast Conference

http://www.cs.fsu.edu/~smiths/acc.html

Big 12 (records)

http://penguin.cc.ukans.edu/Big12_hoops.html

ESPNET SportsZone Server

http://espnet.sportszone.com/ncb

College Basketball Home Page

http://www.cs.cmu.edu:8001/afs/cs.cmu.edu/user/wsr/Web/bball
bball.html

GNN Basketball Home Page

http://www.digital.com/gnn/news/sports/basketballncaaindex.html

NCAA Basketball Home Page

http://www.traveller.com/scripts/pool_db/ncaa_bb?menu=main

CNN/USA Today Polls

http://www.nando.net/newsroom/basketball/1994/col/feat/
usat25.html

Dick Vitale's Polls

http://www.cs.cmu.edu:8001/afs/cs.cmu.edu/user/wsr/Web/
bballdv-poll.html

Sporting News Preseason Polls

http://www.cs.cmu.edu:8001/afs/cs.cmu.edu/user/wsr/Web/bball/
sn-poll.html

NCAA Men's Tournament Pools

http://hoohoo.ncsa.uiuc.edu/NCAApool/NCAApool.html

Schedules

http://www.nando.net/newsroom/basketball/1994/col/feat/bkc/
msked.html/

Standings

http://www.nando.net/newsroom/basketball/1994/col/stat/
standings.html

Collegiate Sports—Women's Basketball

ESPNET SportsZone Server

http://espnet.sportszone.com/ncw

NCAA Women's Basketball Home Page

http://gnn.com/gnn/meta/sports/index.html

Women's College Basketball Home Page

http://www.auburn.edu/~poperic/wbb.html

Top 25 Polls

http://www.nando.net/newsroom/basketball/1994/col/feat/
wt25.html

Collegiate Sports—Football

Conference, Big Eight (statistics)

http://www.cis.ksu.edu/~chiefs/bigeight.html

ESPNET SportsZone Server

http://espnet.sportszone.com/ncf

Darryl Marsee's Home Page

http://erau.db.erau.edu/~marseed/fb_page.html

Division I-AA Home Page

http://www.vt.edu:10021/bev/Users/gunner/1-aahome.html

Gate Cybersports College Football Home Page

http://sfgate.com/sports/sports/ncaa/football/index.html

NCAA Football Home Page

http://www.traveller.com/sports/ncaa_fb

RSFC College Football Home Page

http://www.math.ufl.edu/~mitgardt/rsfc.html

rec.sport.football.college

Football—Pro

Canadian Football League Home Page

http://www.ee.umanitoba.ca/CFL

Eric Richard's NFL Server

http://www.netgen.com/sis/sports.html

ESPNET SportsZone Server

http://espnet.sportszone.com/nfl

Football Information Page

http://www.armory.com/~lew/sports/football

Gate Cybersports NFL Home Page

http://sfgate.com/sports/sports/nfl/index.html

NandoX NFL Server

http://www.nando.net/football/1994/fbserv.html

NFL FTP Server

ftp://vnet.net/pub/football/PRO

NFL Home Page

http://www.cs.cmu.edu:8001/afs/cs/user/vernon/www/nfl.html

NFL News and other information

http://lux.labmed.washington.edu/~shoe/dallas/info/
football_news.html

NFL Schedule

http://www.cis.ksu.edu/~chiefs/nflstat.html

NFL team home pages

http://tns-www.lcs.mit.edu/nfl.html

Tom Jackson's Pro Football Update

http://www.awa.com/arena/jackson

Weekly NFL Pool

http://www.hal.com/~markg/NFL

Golf

Golf courses archived

http://dunkin.princeton.edu/.golf

Public golf courses across the United States

ftp://dunkin.Princeton.EDU/pub/golf

Scorecard archive

http://www.traveller.com/golf/scorecards

Fantasy Golf Challenge

http://caligari.dartmouth.edu/~ryde/ryde.html

ESPNET SportsZone server

http://espnet.sportszone.com/pga

Fore Play Golf Newsletter

http://www.deltanet.com/4play/newsltr.html

Golf Data Online Home Page

http://www.gdol.com

Golf Home Page

http://ausg.dartmouth.edu/~pete/golf

NandoX Server

http://www.nando.net/newsroom/sports/gol/feat/gol.html

The 19th Hole

http://zodiac.tr-riscs.panam.edu/golf/19thhole.html

Covers all pro tours.

Skins Game Information

http://www.cyberplex.com/CyberPlex/Fun/Skins/skinmenu.html

Hockey

Dan's Hockey Page

http://www.pitt.edu/~dtgst1/hockey.html

ESPNET SportsZone Server

http://espnet.sportszone.com/nhl

Hawaii's NHL Home Page

http://maxwell.uhh.hawaii.edu/hockey/hockey.html

Index to hockey links

http://www.wwu.edu/~n9143349/links.html

International Hockey League News

gopher://xavier.xu.edu:79/0074345

Klootzak's Internet Hockey Archive

ftp://ftp.u.washington.edu/public/hockey/homepage.html

NandoX Server

http://www.nando.net/newsroom/sports/hkn/feat/hkn.html

NHL FTP archive

ftp://wuarchive.wustl.edu/doc/misc/sports/nhl

Sports World Bulletin Board Service

http://debussy.media.mit.edu/dbecker/docs/swbbs.html

NHL schedule by team

http://www.cs.ubc.ca/nhl

Complete schedules

telnet://culine.colorado.edu:860

News, features, columns

http://sfgate.com/sports/sports/nhl/index.html

NHL logos

http://web.cps.msu.edu/~vergolin/wings/logo.html

Olympics

1996 Summer Olympics in Atlanta, Georgia

http://www.mindspring.com/~royal/olympic.html

http://www.gatech.edu/3020/olympics/olym-proj/intro.html

1998 Winter Olympics in Nagano, Japan

http://www.linc.or.jp/Nagano/index.html

NandoX Server

http://www.nando.net/newsroom/sports/oly/feat/oly.html

Soccer

Facts

http://www.di.unipi.it/fos/fos.html

French Soccer Web Server

http://www.cc.columbia.edu/~yn25/soccer.html

Games

http://www.atm.ch.cam.ac.uk/sports/games.html

International Soccer Results

http://www.pitt.edu/~rlpst/international.html

International Soccer Server

http://sotka.cs.tut.fi/riku/soccer.html

Italian soccer

http://www.cedar.buffalo.edu/~khoubs/WC94.nations/Italy.html

Laws of Soccer

http://mirach.cs.buffalo.edu/~khoub-s/FIFA_rules.html

Mailing lists

http://www.atm.ch.cam.ac.uk/sports/lists

NandoX Server

http://www.nando.net/newsroom/sports/soc/feat/soc.html

Northern European Rec.Sport.Soccer Statisticians Foundation

http://info.risc.uni-linz.ac.at:70/1/misc-info/rsssf/nersssf.html

U.S. soccer

http://www.cs.cmu.edu:8001/afs/cs/usr/mdwheel/www/soccer/us-soccer.html

Web Page rec.sports.soccer

http://www.atm.ch.cam.ac.uk/sports/

World Cup 1994 information

http://mirach.cs.buffalo.edu/~khoubs/WC94.html

Tennis

UseNet Group

UseNet: clari.sports.tennis

Player rankings

http://www.cdf.toronto.edu/DCS/FUN/tennis.html

UseNet Group

rec.sport.tennis

ESPNET SportsZone Server

http://espnet.sportszone.com/ten

Goddard Tennis Club Home Page

http://epims1.gsfc.nasa.gov/tennis/GTC_homepage.html

NandoX Server

http://www.nando.net/newsroom/sports/ten/feat/ten.html

The Tennis Server Home Page

http://arganet.tenagra.com/Racquet_Workshop/Tennis.html

Weightlifting

FAQs (Frequently Asked Questions)

http://www.cs.odu.edu/~ksw/weightsfaq.html

The Weightlifting Page

http://www.cs.odu.edu/~ksw/weights.html

16

Internet Oddities

IN THIS CHAPTER:

> Link pages

> "Best of" and "Worst of" pages

> Device pages

> Useless pages

IN OTHER CHAPTERS:

< Some Internet time wasters and online distractions are discussed in Chapter 14, "Games."

If you spend enough time searching for information about entertainment on the Internet, you will realize that a new medium of expression has slithered into our lives in the last few years that may eventually overshadow all of the other media for its sheer entertainment value: the Internet itself.

There are now enough lunatics and visionaries fiddling around online that you could merrily spend the rest of your life surfing the Net and never watch another movie or read another book; and yet in the process you can become as hip as the coolest club-goer—or as pacified as the most dim-witted couch potato. Because of its increasing multimedia capabilities, it is not unthinkable that eventually some portable form of the Internet could replace television, movies, literature, the theatre, and music as the dominant medium of "entertainment" on the planet.

Already there are thousands of Web sites that exist solely for amusement and novelty; and there are countless other sites that were originally intended to be useful but are rendered amusing by the ironic sensibilities of the user. There are photo essays of beloved goldfish, cameras posted in people's bathrooms, and self-promoting homesites for every college student with a spare key to the Computer Lab. This chapter comprises a collection of Web sites that have nothing in common but their capacity to amuse or mystify the author of this book. After a while it is likely that you will develop a collection of your own.

Link Pages

Lateral navigation through the Web is a pleasure unto itself, and a good list of links can be a springboard to places you never dreamed of. While almost every Web site has a small collection of links that are related to the ostensible subject of that Web page (for instance, a site devoted to baseball will point you to other baseball pages), many sites on the Internet exist primarily to bounce you off into cyberspace and have little or no actual subject matter of their own. Some of these pages are arranged thematically, according to the developer's particular interests, while others are just a big bag full of unrelated links that the users have to sort through for themselves. Following are some good collections of links that will fling you around the Internet like a drunken cosmonaut and have you begging for more.

Organized Link Sites

The following link sites have some semblance of organization or theme. There are numerous others.

Thematically coherent lists of links are often embedded at the end of a comprehensive site devoted to a particular topic. Chances are, if you find even a crummy little site that is dedicated to the topic you are interested in, it will contain at least a few links to other sites, and one of those sites is likely to be the kingpin site with the best collection of links. So have a little fun and don't be in too big a hurry. Like the Rolling Stones once said in a song, "You cannot always be certain of obtaining what it is that you desire, but if you endeavor with sufficient fortitude, you may obtain what is *necessary*." Or something like that.

Justin's Links from the Underground
http://www.links.net

If you didn't know that the Internet is populated by a bunch of socialist sympathizers and anarchists with a techno-liberal agenda for our collective future, you haven't been paying attention. Pill-popping cyberpunks and left-wing pansexual renegades are in control here, and there's not a lot you can do about it, because they know so much more about computers than you do. My advice: Get with the program, before it's too late.

Justin's Links from the Underground is a well-known collection of links from Justin Hall, a college student who has worked at *Wired* magazine and does a lot of writing on the side. This is not technically a links-only site—there are a lot of Justin's own writings here, including a hypertext autobiography (in which, among other things, he meets Punky Brewster in a Hollywood canteen)—but it's the links collection that makes it such a useful site. Figure 16.1 shows a number of his links—to his own writings and to a handful of new sites he has recently added to the menu.

FIGURE 16.1

This part of Links from the Underground is reserved for pointers to Justin's own autobiographical writings and to the latest cool sites that have come to his attention.

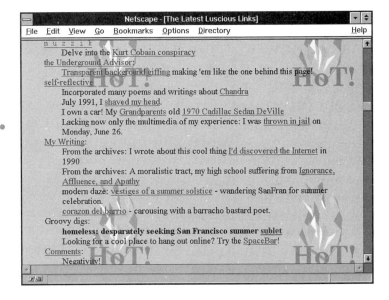

The links cover the hip portion of the Web experience (you won't find a direct link to the Canadian Dairy Farmers Association, if there is such a thing, although you will find links to some helpful general indexes that will eventually get you to Squaresville if that's where you want to go), with a particular emphasis on counter-cultural, youth-oriented stuff. A big "Best Of" section is called "The Weird, the Wild, and the Wonderful on the WWW," which is further divided into such categories as "Sex, Drugz, and Spirituality" and "The Way of a Web Wanderer."

There's more than a little anarchy that can be accessed here (a Guide to Lock-Picking, the Phrack Magazine Handbook on Sabotaging Fast-Food Restaurants), along with lots of intelligent information about sexually explicit material on the Net and everything you'd ever want to know about electronic publishing, Internet culture, and the legal issues that are generated in cyberspace.

WHAT'S IN A NAME?

Besides being an invaluable resource for exploring the Net, Justin's Links From the Underground contains some of the most pertinent information available about the emerging Net culture itself. One of the more interesting original documents within Justin's Links is a series of letters between himself and InterNIC, the organization that grants and administers the rights to domain names on the Internet. In the letters we learn that Justin has been trying to register a domain name that the InterNIC folks consider obscene. (Hint: The name is f**k.com, in which the asterisks are placeholders.)

In the letters, Justin makes a passionate plea for artistic freedom and the unfettered flow of information, contending that the Internet is a global resource that transcends the censure of local jurisdictions or individual morality. Of course, he gets nowhere with these people, but it makes for a provocative read.

Hyper-Weirdness By World Wide Web

http://phenom.physics.wisc.edu/~shalizi/hyper-weird

On the Internet, it's hard to determine what is fringe culture and what is the mainstream, partly because every idea arrives at you from the same source (your computer), and partly because the cyberspace definition of what is mainstream or acceptable keeps moving to the left.

Yet even on the notoriously kooky Web, there is an avant garde of weirdness and speculative thinking. That portion of the cyber community that adheres to conspiracy theories and radical ideologies has a home base at a link site called Hyper Weirdness By World Wide Web.

This dense and well-indexed collection of links will bounce you to sites about religion (mainstream, new age, and cult alike), philosophy, science, unexplained phenomena, drugs, computers, underground music, online magazines, and so on. (See figure 16.2.)

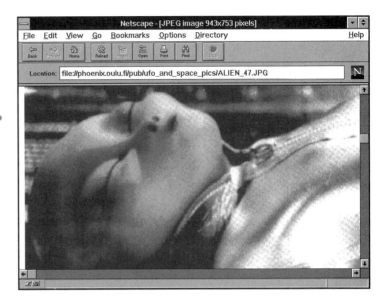

By the way, the most frequently accessed link within Hyper-Weirdness is something called Nekkid Wymmin By World Wide Web at *http://phenom.physics.wisc.edu/~shalizi/hyper-weird/nekkid-wymmin.html*. However, I'll save you the trouble and tell you that there are no longer any dirty pictures at this site. Instead, you'll will find an interesting document about how this site was accessed so frequently that it had to be shut down. Which brings us to...

The Prurient Pages
http://www.links.net/sex/prurient.html

This is actually a subdivision of Justin's Links, mentioned earlier, but it addresses such a popular topic that it deserves separate mention. This site provides immediate access to many of the sex-related sites on the Internet. It is likely to irreparably screw up your life.

The Point of No Return
http://zoom.lm.com

This sex-related gateway is actually a commercial service, but if you think that access to a smorgasbord of online sex resources is worth about twenty bucks a month, don't let me stop you. The "free" part of this site has a lot of ads for European sex videos, discreet photo processing, and a recruitment campaign for nude models (ages 18 to 40, please). Before you dig too deeply, keep in mind that there's a reason they call this site "The Point of No Return."

This site also features a surprisingly comprehensive general link index that seems to have nothing to do with sex whatsoever (unless you're one of those amateur psychologists who thinks that *everything* has something to do with sex). This index, called "Main Street," is divided into Art, Entertainment, Religion, Computers, and so on, just like Yahoo.

By now you should be aware that the most complete and best-organized link resource on the Internet is the Yahoo utility. The 44,000 Web sites to which Yahoo is connected are divided into broad categories such as Art, Business, Computers, Law, Science, and of course, Entertainment. Within these categories there are many subdivisions, down to the level of individual links (for instance: *Entertainment/Movies/Products/The Florida Girls Network*). Almost every site that is referenced in this book can be found and accessed directly from Yahoo (and many of the sites in this particular chapter are listed under subcategories called Useless Pages and Cool Links). Yahoo also offers a choice of a random Web site at the push of a button. (Yahoo can be accessed at *http://www.yahoo.com.*)

Disorganized Link Sites

A lot of the best link collections on the Internet are stuck at the end of somebody's home page.

UnderWorld Industry's Web's Edge
http://kzsu.stanford.edu/uwi.html

This techno-savvy mess of links is at the cutting edge of something, but I don't know what it is. Most of the links at this site will take you to places of eye-popping weirdness. It was here that I learned about Grouchy Cafe (a good-natured send-up of coffee culture), The Speed Trap Registry (where users report the locations of small-town speed zones around the country), the Wall o' Shame, the Yak's Lair, the 50 Greatest Conspiracies of All Time, and much more. (See figure 16.3.) It's nicely disorganized, and I'll award it some bonus points for its mysterious and oft-repeated antipathy towards Netscape.

FIGURE 16.3

A more-or-less random sampling of the interesting stuff that can be accessed via The Web's Edge.

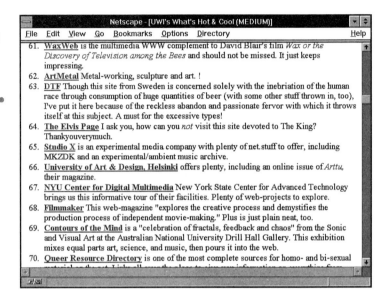

Brittany's Grandaddy

http://www.inmind.com/people/dglass

So there's this guy in Virginia who's a local magistrate and a rock & roll deejay and he's got this home page in which there's a picture of him scaring the heck out of this little kid who's probably his granddaughter and he's got a gargantuan list of links that range from the Jews For Jesus Page to something called the Abuse-A-Tron and I just had to slip him into the book somewhere. Okay? (See figure 16.4.)

FIGURE 16.4

The individual home page with the weirdest snapshot and the longest list of links that I have found. Warning: Most of the links are perfectly wholesome.

The Best and the Worst: Web Indexes

There is a species of Web site that exists solely to critique or compliment other sites. There are now several "Site of the Day" pages, a few "Worst Of" pages," at least one random site generator, and even a site that is devoted to the most *mediocre* Web pages.

Cool Site of the Day

http://www.infi.net/cool.html

Every day, the folks at *infi.net* choose a cool site that gets to wear the crown of Web hipness for 24 hours before passing it on to the next winner. About half of the chosen sites are splashy and well-funded, but there is still a fair number of little eccentric home pages that make the grade. Figure 16.5 shows a recent winner, The Web Dating Game (a cyberspace variation on the odious TV show *Love Connection*), in which online denizens pair off for an actual blind date.

Funky Site of the Day
http://www.realitycom.com/cybstars/index.html

Ostensibly these sites should be a little more oddball than ones
at Cool Site of the Day, but they seem about the same. Recent
selections have included The Surrealistic Excuse Generator,
Amnesty International, and the home page for a British hang-
gliding association.

Cybertown's Site of the Week
http://www.directnet.com/cybertown

This all-purpose lifestyles-and-entertainment site (which features a
space colony visual motif) chooses a notable Web site very
week. Similar to Cool Site of the Day and Funky Site of the Day,
except it's only about one-seventh as much fun. This week: The
Gigaplex, a much-lauded entertainment-news-and-reviews
supersite.

Mirsky's Worst of the Web

http://mirsky.turnpike.net/wow/Worst.html

Mirsky's Worst of the Web celebrates the inane and inept on the World Wide Web. Of course, the definition of what is "bad" is so slippery that even Mirsky realizes these can be some of the most perversely entertaining places on the Net.

Every day there are three or four new sites added to the roster, and the previous winners are indexed for easy retrieval. Past winners have included Kyle's Walkman Server (cited later in this chapter), the Breakfast Cereal Hall of Fame, a price guide to prostitution in New York City, and a press release about the new Sprite soft-drink bottle. (See figure 16.6.)

FIGURE 16.6

A recent winner of Mirsky's Worst of the Web award. (Mirsky, I like the spite in you.)

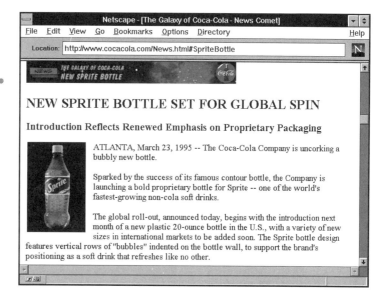

Mirsky also sponsors a contest in which users can nominate sites as the Worst on the Web—and apparently many Net denizens are eager to have their *own* sites declared as The Worst.

A guide to those sites that embody the nerd principle as it is expressed on the Internet. Today's site: Birthplaces of European Mathematicians.

Devices Connected to the Internet

From the early days of networked computing there have been external devices connected to computers, devices that remote users could access and even manipulate. The most famous of these devices was the soda machine at Carnegie-Mellon University that was connected to a computer that reported how many cans of each brand of soda were available in the machine at any given time. Today there are many sites connected to televisions, CD players, video cameras, telephones, toilets, robotic arms, and weather instruments (as well as at least a dozen soda machines).

A general index of Internet-accessible devices is located at http://www.cs.cmu.edu/afs/cs.cmu.edu/user/bsy/www/iam.html.

Camera Pages

These are some of the several dozen sites in which cameras are pointed at objects and linked to a computer on the Internet. (Generally these sites do not offer strictly "real-time" images but rather have images that are changed or refreshed at given intervals—usually every few minutes.)

Niagara Falls Cam

http://fallscam.niagara.com

The Falls Cam is a camera located at the top of the Sheraton Fallsview hotel near Niagara Falls (on the U.S./Canada border). You have to register for this one, but it's worth it. Once you've entered your password, you can see either an MPEG mini-movie of the falls or a still JPG image. (See figure 16.7.)

FIGURE 16.7

An image from the Niagara Falls Cam. I'm sure it's much more lively and impressive in person.

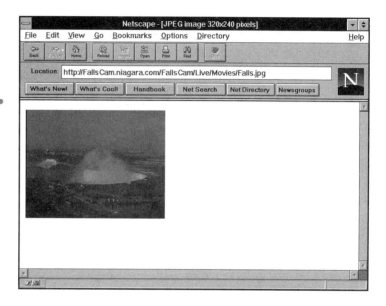

If you're interested in this kind of tourist cam, you might also try the Golden Gate Bridge Cam, from San Francisco TV station KPIX, at *http://kpix.com*, and the Hollywood Sign Cam at *http://www.rfx.com/holly.html.*

Steve's Ant Farm

http://sec.dgsys.com/AntFarm.html

Watch the ants build tunnels, horde bread crumbs, and bury their dead. (Yes, they actually do that.) Updated every 10 minutes. (See figure 16.8.)

FIGURE 16.8

An image from Steve's Ant Farm.

• • • • • • • • • • • • • • •

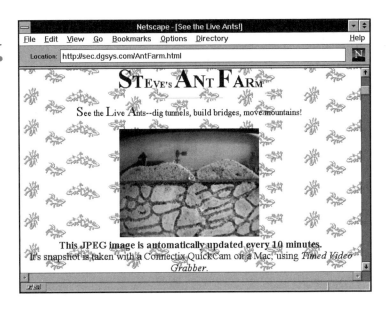

The ORL Active Badge System Map

http://www.cam-orl.co.uk/cgi-bin/mapgen

The Olivetti Research Labhas a system by which the comings and goings of employees are monitored by the badges that the employees wear. At this site you can access a map of the building and see a blip that marks where everybody is. Isn't that diabolical? (No, I don't know if there are automated badge readers in the bathrooms.)

THE LEGEND OF THE POTTY CAM

• •

It is alleged that somewhere on the Net there was once a camera that was placed in the bathroom of a notoriously filthy bachelor pad. On nights when there were parties at this apartment, it was even possible to see partygoers passed out with their heads upon the porcelain. While I have not actually found this site, I have found a closet cam, many fish cams, a cockatoo cam, and a site that shows you what a guy in San Francisco is watching on TV at any given moment. I'll keep searching and let you know.

Brian's Lava Lamp

http://www.arl.wustl.edu/~brian/Office/LavaLamp

A guy in St. Louis named Brian provides us with a new picture of his lava lamp every minute. (See figure 16.9.)

FIGURE 16.9

Brian's Lava Lamp. By the way, if you'd like a lava lamp of your very own, try a store in St. Louis called Hullabaloo.

● ● ● ● ● ● ● ● ● ● ● ● ● ● ● ●

Other Devices

Brian's Phone

http://www.arl.wustl.edu/~brian/Office/Phone

Yes, it's Brian again, the same Web visionary who brought you the online lava lamp. Brian also has his computer connected to his telephone. You can see a report of the last time Brian got a phone call, hear an audio sample of the ringing mechanism itself, and listen to recordings of some actual calls he has received since becoming a big-time Web celebrity.

Paul Haas' Refrigerator

http://hamjudo.com/cgi-bin/refrigerator

Here you can find out how cold it is inside of Paul's refrigerator and get a notion of its contents. However, because it is an extra refrigerator, it is now empty. (As a bonus, Paul tells us the refrigerator is for sale and reproduces the ad. Because the refrigerator is not much fun without a network interface, the buyer will also receive a Sun Workstation and a can of Diet Coke. Honest.)

Paul also operates a hot-tub monitor and a robotic arm that lets you wave to whoever is in his room at the time.

Interactive Model Railroad

http://www-vs.informatik.uni-ulm.de/RR

This site in Germany lets you operate and watch a model railroad as it travels around a multi-platform set-up. This site is pushing the boundaries of inline video images over the Net. Personally, I couldn't get it to run, but I'm a blockhead, and I'm sure it wouldn't exist if it didn't work. Plus, it has a nice home page. (See figure 16.10.)

FIGURE 16.10

The Interactive Model Railroad.

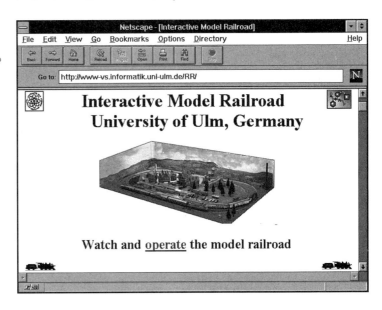

TRAFFIC MONITORS

There are real-time, computerized traffic reports available for several American cities. The Houston traffic server is at http://herman.tamu.edu/houston-real.html. The Seattle traffic report is at http://198.238.212.10/regions/northwest. And the Los Angeles/ San Diego traffic report is at http://www.scubed.com:8001/caltrans/transnet.html. This can come in very handy if you are using your computer while you are driving.

Web Miscellany

The odds and ends that comprise the rest of this chapter include online magazines, cyber diaries, and bonafide time wasters.

Oddball E-Zines and Lifestyle Manifestos

By compiling some images, an introductory text, and a collection of links, almost anyone can create an e-zine, promote a cause, or start a cult. The following are some e-zines and alternative lifestyle sites that are particularly odd or entertaining.

NOTE
Today, there are more online e-zines than you'll ever have time to read, and that's okay, because many of them are the same, with lots of alternative-music reviews, bad poetry, and eye-straining graphics. However, there are plenty of bold and interesting e-zines that are worth your time. A comprehensive list by John Labovitz can be found at *http://www.meer.net/~johnl/e-zine-list/index.html.*

Tum Yet Ghetto
http://www.tumyeto.com

This is a young, fresh lifestyle magazine from San Diego that has just the right combination of cynicism, faux naiveté, and verve for the new generation of skateboard-toting intellectuals.

Included in the Tum Yet Ghetto is Foxy, "the e-zine for chicks," which includes an underwear survey, helpful information about pimples, a guide to dumping a bad boyfriend, a Cute Dictionary (see figure 16.11), and a list of 60 things to do when you're bored. 👉

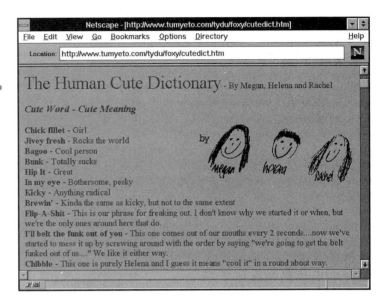

Cocktail Nation: The Lounge-Culture Sites

Unless you've been wearing a bag over your head, you know that all the coolest kids are donning smoking jackets and listening to Mancini records beneath the backyard tiki torch. Two fabulous new Web sites celebrate this subculture of cool. The Roots of Lounge at *http://www.expanse.com/ads/kiwr/rootsoflounge.html* puts the lounge phenomenon that has been rediscovered by the so-called Cocktail Nation into a perspective that even a square could understand.

The Space Age Bachelor Pad Music site is a tribute to the sounds of technorama kitsch that emanated from every suburban rumpus room in the 1950s, in particular the music of Juan Garcia Esquivel. It also includes a priceless gallery of "exotic" album-cover art. (See figure 16.12) 👉

FIGURE 16.12
Space Age Bachelor Pad Music is just the tonic for the over-worked young modern.

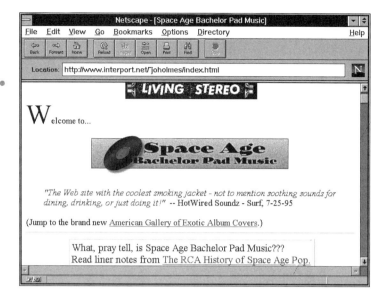

nothingness.org
http://www.nothingness.org

Also known as The Wonderful World of Spud, this is a hip, good-looking arts journal with a firm foundation in existential anxiety and the saving graces of dadaist absurdity.

Fortean Times
http://www.mic.dundee.ac.uk/ft/ft.html

This is the online edition of the British magazine of unexplained phenomena—UFOs, spontaneous combustion, goats that rain from the sky, and that sort of thing.

Rox
http://www.rox.com/quarry

Rox is a notorious public-access TV show from Bloomington, Indiana, that claims to be the first television show to offer an entire episode for online downloading. (Believe me, you don't have the time or the technology to find out if it works.)

The Rox dudes are perhaps best known for an episode in which they smoke a fatty in front of the local courthouse. After this episode aired, the district attorney accused them of "the overt promotion of anarchy," a charge that they warmly accept.

This Web site offers an episode guide to all of Rox's shenanigans, as well as still images of one of the guys running nude across the Indiana University campus, and a between-the-lines defense of small-town revolutionary hi-jinx.

The Church of the SubGenius

http://sunsite.unc.edu/subgenius

The world's first (and still the best) for-profit religion has several sites across the Web, but this is the Grand Poobah of SubGenius pages, administered by the Rev. Ivan Stang, a sanctified Elder of the Church.

For those of you who are too tightly held in the grips of the Conspiracy to recognize Salvation when it's offered to you, a little brainwashing is in order: The Church of the SubGenius is the terrestrial mouthpiece of J.R. "Bob" Dobbs (see figure 16.13), the trickster deity and salesman of slack who, for a $1.00 love offering to a post-office box in Dallas, Texas, will free you from the tentacles of the Conspiracy, will teach you to pull the wool over your *own* eyes, and will prepare you for the arrival of the JHVH 1 mothership.

Sure, there are a handful of wily manipulators making a fortune from this supposed "send-up" of organized religion. But as "Bob" would be the first to tell you, there are a million ways of getting manipulated—and some of them are fun.

FIGURE 16.13

With "Bob," all things are possible.

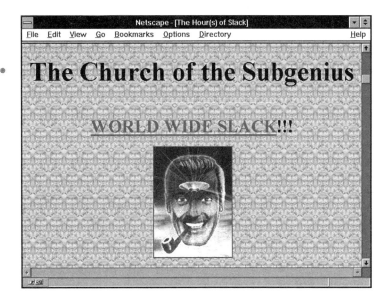

Diaries

There is an increasingly popular kind of site on the Web in which somebody (usually a college kid) posts his daily activities, his deepest thoughts, or snapshots from the road trip he took with his best buddy in the whole world. The following are some diary sites that are better than the usual.

The Spot
http://www.thespot.com

This excellent site is a kind of group diary from the five attractive residents of a California beach pad with a long history of visits by Hollywood merrymakers. (See figure 16.14.) This could have been a dreary exercise in self-indulgence or an attempt to attract financing for an MTV-style documentary, but the folks who live at The Spot have a good feel for the technological potential of the Web. The entries are meticulously indexed by date and by writer, and often the roommates are writing about the same events from different points of view. There is also some chatting with the people who visit The Spot page, which raises some interesting questions about the nature of "community" in a virtual environment. (There's a rumor that the Spot is actually the work of one very Web-savvy individual named Scott Zakorin, in which case it's an even more impressive and provocative achievement.)

FIGURE 16.14

The Spot, which is both the name of a California beach house and the name of the Web site about the people who supposedly live there.

The Adventures of Matthew and Jake

http://www.mit.edu:8001/mj/mj.html

Two MIT students report periodically on their lives, including "Matthew and Jake Fly a Kite" and "Matthew and Jake Go to The IHOP" (which, my sources tell me, stands for The International House of Pancakes).

Look Out! It's Dave's Page!

http://kuhub.cc.ukans.edu/~daten/index.html

This home page of a Kansas college student named Dave Aten earns its place in this book because of Dave's poignant account of a recent trip to Dinosaur World (in Beaver, Arkansas), a glittering tourist destination that was built by '50s B-movie icon John Agar. (See figure 16.15.)

FIGURE 16.15

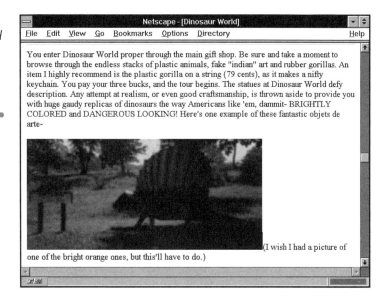

Dave promises to add to his home page a report on his recent trip to the Precious Moments Chapel in Carthage, Missouri, a shrine to traditional American values that will make your jaw drop in disbelief. (To give you a rough idea, imagine if the Smurfs took over the Vatican.)

Ranjit's Lunch
http://oz.sas.upenn.edu/miscellany/lunch.html

This is part of a larger basket of miscellaneous Webfoolery from a student at the University of Pennsylvania. It consists of Ranjit telling us what he had for lunch today and where he ate it. (Personally I think Ranjit could do a lot worse than the scrapple and scrambled eggs platter at the Stouffer Dining Hall on the Penn campus. It got me through some hard times.)

Useless Pages

In Web parlance, to say that a site is "useless" is not necessarily insulting. Indeed, many sites on the Internet aspire to a kind of transcendent stupidity or uselessness, a deliberate inversion of the idea that computers have to be employed in some productive way in order to justify their existence. This is partly attributable to the obscene amount of computer space that is available for free to college students. If they actually had to pay for all the megabytes that their vanity projects were consuming, they'd think twice before posting so many lame snapshots of their girlfriends. But there is also a spirit of irreverence on the Web that has more to do with the joy of self expression than the thrill of stealing gigabytes from The Man.

There are indexes to useless pages in the Yahoo directory and at *http://www.primus.com/staff/paulp/useless.html*. The latter includes links to The Elbow Page, The Keyboard Nipple Survey, The Booger Page, The Mime Page, a page called Give Ben Money, and something I'm very fond of called What's in Joe's Pocket?

Following are some useless pages of note. There are hundreds of others: Go get 'em.

Kyle's Walkman Server
http://www.efn.org/~kpw/walkman.html

This is one of my favorite sites on the entire Internet. Kyle Whelliston is a college student in Eugene, Oregon, who rides the bus to campus every day. Like a lot of people in similar situations, he listens to a headset stereo to pass the time. Every day, Kyle chooses a cassette tape from his extensive collection and pops it into the Walkman (which he bought at the Bi-Mart for $49.99). By accessing this page, we can find out what Kyle is listening to today. As a bonus, he tells us the last time he changed his batteries.

There are a lot of similar sites on the Internet, including one where you can tell a guy what you want him to play on his CD. However, this was the first truly "useless" page I ever accessed, so it will always have a special place in my heart. Plus, Kyle has pretty good taste in music and a fairly tolerant attitude toward people who don't get the joke. (He proudly proclaims that he was named to Mirsky's Worst of the Web index, and his site includes a collection of abusive e-mail he has received.)

Strawberry Pop Tart Blow Torch

http://www.sci.tamucc.edu/~pmichaud/toast

This popular site provides step-by-step instruction for using your toaster to turn a Strawberry Pop Tart into a potentially lethal incendiary device. See figure 16.16.

FIGURE 16.16

The necessary ingredients for a Strawberry Pop Tart Blow Torch.

● ● ● ● ● ● ● ● ● ● ● ● ● ● ● ● ●

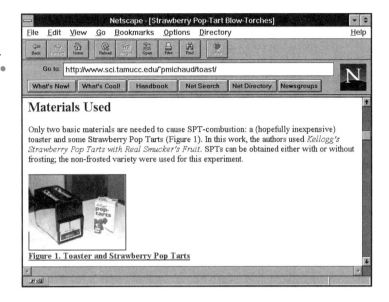

The demonstration is all the more funny for adhering to the basic principles of scientific methodology (hypothesis, materials, experimental preparation, observation of results, and summary).

The Spork Home Page

http://www.intac.com/~cully/spork.html

This guy is such a devotee of this wonderful modern implement—a combination of the spoon and the fork—that he tracked down its inventor.

Steve's List of T-Shirts
http://www.chaco.com/~stev0/shirts.html

All 34 of them, sorted by category.

The List

Link Sites

Justin's Links from the Underground
http://www.links.net

Hyper Weirdness By World Wide Web
http://phenom.physics.wisc.edu/~shalizi/hyper-weird

The Prurient Pages
http://www.links.net/sex/prurient.html

The Point of No Return
http://zoom.lm.com

UnderWorld Industry's Web's Edge
http://kzsu.stanford.edu/uwi.html

Brittany's Grandaddy
http://www.inmind.com/people/dglass

Many URLs
http://www.galcit.caltech.edu/~ta/revdoor/oldurls.shtml
Just what the name says: a steaming pile of *3,000* Web sites with no
organizational structure whatsoever.

Web Tendrils
http://oz.sas.upenn.edu/tendrils/tendrils.html

"Best of/Worst of" Pages

Cool Site of the Day
http://www.infi.net/cool.html

Funky Site of the Day
http://www.realitycom.com/cybstars/index.html

Cybertown's Site of the Week
http://www.directnet.com/cybertown

Mirsky's Worst of the Web
http://mirsky.turnpike.net/wow/Worst.html

Geek Site of the Day
http://chico.rice.edu/~indigo/gsotd

The Web Seeress
http://www.cyberzine.com/seeress

Spider's Pick of the Day
http://www.realitycom.com/cybstars/index.html

Barbara's Best Bookmark of the Day
http://www.shsu.edu/users/std/stdkco/pub2/best.html

Mediocre Site of the Day
http://minerva.cis.yale.edu/~jharris/mediocre.html

Devices Connected to the Internet

Cameras

Niagara Falls Cam
http://fallscam.niagara.com

Golden Gate Bridge Cam

http://kpix.com

Hollywood Sign Cam

http://www.rfx.com/holly.html

Steve's Ant Farm

http://sec.dgsys.com/AntFarm.html

The ORL Active Badge System Map

http://www.cam-orl.co.uk/cgi-bin/mapgen

Brian's Lava Lamp

http://www.arl.wustl.edu/~brian/Office/LavaLamp

Other Devices

Brian's Phone

http://www.arl.wustl.edu/~brian/Office/Phone

Interactive Model Railroad

http://www-vs.informatik.uni-ulm.de/RR

Paul Haas' Refrigerator

http://hamjudo.com/cgi-bin/refrigerator

Traffic Monitors

The Houston Area Traffic Server

http://herman.tamu.edu/houston-real.html

The Seattle Area Traffic Report

http://198.238.212.10/regions/northwest

Los Angeles/San Diego/Orange County Traffic Report

http://www.scubed.com:8001/caltrans/transnet.html

What Miles is Watching on TV

http://www.csua.berkeley.edu/~milesm/ontv.html

What's Liem Watching?

http://www.ssc.com/~roland/other/tv.html

The Internet Monitored Restroom at Vanderbilt University

http://entity.vuse.vanderbilt.edu/project

Although I haven't accessed it, I've been told that this site measures bathroom utilization and doesn't actually take pictures; but when it comes to bathroom surveillance, it's always better to err on the side of caution, if you ask me.

Offbeat E-Zines and Lifestyle Manifestos

John Labovitz' E-Zine List

http://www.meer.net/~johnl/e-zine-list/index.html.

Tum Yet Ghetto

http://www.tumyeto.com

Urban Desires

http://desires.com

The Roots of Lounge

http://www.expanse.com/ads/kiwr/rootsoflounge.html

Space-Age Bachelor Pad Music

http://www.interport.net/~joholmes/index.html

nothingness.org

http://www.nothingness.org

Fortean Times

http://www.mic.dundee.ac.uk/ft/ft.html

The Church of the SubGenius

http://sunsite.unc.edu/subgenius

Rox

http://www.rox.com/quarry

Postmodern Culture

http://jefferson.village.virginia.edu/pmc

An interdisciplinary magazine of media-saturated, apocalyptic double-speak.

Wall o' Shame

http://www.milk.com:80/wall-o-shame

A collection of bizarre true stories, including the following: "A hunter in Uganda is being sought by local authorities for illegally hunting gorillas. He shoots them with a tranquilizer gun and dresses them in clown suits. So far, six gorillas have been found wandering around in this condition."

Grouchy Cafe

http://www.echonyc.com/~cafephrk/cafe.html

Servin' up delicious angst, seven days a week.

BRETTnews

http://www.pathfinder.com

A retro-stylish zine of "pithy fluff," including the requisite cross-county odyssey (in which Brett catches a "performance" by Frank Sinatra, Jr., at the Four Queens Hotel lounge in Vegas), inexplicably associated with *Vibe* magazine, the R&B publication from Time, Inc.

The Frank Sinatra Home Page

http://www.io.org/~buff/sinatra.html

It's the ring-a-ding-dingiest!

Sinatra and the Rat Pack

http://www.interport.net/~sinatra

American Legends #3: Jack Webb

http://www.echonyc.com/~pjames

Diaries

The Spot
http://www.thespot.com

The Adventures of Matthew and Jake
http://www.mit.edu:8001/mj/mj.html

Look Out! It's Dave's Page!
http://kuhub.cc.ukans.edu/~daten/index.html

Ranjit's Lunch
http://oz.sas.upenn.edu/miscellany/lunch.html

Onward
http://sunsite.unc.edu/onward/loop94/loophome.html

Featuring yet another road-trip diary.

Randy's New CD
http://www.aloha.com/~randym/new_cd.html

I see that Randy just bought a Pearl Jam CD.

Rants & Raves
http://www.winternet.com/~faz/rants/rants.html

Confessions of a 41-Year-Old Virgin
http://www.calpoly.edu/~ttokuuke/virgin.html

Sadly, this is an ongoing project.

Useless Pages

Index of Useless WWW Pages
http://www.primus.com/staff/paulp/useless.html

Kyle's Walkman Server
http://www.efn.org/~kpw/walkman.html

Strawberry Pop Tart Blow Torch

http://www.sci.tamucc.edu/~pmichaud/toast

The Spork Homepage

http://www/intac.com/~cully.spork.html

Steve's List of T-Shirts

http://www.chaco.com/~stev0/shirts.html

Keyboard Nipple Survey

http://sync.cs.buffalo.edu/nipple-survey.html

Spatula City

http://www.wam.umd.edu/~twoflowr

With thousands of spatulas to choose from, in every shape and color. (Within this site you will find a site of transcendent uselessness: "The Really Big Button That Doesn't Do Anything.")

Stuff In My Room

http://www.cascade.net/~sunspot/stuff.html

The Mime Page

http://www.umich.edu/~ryandhoz/mimes

The Elbow Page

http://www.mit.edu:8001/afs/athena.mit.edu/user/j/k/jke/www/index.html

What's In Joe's Pocket?

http://ripsaw.cac.psu.edu/~jpn111/pocket.html

See for yourself.

Getting
Connected

IN THIS CHAPTER:

> *What you need in order to access the Internet*

> *Choosing a service provider*

> *Understanding UseNet, Gopherspace, FTP, and the Web*

> *How to use the addresses in this book*

> *How to find additional information on the Net*

Even a blockhead can navigate the Internet. I know, because I used to *be* one. (Like many people in the '90s, I am slowly evolving from a blockhead to a knucklehead to a puddin'head to a disembodied head that is connected to a computer via fiber-optic cable.)

This chapter shows you how to use the software you'll need in order to find entertainment sites and other information on the Internet. It isn't meant to be an exhaustive "How To." Rather, it's intended to give you the basic information about getting started—from choosing a software package to actually dialing up and connecting with the many different types of servers on the Internet. Once you get connected, you'll probably find that the actual process of navigating the Internet is remarkably simple (and it will get even easier in the future as more money is at stake and more neophytes enter the market). At the end of the chapter you will find a list of books that can take you further in your exploration of the Internet.

Hardware for Connecting to the Net

The Internet began as a text-based medium that a user could access with only some basic hardware. Today, however, the Net includes graphics, video, audio, and other multimedia elements. (These are especially common in entertainment-related sites, where you can listen to entire songs or view video clip of upcoming films.) To use the Internet to its fullest extent, you'll need the following hardware:

* A computer with a 486 or stronger microprocessor

* 50 MHz or higher processing speed

* At least 25-50M of free disk space

* 8M of RAM

* At least a 14.4 V.32bis/V.42 modem (although 28.8 V.34 modems are already very affordable and will speed things up considerably)

* A sound card (optional)

* A video card that will handle at least 256 colors

* Speakers (optional)

* CD-ROM drive (optional)

* A mouse

If you're using a Macintosh computer, these same memory, hard-disk, and modem requirements apply. Although you can do many things on the Net with a Mac Classic, it's recommended that you use a higher-end machine such as a Quadra or PowerMac. Many audio and video capabilities are built into these machines.

Software for Connecting to the Net

Much of the data available on the Net is not accessible through a standard connection. In other words, you cannot dial up the Internet with the same modem software you use to call BBSs. For many of these tasks, you need to establish a special connection that speaks TCP/IP (the language of the Internet). To do this, you need special software and a service provider that gives you a more direct link to the Internet.

Many commercial services offer their own software to help you establish a TCP/IP connection; these are discussed in the next section. If you already belong to a service provider and do not have access to TCP/IP software, more and more companies are offering dial-in Internet connections through software programs you can purchase at your local retailer. Other Internet providers offer prepackaged software that is already configured for you to use.

NOTE

Prodigy, America Online, and CompuServe continue to add access to more portions of the Internet via their own graphical software. It's probably only a matter of time before these services offer complete Internet access. Until then, however, the values of these services to people who are interested in the free flow of information and personal empowerment through online computing is open to considerable debate.

Service Providers

Once you have the right hardware and software, you still need a service provider. There are hundreds of service providers to choose from—both local and national—and additional companies are jumping into the marketplace every day. If you haven't yet signed on with a service provider, this section offers some guidance.

What To Look For in a Service Provider

A service provider is nothing more than a company or organization that provides access to the Internet (usually for a fee). Not all service providers are alike. Although they all provide the same essential service—a connection to the Internet—they vary with regard to what they allow you to access, how they charge you for connecting, and what extra services they provide. To determine the best provider for your needs, consider the following criteria:

* Cost. What is the bottom line cost for the service? A flat-rate service is often a better deal than a per-hour service. Many providers offer an attractive fee but charge extra for connect time, higher connection speeds, and direct computer-to-computer access (via a PPP or SLIP account, which bypasses the host computer). When you are considering a provider, it's essential that you understand and determine the hidden costs.

* Company stability. It's important to know that you can rely on a company. If possible, find out how long the company has been in business and how many subscribers it has. Although an old company is not inherently better than a new one, a mature company with a stable base of customers is often a good choice.

* Usability and customer support. Many providers offer free trial subscriptions to their services. You can use this trial period to determine how easy the system is to use. Does the interface provide an integrated menu that lets you access multiple functions from a central application? Customer support is another important consideration. Once you sign on the dotted line, are you on your own?

Does the company provide online help? Does it offer toll-free support? Can you instantaneously determine how much you've used the Internet service at any given time?

✳ Connectivity. It's very important to find out how a provider gives you access. Will you be able to dial a local or toll-free number? These are almost always preferable to a long-distance connection. Make sure the provider has enough lines to support the necessary users; otherwise you may end up getting a busy signal at inopportune times. When talking to potential providers, ask them how often their users get busy signals. If it's a high percentage of the time, ask them if they plan on adding more lines in the future. Also ask what services you can access once you're connected. Can you perform all the major functions of the Net, such as Web-browsing, FTP, Gopher, and e-mail? What type of interface does the company offer to help you use these functions?

NOTE

Unless you are a college student with free Internet access (or a guy writing a computer book from palatial offices on the outskirts of Indianapolis), you'll probably be connecting to the Internet from home, using a dial-in connection. Although there are other ways to connect, this chapter proceeds from the assumption that you will be connecting to the Internet via dial-in access and a conventional modem.

National Providers

Several national providers are listed in table 17.1.

Providers with Custom Software

In an attempt to keep pace with commercial services such as America Online and CompuServe, some providers have developed their own interfaces to make using their services easier. Although it is not intended as an endorsement, this section briefly looks at two such providers: Netcom, a national provider based in San Jose, CA; and Pipeline USA of New York City.

TABLE 17.1. INFORMATION ON NATIONAL PROVIDERS

PROVIDER	ADDRESS & PHONE NUMBER	SERVICES
CERFNET	P.O. Box 85608 San Diego, CA 92186 800-876-2373	14.4 Dial-up SLIP/PPP Toll-free number
JvNCnet	3 Independence Way Berkeley, CA 94704 609-897-7300	14.4 Dial-up SLIP/PPP
PINET	500 Sunnyside Blvd. Woodbury, NY 11797 800-539-3505 or 206-455-3505	14.4 Dial-up SLIP/PPP Menu
Rocky Mountain Internet	2860 S. Circle Suite 2202 Colorado Springs, CO 80906 719-576-6845	14.4 Dial-up SLIP/PPP Toll-free number Menu

Netcom

Netcom offers a product called NetCruiser, a comprehensive package for connecting to the Internet. NetCruiser is a Windows program that comes on a single floppy disk that is easy to install. The software is free, but the service is $19.95 a month, with a $25.00 start-up fee.

An attractive feature of NetCruiser is its connect-time policy. The first 40 hours of prime-time usage are included in the fee, and all of the off-peak hours are free. ("Off peak" is defined as midnight to 9:00 am, and all day Saturday and Sunday.) This policy is handy for anyone who uses the Internet during off hours.

NetCruiser offers WWW, Gopher, FTP, Telnet, e-mail, and UseNet (including the ClariNet e.News service). Whereas you might have to find a separate application to perform each of these tasks with other systems or providers, NetCruiser does it all from one application. This makes cruising the Net much easier.

To get more information, contact Netcom at:

> 3031 Tisch Way, Second Floor
> San Jose, CA 95128
>
> 408-983-5950, 800-353-6600
> Fax: 408-241-9145
>
> WWW address: *http://www.netcom.com*

Pipeline USA

As with NetCruiser, all the software needed to use Pipeline USA comes on a single disk that's easy to install. With Pipeline USA, there's none of the hassle of trying to establish a special PPP or SLIP connection; Pipeline provides its own connection for you.

Pipeline USA offers a free demo account that you can try before you subscribe. If you decide to continue, accounts begin at about $15 a month. Pipeline USA offers e-mail, FTP, online chatting, and Gopher service. Much of its interface has a point-and-click simplicity. As with Netcom, the single software interface successfully replaces separate applications so that you can cruise most places from within one application.

To find out more, contact Pipeline USA at:

> 150 Broadway
> New York, NY 10038
>
> 212-267-3636
> 212-267-6432 (dial-up modem)
>
> WWW address: *http://www.pipeline.com*
> E-mail address: *info@pipeline.com*

How To Access Different Parts of the Internet

If you don't go with a commercial or national provider that supplies its own interface, you will need to get different software to access the different types of information in this book. This section tells you what you need, where to get it, and how to use the addresses in this book. In addition to the locations given for specific software, much of the software can be retrieved from Que's FTP site at *que.mcp.com* and at several other sites such as *wuarchive.wustl.edu* and *mac.archive.umich.edu.*

For more detailed information about the many types of Internet software that are available, you might want to check out the Special Edition of *Using the Internet* from your friends at Que Publishing.

NOTE

World Wide Web

As you've probably figured out by now, the World Wide Web (also referred to as the Web, WWW, or W3) is a multimedia-capable network that makes jumping from site to site as easy as pointing and clicking. It's also the home for much of the best entertainment information on the Internet.

The hypertext format of the Web allows you to move quickly to specific information on your chosen topic, or you can move to another topic altogether by clicking on a line of highlighted text.

To cruise the Web, you need a Web browser. Some browsers are better than others, but it should be obvious that a good Web browser is the most important tool for getting entertainment information off the Net.

Web Browsers and Where To Get Them

There are many browsers that can be obtained via the Internet itself. The following two browsers are the most popular.

* *NCSA Mosaic*, the original Web browser, is an excellent choice that offers many attractive features for Windows and Macintosh users. The Windows version is available at *ftp.cyberspace.com* in the directory */pub/ppp/Windows/mosaic*. The Macintosh version is available at *scss3.cl.msu.edu* in the directory */pub/mac*.

* *Netscape* is a Windows and Macintosh browser that has attracted a large share of the market. That's because it's good and it's free. Among other places, the Windows version is available at *ftp.halcyon.com* in the directory */pub/slip/www/netscape*. The Macintosh version is available at *ftp.3com.com* in the directory */netscape*. Netscape also offers many sites for both versions, including *ftp.netscape.com* in the directory */netscape1.1*.

Using a Web Browser To Find URL Addresses

Every site on the Web can be identified by its URL (Uniform Resource Locator). Basically, a URL is an address; it tells your Web browser where to find a particular Web site.

NOTE

You can glean considerable information from a URL. For instance, the abbreviation "com" in the address *http://www.mcp.com* tells you that this is a commercial or business site. (In this case, the "mcp" stands for "Macmillan Computer Publishing.") Likewise, "edu" means the site is operated from an educational institution, and "gov" tells you that it is a government-sponsored site.

Also, you can also tell if the site is operated from a computer outside of the United States by a code that precedes the first single backslash. For instance, the abbreviation "it" in *http://www.flashnet.it/models.htm* tells you that this "supermodels" site is from Italy. This is helpful information if you are worried about expensive (and sometimes slow) connections to overseas sites.

Netscape and Mosaic enable you to enter an URL to get to a particular page on the Web. Simply type the URL address of the site you'd like to visit, and the browser takes you right to it. You should remember that URL addresses are case-sensitive. This means that if an address has capital letters, you need to use capital letters when typing it. For example, if you wanted to get to the Audrey Hepburn fan page, you would type in the address *http://grove.ufl.edu/~flask/Hepburn.html*. (See figure 17.1.)

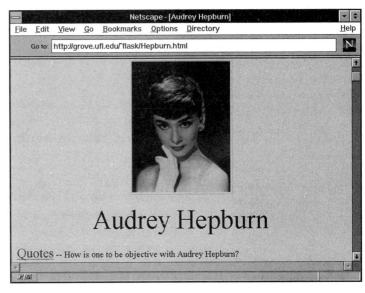

Web sites aren't the only places on the Internet with URLs. You can generally use a Web browser such as Mosaic or Netscape to access FTP sites and other resources on the Net. For instance, if you want to FTP to *wuarchive.wustl.edu* using Netscape, type *ftp://wuarchive.wustl.edu* as the URL. If you want to get to the WELL's Gopher, you would type *gopher://gopher.well.sf.ca.us*. FTP and Gophers are discussed in the following sections. To highlight this capability, all examples in this chapter will use Netscape for access.

FTP

File Transfer Protocol (FTP) software enables you to receive (download) files from another computer and send (upload) files to another computer. These files can be anything from documents to complex audio/video files to software programs.

FTP Clients and Where To Get Them

Although Netscape can do FTP, it does have some limitations. For instance, you cannot upload files via Netscape. Most FTP clients offer many additional options that you might find useful if you use FTP a lot. Some good FTP clients for both Windows and Macintosh users are as follows:

* WS_FTP. This is probably the best Windows FTP program available. For a complete user's guide for WS_FTP, see Que's *Using FTP*. Among many sites, WS_FTP is currently available at *ftp.halcyon.com* in the directory */pub/slip/ ftp*.

* Fetch. The original Macintosh FTP client, Fetch offers a good user interface along with automatic decompression and execution of downloaded files. It can be found at *bitsy.mit.edu* in the directory */pub/mac/fetch*.

* Anarchie. This program allows you to first locate programs (using an FTP search client called Archie) and then instantly access the FTP site once it has been found. This is an excellent program to use if you don't know exactly where a file is located—or even if you do. It can be found at *nic.switch.ch* in the directory */software/mac/archive*.

Using an FTP Client To Find FTP Addresses

Using FTP has become easier with the new graphical-interface clients that are available. When getting a file from an FTP site, there are several things to consider:

* First, you should know the whereabouts (that is, the *host name*) of the FTP site itself. This is the place where you actually find the file.

* It helps to know the *path*, or set of directories, that lead you to the file. For instance, let's say you want to read the *Seinfeld* episode guide at the Cathouse FTP archives. You would first tell your FTP client to find the host *ftp.cathouse.org*. You would then proceed through the */pub*, */cathouse*, */television*, and */seinfeld* directories before you arrive at the choice called *episode.guide*.

* The last thing to be aware of is the *file type*. A text file (the type of file whose name often ends with *.txt* or *.doc*) can be downloaded as plain text. Most other files should be downloaded as binary data. For instance, if you see a

directory with a file in it such as *pub/music/lyrics/text/ highway66.txt*, the file can be downloaded as text. However, if a file has a different extension, such as in */pub/ music/soundfiles/highway66.wav*, you should download the file as a binary. If you're unsure, download it as a binary, because a binary download also can handle text data. All of the FTP clients listed in the previous sections enable you to define the file type both automatically and manually.

NOTE

When using FTP, you're a virtual nobody. All of the FTP sites in this book are referred to as *anonymous FTP sites*. This means that when you log on to the host, you enter **anonymous** as your user name. Also—although it isn't required—proper etiquette dictates that you use your e-mail address as your password.

UseNet Newsgroups

The UseNet newsgroups contain more discussion and raw information than a thousand talk shows, tabloid magazines, and kitchen-table conversations combined. As of this writing, there are more than 13,000 UseNet newsgroups in existence, covering almost every aspect of society, technology, and culture.

If you're looking for serious nuts-and-bolts information on a particular topic, a good place to check is the list of FAQs (frequently asked questions) for the newsgroup that's most closely related to the subject matter that you're interested in. Many newsgroups provide a FAQ list within the site itself on a periodic basis. You can also access a central repository of every known UseNet FAQ list at the following addresses: *rtfm.mit.edu/pub/usenet-by-group/ news.answers* (anonymous FTP site) or *gopher.well.sf.ca.us:70/11/matrix/ usenet* (Gopher site).

Not only can you get current information from these newsgroups, but you also can let your opinions be known as well. (Just do me a favor and don't get bamboozled into the subculture of "flaming,"—that is, online insults. A recent edition of the Project McLuhan newsletter referred to flaming as "a new form of intellectual violence in pursuit of identity," and that's essentially what it is—fascism for weaklings. People can be so darn *unfunny* when they're trying to score points against strangers.)

Newsreaders and Where To Get Them

Newsreaders are software packages that help you sort through the messages that are posted to UseNet. More than that, though, they help organize the newsgroups so that you can easily pick out the topics that interest you. (For more information about newsgroups, see Que's *Using UseNet Newsgroups*.) Although most Web browsers will enable you to read postings from the newsgroups, some newsreaders have expanded capabilities, such as on-the-fly decoding. Popular newsreaders include the following:

* WinVN. This is one of the best Windows newsreaders available, enabling you to do just about everything with a click of your mouse. The most-recent version is available at *ftp.ksc.nasa.gov* in the directory */pub/winvn/win3*. (The most current version is wv16_99_03.zip.)

* NewsXpress. NewsXpress is a new Windows entry into the newsreader market that already enjoys widespread popularity. You can find it at *ftp.cyberspace.com* in the directory */pub/ppp/windows/newsreaders*.

* Newswatcher. This is the easiest-to-use and most complete Macintosh newsreader. The multi-window design helps you read news quickly and easily. It can be located at *ftp.switch.ch* in the */software/mac/news* directory.

* Nuntius. This is another Macintosh newsreader. It may not be as widely used as Newswatcher, but it contains some attractive features. Nuntius is located at the same FTP site as Newswatcher (*ftp.switch.ch* in the */software/mac/news* directory).

Using Newsreaders To Find UseNet Addresses

Once your newsreader is operational, newsgroups are very easy to locate and to read. Most of the entertainment newsgroups reside in the *alt.* and *rec.* hierarchies of UseNet. A *hierarchy* is simply a way of organizing related newsgroups within the UseNet jungle. Newsgroups about society and culture are in the *soc.** hierarchy; groups about computers are in the *comp.** hierarchy, and so on.

If you wanted to read *alt.conspiracy.jfk*, you would instruct your newsreader to go to that group. Many newsreaders have a Find option that lets you look for a group by name. You may also run into a newsgroup while scrolling through all the possibilities.

Once you have found a newsgroup, subscribe to it (usually by selecting the group and choosing the Subscribe option in most newsreaders). After you've subscribed, you're off and reading.

There are a couple of things to keep in mind when finding, subscribing, and reading newsgroups.

* A lot of news servers don't carry many of the *alt.** hierarchy because of the high traffic. If your news server doesn't carry a group mentioned in this book, contact your provider and request that they carry the group.

* You may want to lurk for a while on the newsgroups before subscribing. (To *lurk* means to read some of the messages and get a feel for the group before you plunge in and start contributing articles.)

* Remember that individual taste in the arts can be a very emotional topic—try to keep your cool.

Gopher

Gopher is yet another means of finding your way around the Internet. It's called Gopher because it was set up at the University of Minnesota—home of the terrifying Golden Gophers—and because it's a way to *go for* files on the Internet.

Instead of using command lines to get you where you want to go, Gopher uses a menu-driven system. Getting from place to place is merely a matter of choosing a menu item.

Gopher Clients and Where To Get Them

Despite the inherent simplicity of gophering, there are Gopher clients available that make it even easier. They streamline the process with point-and-click interfaces that are often very similar to Netscape's. The following two Gopher clients are the most popular:

* Hgopher. This is the most popular Gopher client for Windows. You can save electronic bookmarks and use Gopher by using your mouse. Hgopher is located at *ucselx.sdsu.edu* in the */pub/ibm* directory.

* TurboGopher. TurboGopher is a simple Macintosh Gopher client that creates separate windows for each menu. TurboGopher can be found at *bitsy.mit.edu* in the */pub/mac/gopher* directory.

Using Gopher Clients To Find Gopher Addresses

Gopher addresses work much like FTP addresses. You need to find a Gopher address you would like to use as your home Gopher. In other words, you want to tell your client which Gopher menu you would like to have appear when you first start. Most Gopher clients usually have a preset home Gopher that the user can easily change.

Obviously, you'll want to access more than one Gopher site. There are two basic ways you want to do this:

* Gopher clients generally enable you to go to a Gopher site other than your home Gopher. Choose the menu option that enables you to type in the address of the Gopher site you'd like to go to. This is the best method to use when first looking at a Gopher site.

    For instance, if you had an interest in cyber culture and fringe Americana, you could point your Gopher client to the well-known repository called The Well at *gopher.well.sf.ca.us*. From there you might choose the *Periodicals* subdirectory to read the electronic version of *Factsheet Five,* the bible of fanzines and oddball literature.

* The second way to use Gopher sites is to make bookmarks in your Gopher client. Suppose you browse a Gopher site and decide you like it and will probably look at it again. Instead of writing down or remembering the address for future use, set a bookmark using the Gopher client. Once a bookmark has been set, you can instantly access that Gopher site again.

Mailing Lists

It is likely that the e-mail capability is used more often than any other function on the Internet. People use e-mail to communicate, transfer files, access information, and so on. While most e-mail is transferred privately between two individual users, there are also instances in which groups use e-mail in a more public way. One such application is the LISTSERV mailing list.

LISTSERVs (sometimes simply referred to as mailing lists) are very similar to newsgroups, except that all of the LISTSERV postings are delivered directly to your mailbox.

When you find the e-mail address of a LISTSERV that you are interested in, you send a message to that address in order to subscribe to the list. From that point on, all of the e-mail discussion that is sent to that LISTSERV address will appear in your electronic mailbox (either in more-or-less real time or in packets of collected messages at regular intervals). In order to use a LISTSERV, you should have a good e-mail client.

E-mail Clients and Where To Get Them

Surprisingly, there aren't many good e-mail clients out there for public use. One very good one does exist, though:

* Eudora. This is the most widely used Windows and Macintosh e-mail client. Although Eudora is now available commercially, a functional shareware version is still available. Eudora, both the commercial and shareware version, is available for both Windows and Macintosh platforms.

NOTE

Shareware is software that enables you to use it free on a trial basis, after which you can pay a fee for its continued use and for technical support. The whole concept of shareware is essentially a test of our character.

The best place to get Eudora is from *ftp.qualcomm.com*. This FTP site is run by Qualcomm, the makers of Eudora. The Windows version can be found at */quest/windows/eudora/1.4*. Version 1.4 is the latest shareware version. For the Macintosh version, go to */quest/mac/eudora/1.5*.

Subscribing to Mailing Lists

You can find addresses for various mailing lists throughout this book or at mammoth archives such as the one at *http:// www.NeoSoft.com/internet/paml/*. Once you find the address for a group that you are interested in, using a LISTSERV is really quite easy. There are several important things to keep in mind, however.

* LISTSERVs usually have two addresses. One address is used to subscribe, obtain archives and help files, and so on. The other address is used to post messages to the rest of the subscribers.

* Always read the introductory message (and keep a copy) that you receive when you first subscribe to a LISTSERV. It could save you a lot of hassles.

* When you join a LISTSERV for the first time, check your e-mail every day for a few days after subscribing. This way, you'll know if you've subscribed to a list that either has too much traffic, isn't interesting, or gives you any other reason for wanting to unsubscribe right away.

As an example, suppose you want to subscribe to Digital Graffiti, the e-mail discussion group for an obscure English art-rock band called Led Zeppelin. (Remember, this is purely theoretical.) You would follow these steps:

1. The contact information for Digital Graffiti is:

   listserv@cornell.edu subscribe zeppelin-l your_name

2. To subscribe, open your e-mail program and type the address **listserv@cornell.edu** on the "To" line. Leave the "Subject" line blank.

3. In the body of the message, type **subscribe zeppelin-l your_name** (in which "your_name" is a placeholder for your first and last name, e.g., "Aleister Crowley"). Because the subscription request is processed automatically, no other message should be included.

4. Now send your e-mail message. You will usually receive a message that welcomes you and provides instructions on how to send mail to the list. (In this particular case, you may even be sent an ancient Celtic incantation that will grant you a personal interview with Beelzebub.)

How To Find Other Entertainment Information on the Internet

Although this book is full of information, it touches on only a fraction of the entertainment, arts, and cultural information available on the Net. To make matters worse (or better), the available information is likely to double in six months. Given this rate of growth, it's helpful to be able to find new and additional sources of information from the Internet itself. Fortunately, there are ways to do this on the Web.

Using WWW Directory Pages To Find Other Sites

There are lots of directory offerings on the Web to help you find what you're looking for. In fact, many Web browsers—such as Netscape—have collected a number of directory pages and made them available at your fingertips.

The Yahoo Web Site

The Yahoo Web site is a popular and well-organized subject directory. Frankly, this book could not have been written without it. It offers a wide range of subjects that comprise over 44,000 Web sites. (The entertainment subdirectories are the most popular.) You can find the Yahoo directory at *http://www.yahoo.com* or you can access it directly from the Netscape browser by selecting the button marked "Net Directory."

The CERN Full Server List

Probably the most complete directory page is the full server list available at CERN. It lists the servers by geographical region. Be warned, this is a big site and you may have trouble connecting. You can get this directory at *http://info.cern.ch/hypertext/DataSources/WWW/Geographical.html*.

Sun Microsystems's Web Site

Another useful directory is Sun Microsystems's Web site at the University of North Carolina in Chapel Hill. It connects to many cultural resources, both in the United States and in other countries. It is located at *http://sunsite.unc.edu/unchome.html*.

The Whole Internet Catalog

One of the better directory pages on the Web is The Whole Internet Catalog. This site is an online adjunct to a book by the same name, and even though the book competes somewhat with the stylish volume that you are now holding in your hands, it's a well-done guide and it deserves a plug. The online version offers information on a tremendous variety of subjects, including entertainment. The online Whole Internet Catalog is available at *http://www.digital.com/gnn/wic/index.html*.

Using WWW Search Pages To Find Other Sites

In addition to using directories that give you pre-selected sites, you can also perform keyword searches on the Internet. There are many of these search engines available on the Net. Keep in mind that every search engine works differently, so the same query will give different results with different engines. If you don't find what you want on one, you can always try another.

Carnegie Mellon's Lycos

The most popular and well-known of the search engines is Carnegie Mellon's Lycos catalog. (See figure 17.2.) Currently, Lycos has the capability of searching more than 3.7 million link descriptors and 700,000 document pages. (There is also a "small catalog" option that is less comprehensive and less time-consuming.) To use Lycos, point your Web browser to *http://lycos.cs.cmu.edu*, or you can access it directly from Netscape by selecting the "Net Search" button.

FIGURE 17.2

The Lycos catalog at Carnegie Mellon can search millions of documents for what you want.

● ● ● ● ● ● ● ● ● ● ● ● ● ● ● ● ●

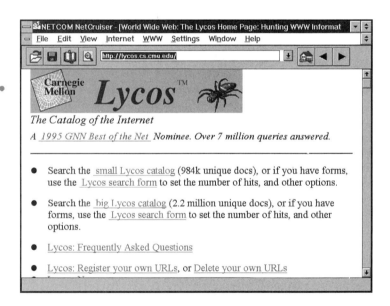

WebCrawler

The WebCrawler is similar to Lycos and is particularly easy to use; you just enter one or more keywords and click the Search button to get a list of sites that contain those keywords some-where within the site name or body text. The address for the WebCrawler Search page is *http://webcrawler.cs.washington.edu/WebCrawler/WebQuery.html*, or you can access it directly from Netscape by selecting the "Net Search" button.

The Centre Universitaire d'Informatique at the University of Geneva

The Web even has a directory of search engines to help you locate even more search engines. CUI (The Centre Universitaire d'Informatique at the University of Geneva) maintains one of the best "search for the searchers" sites. Its URL is *http://cuiwww.unige.ch/meta-index.html*.

Recommended Books on Using the Internet

This chapter has given you a peek at the technical underbelly of the Internet and provided a brief description of some tools that you might use to obtain entertainment information from the many online resources that are available. But, like the book itself, this chapter doesn't pretend to be comprehensive.

If you want to explore the Internet and the resources mentioned in this chapter in greater detail, you may want to check out the following helpful tomes:

* Que's *Using the Internet* is a concise, user-friendly reference guide to the Internet. It includes a disk with Windows accessories for cruising the Internet.

* Que's *Special Edition Using the Internet, Second Edition* is more than 1,300 pages of Grade A cyberbeef that includes everything you need to know about the Internet. For dessert you get a CD with hundreds of megabytes of software to help you out.

* Que's *Special Edition Using the Internet with Your Mac* focuses on accessing the Internet via the Macintosh.

* Que's *Special Edition Using the World Wide Web* will save you time and effort by walking you through the processes of connecting to the Web and utilizing its far-flung resources.

And Finally...

As a final note, it should be pointed out that human beings are alleged to have free will and that most of us have the ability to walk away from behaviors or circumstances that are unproductive. A book about entertainment sites on the Internet isn't likely to straighten out the priorities of the modern world, but your author wants to suggest (for those of you who might have forgotten or didn't already know) that there's a whole lot more to life than an endless stream of multimedia "entertainment" pouring out of your television, your radio, or your computer screen. When the Net isn't meeting your deeper psychological or spiritual needs, you might want to consider taking a walk outside to reacquaint yourself with the larger world, the world that provides the raw material for our arts and entertainment in the first place.

Have fun.

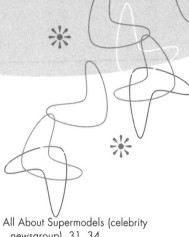

E

H

Hart, Buddy (Harrison Ford stage name), 84

Harvey, PJ (singer), mailing list, 265

Hawaii Five-O (TV drama), 178

Hawaii's NHL Home Page (hockey), 463

Heather Locklear Home Page, 153

Hendrix, Jimi (singer), mailing list, 261

Hepburn, Audrey, fan page, 509

Hereeeeeeeeee's Conan (Conan O'Brien; talk show host), 140, 143

Hersh, Kristen (singer), mailing list, 267

Hgopher (Gopher client), 515

Hiatt, John (singer), mailing list, 261

hierarchies (UseNet newsgroups), 514

Hip-Hop Links (R & B music), 274, 297

hip-hop music, newsgroup, 211

histories, *see* movies, histories

History of Country Music, 312

History of Rock n Roll, 235, 254

Hitachi, Noru, 102

Hitchcock, Alfred (movie director), newsgroup, 97

Hitchcock, Robyn (singer), mailing list, 261

hockey, *see* sports, hockey

Hollyweb (movie promotions), 58-59, 72

Hollywood Online (movie promotions), 59-60, 72

Hollywood Sign Cam (camera connected to Internet), 479, 494

Home Improvement (TV sitcom), 178-182

Home of Soul (R & B music), 297

Homicide, Life on the Street (TV drama), 177

HOMR Music Recommendation Service, 205

Hong Kong Cinema, 96

Hong Kong Movies Home Page, 87, 96-98

Hoop Dreams (documentary), 67

HORNS (International Horn Society maillist), 217

Hornsby, Bruce (musician), newsgroup, 210

horror movies, *see* movies, horror

horse racing, 441, 450-451

Houston Area Traffic Server, 483, 494

humor
archives
Cathouse Humor Archive, 363, 384
Funny Pages, 366, 384
LaughWEB, 364, 384
Mother of All Humor Archive, 365, 384
jokes
categorized lists (canonical), 364, 367, 385
classical music (WWW Virtual Library of Classical), 338
Imagine Publishing's Joke Board, 382, 387
newsgroup, 380, 386
rednecks, 367
Roger Ebert's Movie Laws, 365
magazines, 376-378, 386
newsgroups, 379-381, 386, 386-387
political, *Pathfinder* magazine, 16
resources, 383-384, 387
TV shows archive, 121
see also cartoons

Husker Du (musical group), mailing list, 267

Hype! Online (Oscars, The; Academy Awards), 74

Hype! Reviews (rock & roll reviews), 254

Hyper-Weirdness By World Wide Web (miscellaneous topics link site), 471-472, 492

Hypertext Who (rock & roll band), 255

I

Idea Futures (online game), 415

IHL (International Hockey League), *see* sports, hockey

ImagiNation Network (gaming service), 395

Imagine Publishing's Joke Board, 382, 387

IMPULSE MUSIC JOURNAL (mailing list), 217

Independent Film and Video Makers Internet Resource Guide, 50, 53

INDEPENDENT MUSIC (Indie-List; mailing list), 217

Index of Useless WWW Pages, 497

Indian classical music, *see* music, Indian

Indiana Jones WWW Page, 75

Indiana University Music Library (general interest music links), 342

Indiana University School of Music, classical music, 341-342, 355

Indie Label List: A Partial Guide to Independent Record Labels (Music Resources on the Internet), 188

Indigo Girls (musical group), mailing list, 261

Indy Car racing, *see* sports, auto racing

Influence of Jazz on the Beat Generation, 302

Information Age, 102

Infomercial List, The (TV), 124

installing software (Toolkit), 60

Institute for Propaganda Analysis, The (news analysis), 127-128, 141-144

Interact with Sandra Bullock! (movie actress), 47

Interactive NBA Schedule (basketball), 458

Interactive Week (magazine), Internet/cyberspace movies report, 14

International Hockey League News, 463

International Soccer Results, 464

International Soccer Server, 464

International Soccer Site, 452-453

international telecommunications resources (WWW Virtual Library Telecommunications Index), 115

Internet access, 4
FTP (File Transfer Protocol), 510-512
Gopher, 514-516
mailing lists, 516-518
recommended books, 521
resources (BBC Networking Club), 110
UseNet newsgroups, 512-514
World Wide Web, 508-510
directory pages, 518-521
see also service providers

Internet Anagram Server (games), 427

Internet Baseball Information Center, 456

Internet Casinos (gambling game), 421

Internet Chess Club, 410, 434

Internet CNN Newsroom (cable news), 122, 130, 142-144

S

• • • • • • • • • • • • • • •